TRIGGER

Robert Dannin and Tony Gawron

ISBN: 978-1-7321708-8-9
ISBN: 978-1-7321708-9-6 (ebook)
Library of Congress Control Number: 2020923718

Edited by Joanmarie Kalter

Frontispiece photo by Charlie Steiner (c) 2020

Author photo by Jolie Stahl (c) 2020

Cover design by Dana Bree, StoneBear Design

StoneBear Publishing LLC - 01/2021
Milford, PA 18337

www.stonebearpublishing.com

For Tony Gawron

Table of Contents

Dedications iii

About the Author ix

INTRODUCTION - "Just Like Humphrey Bogart" 1

PART I   Good People, New World 31

Chapter   1.   Newark Undercover 32

Chapter   2.   Central Casting 40

Chapter   3.   Brooklyn Deli 54

Chapter   4.   Kishke Max 59

Chapter   5.   Stein's Tadek 69

Chapter   6.   Max's Tadek 92

Chapter   7.   Monty's Tadek 101

Chapter   8.   Tadek's Johnny 111

PART II   Good People, Old World 123

Chapter   9.   Juraski's Tadek 124

Chapter   10.   Johnny's Lucini 181

Chapter   11.   Mustapha's Ted 192

Chapter   12.   Sturmbannführer Schlaube's Hans 208

Chapter   13.   RAF 248

Chapter   14.   Johnny's Ted 256

Chapter   15.   Ted's Communist 269

Chapter   16.   Winarski's Adam 292

PART III   The Promised Land 311

Chapter   17.   Sol's Adam 312

Chapter   18.   Greenberg's Prize 332

PART IV   The Package 341

Chapter   19.   Lucini's Ted 342

Chapter   20.   The Professor's Entourage. 353

Chapter   21.   The Five Days of Freedom 368

Chapter   22.   Johnny's Ted Again .424

PART V   The Incorruptibles 431

Chapter   23.   Harris's Threat 432

Chapter   24.   Donaldson's Plan 436

PART IV   The Puritans 457

Chapter   25.   Cop or Friend? 458

Chapter   26.   Ted's Adam, Adam's Ted 466

Chapter   27.   Whose Millions? 483

EPILOGUE   The Cleaning 493

Chapter   28.   Ted's Final Solution .494

Glossary   513

About the Author

Robert Dannin taught linguistics and anthropology at Brown University and New York University. He studied for his doctorate in Paris and paid for his education by working as a cook and journalist. That's where he met Tony Gawron and began the collaboration that would result in *Trigger*, which Dannin continued to work on and finally completed after Gawron's death.

Among Dannin's scholarly publications, *Black Pilgrimage to Islam* (Oxford 2002) was the first ethnography of Islamic religious conversion in America. He was the editorial director of Magnum Photos, where he produced Sebastião Salgado Jr.'s *Workers, An Archaeology of the Industrial Age*, (Aperture 1993). His other editorial credits include James Nachtwey's *Inferno* (Phaidon 1999) and *Arms Against Fury: Magnum Photographers in Afghanistan* (Powerhouse 2002. In 2009 Dannin was an inaugural fellow at the Norman Mailer Writers Colony.

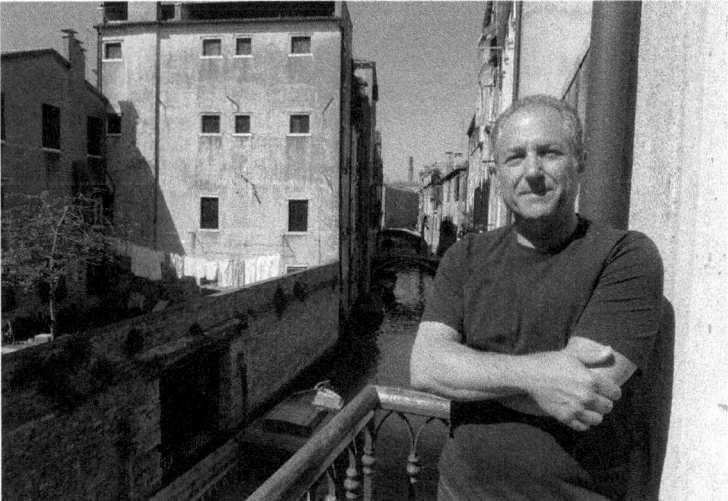

"Just Like Humphrey Bogart!"

An Introduction to Edward "Tony" Gawron's *Trigger*

Robert Dannin

Foreign students came looking for mentors. They saw Foucault, Barthes, and Lévi-Strauss lecture on consecutive days at the Collège de France, then finished the week boozing with disheartened Mai'68ers at intergalactic bars like Boucher's L'Aquarelle on rue de Seine. Around two in the morning, closing time, Boucher began to cajole and plead for people to go home. Sometimes he resorted to bribes and promised free drinks the next day. The drunken hubbub rose deliberately to interrupt his entreaties. Yet Boucher persisted, never losing his cool. Needed to go home to his wife, sleep, get to the bank early. Plastered fools usually inclined to his comradely gestures. He'd enlist someone slightly less inebriated to escort a stumbling *goguette* home, or just arm-over-shoulder separate a death-clench drunk from the zinc bar, docilely spin him around and coax him out the door. The finale of a night at L'Aquarelle was an unchoreographed ballet set against the backdrop of a Doisneau barroom scene – stumbling fools shrouded in a thick tobacco haze to the arrythmic accompaniment of insects sizzling in the overhead electric snare. Zap.

The contrast with the tile-and-mahogany floozy across the street could not have been greater. Every barfly worth his reputation had been eighty-sixed from *La Palette,* booted out violently by the young National Front waiter. Jean-François played the role perfectly – a full-length apron, Marechal Pétain mustache – regularly spewing his bigoted venom on *nègres, bicots et youpins* (Africans, Arabs, and Jews). He made change and ripped the bar tab with one hand while surveying the scene above his patrons' heads. When I showed up with visiting friends, he tolerated me as an Americanski with cash to spend. A week later I once again became "Mustafa Bob," reproachfully disdained for speaking French "like an Arab."

In 1977 only political hacks expected anything positive from the Socialist-Communist united front, the so-called *Programme Commun*. Some secretly applauded Baader-Meinhof but not the Red Brigades. Structuralism was dead. Louis Althusser, author of *For Marx* and *Reading Capital* and the presumptive renovator of revolutionary philosophy, reasoned himself into strangling his wife to death over their morning coffee. Confined thereafter to St. Anne's psychiatric hospital, he wrote a grim epitaph entitled *The Future Lasts Forever*, "to be read," according to one reviewer, "as a complement to Michel Foucault's *Madness and Civilization*." Outside the asylum, Jean Baudrillard had seized young imaginations and was busily deconstructing Marx, sinking would-be rebels ever deeper into an overwhelming postmodern funk. In the dying gasp of its Bohemian splendor, Paris in the seventies was the doldrums where I ended up grilling ham-and-cheese sandwiches and taking notes in the apartment of a demented Holocaust survivor.

Edward "Tony" Gawron was born in 1926 to a Polish aristocrat and his Jewish wife on an estate near Lodz. His father died before Tony reached the age of five, leaving his mother to raise her son and manage the family holdings with the assistance of a feudal retainer. In 1939 Hitler invaded Poland and confined its three-and-a-quarter million Jews to urban ghettos, the first stage in his plan to wipe out European Jewry. Tony's mother obtained an apartment in the Warsaw Ghetto and enrolled him in a Jewish school, an alienating experience for an adolescent theretofore educated in a secular Polish academy. In 1943, at the age of seventeen, Tony escaped the Warsaw Ghetto just as the Nazis began the final liquidation of its population to the death camps. As a fair-haired, blue-eyed boy fluent in Polish, German, and English, he survived by his wits on an odyssey that included service with the underground Polish Home Army, the Communist resistance, and even the German SS occupation forces.

As the Third Reich crumbled, he disguised himself as an American MP and smuggled contraband from occupied Germany to France. Eventually someone blew his cover, he was arrested and sent to prison. Once released, he recuperated his well-hidden profits and settled in Paris where he opened La Bohème, a discothèque catering to African-American GIs. As a Jew and war refugee, he identified with black Americans who, despite their heroism in combat, were disrespected and segregated by the U.S. Army. In 1969 the SNCF, the French national railway company, purchased his club to clear the way for the new Montparnasse terminal and its crappy office tower. He invested the funds in 8% Swiss CDs and drove his little Fiat to Geneva every six months to get cash and roll the securities over. The German Federal Republic also paid him reparations. In 1978, the year we met, he was a retired gangster in a third-floor walkup next to Paris' sleazy Gare de l'Est.

Unlike many survivors who wanted to forget their nightmares and never talked about their experiences, Tony was obsessed by the war, concentration camps, Hitler, Stalin, and especially the American liberators whom he idealized as the Hollywood characters played by Humphrey Bogart. Another of his heroes was Patton, or maybe it was George C. Scott playing Patton in the movie. By 1980 Ronald Reagan was right up there in his pantheon too.

Fighting the war over and over, battle by battle, ghost for ghost, left him little time to sleep. With all this stuff going on in his mind, Tony needed a therapist. Gérard Mendel wasn't a university mandarin, rather a renowned, practicing psychiatrist. He authored a dozen books, most notably *Revolte Contre Le Père (Revolt Against the Father)*, meaning Freud himself. His theories coincided with those of radical hipsters, Gilles Deleuze and Felix Guattari whose book, *Anti-Œdipus*, identified schizophrenia as the prime malady of capitalist society and underpinned the May '68 generation's beliefs. Mendel called himself a socio-psychoanalyst, saw patients like Tony and even wrote prescriptions.

Tony's evening cocktail of muscle relaxants and barbiturates knocked him out cold for hours. Sometimes he'd overdose and remain unconscious well into the next day. Friends who were unable to rouse him on the phone or by ringing his buzzer would call the fire department to break down the door. This pissed him off to no end, not only because of the hassle of replacing the lock but the firemen always took him into custody as a potential suicide. Once hospitalized, it was a bureaucratic nightmare to get discharged. Several times he left the hospital in his nightgown and walked home barefoot. Depending upon where you stood with him, each hook-and-ladder incident became an excusable misunderstanding, an endless complication, or a humorous introduction to the collected tales of his life, "Mr. Gawron's Mad House." Sometimes, he confessed, he really did want to end it all, but this was nothing more than a mere test run. When he really wanted to die, not even the firefighters would stop him from implementing his own final solution.

Meanwhile, he continued Dr. Mendel's pharmaceutical regimen with all manner of unintended and bizarre consequences. Tony was a middleweight, about 5'10", 225 lbs., cropped blond hair, blue eyes – not your average Polish Jew. He liked to chase his bedtime pills with a mug of strong Russian tea and a slice of lemon. Distinctive gold and black tins of Indar, his favorite brand, were piled on the kitchen counter where he would brew a pot and take a glass back to his bedroom. Then he would turn on his television, pop an American movie into the VCR, sit back, and wait for the pills to hit. From time to time he'd get anxious waiting for this to happen, or perhaps over-stimulated by the movie, he'd return to the kitchen for another glass of tea. All at once the sedatives would topple him somewhere between the kitchen and bedroom. He'd collapse in a heap and remain there for hours.

One Friday, a skinny little man was folding his bedsheets when I showed up. Stashu, the Polish tailor, sometimes slept on Tony's living-room couch. Another zonked-out survivor in his late sixties or early seventies, Stashu worked in a Belleville shop but had no fixed home. Normally he probably looked no different than the day he'd left Auschwitz, yet he was in particularly bad shape the day I met him because Tony had collapsed unconscious right on top of him the night before. Unable to wriggle free, Stashu had spent part of the night crushed under his friend's dead weight. When the narcotic effects had worn off sufficiently, he rousted Tony aside and liberated his slender body from captivity. Tony finally came to and made breakfast – more tea and his daily dose of amphetamines to get the madness rolling.

Stashu looked like a crumpled cigarette and seemed annoyed. But Tony had a different perspective. This was the price of freedom, and Stashu's account was now balanced again. "He gets women almost all the time," Tony marveled. "Sometimes he quarrels with one of his girlfriends and has to leave her house. When that happens, he comes here. I'm always grateful for the company but I can't change my routine just for a fellow Pole," Tony explained to me in English while simultaneously translating into Polish for his pal.

Tony's attitude toward Stashu's luck with the opposite sex fell somewhere between admiration and disinterested clinical observation as a counterpoint to his own inability to handle a woman's affections. They always made him anxious and jealous. "My psychiatrist," referring to Mendel, "explained that it's better for me to eliminate sexual relations altogether. He turned my libido off ... just like a plumber shuts a valve. And then he gave it an extra twist, just to make sure!"

In addition to this practical anti-Freudian treatment, Mendel had also prescribed group therapy in the guise of regular acting lessons. Consequently, Tony had become a long-time member of the Paris Actors Studio, dedicated to teaching the Stanislavski-Strasberg theories of method acting. Years of rehearsing the many personalities that played important roles in his life had prepared Tony to write his autobiography.

Tony began writing after the war and by the early 1960s had assembled two draft novels and a collection of short stories. Around 1966 he met James Jones, who was living in Paris and who became fascinated by Tony's wartime experiences. Jones read his stuff and quickly became an advocate. He sent a manuscript entitled "Angry Old Men" to Ross Claiborne, his editor at Dell Publishers in New York. A year and half later, Claiborne informed Jones that it had been rejected. Undeterred, Jones insisted he read it again and impatiently went above his head. Writing to Manon Morrison Tingue, the newly appointed executive editor, he described the book as "a tight, most enjoyable read that would more than pay for itself as a detective novel in Dell paperback. But with the proper exploitation as a picture of the present and recently past Paris underworld it could be a success in a hardcover edition. Meantime I am finishing up my reading of his other novel. I need not tell you what a great shot in the arm it would be for the author if 'Angry Old Men' were accepted, even if only as a paperback edition."

Another "much more comprehensive novel," to which Jones referred in his second letter to the publisher, was a rough draft of the present book. It was a longer manuscript that "tells an incredible tale, a rather fantastic life, [the author] having escaped first from the Poles as a Jew, then serving as a conscript in the German Army as a Goy, then having escaped to Paris where he became one of the kings of the black market, still during the war. He has made himself enough loot in these semi-criminal (and perhaps other criminal) activities to buy himself a couple of good bars in Paris – so that he doesn't really need money and is doing his writing because he is compelled to do so by some inner, bitter force. In some ways it reminds one of Kosinski's *Painted Bird*, though it is much more realistic and factual. It's going to need a massive re-write and cutting job before it can even be submitted. I intend to help him as best I can. Point is," Jones concluded, "I think that Mr. Gawron, who certainly now no longer has any problems about money, is fiercely determined to write and is a voice which I'm sure will be heard from eventually – if in a somewhat Céline-esque approach. He is aware of his inadequacies in English (American)" … but the "antidote" is to get an "American kid here to help."

Several years later, the 26-year-old "American kid" was me, recruited for the job by Jones' literary agent, Alain Bernheim, who had placed an ad in the *International Herald Tribune* in the spring of 1978. I answered with my CV and a letter citing my experience as a translator for UNESCO, the first position I'd held in Paris. Bernheim invited me to meet at a café outside the rue de Rennes Métro station at the intersection with Boulevard Raspail. Our interview lasted about 25 minutes, enough time for a *café-calva*. Mostly he told me about the expats he'd worked with – Jones, Ralph Ellison, and Peter Matheson. Then he handed me Tony's address (12, rue du 8 Mai 1945) and phone number (607.78.20) with a word of advice about Tony's eccentricities. Ignore them because he had an important story to tell and was willing to pay for my editorial services.

Thrilled at the prospect of a new job, I returned to my apartment on Square Grangé in the 13th *arrondissement* and phoned Tony to introduce myself and arrange an appointment.

Max the Doberman

He lived next to the Gare de l'Est, a grungy neighborhood haunted by aging prostitutes, addicts, and homeless transients. It was all shades of grey like a Eugene Atget photograph. When I located Tony's building, a lone newspaper vendor was sheltering himself from the rain just inside the *porte cochère* leading to the courtyard of his apartment building. Mid-thirties, about six feet tall, clad in a weathered black trench coat, the guy was hawking *Minute*, the monarchist-fascist weekly. I ignored the array of past editions and pamphlets laying on his small table and glanced up at the used books displayed in a wire contraption hung on the side of the arch. The only title I recognized amidst names of right-wing authors – Sorel, Drieu La Rochelle, Paul de Man – was the French translation of *The Protocols of the Elders of Zion*, a book I had often heard about but had never seen at home and would henceforth notice wherever I traveled in the world. After a few seconds I became self-conscious, stepped back on the sidewalk to confirm the address and, without making eye contact, quickly trudged inside to the "A" staircase, past the concierge's window and up to the third floor. I drew breath and rang the bell.

Loud barking erupted immediately from within, followed around thirty seconds later by shuffling and scratching on the other side of the double doors. "*Assieds, Max*!!" (Sit!) a Peter Lorre-type accent shouted. The scratching continued furiously as the voice pulled back a heavy spring-loaded deadbolt and swung the door inward. Striving with one hand to control a menacing Doberman was a smiling paleface with red bruises where the dog had pawed his forehead raw. "Don't worry about Max. He's just a rambunctious puppy," he greeted me in a staccato voice. He gripped the beast's collar and yanked him away from the opening so I could slip inside between him and the suddenly submissive dog.

"I'm very happy to meet you, Mr. Dannin. I'm Edward Gawron, but call me Tony. Welcome to my home." He wore a wrinkled Oxford long-sleeved shirt and tailored dark wool trousers. I entered a spacious, high-ceilinged apartment. As he conducted me from the vestibule, we passed a room occupied by a piece of homemade furniture about the size of two ping-pong tables. Strewn across the surface of a painted schematic of Europe were carved miniature World War II armies of planes, tanks, infantry divisions, railroads, etc. On the near right corner, corresponding to the geographical southeast, German forces were clashing with the Red Army at Stalingrad. "It's my war room," he paused to explain. "I invented this game. I'll teach you the rules and maybe we can play sometime." The room's four walls were lined by bookshelves filled with reserve miniatures awaiting deployment and also a veritable library of historical literature. The next room was a smallish kitchen overflowing with garbage and dirty dishes. Escorting me to the main living room-office, he gestured to the sofa and, bending down to clear away some old newspapers, offered me something to drink. "Would you like some tea? I was just brewing a pot. Do you take it with lemon or milk? I'll be right back."

Watching Tony head to the kitchen, Max reversed direction and sauntered past me, then disappeared into a darkened room in the back. Grateful to be ignored by this beast, I stood up and surveyed the room. More bookcases filled with historical works in English, French, German, and Polish. One wall had a built-in armoire, half-opened with assorted jackets hanging flush against the door. A leather trench coat reminded me of the fascist book-dealer downstairs. There was a business suit draped in plastic just back from the cleaners and behind it, a dark woolen military tunic with SS lightning bolts affixed to the collar. A U.S. Army battle helmet sat on the upper shelf beside what looked like a Luger pistol. Perpendicular to the armoire, an office desk jutted out into the middle of the room. I saw an IBM Selectric with a pile of manuscripts to one side. A pineapple hand grenade weighted down a mass of disorganized papers and letters on the other side. I was examining the ordnance when Tony reentered the room carrying two glass mugs filled with amber tea.

"Go ahead, pull the pin but keep your hand on the grip. It's a live one," he said, a feverish smile crossing his face.

I placed the grenade gently back on the papers and returned to the couch. Steam wafted from the tea. Through the haze I stared at Tony. At fifty-two, he resembled one of those ghoulish Gahan Wilson drawings from *Playboy*. His facial outline was blurry, and his expressions vibrated into and out of focus to the rhythm of his near-perfect English. As I began to wonder whether I was going to leave the place alive, Max loped back into the room and nudged himself between the coffee table and me. He lowered his head onto my lap. I took it as a vote on behalf of sanity, a canine recognition of his master's infirmity, and offered him my palm to lick.

"This is the only tea I drink. Good Russian Caravan tea. The Bolsheviks would have ruined it, but it's made here by White Russian exiles now." He put the glass to his lips and slurped through the lemon slice. He surveyed the room, then looked back at me. "This is my little world. I don't go out very often, just to get supplies or to see a movie. Otherwise I have everything I need right here. My television and VCR are in the bedroom so I can watch movies all night long. I love anything *série noire*. Do you like Bogart?"

"His daughter Leslie was in my class at university," I replied. I recalled the girl's face and the apartment on Spofford Road in Allston that she shared with my friend Nancy, another B.U. student. Copies of *Screw* and other pornography had littered their floor. I knew very little about Leslie Bogart, had met her just once in passing, and was trying to recover all the details of our encounter when Tony interrupted my reverie.

"Bogie must have been dead by then. Great actor, and a tragic loss. By the way, I have all his films here. Sam Spade, Rick Blaine, Philip

Marlowe and his other characters were my heroes as a kid. I tried to live according to their principles. I admired them as Americans too because they accomplished things, unlike the French who are forever procrastinating. Sometimes I can't even get my laundry back on time. They should have Chinese laundries in Paris. The modern French let action take a backseat to contemplation. Existentialism was okay but taken to the extreme it became more style than substance. True philosophy, on the other hand, is mostly a demonstration of conscious will. Like Napoléon, the Germans tried and failed to impose their will on a reluctant Europe; but the Americans have it in their blood, it's part of the pioneer spirit that induces immigrants to carve their place into the physical and social wilderness." He veered back to the nature of our meeting. "My project is an autobiography. I've written stuff already and used to have an American girl helping me, but she got married and went back to the States. That explains my ad in the *Trib*. "So, what about you. Bernheim said you're studying here?"

I explained my presence in France as a doctoral student in anthropology at the École des Hautes Études en Sciences Sociales. It was a naïve, rambling discourse of my quest for intellectual sustenance, a rebellious soul looking for a revolutionary fix in Paris. He listened politely for about ten minutes, then launched into his own theory of ethnicity.

"I'm Polish. We hated the Nazis, but we hate the Russians more. Many Poles were happy that Hitler got rid of all the Jews. They said, 'Thanks! You did our dirty work, now please go home. Leave!' I was in the Home Army. That was their attitude. Hitler solved our biggest problem, but instead of leaving he invited the Soviets in. Stalin was worse. He hated anyone who wasn't Communist. The Americans should never have stopped moving east. They only stopped to please the French who had too many Communist sympathies. The GIs should have kept going, even to Moscow. They would have succeeded because the Red Army was exhausted, and the Soviet Union was already on its knees. I still hope, I never pray by the way, that NATO will someday liberate Warsaw. I want to be sitting on top of a tank, waving an American flag when NATO rolls into Warsaw." He thrust both arms victoriously into the air and grinned. When he motioned to a huge

American flag hanging like a curtain over one of his floor-to-ceiling bookshelves, I got the message. Better to remain politically neutral if I wanted this job. Being American seemed qualification enough for him, so there was no need to compromise the deal with my anti-Cold War polemics. Tony disdained ideology and represented, more than I knew at that moment, a salutary defense against French intellectual arrogance whose reign was already in rapid descent. He was chugging full-throttle on the same track as Zbigniew Brzezinski and Pope John Paul II, a couple of other Polish expats who probably wanted to be riding shotgun on that same American tank. Tony articulated their strategies and hoped they would be carried to fruition by another one of his Hollywood idols, Ronald Reagan.

He stood up and grabbed a Marantz cassette recorder from the shelf. It was the black professional model one always saw hanging on the shoulders of radio journalists at the time. It made the high-quality voice registrations heard on stations like NPR, BBC, and France Inter. "Do you have a cassette player and typewriter at home?" he asked. "If not, I'll buy you a tape player, not like this but something you can listen on. Or you can work here. This is the way I write."

He wanted his autobiography written in the style of a political thriller like a John Le Carré or Robert Ludlum spy novel. He had rehearsed all the roles and characters for years at the Actors Studio. The plan was to work a three- or four-hour day once a week, recording dialogue according to his plot outline. I was to take notes and study his gestures. His familiarity with the dialogue was such that I could interrupt him at any point to interview the character about his physical appearance, attire, personal background, motivations, feelings, posture, opinions, and whatever else might contribute to drawing a full description of the persons and places in the novel. Following our session, I'd take the cassettes home for transcription, editing, and narrative embellishment. The following week I would return the typewritten draft in exchange for 50 French francs per double-spaced page. Tony would photocopy the pages so each of us had a full set to discuss during the next phase of editing. He offered me a cash advance to get things started. Although we didn't use a written outline, Tony was working through numerous episodes and adventures toward a definite conclusion in which one of his alter egos, Tadeusz Szczepanski, drags humanity to the brink of annihilation while the other one, Johnny Miller, makes off with millions.

Tony wanted to be social and invited me to stop by his place, even bring my friends, and help myself to his food, books and movies. His VCR library contained at least 200 films, most of them in English, purchased on dedicated missions to Amsterdam and London. Between the Actors Studio and watching Hollywood movies, he easily portrayed an assimilated Polish-American expat living in Paris. "Last time I went to London," he said, "I got in a taxicab and began talking to the driver. His Cockney accent was so thick that I couldn't understand a word. 'Talk to me in BBC English, I told him.' Just like that, he switched. I hired him to be my driver for the entire weekend."

He proposed we watch a movie and then perhaps eat dinner together somewhere. We decided on *Key Largo* with Bogart and Bacall playing hostages to Edward G. Robinson's gangster in the middle of a Caribbean hurricane. Tony poured us another round of tea and fired up the VCR in his bedroom. I sat down in a comfortable Eames chair. Tony pushed "play" and propped himself up on the bed. Max settled onto the bed and put his head on Tony's lap.

After the movie Tony prepared for one of his rare excursions into Paris nightlife. He fished a khaki trench coat from the closet and cinched the waist much tighter than fashion allowed for a middle-aged man. He donned a grey fedora, leashed the dog, and we set out. First he had to walk Max around the block. Down the stairway onto the street, we passed the concierge and also the fascist book dealer already packing up for the day. They seemed to be on familiar terms, and Tony acknowledged him with a few words about the weather. We walked east along the boulevard, then took a right up the rue du Saint Quentin. Max found a curb. Retracing our steps back toward the apartment, I surveyed the shabby Gare de l'Est. It was the dull underbelly of working-class Paris. Owning a Doberman in this neighborhood made sense. I waited downstairs while Tony deposited the dog and returned. We crossed the station's slippery cobblestone esplanade and entered the Métro.

Aboard the Orléans-Clignancourt line, Tony appeared tense and formal. A bit paranoid even, he had an unmistakable straphanger's gaze that warned other passengers not to trespass his space. It was an icy, defiant stare, complemented by a slightly quivering upper lip broadcasting the menace of someone familiar with violence. Though the car was moderately crowded, even the usually pushy commuters conceded him a substantial radius. At one stop, a group of boisterous teens entered the train. Tony made brief eye contact with one of them. They exchanged a few words with each other in Arabic and then moved away as if he were radioactive. At Châtelet we changed in the direction of Gare de Lyon and, after a couple of stops, got off at St. Paul.

We walked down rue des Rosiers into the Marais, heart of the old Jewish Ghetto. Merchants were pulling down iron shutters over windows painted in fading Yiddish letters. A few people acknowledged him, not personally but as someone who might have once belonged there. He responded with clipped salutations in French. No one ventured conversation. Tony stopped outside a brightly illuminated restaurant whose windows were framed in yellow paint. Jo Goldenberg was Paris' only surviving Jewish delicatessen. He opened the wooden door slowly and stepped inside. A thin, grey-haired woman behind the cash register lifted her eyes and recognized him almost immediately.

"*Monsieur Gawron, c'est un plaisir de vous voir.* Michel, Sasha," she called excitedly to a pair of aging waiters standing just near the kitchen. "*C'est Monsieur Gawron!*" She angled from behind her podium and did a half-bow before Tony, who lifted and kissed her right hand. The men stood motionless until this ritual was over and in turn kissed him on both cheeks. They exchanged a few words in Yiddish and surrendered him back to the hostess, who escorted us past the deli counter into the dining room permeated by the odor of pickles and meat. The hostess' attitude bordered on reverence. She made some small talk about common acquaintances, then left us to the wait staff. A few years later she would die in the PFLP (Palestinian terrorist) bombing of this famed landmark.

We feasted on stuffed derma, cholent, a hot meaty borscht, a platter of smoked fish and a bottle of kosher Burgundy. Loosened up a bit by the alcohol, Tony began to recount his post-war experience in Paris. With money from smuggling and distributing contraband across the German-occupied border, he opened his Montparnasse discothèque specializing in the latest jazz and soul music. He was very strict about rules in the club – no drugs and no pimps. This was not his moral judgment, rather a way to avoid complications with the cops. He played by French rules with guarded respect for officials. Except for the small core of resisters surrounding de Gaulle in London, he knew that many French men and women had swung both ways during the war. He was unmoved by the subsequent rebellions in Vietnam and Algeria. The French generals, he declared, were too soft in the face of the continuing global Soviet threat. 1968 showed how weak France was without NATO forces on the ground. Shamefully, de Gaulle had made them leave. GIs were good for his business and it gave him something to do, people and new friends every night. But the American servicemen were gone by the time the government railway offered generous compensation for him to close down. That money was Tony's legacy, and he intended to use it to set the record straight about who he was and just what he wanted.

It took another two weeks to get the project moving. When I showed up the following Friday, Tony had written a letter that needed my urgent attention. Composed in acceptable French, he needed an English version too. He was looking for a part-time job and wanted to solicit a few multinational companies now established in and around Paris. The letter explained that although financially secure, he sought employment to occupy his time. A night watchman's job would be perfect since he was an insomniac. His qualifications included familiarity with firearms and possession of a trained Doberman, whose services would be included in the deal. In short, he was a perfect match for the security duties any company might need.

The ham-and-cheese-on-rye sizzled on his electric grill press while I tried to imagine how a Fortune 500 personnel manager was going to react. The only thing missing, I thought, was a snapshot of Tony holding the Luger across his chest with Max faithfully at his side, like Marina Oswald's picture of her husband, Lee Harvey, with the high-powered rifle and target sheet taken a couple of weeks before he squeezed behind some boxes at the Texas School Book Depository. "Wrong approach, man," I advised, returning to the desk. Dijon mustard dripped onto the plate from my crispy sandwich.

Tony flashed a boyish smile that demolished my sophomoric judgment. We laughed at how ridiculous unincorporated truth always sounds. The fact of the matter was that Tony was probably willing to pay some company for the opportunity to spend his nights strutting around their offices with Max and a sidearm. On the other hand, I was in no position to be charitable. "Fifty francs a page for this too?" I inquired and, upon hearing his assent, rolled a clean sheet of paper into the Selectric. Who cared if the only response he got was a visit from the police? He'd simply enact another role he'd rehearsed or use the occasion to talk shop with the gendarmes. French cops watch American movies too. They'd love his skillfully improvised wisecracking and blunt humor.

I wrote most of Tony's correspondence for the next couple of years. Later I also undertook the additional task of trying to secure him a U.S. tourist visa. Visiting the States was the one thing he wanted above all others, yet it was impossible unless someone could persuade the U.S. consul to grant him a waiver for his old smuggling conviction and issue the visa. He'd exchanged letters and arranged interviews at the embassy many times, but the response was always the same. In view of his past "crimes of moral turpitude," Edward Gawron was ineligible to travel to the U.S. He was a stateless person with no permanent employment, travelling on a French passport moreover, and therefore a risk to remain in the U.S. as an illegal immigrant. He always put the same name and address in New Jersey as his intended destination on the visa applications, and in the course of writing the novel I surmised that this might have been the individual who ratted him out to the MPs years before. But Tony would probably have greeted him as a long-lost war buddy, might even have brought him money. Yet, if anyone alerted the guy in Jersey about Tony's imminent arrival, it's likely he'd have immediately taken to the hills.

Trigger revealed enough details to give one pause about the nature and extent of Tony's underworld deeds. Regardless, I grew indignant over the idea that smuggling Lucky Strikes and silk stockings amounted to the capital offense the consular bureaucrats were making it out to be. Here was someone who ached and breathed patriotic American values – an anti-Communist ready for hand-to-hand combat against the Warsaw Pact forces – yet they refused to let him spend his blood money on Times Square souvenirs and videotape movies. All those Nazis scurrying along the infamous CIA ratline into the States, while one of their intended victims remained confined to European house arrest. Poor Tony couldn't even get as close to Hollywood as the notorious, shoe-banging Nikita Khrushchev, who reportedly flew into a rage when denied entry to Disneyland.

The following week we got down to business. Max went wild again when I rang the doorbell. Tony stood there with his ghoulish smile and offered a handshake. The Battle of Stalingrad was still raging in the war room. The kitchen was dirtier than ever, but the refrigerator was freshly stocked with good Polish ham and a choice of aged Gruyère or fresh Gouda. The living-room coffee table was laid out in surgical precision with a notepad, pens, tape recorder and microphone, and a liter of clear Polish moonshine. Dropping a handful of Dexedrine into his mouth, Tony poured about three ounces of the alcohol into a highball glass to chase them down. "It's not vodka. It's the distilled spirits they use to make vodka," he offered, bringing to mind the cadenced descent of Josef Roth's characters, who all ended up drinking themselves to death on *neunzig grad* (90-proof). Not far from Tony's on the Left Bank, Roth had himself succumbed to alcohol in 1939 rather than join the collective European suicide instigated by mad ideologues. His pages are haunted by discontents: men willfully disobeying the unwritten rules of filial piety, foisting themselves into unrequited love affairs; derelicts vomiting on their imperial uniforms; resentful sons; incapable parents; miserable failures; and fools. Unlike Roth, however, Tony had endured, and within a half-hour resembled a schizophrenic train wreck, a bug-eyed four-star general re-running the war in one room, while down the hall his Humphrey Bogart rehearsed lines with Grace Kelly or Lauren Bacall, furiously marinating his brain for an altogether bizarre experiment in Method Acting.

He hit the "record" button and introduced Johnny Miller, the anti-hero, friendless, mean and without purpose until plucked from a low-level undercover job by an FBI supervisor who spots his war record and inserts him into the eye of a world-historical storm. Miller is reluctant and fast-talking. Demons in the form of dead war buddies haunt his dreams. Uncomfortable with any professional calling, he views history through the lens of personal opportunity. Emerging from his depressive funk, Miller craves sex and money. Money is shit, he says, but without it you've got nothing, you're just taking orders. But to get some quickly requires violence and ruse. Consequently, Miller sets out to deceive everyone but himself. On the surface he resembles the prickly Rick Blaine character in *Casablanca* whose dedication to freedom and the American way smells like expat nostalgia, the right stuff to justify killing Nazis and Stalinists. His moral core, however, has melted into a dangerously unstable magma of confusion and egotism. He's a drunken lover and a treacherous partner. He reeks of post-traumatic stress disorder. The bespoke business suit and soft fedora compare somehow to the hardened sarcophagus encapsulating Chernobyl's sputtering radioactive core.

After 45 minutes, the speed and alcohol dissolved Johnny Miller into a rambling drunk. It seemed he couldn't remember to whom he was speaking. He continued to recite all the lines, but it looked like he was delivering them to an unknown person or camera off-scene. I would soon learn not to interrupt because everything sounded different when I listened to the tapes at home. Besides, Tony never permitted his characters to wander off without showing them the way home. But now I stupidly suggested a break. Tony turned off the recorder. He poured another drink. It was difficult to know what remained of Miller beyond the hardboiled stereotype that he started up again almost instinctively. "I like a drink now and then. It hones the rough edges and keeps me sharp. But I don't drink all the time, and here I'm only doing what my actor's sense tells me to do. Miller was miserable before he got this case. It's the kind of work he enjoys because killing is always a possibility. Money and women too. Maybe he can't stop drinking long enough to get things done the right way and he'll end up back in the shit. His past is shit too because his friends died while he escaped. That guilt is tacky but still haunts him but not as much as the slow death by aging he faces in the present. He's got a situation where he's free to romance and screw these young women. They don't see much in the younger guys they're with, so he's kind of interesting. He strings them along but also realizes that these affairs don't go far enough or relieve his anguish. If he falls asleep or gets distracted in another way, the ghosts will start bugging him again. He was trapped until the CIA invited him back in the game. They have high standards, or so he believes. That's what scares him at the beginning."

Miller comes to view the inter-agency squabbling among the intelligence services as detrimental to national security matters. The competition and backbiting he observes have more to do with career opportunities than law enforcement or counterespionage. This realization quickly leads him to target the top operatives, not for the personal threat they pose, rather on account of his resentment of their abject dishonesty. Who put them in charge! He knew about government corruption. All relative, he would say, not really wanting to engage a political debate that might jeopardize his beliefs. Their machinations nonetheless disgusted him. Despite his personal ambivalence, he always assumed a commitment to loyalty and higher ideals among top cabinet officers. Unlike the prevaricating and weak European governments before and even after the war, the Americans were the foremost patriots dedicated to eliminating the Nazi war machine. They saved everyone else from their own foolishness. Minus cowards like Chamberlain, the Brits were good people. Churchill was a mellifluous orator and dedicated killer. Then came the rest of Europe, its moral deviancy masquerading as the ontology of freedom that excused dissociative behavior, spying on one's fellow citizens, blatant anti-Semitism, and then in 1940 outright collaboration with the enemy. By the 1960s, however, French popular memory had all but erased this ugliness by substituting a bogus narrative of general *résistance*, the textbook fantasy where millions of people fought the Occupation tooth-and-claw. It left no one to count the real collaborators who were still out there running not only the banks and the government but also the Socialist and Communist Parties. It was hard to sort the good people from the bad people. Someone needed to clean things up.

Enter Tadeusz "Ted" Szczepanski, promised messiah in the guise of the Big Janitor who never slept, didn't bother with sex, and lacked any feeling for such things as a perfect autumn day: "I saw people starving to death on warm sunny days. I smelled rotten corpses, then turned my face upwards into a cloudless sky. Don't talk to me about nice weather or similar bullshit, okay?"

Ted is the maniacal Frankenstein begat by war, religion, animal territoriality and parental repression. He's a self-conspiring assassin plotting to scour the world clean with a solitary homicidal swipe designed to trigger the ultimate world war. His experience as a ghetto inmate and subsequent refusal to accept mere survival as a gift from the Almighty provoke a monstrous outburst of adolescent immaturity worthy of the fractious demiurges of Greek myths. A single act of revenge is his only response to the call for justice and reparations – otherwise meaningless gifts – because they cannot redeem but rather only intensify the feelings of loss and suffering.

Ted weaves his plot remorselessly and sparks an international crisis whose resolution demands that he be stopped from creating further mayhem. The world's most powerful brokers begin to counter-scheme furiously until the practically derelict, low-level operative Miller is hired to neutralize him. Tony enacted the role with the physical intensity of Burt Lancaster's *Elmer Gantry*. He moved around the room shaking and gesturing one moment, then morphing into a prisoner frozen in chains. Several minutes later, he collapsed on the sofa, mercifully depleted by this amphetamine-fueled performance. I scribbled some notes quickly for future reference. How was I going to include all his facial gestures and eye movements? These characters came from a world I did not know.

I made my sandwich and tea. Returning to the living room, I mentioned to him that I'd seen a bunch of mice running around the kitchen floor. "Really. That's so nice," he mumbled dreamily. "If I had any more energy I'd go in there right now, get down on my knees and shake their little hands in gratitude for coming to visit. I love guests." Pure Tony. Then he explained that his housekeeper usually came late on Fridays to clean up.

I finished my snack and left with two cassettes. The fascist book dealer intimidated me less when I breezed past this time. I spotted a café across the street and decided to have a beer before descending into the Métro. Like most establishments around the Gare de l'Est, the place was grungy and filled with pungent black tobacco smoke hovering like a cloud over the pockmarked bar. The clientele were mostly union workers. By the look of things, they had just finished a shift in the rail yards. I nursed my beer slowly while they socialized around me. The counterman seemed to know everyone, Tony perhaps, but definitely not the two characters who'd been sharing his apartment and were now accompanying me back to the 13th.

The ghetto did not believe the rumors

Tony died of smoke inhalation on April 20, 1983. He was asleep when a blanket left on the gas heater in his living room ignited a fire that rapidly consumed his floor-to-ceiling library. The firemen broke down the door again but couldn't save him this time. When they arrived, the entire apartment was engulfed in smoke. According to the concierge, Max had tried to rouse him and then moved to the front where his loud barking alerted the neighbors. The fire brigade extinguished the flames and prevented the fire from spreading throughout the building. They found Tony's corpse in bed, called a doctor to issue the death certificate and removed him to the morgue. There is no trace of what happened to him next, where he is buried, or whether anyone contacted his next of kin, a cousin in Israel.

I had left Paris in June 1981 and got my first teaching job at Brown University in Providence the following autumn. Tony and I exchanged letters every few months. I was still advocating for a visa, and our correspondence focused on those efforts. I wrote to both Rhode Island Senators and the state's lone Congressman describing Tony's case succinctly. As a teenager, he had fled Warsaw just days before the Nazis burned down the Jewish ghetto, I explained. He had spent the rest of the war in different armies and ended up finally in

France where he parlayed his black-market profits into a Parisian nightclub. He'd catered to American servicemen whose friendships he maintained until de Gaulle ordered NATO forces out of France in 1966. Owing to his affection for Americans as the liberators of Europe, Tony had befriended and aided many American students, including me. Mr. Gawron, I explained, demonstrated the sort of hospitality rarely extended to foreigners in Paris. I was neither the first nor the last to benefit from his kindness and felt compelled to bring his case to the attention of those with the power to act on it.

To my astonishment, the three politicians responded immediately. Senator Chafee corresponded with the outgoing and incoming U.S. ambassadors to France while Sen. Pell and Rep. St. Germain directed their efforts to the State Department in Washington. Within two weeks we had answers from the responsible parties, but unfortunately they were all negative. The State Department liaison explained that Tony couldn't have a tourist visa because the embassy had designated him as an "intended immigrant" in the 1950s, and this designation had never changed. Evan Galbraith, the newly appointed ambassador to France, sent a cable with more details, citing Tony's conviction for "crimes of moral turpitude" and for making "false statements" on previous visa applications. The latter were probably omissions as to the questions about the former: Had he ever been convicted of a crime? That French justice had erased his conviction was of little consequence to the Americans who would never get over his impersonating a GI. I doubted there was a more serious infraction that Tony hadn't told me about because, even in the 1970s, the French cops enforced very strict background checks for firearms permits, and he possessed a registered handgun. Tony wasn't going to see his Polish wartime buddy now residing in New Jersey. I sent him copies of the correspondence and said there was nothing more I could do, encouraging him instead to get *Trigger* published. Perhaps if it became a bestseller or a movie, the State Department might change its tune.

In November 1979 I had delivered the *Trigger* manuscript to his agent Alain Bernheim at the same café on rue de Rennes. It was around Thanksgiving because I joked about "La Fête du Merci-

Donnant," Art Buchwald's humorous *franglais* explanation of the all-American holiday that was republished annually by the *International Herald Tribune*. Buchwald, another of Bernheim's famous clients, had befriended many famous American expats while living in Paris, and I wondered if he could be persuaded to help with publicity for *Trigger*. "We'll cross that bridge later. Let's get this copyrighted and find a publisher first," the agent had replied.

That was the last I heard of *Trigger* except for my copy of the manuscript that I shipped home before leaving France. In the spring of 1981, I had purchased an old leather courier's bag at the flea market. It was very sturdy with a chrome frame and precision lock and, weighing almost ten pounds empty, large enough to accommodate my doctoral dissertation alongside *Trigger*, some other documents, and my set of carbon-steel kitchen knives. Along with several more boxes of books and clothes, I carted it to the PTT post office on rue Cherche-Midi around the corner from my school. The clerk attached a few labels and sent it off by slow boat across the Atlantic. The charges were about $100. A few months later, the pouch and boxes arrived intact in Rhode Island. Eventually I carted this stuff to New York, but it was another twenty years before I scanned and OCR'd the pages of *Trigger* to begin the process of editing for this publication.

Neither Tony nor his agent ever managed to find a publisher, and Tony was dead by the time I returned to Paris on a business trip in 1984. Piecing together the details of his demise was nearly impossible. The concierge told me about the fire and having trashed the remaining contents of his apartment. She had no idea about the body and explained how his mail delivery had been cancelled immediately. There was no forwarding address and she did not record the handful of individuals who, like me, had come afterwards. Max had escaped unscathed and went with the firemen, she added. The fascist book vendor by the *porte cochère* was gone. There was no obituary in the papers. I didn't have the time or patience to muck around the bureaucracy to dig deeper. Who knows what happened to his Swiss bank account?

The date of the fire told me what I needed to know. April 20, 1983 was the anniversary of the Warsaw Ghetto uprising that began on the first night of Passover in 1943. It had also been Hitler's 54th birthday, giving reason to ultimate cosmic alignment of sacred and profane, interpreted by leaders of the Jewish underground army as a divine signal to unleash their improvised yet considerable firepower on the enemy.

By 1943, the ghetto had been mostly liquidated. Its dwindling population consisted of either stragglers who had escaped the selections or members of the covert Jewish underground. Having concluded they were doomed anyway, this well-organized latter group decided to give Adolph Hitler a birthday present of dozens of corpses of his murderous SS accomplices. News of the uprising arrived the next day in an Associated Press dispatch filed from Stockholm, reporting on an interrupted radio broadcast from Warsaw. "Secret Polish Radio Asks Aid, Cut Off," it read: "The last 35,000 Jews in the ghetto at Warsaw have been condemned to execution. Warsaw is again echoing to musketry volleys. The people are murdered. Women and children defend themselves with their naked arms. Save us!"

Thanks to a cadre of young smugglers like Tony, the Jewish underground had stockpiled a vast munitions depot and even built a clandestine bomb factory during the preceding eighteen months when the Nazis had begun herding weekly quotas of ghetto residents into the *Umschlagplatz*, the open-air deportation center, and forced them onto trains bound for Treblinka and other concentration camps. Despite persistent rumors, the ghetto residents did not believe they were to be gassed in mass death factories and accepted instead the official lies that they were bound for work details with a promise of decent food and better accommodations. Although they knew better, illusions had proved critical to their own sanity and to protect their loved ones from the truth of annihilation.

Tony's mother was among the bourgeois matrons who had denied reality until the moment they were separated in the *Umschlagplatz*. A victim of one of the last organized selections, she saw her son disappear into a line of young men ordered to remain in Warsaw. Until then her money had secured a relatively exalted status for the families of professionals and landowners thrown into the ghetto. It could not last. Now she was gone.

By his own account, Tony had resented his mother's preoccupation with maintaining appearances within the grotesque caricature of ghetto society. He disliked her friends, mostly doctors' wives, and detested her card games, her precious furniture and baubles. The makeshift Hebrew school she had made him attend was an annoyance despite the recognition and friendship offered by one of his teachers. He preferred the company of tough guys who resembled in real life the fictional antiheroes of American gangster movies. Their criminal mindset eschewed the judgment of his mother's circle and was better adapted to the contingencies of survival. Wartime or not, the seventeen-year-old Tony was a paragon of adolescent rebellion, his rage intensified by the incomprehensibility of the situation. No sentimental attachment had survived the gravitational pull of a bare ego foraging the ruins for anything, or anyone, that promised the elusive ideal of freedom. Not to cry – even for his mother – meant not to bemoan one's fate. It could be likened to the unforgiveable remorselessness of the convicted murderer in Camus' *The Stranger*. Or, possibly, an expression of foolish self-confidence in the existence of a world beyond the human transports and extermination camps.

Was Tony indifferent to his mother's demise?

His psychiatrist, the eminent Dr. Mendel, thought Tony had been involuntarily complicit in his mother's assimilation into pre-war gentile society. The very basis of his malformed unconscious was rooted therefore in a deception. Tony had lived this deception as a type of dependency from which there was no escape. He was raised in the shadow of his father's image as a Polish patriot and landowner and had little or no knowledge of Judaism. He had certainly never been exposed to the Yiddish-speaking communities that constituted a majority of Polish Jewry. Yet pre-war Poland was rife with anti-Semitism and even under normal conditions any exposure of his mixed heritage might have provoked disillusionment and confusion.

The Nazi occupation accentuated these pathologies. Its race laws erased any possibility for him to ever assimilate his father's identity as a Pole. Unable to conceal their Jewish identity, his mother moved them from Lodz to Warsaw. Despite Tony's everlasting resentment at being deprived of his childhood, it was a wise choice reflecting her prescience for survival and also the street smarts he would inherit.

When Hitler and Stalin carved up Poland in 1939, Lodz was incorporated directly into the German Reich. Known previously as the "Manchester" of Poland, the Nazis turned the city into a massive factory for their war machine. The security police sealed the Jewish ghetto hermetically and issued orders to shoot anyone who approached the barbed wire fence. In late 1941 half the already starving population were liquidated to the death camp at Chelmno. Jewish deportees from Germany and other western European countries replaced them and in turn went to gas chambers at Auschwitz-Birkenau in 1944. In this scenario Tony could have been one of the earlier victims of the Final Solution rather than the crafty teen who lived to tell his story, or perhaps an embellished version thereof.

By contrast Warsaw remained under the *Generalgouvernement*, the rump Polish state, where his mother's wealth secured relatively better living conditions, more food, and the semblance of an education for Tony. Crucially, Warsaw's chaotic administration resulted in a porous barrier between the ghetto and the Aryan population outside. Little surprise that compulsive role-playing became Tony's formula for survival. His social repertoire was paradoxically a flight from his mother's affective relations and simultaneously a tribute to the decisions she made to increase the probability for her son to prevail. Once beyond the ghetto walls, constantly on the run, he switched from the Home Army to the Communists, the Germans, and then the Americans. In cosmopolitan Paris, he hung out with Algerians, Corsicans, and black GIs. Holocaust survivors there viewed him as one of their own, yet, despite an occasional taste for Kosher delicatessen, he preferred a steaming Polish *bigos*, laden with stewed pork and kielbasa.

The melodramatic movies he enjoyed in his youth were more grist for possible roles. He took the characters very seriously and elevated their morality plays to a modern exegesis of Maimonides' *Guide to the Perplexed* updated by Howard Hawks. The lesson was, you had to be a bastard to subdue all the miscreants and lowlifes. "Just like Humphrey Bogart!" he insisted, alluding not only to the actor's hardboiled persona but more deeply to the honorable rogues he so often portrayed. Obtaining the gold was sufficient reward, having a heart optional as long as you could be admired for doing the right thing. A streak of irony, often manifest as gallows humor, was the residue of any compassion that emerged from his experiences. If there was any remorse, as in survivor's guilt, *Trigger* transfers that emotion to Johnny Miller, the American protagonist who suffers nightmarish apparitions of the platoon mates whom he has killed, indeed murdered. The character drinks and fornicates to escape his demons. Tony swallowed massive doses of uppers and downers and washed them down with 90-proof vodka. By doctor's orders, he avoided sex that would have been impossible anyway with his steady pharmaceutical intake. Only once did he lament his solitude in a hazy comment after watching Woody Allen's *Interiors*. "I wish I had a family like that," he slurred.

A hellish desire if you know the script.

Trapped in his portable ghetto, Mr. Gawron's *Mad House* (his cycle of short stories consumed by the flames), Tony seemed unconcerned by current events other than what he perceived as the limitless atomic power of the USA. Through the lens of his fictional Hollywood heroes and the actors who portrayed them – Humphrey Bogart, Ronald Reagan and the others – he viewed that power as the world's singular positive force. It was the last, best hope for a kid who fantasized his own survival as an achievement worthy of Olympic gold. Ironically, the American diplomatic corps, the "deep state," blindly dismissed his patriotic zeal, his emulation of everything red-white-and-blue, because of a crime of "moral turpitude."

Having exhausted the diplomatic avenues for getting Tony a visa, I filed the manuscript and turned to my own publishing agenda. On the advice of Prof. Claude Lévi-Strauss, I translated several chapters of my dissertation into English and submitted each to professional anthropology journals. Endless revisions followed, and they led me away from the novel in both spirit and style. Pursuing a career in the social sciences is a continuous writing project ruled by deadlines, job applications, grant proposals, and new research-based articles. In the months that followed I did not realize that time had lapsed beyond the date which Tony and I had agreed upon for *Trigger's* suspenseful denouement. Originally completed in 1979, the plot unfolds in the near-term future, October 1983.

Then I switched abruptly from academia to journalism with yet another set of demanding editorial priorities. After the 1984 visit to Paris when I learned of Tony's demise, any concerns about preparing *Trigger* for publication barely registered. The manuscript lay untouched, locked inside my postal transfer pouch until two decades later. I was teaching at New York University when a few students invited me to participate in a literary soirée at a Lower East Side café. Needing something not too scholarly, I pulled out the manuscript and zeroed into the "Five Days of Freedom," Tony's novel-within, as a provocative reading for my Gen-X audience.

The manuscript was now back on my desk, and soon afterwards I deconstructed its binding and scanned the pages to generate a workable electronic copy. Recalling Tony's generosity during those years in Paris, I began the process of editing and rewriting, sporadically, until deciding that the time had come to ready his sui generis novel for publication.

To Tony, the calendar never advanced past 1943. I am convinced that escaping from the real ghetto was a scene Tony rehearsed and reenacted almost obsessively. He had few if any diversions that could repress the memory of those events. To James Jones, it had appeared as the "compulsion" underlying every good novel – the "inner, bitter force" that drives a captivating narrative. For Tony, the book was to become the basis for a cinematic interpretation. As its director and producer, he would command the lights, camera, action; he would review the daily rushes, rewrite the script, coach the actors, design the movie poster, oversee film distribution, and saunter down the boardwalk during the première at Cannes where he would receive the Golden Palm award. Somewhere north of middle age, he conceded the fantasy and chose another ending, this one a suicide contrived to look like an accidental fire but revealed to the cognoscenti by a coincidence of dates: April 20, 1943, April 20, 1983.

The Warsaw Ghetto Uprising came as the furious last gasp of the fifty Jewish "battle groups" composed of wily survivors who fashioned an underground army in basements and dugout shelters beneath the ghetto streets. Tony had assisted them by smuggling ammunition and, with their encouragement, had escaped through one of the unguarded gates. As the SS marched into the ghetto, the defenders ambushed them from concealed positions. Their bullets forced the invaders to bivouac at exposed intersections that they then bombarded from rooftops with improvised hand grenades. Jewish resistance squads isolated the Germans by cutting off the adjacent streets. When Nazi tanks arrived to facilitate a retreat, more homemade bombs blew them to smithereens. A massacre ensued. Other urban guerillas deployed similarly wherever the Germans attempted to enter the ghetto. Nearly a thousand SS Einsatzgruppen died during three weeks of combat. Then the Germans torched the ghetto. From the other side, Tony watched it burn.

March 2020

Part I - Good People, New World

"Communism is at our door. We shouldn't let it in. We got to organize and resist. We got to defend America and keep it intact. We have to take care that its mentality remains healthy." – Al Capone

Monday, October 3, 1983 – **"We interrupt this WABC radio broadcast to bring you a Special News Bulletin from the United Nations in New York. This morning at the General Assembly meeting, Soviet Premier Dimitri Berisov was assassinated. A United Nations envoy is being held in connection with the shooting. The man in custody is reported to have said, and we quote, 'Listen to me, everybody. I did it. I was ordered to do it by the CIA. The CIA!' This station will keep you informed of any developments as they break."**

Chapter 1. Newark Undercover

Moscow, October 4, 1983 – "The cold-blooded assassination by the CIA of our beloved Premier Dimitri Berisov demonstrates the implacable character of encroaching Western imperialism. The Soviet people and all socialist peace-loving nations condemn this cowardly act which will not go unpunished. Nothing can eradicate the responsibility of the American government and the American nation." – *TASS*

Washington, October 4, 1983 – "On behalf of myself and the American people, we express our deep and heartfelt sympathies following this tragedy. The search for friendship and peace with the Soviet peoples and the Soviet government will not and should not be deterred by this senseless act caused by an irresponsible individual. These events were beyond our control and beyond yours, neither urged nor condoned by the American nation nor the American government nor any of its agencies." – *President of the United States*

I saw their bodies, the Germans, Billy's and Jimmy's together. They weren't moving. There was blood everywhere. Blood flowing from their bellies, from their heads. All over ... blood all over. Then two hundred yards on, toward the bridge, I saw Frankie's body. His brain slowly oozing from his smashed skull. He was dead too.

He turned to me and said, "Johnny. Johnny, come. Please join us. Join Billy, Jimmy and me. We're waiting for you. Come join us ... Come on."

"Wake up. Come on." It was Maggie pulling me out of my nightmare.

I was still sleepy. Maggie was beside me on the bed, pushing and pulling me. "What's the matter with you? The phone's ringing. It's for you. It's important. Come on. Wake up!"

"How do you know it's for me?" I yawned.

"I answered it before. He said he'd call back in ten minutes."

"Okay, Maggie. I'm getting up."

Semi-consciously, I tried to guide myself into the bathroom, plodding through a morass of year-old newspapers, wet with catpiss. I had cottonmouth and needed a drink. The bathroom faucet was useless, however, just as were all the others in this squatters' tenement in the middle of Newark.

I surveyed the room. It was filthy. The garbage had already been trampled into a sediment and a new layer was building up from empty food containers. Greasy Colonel Sanders buckets twice recycled. Once as salad bowls, afterwards as hovels for the mice. The television glared at me. New Jersey Public Access Channel 38 was running the daily employment bulletin board. In Queens, the New York Department of Sanitation was recruiting for a rodent-control team. For applicants with valid green cards, firearms permits were being offered.

I turned away and looked at Maggie. We had been alone together for an entire night. The others had left the previous afternoon on what they called a squatters' coordinating mission. In spite of this past night of quiet, she seemed nervous.

"Who's Jimmy?"

"Huh?"

"Who's Jimmy?" she persisted.

"Don't know. My connection maybe." Of course, I knew who Jimmy was. I scrounged around for some clothes, got dressed, and went out into the hall to wait. The phone rang again, and I picked it up.

"Johnny?"

"Who?"

"This is Jimmy. Where the hell have you been?

"Would you believe ... in bed? Asleep!"

"Cut the crap, Miller. This is important. I want you to change, shave, and do whatever it takes to make your ugly face presentable and get over here fast."

"I can't talk now. I gotta piss. I'll call you back." As I put the receiver down, I could hear him swearing. I went back to the room. Maggie, her black hair greasy and dirty, was up and pacing the floor, walking back and forth, naked and smoking. The pungent odor of her cigarette and the stench in the room nearly made me puke.

"Who was it?"

"My connection. I've been waiting so long for that guy of yours to show up ... well, I made my own contact. I'm going out."

"Be back soon?"

"Soon as I can." I went out onto the fresh air, found the nearest telephone booth and called the office. "This is Johnny speaking. Johnny Miller. That you, Jimmy?"

"Yes. Like I told you before. Get over here right away." I started to count the number of Chevys going by. "Berisov's been wasted. We want you on the job. So, get over here. The brass will be there."

"And just who is the brass?"

"Shut your goddamn mouth and get your ass over here. These are VIPs and we don't keep them waiting," he said.

"Well, well. All to see me?"

"Miller, I haven't got time to bullshit with you. Just clean up and come at once."

"Hey, listen. Don't fucking blow up. Cool it man ..."

"Goddamn it, Miller!"

"Look pal, you've had me here in Jersey for more than a month living in a rat-hole, trying to get the man who's commandeered every drug manufacturer on the East Coast. The connection is due anytime now. I'm not going to screw up everything now. You don't need me on this political job. I'll come to see you, but just the way I am. Take it or leave it."

I hung up and went back to the room. Maggie was curious as ever. Women are always asking questions. I sometimes wonder why they aren't used more often as spies. Always questions. Questions, questions, questions. When I ask a question, everybody looks at me like I'm nuts.

"It was my connection. Your man hasn't shown up yet, has he?"

Before she could answer, the door burst open. It was the rest of the gang, and a few others whom I didn't know. Ellie, a black homosexual, addicted to morphine and amyl nitrite poppers. Clint was a runaway from a psychiatric detention center in Kansas. His ideas were convoluted to the nth degree and on top of that he had a guilty conscience. About what I never knew, but I liked him anyway. It takes courage to refuse hormonal reequilibration. The most dangerous and reprehensible of these characters was Gary.

He came in all excited. "Hey, people. Berisov's been dropped. They say the CIA did it. The government is up to its ears in shit. The autonomists will be hot to strike. Maybe you folks want to flash out in a neutron storm, but not me. We can exploit this situation to make contact with the New England cells. Our priority targets can be coordinated."

Same old Gary. Any excuse for a terrorist's fantasy. He was usually the first to plan a target list and the last to want to put his voice on the cassette claiming responsibility. The name of his organization changed with his mood. He wore ideologies like dirty underwear but the one that fit him best was fascist. I hated that motherfucker.

"Honey, you can do as you like," said Ellie. "I'm just gonna stay here and sizzle, and when you jive-ass turkeys have done each other in, we'll have pie-in-the-sky. Jobs, dope, food and plenty of boys."

Ellie sat down in the corner, took out a small disposable hypodermic from his pocket as well as an ampule of colorless liquid. He plunged the needle into the rubber socket and withdrew about 2 cc's which he methodically injected into his arm. Ellie was together. He did as he pleased. Never bugged anybody, but he wasn't the type to let people walk on him either. If need be, he could be a real bastard.

Clint was staring out the window.

"War! Peace! I can't understand this obsession with social discourse. What does it change? Nothing. Technological expertise is what we need. Ad hoc interventions into the real and scientific nature of the world. None of this nineteenth-century bullshit about social organizations and their theologies."

"You're so fucking myopic," retorted Gary. "Can't you see where technological progress has gotten you? Emotional modulation, dial-an-orgasm, psychotropic diets. That's your future. Autonomy and self-determination are the name of the game. The only way is through revolutionary action, and that means turning to the attack, neutralizing the elite. Isn't that right, Johnny?" Gary looked me in the eyes.

"You're right, Gary. The only way to get peace is to fight for it," I assured him. I had to humor this guy carefully because he didn't trust me and probably never would. He thought I was too old to be in the group. It was Maggie who brought me in.

This was my first assignment in the New Jersey District. I had been in Boston for three months working on a case connected with this one. We scored big, knocking off a warehouse full of drugs in Watertown. Two or three guys at the top had been fingered. They were based in Providence and had managed to brainwash the executive of a chemical firm. They rewired the chain of command. A pharmaceutical compounding factory converted into a clearinghouse for illegal narcotics. We passed the word on to the Rhode Island Coast Guard station and let them take care of it.

Wilson wanted the entrepreneurs, the guys who made the profits. We left the small fry to the DA. The only one who got away was the trigger man. A special trigger man who used hypnosis and drugs instead of a .38-caliber. Word got back that he was in New Jersey. I checked with HQ and they'd given me clearance to come down here. I zeroed in on this gang and found my man. It was Gary.

Getting off the Amtrak at Union Station I'd booked-in at a fleabag in downtown Newark. The Albert Hotel was furnished wall-to-wall in semen. After a two-hour rest, I was back on the trail, cruising bars in the early evening and the disco circuit later on. Nothing. This continued for days. I had a routine. Murphy's, Hurley's, and the Salt-and-Stew, then over to the Raunch, the Phunk and Moss Eisely's.

One night at the Phunk, I was alone as usual when a girl came over to me. "Hi. I've seen you around a lot. New in town?"

"Yeah."

"Thought so. Where you from?"

"Boston."

"Pretty hot up there now."

"That's exactly why I'm here. I live in Watertown and got out just in time. I'll give it another week or so and then go back. But in the meantime, I, uh ... it's tough not to have ..."

"But you just got here."

"Don't know anybody here."

"I'm Maggie."

"I don't know anybody but Maggie."

She smiled.

"But I'm established up there. I've got my own thing going for me. And here ..."

We met frequently, though mostly by chance. Neither of us pried too deeply into the other's affairs until one night she invited me to a party.

Five weeks ago, in this same hellhole ... the place had more drugs than Smith, Kline & French. I was soaring before I even felt the syringe. I got a weird sensation. I could feel the synapses firing up and down my spinal cord. Fucked up, hon? I laughed hysterically and then came in my pants. Time-lapsed orgasm. It felt like hours. Lou Reed and the Velvet Underground in the background. Maggie to the front through the haze, another face, asses jiggling, mouths moving, finally no sound at all. Frankie calling ... a black shadow ... Mister Jimmy

Wilson ... and a very unhappy, un-birthday to us, to us. Maggie's body moving in and out of mine ... no control.

The next day I met Gary and Ellie. "We met last night at the party," stated Gary coldly.

"I don't seem to remember."

"I bet your sweet, sweet ass you don't, hon. Your first rave?" Ellie smiled.

"What?" I looked at my surroundings.

Gary and Maggie were sitting on the floor in the corner. Gary looked at me suspiciously. "Who's the grandpa?" He turned to Maggie.

"Congressional Medal of Honor winner. World War II."

"So, who gives a fuck?"

"You want to know about him, don't you?"

"Okay, Maggs, okay."

"I was thinking we might be able to use him. He's ex-military ... he might be able to ... It ..."

"Doesn't look like he can even get it up."

"What do you mean? He can fuck all right. Veteran. He's got all his limbs intact. No paraplegic, this Johnny. As a matter of fact, he's a classic stud."

Maggie got up and draped herself over my shoulders. She hung there for hours it seemed. Then she went away. "Yeah. He's not used to it, but I'll teach him."

"I'm sure you will," said Gary with a ton of sarcasm. "When's he leaving?"

"Next week. Maybe."

No, Gary never liked me. Jealous? Perhaps. But I tend to think that my age was no threat. On the other hand, he was so wrapped up in terrorist folklore, he might have taken my liaison with Maggie as a direct challenge to the Ulrike Meinhof she was playing to his Andreas Baader. Eva to Adolf. No, I don't think it was the cockplay that bugged him. Just a change in his rather infantile fantasy. One

thing was certain; he was keeping an eye on me. If I made one slip …
well, I just had to be careful. So now when he proposed a bombing,
I agreed to go along with it. "Sure, Gary. I'm with you, but I've got a
little errand to run before we get to work."

"Where ya' going?" he asked, staring at me.

"There's no more shit and since your connection hasn't shown, I've
made my own contact. I'll be back later."

"Are you sure it's not another girl?" drawled Maggie.

"Only my contact, pet."

"Kiss me before you go."

"Me too," chimed in Ellie.

"Kiss my ass!" Gary had to have the last word.

I gave Maggie a quick kiss and stopped holding my breath once
outside the room. I hated that bitch. She smelled so bad. One thing I
could never understand was why those people never fixed the faucets.
They'd probably have no further excuses for not washing.

Chapter 2. Central Casting

It took about fifteen minutes to Manhattan on the PATH train to the World Trade Center. When I reached the North Tower, a guard stopped me. I didn't blame him with my disheveled appearance.

"And just where do you think you're going?" he said nastily.

Suddenly it occurred to me that he might call the pigs.

"If you would call Mr. James Wilson at the DEA[1] office, extension 3410."

After a minute, he told me I could go up.

When the elevator door opened on the 23rd floor, Jimmy my boss was waiting for me.

"Jesus Christ! I told you to clean up. Do you know who you're about to meet?"

I looked at him. I hated him even more than Gary. More than anybody in my entire life. I had the urge to rearrange his face so that even his own mother wouldn't recognize him.

"Didn't you at least wash?" He sensed my anger but didn't try to placate it. "Boy, do you smell!"

"Look, you put me on this thing. I'm trying to do the best I can. Now you call me into some international murder. God knows what for. Why me? Besides I'm not going to ruin my cover for some stupid-ass meeting. So if you or anybody else wants to talk to me, here I am."

"Just try to act civilized in front of these people," he said as we steered toward the door. "They can do a lot for you."

"They can do a lot for you, you mean!"

He was right, this certainly was the brass. I immediately thought of

Gary and how he'd react if he saw my connection. A bunch of Grade-A political turkeys. The room too was quite a contrast from my former surroundings. Plush carpeting and a mahogany conference table. Some difference from the catpiss and apple crates. I was struck by the smooth complexion each one of the faces wore as I gazed around the table. Some of the bodies were in suits, others in uniform. It looked as if they all came from central casting, a Hollywood make-up man had just added the finishing touches. They stared back and seemed amused by my appearance. By the time Wilson had finished bowing and scraping, apologizing for my demeanor and ass-licking in general, I had associated the principal ranks with the faces.

The William Holden type in the dark suit was Haverson, Director of the FBI. The schnozz was undoubtedly Goldman from Secret Service. The fat guy in uniform was O'Brien, chairman of the Joint Chiefs of Staff. I recalled a news photo of this guy which appeared right after Vietnam. He had really fattened up. No question about the chic joints he holed up in. Berlinger, the Energy Czar, was in a tailored suit that must have cost taxpayers $3,000 at least. I thought about the last time I filled my gas tank. Next in this chamber of Hollywood dummies was Steve Kramer of the DIA. Then Secretary of State McClellan and finally Tarnovsky, the National Security Advisor. The latter stood out. His open-neck shirt and sports jacket made me think that he probably arrived too late for the puff-man to touch up. Of course, I can't forget Donaldson of the CIA, the man in the hot seat, whose intelligent look compensated for the blank, Ivy-League stares of the rest.

"I thought this was a secret meeting," shouted O'Brien. "Why have these guys been brought in?" He motioned to Wilson and me.

"Yes. Mr. Wilson can leave the room," Donaldson answered. "But Mr. Miller is our special guest today. In fact, I think you should know that his presence may determine the outcome of this little crisis.

"John Miller," he directed himself towards me, "you have an excellent record of government service. We have all your files here. Let's see." He opened the dossier. "Twenty years old when your father was murdered by the Bund. Volunteered for active duty. Transferred to OSS. Parachuted into France, then Germany. Captured by the

Germans. Repatriated. Congressional Medal of Honor. You were the man at the bridge. Remember the bridge?"

"Yeah, I remember it."

"Well, we need you on this one."

"On what?"

He began again, very deliberately this time. "I presume you know that Berisov was killed by a man who claimed to have been directed by the CIA. This, to say the least, has caused a very serious international incident. The man stated before the witnesses, before the world, that the CIA ordered him to do it. He was taken into custody by a federal agent. Of course, they got him out of the UN building. So, we've got the Soviets breathing rather heavily down our neck because we had no right to take him out of there. We're holding him on a technicality. Entering the country on a forged passport."

"In fact, this matter of a forged passport is our first lead," interrupted Kramer.

"Yes," added Tarnovsky, "it seems that our killer used a diplomatic passport to infiltrate the UN building as a member of the West German delegation."

"If it's a forged passport, then I have no doubt about the CIA's responsibility," snapped Haverson.

"I can and will swear on my mother's grave that we never gave such orders," insisted Donaldson. "Killing Berisov was senseless. We want coexistence. We don't want to have to fight them. Besides the passport was legitimate enough. It belongs to a Rudolf Schleyer, a real member of the West German UN delegation. The suspect was in possession of all of Schleyer's papers when we picked him up. This confirms my idea of a plot, because from the information coming from Germany, the Rudolf Schleyer in question disappeared and never arrived in New York. He was most likely kidnapped by the Red Army Faction."

"Has the German RAF made any claims in connection with this affair?" asked Haverson.

"No. But I suspect that an affirmation will be made shortly," assured Donaldson.

"You mean to tell us that this is part of an international conspiracy?" attempted Berlinger. "Personally, I don't believe it. It was another lunatic killer. A publicity hound like in the Kennedy assassination."

"Directed by your agency. You do seem to specialize in morons and psychopathetic types, don't you?" Haverson pointed at Donaldson.

"I protest," shouted Donaldson. "Our agency has been smeared for many years by exactly this sort of accusation. Barring that kind of mindless criticism, we wouldn't be in this position of weakness right now. We'd have a strategic advantage over the Reds.

"I repeat. Killing Berisov was senseless. There were no orders. But I firmly believe that we are dealing with a wide-ranging plot to undermine world order."

"Okay, okay," I interrupted. "Before you pick up where you left off before I arrived, please tell me, I mean, why me? What's this got to do with me?"

There was a pause. Everybody looked at Goldman who looked at me and began. "You know the suspect."

"I know him? But from where? Where?"

"You should remember him. He saved your life," said Haverson.

"Saved my life. Somebody saved my life!" It was someone I couldn't remember. "So he saved my life. But where and when? I don't remember." I tugged at my beard, trying to think when this could have happened, but nothing. "Even so, that doesn't explain why you need me," I blurted out.

Then Donaldson took over. "We chose you for many reasons. Some you already know; some you'll never know. But the main one is that you know the man who assassinated Berisov," he said briskly. "We feel that you are perhaps the only man who can approach him simply because he saved your life during the war. He might listen to you. We can't get anything out of him. We don't want much. Just get him to back off his statement, to say that the CIA did not order it, that his motive was a personal one or that he acted for the Red Army Faction.

You can offer him anything he wants. But keep in mind that we don't want a war. We don't want any trouble."

"How did you connect him with me?"

"You signed an affidavit for an immigration visa in June 1945, applied for by a Tadeusz SSSzzz ... what is this name anyway," he said, handing a piece of paper to me. "Those damn people throw 20 consonants together, tell you it's a word and then have the audacity to expect you to pronounce it."

"TADEUSZ SCZCEPANSKI" said the name on the paper. I couldn't pronounce it either.

"The name is Shipansky, Mr. Director," interjected Tarnovsky. "And I hope that you weren't referring to me as an audacious Polak ..."

"Gentlemen," Haverson broke in, "Mr. Miller has the right to a full explanation. Also, I think that he should be spared from our petty quarreling."

"My apologies, Mr. Tarnovsky," Donaldson extended his hand across the table." The insulted party accepted it with a patronizing smirk.

Haverson began again. "He saved your life. In return you probably managed to get him out of the Russians' hands. That we know. You may have wanted to get him into the US.

"1945. Tadek Shipansky. Application for an immigration visa. Affidavit signed by John Miller, US Army - Polish Labor Division[2]. Does that refresh your memory, Mr. Miller?" He paused.

"In fact, this is a good opportunity to review what the computer boys have sent us. The next thing on our man:

Belgium, January 1947. Arrested in the company of Jacob Stein and Haim Lucas. Convicted of smuggling and forgery. Served 3 months.

Paris, December 1949. Arrested with Franek Juraski. Convicted of illegal trafficking of controlled merchandise. Served 3 months again. Here's his photo, Mr. Miller ..."

Haverson continued as I racked my brain trying to put the name and picture together ...

April 1945. We were on reconnaissance patrol in a Greyhound M-8. Something had gone wrong. Our last mission was to be a parachute drop on Berlin, but the orders were canceled. Eisenhower said that Berlin was going to be in the Soviet zone. We were to move in there peacefully. I was riding along with my buddy, Fred, and an officer. We had just crossed the Elbe. Suddenly everything was quiet. No enemy. No wind. No gunfire. Nothing. Then we hit a mine. I was thrown clear. There was machine gun fire. I covered my head. When the firing stopped, I looked around. The officer was dead. I thought I was the only one alive. But as the haze of dust and smoke settled, I saw Fred slowly emerge from the vehicle's lower hatch. His clothes were shredded and exposed a bloody gash in his left shoulder. Yet he was alive and appeared otherwise unscathed.

About twenty Germans surrounded us, looking as scared as I was. I had no intention of trying to fight them. It was stupid to die in the last days of the war. So I raised my hands. One soldier moved forward and spoke to me in English. "American?"

"Yes."

"We surrender." He still had me covered. "Take us there."

He pointed in the direction from where I had just come. "Russians come fast. Not gut fur you. Not gut fur us. We surrender. Go west."

It was a nice offer ... always better to capture a prisoner than to be one yourself.

"Okay," I said.

Just as we were about to switch places, a big SS man with a machine gun appeared. "Nobody's going west. We're going east to Berlin. The Führer is in danger. Anybody who moves west will be shot. You're going east to fight the Russians."

Following this little pep talk, they started moving east.

"What about the prisoners?" asked one of them.

"Take them with us. We might need them later," said the SS man.

After walking for three hours, someone sighted a village. Cautiously we started making our way toward it. Russian soldiers appeared from nowhere, surrounding us on all sides. The German soldiers dropped their guns and put up their hands, but the SS man opened fire. He was cut down still shooting. The rest of us were lined up and searched. The Russians took anything and everything of value. "Heroes of the Third Reich," said a voice in broken German. I looked in the direction from where the voice came and saw that the speaker was a stocky Russian captain. "The war is over for you." He hesitated. "Now you're going to die." Preparations for the executions were already in progress.

But I wasn't German nor was Fred and I wasn't about to be killed like one by an ally. My protest, however, was cut short by the fist of a Russian soldier. I tried to attract the attention of the captain without causing any trouble, but I couldn't. He was busy preparing the show. "Shoot them all," he ordered his sergeant. "Shoot all those bastards."

At the same moment the order was given, a young interpreter wearing a white-and-red arm band came up and spoke to the captain. An expression of disbelief crossed the Russian's face. He pointed and called out in English. "Americansky, Come here."

I ran to him. Fred was taken away, presumably to a medic. I stayed with the captain during the execution. I was alive. It was a miracle. The Russian smiled. "Americansky. You our friend. Good. Good. Polsky save your life." He pointed to the young civilian. "My men. Mongol from Siberia. Very stupid. Not intelligent. No kulturny. We give them orders, everybody you meet you shoot. So, they shoot. We not know you Americansky. Come to the house," he said, grabbing me by the arm.

The civilian and about twenty soldiers walked to the edge of the village with us. Once inside the house where the Russians made their headquarters, we sat down. I thanked the man who saved my life and asked him questions about himself. He learned English in school and hadn't had much practice since. Therefore, he didn't speak it well, or so he said. But as far as I was concerned, he spoke it well enough to save my life and that was all I cared about.

"Americansky," interrupted the captain. "You first I see. You help us. Good. You drink vodka?" Three glasses were filled. I hadn't had a drink for a long time. It burned like hell, but I didn't care. An hour ago, I thought I was going to die, but now I was sitting at a table surrounded by foreigners, a Pole who saved my life and a Russian captain, who kept slapping me on the back saying, "Drink! Drink! You not drinked for a long time. Good Russian vodka!"

"Where you come from?" he asked.

"I was a German prisoner."

"Ooooh! You was a prisoner of war? No woman for long time. You need woman. We give. Plenty Fräulein here." It was only then that sounds from outside, which had surely been audible when I came in, sank in. There were screams and shouts, but nothing you could identify. Except for sporadic bursts of machine-gun fire and rifles, it was one big continuous noise. The vision that it brought to mind was so ...

"You want new one?" continued the captain. "Nobody take yet, we give to our ally. I like to be nice to our ally." He got up and returned to the table dragging a young girl by the arm.

She was frightened. I was embarrassed. The Pole leaned over and whispered, "Don't object. They're crazy. Do what they say. Drink with them. You never know what can happen. Do what they say. Always!"

I pulled the girl onto my lap and kissed her. "Good. Good," laughed the captain, "Americansky like us. Like women."

"It's hot in here. I'd like to go outside."

"Da! Da!" The captain downed another shot of vodka and wiped his mouth with his sleeve. "We go, out. We walk."

As soon as I put my foot out the door, I was sorry. It was like a slaughterhouse, only the victims were humans. Bodies strewn all over the place, women screaming, children crying. The smell of burnt flesh was sickening. We came to a man nailed on a cross. "Why did you do that?" I asked the captain.

"He say he believe in Christ," the captain explained with a stupid giggle. "We say there is no Christ. Man say yes. We say no. We do him favor. Da? Favor, it's good, no?" The captain laughed and pointed at the dead man. "We make him happy!"

I felt sick. "Why do you kill civilians, though?"

"Good Americansky," he laughed. "You no understand. Twenty million. Twenty million Russians, they kill. Is justice to kill Germans."

"I guess you're right," I said weakly.

"We kill them all," he shouted. "But for woman, before we kill we give fun." He chuckled and poked me in the ribs with his elbow. "But they not deserve," he added sullenly.

Just as I was about to make another comment, the Pole said softly, "Don't say anything even if you disagree." So I kept quiet.

"Americansky, woman, I give her to you. Take, sleep, fuck. Tomorrow you go east. To camp. Back to America. Remember the Russian people, good hearts. We give you drink, fuck, everything."

When I returned to the house, I took the girl upstairs. She didn't speak English, so we conversed in German.

"What are you going to do to me?" she asked timidly.

I looked at her. It was true that I hadn't had a woman for at least a month. Nevertheless, my rescuers had turned me off to sex completely. "Look," I said, "we'll just pretend. We don't have to do anything."

"Okay, you're nice. What's your name?" She was suddenly relieved that she would not meet the same fate as her fellow villagers.

"Johnny Miller."

"But that's a German name."

"My father was German," I told her as we sat down on the bed together. "What's your name?"

"Ilse!"

I explained to her that there was nothing to fear and confided that the Russians were as crude to me as they seemed to her.

"It's okay if you make love to me... I prefer making love to you than being brutalized by them."

In the morning she asked me for my address in the States, saying that she would write to me if she survived. I kissed her goodbye and went downstairs.

The captain and the Pole were waiting. "You had good time, Americansky?" inquired the captain. "We Russians good to you. You help us in the war, but late ... late in '44. We were fighting since '41. You come late. But it better late than never," he laughed. "Old Russian saying!"

He took me by the arm and led me to the table. "Eat breakfast. Russian breakfast. Much milk. Much food. Eat."

Two GI's entered. When they saw me, they greeted me like a long-lost friend. "Take them east. East. Take them to Warsaw, Polsky," said the captain. "War in the west. They go home." He sat down and wrote something. "I give you official papers."

"Let's go," said the Pole anxiously.

I hadn't even finished my breakfast. We marched east across the old Polish-German frontier, stopping now and then at Russian military installations where we were warmly welcomed. But we never stayed too long because the Pole was nervous. "You never know what's going to happen around them. Keep moving."

He explained that Warsaw had been a city of about two million people, but all of it was destroyed. We stopped just at the outskirts of the city.

"Where are you going now?" he asked.

"To be repatriated, I suppose."

"I'd like to go with you."

"Okay. Why not?" I replied. I was beginning to like him despite the nervousness.

"But I can't go dressed like this in a Soviet uniform! They'll never take me." We traded pants. One GI gave him his jacket, the other his dogtags. Now we were four Americans walking toward Warsaw. Not far from the city we encountered a reconnaissance team from the Polish State Police. They belonged to the pro-Moscow provisional government and wore Soviet uniforms. Ironically, just before they picked us up, our new friend had declared that he'd never speak Polish around the Russians again.

They took us to the Central Police Station in Warsaw. No one spoke English, we had to make do with a little German. They gave us food and bunks for the night.

Next morning, we were taken to Rembertow, the big POW camp that was full of British, French and Yugoslavs. We were put in the American section which got special treatment. We were lucky because the adjacent area was filled with men the Russians called bandits, most likely suspected Nazi collaborators. It was clear from the prisoners' screams that their captors were torturing them to extract confessions. The periodic shots confirmed the rough justice being meted out by the victorious Red Army. After we had been there a few days, a Russian colonel visited our section. "Americans, we're going to repatriate you first. You fought like we did. Then the British. The French and the Belgians didn't fight, cowardly dogs! They capitulated."

The next day they put us, including the Pole, on a train. In three days, we arrived in Odessa, which was in the British zone. British intelligence interrogated us. When my turn came, I answered all the questions satisfactorily. Then I told them, "There's a Polish guy with me. Dressed in an American uniform. His name is Tadeusz Szczepanski . Ted for short. He saved my life. I want to take him with me. If you reject him, he'll be sent to Siberia."

"Not to worry, Sergeant Miller. We'll see that Ted isn't sent to Siberia. We appreciate lads like your friend," he said in a BBC accent. "Just tell your chap not to open his bloody mouth and not to speak Polish or Russian and we'll get him home safely.

"Frankly old boy, we think that a war with the Russians is not far off. Old Blood-and-Guts is all for it. We can't stop halfway. We'll need his sort. Of course, we'll want to question him first, but as I said before, if he's cleared, we'll see he stays out of harm's way. And by the by, if he makes it, he'll have to chuck that name. He'd never get past the Russians with that. Let's see, is he dark or fair?"

"He's blond, if that's what you mean."

"Nordic type. Hmmm. Per Andersson. How does that sound?" Without waiting for a reply, he made a note on the file.

We stayed in the camp sixty days. Every night we were entertained by Russian movies of Russian victories in the war. Sometimes they sent a band to play Russian music. Finally, we were on a boat headed for Marseille. Ted was with us.

By the time we reached our destination, the war was over. I left Ted in Marseille saying, "Come join me in the States." It was difficult to get a visa, and everybody had to have one. He applied for his and I gave him an affidavit. While waiting, he worked for the Polish Labor Division[2]. I finally went home, leaving him in Marseille.

That wasn't the last time I saw Ted, but I don't think anybody now in this room knew about it.

"Stop daydreaming, Miller!" snapped Haverson. "What were you thinking about?"

I don't believe that I was thinking anything at that moment. All I felt was fear. Fear of the past or future? Not really. It was a chilled-to-the-bone paranoia about the present. I was guilty of certain things. Things that would have mattered for my career. But cops have always got the goods on one another. It keeps them loyal among themselves. A commissioner, for example, can be held in check by a stupid flatfoot, nevertheless it stays all in the family. No. It was this word-spitting computer, reeling off information to anybody who'd ask and squealing like an unconscionable cunt who doesn't know how to keep her mouth shut. I know better than to expect anyone's purpose to be served, all the more, my ass, if seamy little politicians and creep journalists probe my biography.

Having a computer sheet translated into speak-ease is like hearing the results of an autopsy. No doubt that Ted, distant as he was to me now, would in all probability be more distant at the end of this affair. More distant from me and everyone since he would probably be dead. Here was his post-mortem in the present. But what did they have on me? Had my own post-mortem come to their attention yet?

To hell with the free world, communism and nuclear warfare. Since they were so convinced of my indispensability to this case, maybe I could use that position as a means to delay the payments. Take out a second mortgage on my ass, so to speak.

"I was thinking, gentlemen, that I will not be able to work on this case for you unless I can be assured that all computer references to myself be handed over to me and deleted from the files."

"And if not?" demanded McClellan.

"The choice is obvious, gentlemen," I was suddenly dealing the cards to these over-ranked dummies and even before they acquiesced, I could see the further possibilities in terms of pure cash that this affair offered.

"One more thing, Miller." McClellan was obviously rankled to discover that the Freedom of Information Act had not been repealed. "We're assigning another man to work with you."

"What for?"

"We know you like to play around, Miller. We think you need someone stable with you. We also need the FBI on this."

"What's his name?"

"Dave Harris."

I didn't like the idea much, but I really had no choice in the matter. "Okay ... but sometimes ... I meet people who'll talk to me and only me."

"We'll worry about that later. For now, we want you to start with this man Stein. He lives in Brooklyn and was once arrested with the suspect for smuggling and forgery in Belgium in '47."

These were Haverson's orders.

"Something else you want to say, Miller?"

"Yes, it's Wilson. I don't need his assistance. Promote him, demote him. Just keep him off my back."

"One more bit of detail, Miller," persisted Donaldson. "I don't believe this theory of a lunatic murder. I am convinced that the

German Red Army Faction were contract players in this one. The Palestinians and Jap Red Army could also be involved. These groups all work together. The guy, Schleyer, whose passport the killer has, was on the RAF's hit list. Why, we don't know, but I suspect that this plan has been in the works for months, even years."

"We still believe that it was a one-man job," insisted Haverson.

"You never admitted that organized crime existed either, did you?" retorted Donaldson.

Chapter 3. Brooklyn Deli

Wednesday, October 5, 1983 – "... increase in tension due to the 'bloc' policy which had been predicted and soundly condemned by our former leader, General De Gaulle, has risen to the surface. ... France has offered her services to preserve peace. ..." – *President of France - TF1*

"As of 6 AM, all cultural and economic links with the Iron Curtain countries have been suspended. In Beijing, the Chinese Minister of Foreign Affairs, Wing Lo Pin, declared 'socialist imperialism' as the greatest danger to world peace. ..." – *The New York Times*

"Berisov's assassin has been identified as a Polish refugee, Tadek Shipansky. Shipansky entered the UN Building under the identity of Rudolf Schleyer, a West German diplomat. It is widely presumed that the missing Schleyer was kidnapped in Germany by the Red Army Faction although no official claim has been made." – *WCBS*

In order to avoid any potential interference with my work, the FBI had planned to extricate me from the case I was working on. A bust was planned and once at the station, I would be separated from the rest of those creeps and freed to pursue my investigation with Harris, whom I had not met. It was sometime before dawn when I returned to the apartment. Maggie was waiting up for me. She was as dirty as ever.

"Everything go all right, Johnny?" she asked as she put her arms around me.

"Not really," I mumbled as I pushed her away. "Don't sit down. We have to go."

"Where?"

"Our target is the oil tank farm in Raritan." I continued my charade as a radical provocateur.

"What purpose is sabotage?" piped in Clint.

"Sabotage! You wanna talk about sabotage! The fascist government sabotages our lives everyday. Fight fire with fire!" Gary always had the answers.

Clint was wavering again, but he was too unsure of himself to resist for any length of time. "What you guys do, I'll do, because I know you're right."

There were times when I wondered just what Clint had for brains. They must have scrambled them but good at that detox clinic he was always talking about.

By contrast, once I pushed a challenge, Gary became insistent. "Come on. We got to go now."

When nobody moved, he sat down.

"I want you to explain the details while we're here. Have a drink, old buddy," I said. I knew that the cops would arrive shortly.

As we were sitting on the bed, Maggie turned to me. "I love you."

"Why? Because of my medal ... or because I'm an aging war hero turned urban terrorist?"

She looked hurt and didn't answer.

A moment later someone in the hall was shouting, "Pigs! Pigs!"

The door burst open and we were surrounded by a ten-man anti-terrorist squad dressed in flak. Gary reached for his pistol. A shotgun blast ripped through his chest. He dropped immediately. That shook the rest of us, and we offered no further resistance as the handcuffs were secured and we were escorted downstairs past the waiting TV cameras and into the paddy wagons.

At the station, when they began filing charges, I was taken to a small room where I found Wilson waiting for me.

"Phew, boy! Do you need a wash."

"Fuck off!"

"Don't forget, Miller, I'm your boss."

"Somebody's been putting you on, baby."

"Watch your step."

"Get off my back, Wilson. If you don't, I'll ..."

"Try it son, and I'll see that you're sent back to pencil-pushing in 24 hours. Berisov or no Berisov." He stared hard at me.

"Motherfucker, you've been asking for this." I hit him twice and he fell to the floor. I had been itching to do that ever since being assigned to his section. "Now you have a reason. Sorry, but you can't do a damn thing. I'm not under your orders anymore. This is goodbye, sweetheart."

I bent over him and lifted his billfold out of his jacket pocket. "Since you've been so vocal about my wardrobe, I think you won't mind paying for some new duds, will you?" I laughed as I counted off the Ben-Franklins and shoved the empty wallet back into his pocket.

I left him there fuming and quit the station. As I hustled through the corridor, I heard Clint screaming. They were probably interrogating him. Poor freak. He couldn't tell them a thing and for that he'd get a free trip back to that mental hospital in Kansas. Finally, I made my way into the street. I stopped at the first barber shop and took a shave and a haircut.

I went to Brooks Brothers on Fifth Avenue for a new suit, some shirts, ties, and shoes and then to Carnegie Hall for the designated rendezvous with this man, Harris. It was at the Russian Tea Room, a table to the right of the revolving door. I entered the restaurant and sat down. I turned to see an athletic man in his forties with brown hair and eyes standing by me. He was conservatively dressed. The only thing that was odd about his manner was his posture. His head seemed tilted toward the left.

"Glad to meet you, Miller." He extended his hand, which I purposely and rudely ignored. I turned back to the table. "I've already eaten, but if you ..."

"No time for that now. Let's go." I really was in a hurry.

We left the restaurant and I followed Harris around to his steel-blue Camaro parked on West 56th Street.

"Who's first on our list?" he asked as we entered lunch-hour traffic.

"Jacob Stein. He owns a delicatessen in Brooklyn. I don't think it's wise for you to come along."

"My orders are to stay with you," he insisted.

From that point on, I realized that he would be an albatross around my neck. I saw that he would interfere with my investigation as well as ruin any fun I might be able to have at the same time.

We arrived at Stein's about 1:00 and ordered coffee and sandwiches. It was a medium-sized place with lots of customers. Stein was, I presumed, the man behind the counter making sandwiches. He was tall and wiry with greying hair. I would have placed his age somewhere around early to mid-sixties. His eyes were shifty. I didn't like them. They were cold and always darting about. I thought that the woman at the cash register might be his wife. People were coming in with orders for the surrounding offices and shops. The restaurant was clean. He probably had a nice turnover. Fairly low overhead. "A nice tidy profit here," I said to no one in particular.

"Yeah," responded Harris.

"He can't talk now, he's too busy. Let's go."

We returned two hours later. There were only a few people lingering in the place then. Harris ordered more coffee and sat down. I approached the counter and showed my ID. "Special investigator, Mr. Stein. I'd like a few minutes of your time."

"Go ahead," he said without apprehension.

"Have you read the papers lately?" I asked matter-of-factly.

"Yeah."

"Know who killed him?" I popped the question like a gunshot.

"Who? Berisov?"

"Yeah, Stein. Berisov."

"Some nut. I don't know. What's it got to do with me? With my business?"

I didn't want to go into the details at that moment. The place was beginning to fill up with a new crowd. "Look, Stein, we need your help. You've got a nice place here. A wife. Children born in the country perhaps. All we want is a little cooperation."

"And if I don't cooperate?"

"We'll deport you."

"Whaddya' mean?"

"When you applied for your visa in Paris, did you mention that you had done time?"

"What's it to you!"

"You were in jail in Belgium. So, we can kick you out on a technicality like that because you lied on the visa application. Anytime we please."

"If you want to make a federal case of it, go ahead. But I'll get a lawyer. It'll take you years to get me, if you're right. I have nothing more to say."

He was right. I motioned to Harris that I was ready to go. I looked at Stein. His face showed no emotion. Harris had already opened the door and was halfway out when I showed Ted's picture to Stein. He went pale. "We want to know about him."

His face swelled with anger. "I don't know him from nothing. Get out from my place." He was still shouting when I closed the door.

"Well, what now?" said Harris.

"Stein's got to talk, but my hunch is that he's more afraid of Ted than being deported."

"Wonder why."

"We'll have to find out. Come on. If I know Stein, he'll go to the mob for protection." We got into the car.

"Are you still hungry?" asked Harris as he saw me place a small package on the dashboard.

"Nope."

Chapter 4. Kishke Max

We drove to a street just on the edge of Williamsburg and stopped in front of the crummiest house on the block. It didn't look like it belonged to a mobster. At the door we were stopped by two young hoods.

"Going somewhere?"

"Yeah, to see Max."

"Max ain't interested in seeing nobody."

"Okay, just give him this package."

The older of the two hoods took the package and left us facing an acne-faced kid on the stoop. A few minutes later he returned and motioned us to come in. We followed him into a large room. It was poorly decorated. All the pictures hung crookedly on the wall. Papers and books were strewn about on the furniture and the floor. They covered every available inch of flat space. There were a few old suitcases, a few shabby chairs around a rickety-looking dining table that was littered with dirty dishes, glasses, and ashtrays. When the door closed behind us, a man appeared. He was in his late fifties, about six feet tall and, Christ, was he huge – at least 300 pounds. His face was surrounded by multiple chins and his stomach made him look like Sidney Greenstreet. "Hi. You the guy that sent the kishke?"

"Yeah."

"You not Jewish!" he stared at both of us.

"No."

"How do you know that I'm Kishke Max?"

"Later. I'd like to ask you some questions." I was not going to reveal information from confidential sources.

Max smiled and slapped my back. "Anybody who knows I'm Kishke Max already knows a lot. What do you want?"

"We're special investigators working for the State Department on the Berisov case. Look, Max, we're on the brink of war."

"I don't talk business under any pretenses whatsoever. Not with the feds especially," he added. "Were not exactly legitimate, but we ain't wrapped up in stinkin' political affairs either." Max was getting heated under all that fat.

"If a war happens, Max, all Americans – queer or straight, black or white, guinea or dago – we all go up this time. It's your own ass you'll be saving by cooperating with us."

"So who's a better patriot than Max!" he proclaimed, making light of what he had said before. "What can I do for you?"

"We came to talk to you about Jacob Stein. He seems to have had some connection with Berisov's murderer, but when we showed up at his deli and flashed him the picture, he clammed up. He got uptight and threw us out of the place. I can't say we were overly genteel with him. We threatened to deport him on a technicality. No doubt he'll come to you. Please convince him to cooperate." I stared at him in expectation of an answer.

"Stein?" he slapped his forehead. "Stein? He's messed up in this? I don't believe it. Listen, why don't you guys sit down. If and when he calls, I'll see what I can do."

I chose an overstuffed chair long overdue for an appointment with the upholsterer. Harris sat on a wooden settee which was stacked with old newspapers at the other end.

"You brought a kishke. That's my password. Okay, we'll talk about Stein. Want a drink first? Vodka okay?"

He poured out three vodkas.

"This isn't entirely in my line, you know," reflected Max. "I usually protect my people, all of them.

"Sometimes though, we sacrifice one or two for the common good. It's a kind of moral obligation and there's no organization that can last without it. I learned that early. Do you know what a kapo was?"

"No," I lied to keep him talking.

"A kapo was the master of death for every deportee in the concentration camps and was appointed by the SS. I was the strongest when I was younger, and I thought that being a kapo was the only way to survive.

"The last camp I was in was Chelmno, run by an SS man named Horst. The first morning after our arrival he ordered everybody outside for inspection. Six hundred of us were standing there in the cold and sleet but he didn't give a damn. 'Everybody stays here for six hours!' he ordered. Some froze. Some just died. Others fell. SS men came around and beat those on the ground. Some of the deportees stood up again because the beating was worse than freezing to death. I mean when you're dead, you're dead. You don't feel nothing then.

"Some hours later, Horst came back. 'I need an assistant here. Any volunteers?' Two or three guys stepped forward. Horst beat them until they fell. 'You're not good for anything but the gas chamber, kikes,' he snarled.

"Then a good friend of mine, Levi, stepped up. 'I'd like to be a kapo,' he said.

"'All right. Let's see what you're made of.'

"Horst started to beat and kick him, but Levi stood his ground. It was strange. Horst hated the guys who fell and was enraged when a guy didn't fall. He couldn't beat Levi though. No matter whether he hit in the belly or in the balls, Levi just stood there smiling. Then Horst called some SS man to help him. They beat Levi with sticks until he went down. Then they took him to the gas chamber.

"I didn't know exactly what to do, but I hoped I had Horst figured out. So I stepped out. 'Hauptsturmführer Horst, I'd like to be a kapo.'

"'You would, would you?' He looked me over. 'To be a kapo for me you have to be able to withstand pain.'

"I understood the son-of-a-bitch. Pain or no pain, he just wanted to send people to their deaths personally. Anyway, I just took half-measures, just between the Jewish mite[3]. Anti-Semites understand what that means.

"He hit me five or six times. I didn't move. When he hit me the next time, I figured that if I didn't move, he would be so mad that he'd kill me. The blow didn't hurt me as much as the others, but I pretended that it did. 'Hauptsturmführer Horst, please don't hit me again. You've hit me enough already. You really hurt me.'

"He looked at me. He knew I was on to his little game. 'Stand up, Jew!' he ordered. I stood up. 'I think you'll make a good kapo.'

"So, I became a kapo. I didn't want the job. If I could've done something else, I would've, but I wanted to live. Being a kapo wasn't fun, believe me. Some people considered them worse than Nazis. But all I could think of was survival."

Max stood up and wandered toward the bathroom. He seemed to be enjoying himself, reminiscing about the old days. When he had disappeared from sight, Harris leaned toward me and whispered, "What's this got to do with Berisov? A fat old mobster telling war stories?"

"Listen, Harris," I confided, "you're new-school, all textbooks, computers and torture. I like to play shrink. Maybe it's perverted, but let the guy go on and we'll fish for whatever is useful. Besides, maybe you should listen. Organized crime isn't as awful as they teach you. You think that Henry Ford would cooperate with us like that?"

We shut up when the toilet flushed. As he returned to the room, Max picked up the story as if it had never been interrupted.

"I'll tell you something perhaps you didn't know. In every camp there was a guy with a vice. Real sadistic. In some camps they cut people in half with butcher knives. In others they drowned them by holding their heads in a bowl of water. Sometimes they punched a wooden stick through their bellies. They liked to see the prisoners die slowly.

"Horst liked dogs. He had some *Schäferhunde* in the camp. He wanted to keep them happy. So everyday ten or twenty men were tied to a pole, naked from the waist down. The dogs bit off their dicks and balls. These men died in pain and agony. In comparison, those who went to the gas chamber or who were shot had it easy. It was my job to choose men for this also. He made me kapo. What else was I going to do? If I hadn't done it, I might have died like those men, and I wanted to live. If I hadn't been kapo someone else would've taken the job."

There was a noise outside the door. I thought it might be Stein, but nobody came in. Max offered us cigarettes. "Go on, Max, tell us about Stein."

"I was returning to the barracks after talking to Horst. There was a tremendous ruckus coming from inside. It sounded like the place was being demolished. I rushed in to find the prisoners beating up two newly arrived inmates. That was nothing new, but then I heard, 'You goddamn Jewish policemen. We'll tear you to pieces, you bastards!'

"Looking out the window, I saw two Germans heading my way and, being responsible for peace in the barracks, I couldn't allow this to continue. I stopped the fight and told the new guys to clean up before the SS men arrived. Although they knew I was right, the others protested. 'Let us finish them off. Come on, Max. Those guys were policemen in the Lodz Ghetto. They put us on the train for the camps. Our families were destroyed because of guys like them. Let us kill 'em.'

"I told them that here in the camp, Germans did the killing, not us. I went over to talk to the ex-policemen. I needed some help and knew that they would be devoted to me since I saved their lives. One of them was Stein. He was strong. He should have been. Stein made it because he stole potatoes from those weaker than him. He was in my barracks and I saw what he did. When we gave the ration of bread and potatoes, anyone who didn't grab theirs right away, Stein snatched and ate. That's how he survived. At first, I put him only on the gold teeth detail. With this gold, we could maybe buy off the Germans or buy some weapons. But afterwards I put him and some other men in positions so they could get hold of the ammo if need be. You see, my position in the camp gave me access to many places and with a little patience and keeping my eyes open, I found out where the Germans kept their weapons. I knew that someday we would all be free or all dead.

"Horst was a very strange man. When he was drunk, he would come to see me. 'Max, you're a good man. You're like me. You're like an SS man. Whether Germany wins or loses the war, we're buddies. You're like me even though you're a Jew.'

"I said nothing, just smiled.

"'What would you like to do after the war, Max?'

"'Hauptsturmführer Horst,' I said, 'the one thing I want to do is have a kishke.'

"'What's that?'

"'Jewish food. It looks like a würst and it's filled with rice and meat. It tastes good.'

"'Max, if we survive, and you will survive because I can order it, we're going to eat a kishke.'

"'Yes, sir.'

"Trying to keep Horst happy wasn't the only problem I had. Something was always cropping up. Never a dull moment. Can you imagine where it came from next? Would you believe the Communists? You see, there were a lot of Reds in the camp. In certain barracks, they served as kapos too. They also selected men, but not like I did. Their thing was to protect the party politicians and save men who were devoted to their ridiculous cause. One day a Communist kapo came to see me. He was big and strong like me. I think that's why the Communists chose him to talk to me.

"'Max, you have to change your selection system.'

"'Why? What's wrong with it?'

"'Sometimes you send to the gas chamber some very important people that we should try to keep alive for the future.'

"'Look, pal, you run your barracks your way and I'll run mine my way. We'll leave things just as they are.'

"'But we can't let you do that. The party wants to save our intellectuals. Some aren't very strong and you're sending them to the gas chamber. Don't you understand? We should try to save them.'

"I started to laugh.

"'What's so funny?'

"'You Communists, I've met you before in Warsaw. You were always moralizing and accusing me of cheating the people in the ghetto whom I risked my life to feed. Now you're questioning my judgment. Under these conditions? But what you are doing is exactly the same, only you select them in another way.'

"'We can't stop people from dying, but we can try to be rational, to keep the best ones for the future. You should help. Don't forget the war will end one day and we will run the society.'

"He thought I was stupid. I always hated those scholars and intellectuals before the war. Who was I then? I was a nobody. Here in the camp, I was somebody. I was kapo and now they could kiss my ass. I had plans for him and his comrades. 'Okay, I'll cooperate with you guys, but you'll have to introduce me to your committee so they can tell me who I'm supposed to protect.'

"You know what I did? The next day, I went to see Horst and told him the Communists were pressuring me. Horst was furious. He ran around the room like a madman. 'Who do those bastards think they are?' he shouted. He turned to me, 'They're trying to run the camp. You can never tell what these people will try to do.' He paused. 'Good, you just go along with them for the time being. We'll get all of them.'

"Within a week all the Red leaders were executed, and then I had a little peace and quiet … at least from the Communists.

"We lived like a big happy family, if you can call it that, until we heard on the hidden radio that the Soviets were heading in our direction. The Germans, of course, had been alerted, and the number of gassings and shootings increased. This was the time to strike. I had two possibilities, to be killed by the Germans as a Jew or by the Reds as an anti-Communist kapo.

"When we heard that the Russians were only a few miles away, we stole guns and killed or captured all the SS men and guards. I took Horst prisoner. Everybody was trying to kill the surviving SS men and guards, but I had plans for Horst. 'Okay, Max, you take me prisoner, but don't forget, I saved your life.'

"'I won't. But remember, I promised to eat kishke with you.'

"'Yeah,' he laughed. Are we going to have it right now?'

"'Uh-huh.' I thought about what the French Jews told me about what the Arabs did in North Africa. I found a knife and cut off his dick. When he opened his mouth to scream, I shoved it in.

"At just about the same time, the Russians arrived. They were horrified at what they saw. Prisoners looking like skeletons, dead Germans all over the place. A young sergeant stopped the prisoners from killing the rest of the Germans. Now justice was coming. And like they say in all good Westerns, which I like so much ..."

The telephone was ringing. Max didn't finish his sentence but spoke into the receiver. "Yeah, this is Max. That you, Stein? Well, why don't you come over. We'll talk about it. See you."

He put down the receiver.

"You were right. You knew he'd call me for protection."

I'm not certain why, but Harris had become engrossed with Max and his story. Maybe he had never met an organization man like this. Perhaps the macabre stories of concentration camps triggered a spark in this criminologist's fantasies. Whatever it could have been, he was now playing my game. "So, tell us, Max, how did you get involved with the mob?"

"When the war was over, I had to prove to my brothers that I too was against the Germans. Only a few people were still against me. Some said I had contributed to the deaths of their relatives. Other survivors told the courts that they wouldn't have made it without my help. And that was the truth.

"I settled in Germany near a camp in Salzheim. You know how Jews are. They argued and fought among themselves. If they couldn't find an answer, they went to the rabbinical court for help. This was okay but the rabbis didn't have anyone to enforce their decisions. I mean, rabbis don't go around beating up people, do they? Since they knew my background, they came to me. 'The Court said Isaac owes Moishe two thousand dollars, but Isaac doesn't want to know. Will you convince him to pay up?'

"'Sure, for twenty percent, I'll convince him. I'll see that Moishe gets his money.' And that was my job. The rabbis were the Court and I was the Enforcer. I didn't kill anybody though. I just worked a guy over until he paid. I did this until my American immigration visa came through. I came to Brooklyn and the same thing happened. They'd heard about me from the old country. One guy owed another and wouldn't pay up, or when just anything went wrong, someone called me. I'm not an intellectual. I was a railway porter, then a kapo, but I beat a guy's head and he pays. When they lend money, they ask me for support. When they make bets, I back them. People know if Max is on the scene and if you don't pay up, Max'll beat your brains out.

"One day you know what happened? Two hoods came to see me from a guy called Pasquale. Yeah, the Mafia. They told me that I was cutting in on Pasquale's territory and that I 'shouldn't oughta do that' and 'lay off or else.' I grabbed them, knocked their heads together and took their guns. 'If Pasquale wants to talk to me, you schmucks, then take me to Pasquale.' I finally met the man I knew only by reputation, whom I admired very much. 'Pasquale, here are your errand boys ... and their toys.'

"Pasquale wasn't angry. On the contrary, he grinned. 'Max, if you can handle my boys like that, I'm sure you can handle Brooklyn. Lately I've had a hard time with the new immigrants who come from the camps. I tried to be nice to them. I used all kinds of persuasion, but they won't cooperate.'

"'I'll give you a bit of free advice. People who lived in camps will never be impressed by you guys. Your kind of persuasion will never work. But if you want, we'll make a little deal and I'll handle them for you.'

"'Okay Max. You do Brooklyn for me, and I'll cut you in on the profit.'

"'I'm an old Polish Jew. I don't ask for anything else,' I told him.

"That's how I'm in the Mafia. I'm a gangster. Maybe I'm no good, but I'm still a patriotic American. Like I said before, I tried to get rid of those goddamn Reds even before I came to this country. But then most of the Mafia men are very patriotic. They're not like those hippies who raised hell and closed universities. You have to realize that we old-timers, we gangsters, are good Americans."

Harris and I smiled at each other.

"So, Stein's coming?" I asked, getting up to stretch my legs.

"Yeah. But it'll take some time before he gets here. It's not far but he moves slowly."

Chapter 5. Stein's Tadek

I was trying to build a mental picture of Max and Stein during and just after the war, but my thoughts were interrupted by the doorbell. A few minutes later, Stein appeared and went directly to Max, who was staring at us. When Stein turned around to notice Harris and me, he was terrified.

"I see you've met before," Max said sarcastically. "Stein, let's make a deal."

"What kind of deal?" He was visibly shaken.

"Sit down. Take it easy, boy. Have a drink." Stein eased into an upright Windsor chair, gripping the arms so tightly that his knuckles were almost white. Max got up and filled a glass with vodka. "Listen, I can't cover you on this thing. It's too big." He spoke slowly and deliberately. "I think you'd better tell them what they want to know. Something's happened that nobody could foresee. Something that involves all of us ... Americans, Russians, Germans, the organization – everybody. These men are investigating it. Cooperate. They know nothing."

"He's okay?" Stein glanced from me back to Max accusingly. "They came to my place. They talked to me already."

"He came to your place. He talked to you. So what'sa matter!" Max shouted.

"Listen, I pay you every week, every month for protection and this is all I get!" Stein shouted back. "Where is your protection when I need it? How can I have faith in you?"

"Stein, remember the camp? Nobody can have faith in nobody. Do you think the camp is finished? The concentration camp was, is, and will be forever. The methods have changed, the people are different, but everything is still the same. I was your kapo, right?"

Stein nodded.

"Did I save your life?"

Stein nodded again.

"Okay, now I want to save it again."

"I don't know," Stein hesitated weakly, his cold eyes now glaring at me. "If I talk, I might go to jail."

I interrupted them. "Nobody's going to jail. This is a very special investigation. We only want some facts. We'll overlook anything you say that might be incriminating. But tell the truth. That's all we ask." There was something about Stein that made me instinctively mistrust him.

"You see, Stein. No problem. Look, he even brought me a kishke." Max ratified our bonafides.

"No. Impossible! A goy brought you a kishke?"

Max nodded affirmatively and showed him my package. Stein looked at it and then at me. His face registered even more surprise when he saw the name on the bag. "You bought this at my place!"

"That's right."

Okay, I'll tell you what I know about him on one condition – that nothing I say is going to be held against me and ..."

"For Christ sake, we told you once," Harris reprimanded him in annoyance. "All we're interested in is the man whose picture Johnny showed you this afternoon."

"As I was going to say before you interrupted me," Stein continued, "... and protect me from him." He motioned back toward Max.

"You'll have all the protection you need." Harris's face tightened. "Tell us about him."

Stein got up and poured himself another drink, then returned to the wooden chair. "Well, I don't know where to start. You know I was in a concentration camp."

"You're making my heart bleed," I interjected. "I went to one of the camps during the liberation. I saw you people. Just skip the sob stuff and get on with it."

"Where you want me to start?"

"From the moment you met the man we asked you about."

"When the Russians closed in on Chelmno, the Germans scattered. We seized their weapons and escaped west. A truck picked up me and two of my friends and drove us to Paris where the Jewish Relief Agency took care of us. The three of us got jobs with the Americans in Paris. I worked for an optician. The others did various jobs. We made about twenty dollars a month each, which was more than the average Frenchman got then. We slept in a house on the rue des Rosiers in the Marais area that soon became a meeting place for Jewish refugees. There were about fifty in our house and almost no privacy. But it was better than being dead.

"Every so often we made a buck on the side, selling cigarettes, whiskey or anything else we could get from the American soldiers. Somehow, they knew about our place and came regularly with all kinds of stuff – candy, blankets, anything. In '45 there was nothing in France.

"One day three American soldiers came in with a load of cigarettes. I'd seen them before but never paid any special attention to them. One of them looked at me and smiled. He smiled ..."

"So, he smiled," interrupted Max. "I smile, see?" Max's triple chins arranged themselves into a smile. "Ha, ha, ha. I laugh too. The Feds smile, don'cha? Show him." Harris and I smiled. "See. Everybody smiles."

Stein glared back sullenly at Max. "We bought his cigarettes, and I struck up a conversation with him. Although he was in an American uniform, he spoke to me in perfect Polish. 'How are you guys getting along here?'

"It was the first time a GI had spoken to me in perfect Polish. It took me by surprise. 'Hey! Where did you learn to speak Polish like that?' I asked.

"'I'm not here to talk about Polish. I'm here to make money, and I need some help. I've had my eye on you and I like the way you operate. How about it?'

"'Sounds okay with me, but my buddies ...'

"'Come over here,' he said, pulling me by the arm into a corner. 'I don't want the guys I'm with to hear me speaking Polish. Look, we have a lot of cigarettes, gasoline, and other American things to sell. This is the time to make some quick money.'

"'Why pick me?'

"'I told you. I've been watching you. And you're Jewish.'

"'Yeah, that's right.'

"'Were you in the camps?'

"'Yeah.'

"'And your buddies?'

"'Same thing.'

"'Their names?'

"'The short one is Bloom and the other one is Lucas. He's Lithuanian and speaks very good English.'

"'I've got a proposition for you. I'll drop by tomorrow with ten cartons of cigarettes. We'll talk then.'

"The next night he came just as he said. Of course, I trusted him, but nobody gives something for nothing.

"He greeted me with a question. 'You think I'm American, don't you?'

"'Well, you're wearing an American uniform. You speak good English. Of course, you're American.'

"'I speak good Polish too, don't I?'

"'Sure, but there are a lot of Poles in America.'

"'I'm as much a Polish-American as you are,' he laughed. 'I'm a refugee like you. I'm in business. Like I told you yesterday, I need some help. I want to organize my own outfit. I have a lot of stuff to sell but nobody I can trust to handle it. Are you with me or not?'

"I looked at him and smiled. 'Naturally we want to make money. But we don't want to take risks.'

"'What's your name?'

"'Stein. What's yours?'

"'Tadek. Look, Stein. No risks, no money. I mean, after all you went through during the war, a little smuggling, a little black market … what kind of risk is that? You stick with me and I'll make you some money. Call your friends over.'

"I called Lucas and Bloom over and told them what Tadek had just told me. 'By the way, what are you doing now? Jobwise, I mean?' he asked.

"'I work for an optician, they're stock boys at the PX,' I replied, gesturing toward Lucas and Bloom.

"'You dopes! Did you suffer for four years just to work for a glass grinder or in some lousy warehouse? That way you'll never be covered with gold,' he upbraided us.

"'Gold? What gold?' I asked.

"Then he smiled again, a very strange smile. 'The gold they were supposed to cover you with …'

"'Huh?'

"'Oh, it's not important.'

"'What the fuck are you talking about, Tadek?'

"'Forget it. Look, from now on, I'll come to Paris every week with the stuff. I want you guys to sell it for me.'

"He kept his word. Every week he came with different things. The money was good and easy to make. He was the brains of the outfit. He was everything. Finally, we gave up our jobs with the Americans. It didn't make sense to work for them for twenty dollars a month if we could make two hundred with Tadek. But some things about him worried me. I mentioned it once. 'Why do you wear that uniform all the time?'

"'I'll tell you one day,' was his only response.

"I wasn't put off so easily and probed continually for a serious answer. In '46 the Americans began pulling out of France. There would be no more supplies available, no more depots. Tadek came up with a new idea. 'We're going across the border with fake American papers to Belgium and Germany or to any country where US troops are stationed.'"

"Do you know where he got the travel orders?" asked Harris.

"I didn't ask. We trusted him. It was a very simple operation. We went to Brussels, bought two thousand pairs of nylons, returned to Paris and sold them on the black market for double the price.

"Then we noticed that the French and Belgian officials were now checking everyone's papers more thoroughly than ever.

"'From now on, we're going to have a new cover,' he told us one day. 'We're going to be non-commissioned military police.'

"'I don't know how he did it, but he got the uniforms and badges, the whole outfit. It was very funny, because Bloom and I couldn't even speak English. Tadek told us to keep our mouths shut. In an emergency to let him do the talking. So, dressed as American MPs, we carried things across the border, and nobody bothered us.

"Sometime later on, Tadek decided that Belgium was getting too hot. 'We'll go to Germany now and resume in Belgium later.'

"In Germany we got cameras and other photographic equipment. We traveled by train. It was hard to get around in Europe in those days. Nobody had passports, and Germany was a special area. Yet with the papers Tadek gave us, we went back and forth without any trouble. If the police wanted to check our bags, he told them that we were military couriers carrying mail from Germany to Paris. We looked so goddamn official that French cops didn't even check us anymore."

"Who gave you the uniforms?" asked Harris.

"I really don't know. Tadek provided the cover. There was a black MP in Paris I never met or spoke to. But it was him probably. He and Tadek were very close."

"Did you know his name?"

"I asked around because I was interested in how we got the stuff too." Stein closed his eyes and put his head in his hands. "No, I can't think of it now. It'll come back to me."

"What kind of name was it? American, English, French? Was it a nickname? Come on, man, think," Harris persisted.

"Wait, it was ... English. No, it was both English and French. That's right. He had a nickname too. I remember thinking how funny it was for a black guy to have such a name."

"Try for the nickname first."

Harris, Max and I came up with all sorts of wild names but ... nothing.

"I know what it was," Stein blurted out suddenly. "He had the same name as an English general during the war. No, not a general. He had a rank the Americans don't have ... I think."

Max and I were stumped. We were drawing blanks. "Was this man Army, RAF, or Navy?" asked Harris.

Stein looked blank.

"Was he a fighting man? Was he with Eisenhower?"

"Now I have it. It was Montgomery."

"The MP was named Montgomery?" Harris stated quizzically.

"No. His nickname was Monty and his real name was Montague, and the name of an American president, Jefferson. That's it. Montague Jefferson from New York."

"Hey, I know a guy by that name," announced Max. "He's a pretty big wheel. Owns a few hotels, laundromats, stores."

"Do you know him well?"

"Fairly well. We've met a few times."

"Okay, Stein. What happened next?"

"Well, things started to go wrong. Tadek wasn't like us. He was different. You see, all of us had been in the camps. We talked to him about it once or twice when we were in Germany looking for goods, driving along and trading different stories about what happened to us during the war. 'Wouldn't you like to kill a German?' he asked.

"Just like that, out of the blue. He was mocking us, understand?

"'Sure, but the war is over. We've suffered enough. We don't want to spend the rest of our lives in jail. We want to marry, have families, make a nice life for ourselves, like before the war. We've suffered enough.'

"'Is it okay with you guys if I kill a German?' was his surprising response.

"What could we say? We hated the Germans. Later that day we drove through a German village. We passed a man on the road. Tadek always carried a gun. He pulled it out and asked, 'Who's going to kill him?'

"We didn't dare. So Tadek fired and the German fell. 'See? It's easy,' he smiled.

"I tell you he smiled. He did it so seldom, but he smiled then. I guess I shouldn't call it that. You know when a dog or a wolf bares its teeth? That was his smile.

"Soon afterwards Tadek met some intellectuals in Paris who gave him some books. We were simple guys; we didn't read much. We didn't even finish junior high school. But he always had his head stuck in some book between trips.

"'Tadek, what's that you're reading?' I asked once.

"'A book you wouldn't understand. I don't understand it myself,' he confessed.

"When he made contact with the French underworld, we didn't want to have anything to do with them. Finally, on one trip to Belgium, we were arrested. Somebody tipped off the cops. Three months for possessing fake American ID papers and stolen uniforms. Three months of decent food in comparison to what we had before in the camps."

"What year was that?" I asked.

"1947."

In 1947 I was back in Paris at the Graves Registration Command working with a French officer of the Police Judiciaire, André Jouvert, on MIA cases. There were no more Americans in Belgium by then. "Johnny, they've arrested four men in American uniforms in Brussels," André had said while handing me the files. I remember looking at the pictures. Surely it must have been Stein, Lucas, Bloom, and Ted. I didn't want to get mixed up in that case at the time and told Jouvert to send another American liaison with the excuse that I had too much work. Now, I was so deep in my own thoughts that I didn't realize that Stein was still talking to us.

"After our release, Tadek told us that he knew who had turned us in. It was a man called Nathan. 'What should we do with him?' Tadek wanted to know.

"'Beat him up,' I suggested. 'But if we do, he'll complain to the police.'

"'During the war, when someone betrayed us, there was only one punishment, death,' he offered.

"'But the war is over, Tadek.'

"'War is never over. You are always on about the books I read. Well, in one of them there was a German military tactician who said, War never ends. To me, that doesn't only mean military war, but life, because if nothing else, life is a continuous war. This guy betrayed us, and we have to do something about it.'

"'We're in France now. We can't do things like that. They'll chop off our heads,' I ventured cautiously, not wanting to anger him.

"Tadek smiled that smile again. 'You disappoint me,' he exclaimed. He stared at us so that it scared the hell out of me. 'You're going to kill this guy with me, exactly like we did during the war.'

"None of us were too hot on the idea, but we went along with him because we didn't want to think about what might happen if we refused to cooperate.

"I remember Nathan. He tried to join us once. But four was already too many. Maybe he did give us to the Belgians and maybe he didn't. I'm not certain. Anyway, we arrived at his place and knocked on the door. He didn't act scared when he saw all four of us. I don't think that he imagined that anything could happen to him, it being 1947 and all.

"'Come in, come in. Sit down. What can I do for you?'

"'You turned us in to the Belgians. We got three months for it,' Tadek charged firmly. 'It wasn't much, three months, but the act, the betrayal matters. We sentence you to death.'

"At first Nathan was surprised. Then he took it as a joke. He laughed, because he was sure it was a joke. We still thought the same thing. Then Tadek turned to us. 'Who's going to shoot first?'

"'We give you that privilege.'

"He shot Nathan through the head without even batting an eyelash. And then he smiled that awful smile. I couldn't believe something like that could still happen, especially after the war.

"'You people ought to shoot him too, but that would make too much noise. Instead, why don't you hold the gun so your fingerprints will be on it also!'

"We did what he wanted, and fast. The thought of shooting a corpse ... That's why I said he smiled, because he seemed to smile only when he was killing or planning to kill.

"Right after that episode Lucas, Bloom and I had a little discussion. We decided that Tadek was crazy and should be locked up. He was crazy in the way he did everything, even the way he amused himself. We didn't even believe that he was Jewish. After all, we knew our people and they couldn't act like that. 'Tadek,' we asked him one day, 'Are you really Jewish?'

"'Does it make any difference?'

"'It does to us. We do everything together. We like to stick together.'

"'Yeah. I'm Jewish,' he answered.

"'Got any proof? You don't act like one of us. You don't even think like us.'

"'How much is this proof worth to you? One hundred dollars? That okay?'

"I looked at the others. That was a lot of cash to throw around in those days, but we put it on the table.

"He slowly opened his fly and showed us his dick. It was cut properly. 'Proof!' He put the money in his pocket, stood up and urinated on the floor right in front us.

"As time went on, he acted stranger. He got more uniforms and stuff from the black MP, and we would make quick trips to Germany and Belgium, come back with the goods and then change into civvies. But not Tadek, he loved to parade around in that American uniform, even when it was risky. 'Get rid of that uniform. It's of no use now. We've made the run,' we told him.

"'But it is of use to me now. All the chicks look up to American GIs as big heroes. They conquered Germany, liberated France. During the war, I was in the underground. I didn't have the privilege of wearing a uniform. I didn't have the privilege, the glory that a uniform carries with it. Now I want a bit of that glory. In this uniform, I can steal it. You know, sometimes the uniform means more to me than money.'

"And steal it he did. Every night he went to Mimi Pinson's on the Champs-Elysées. I suppose it doesn't exist now. It was a dance hall. There were girls of every shape and size, and GIs of course. We went there too but in civvies. We'd see Tadek in uniform with a girl on his arm. That wasn't so bad, but it seemed that every time we turned around there was a different girl.

"'Aren't you satisfied with just one? Every time we see you it's a new one.'

"'There's two billion people on this earth and half of them are women. Even if I changed women every hour, I'd never have them all. I have a lot of catching up to do. During the war I couldn't fuck. I was scared.'

"'Well, you could've done it in the dark.'

"'I had to wait till the end of the war. I had a feeling that something bad would happen to me if I had fun.'

"Now he was having his fun. Sure, we had girlfriends, sometimes long relationships, but with Tadek it was different. He never had a steady girl.

"And another thing, holidays. I don't say we went by the book, but on Yom Kippur, we fasted. And on Rosh Hashanah, we went to synagogue. One year we invited him to go with us.

"'I don't celebrate Yom Kippur or Rosh Hashanah or anything else,' was his answer.

"'But you're Jewish like us.'

"'So? You guys are a bunch of hypocrites. If you're going to be religious, be so all the way. I don't like people who go to service one day in the year to confess their sins so that they can start all over doing the same old thing.' He laughed. 'You want to reserve yourselves a little place close to God, don't you?'

"We shrugged our shoulders. He was crazy. Why bother to answer him?

"About a week later, he came out with some very weird stuff. 'I want to be clean, clean all over. Pure. Do you understand?'

"Those were his exact words. I have never forgotten them. Of course, I told him that I understood but I didn't understand one goddamn thing. Him? Be clean! That was an impossibility. There was the German he killed for no other reason than that he was German. Nathan too. And God knows what he got up to when he was on his own. 'You smuggle, murder and do all sorts of things. Is that what you call being clean, Tadek?'

"'Sure, I have to feel clean inside, in my conscience. But you wouldn't understand. When I hate somebody, and I don't commit an act of hatred, I'm unclean. Anything I feel is good, I have to do. I have one law, never change your principles. If I stick to it, I'm clean.'

"Maybe he was talking out of the books he read. Maybe. But we never understood him. He was different. It was one thing when he started to mingle with the Parisian intellectuals. Dragging us to all those Bogart pictures didn't bother us either. He always claimed that Bogart's characters were the precise image of who he wanted to be.

That he lived by his own rules and didn't take shit from nobody. We couldn't understand that. Yet when he became too friendly with the underworld, we decided to draw the line. We couldn't go on with him under those circumstances.

"'Tadek, we want out. We don't understand you. And if we don't understand you, we can't work with you. We simply don't live the same way.'

"'Suit yourselves,' he replied. Then he went all funny. 'You know why you don't understand. It's because you were never free. You were always slaves. When the Germans told you to go to the ghetto, you went to the ghetto. They told you to go to the camps. You went to the camps. The Americans came and rescued you. They told you to go to refugee centers and you went. Ask for a visa, and you did. You were like sheep. Me, I'm Jewish sure, but there is a difference. I went to the ghetto, but I escaped. If they tried to kill me, I tried to kill them. I was nobody's sheep, nobody's slave. I can't escape being what I was born, but I never let anybody dictate my life. In the past year, you've done what I wanted you to do. Well, you're free to go. But don't tell me that because we're all Jewish that we are the same. We're completely different. Get out!' he shouted. 'Make a new life without me.'

"His whole little speech pissed me off. 'Listen, Tadek, where do you get off saying things like that? What gives you the right? We're all equal, you're no better than us. Who do you think you are, speaking to us in that tone of voice, a prince or something?'

"He smiled. 'No, not a prince. A count is more like it.'

"We knew better than to continue, so we just left. He continued smuggling with a new partner, a Polish guy. Lucas and I were still dealing on the black market but in Paris only. Finally, someone else informed on us and we were arrested again. The French police were very understanding. 'We suffered the most during the war,' they said. 'We weren't bad guys.' They asked for information in exchange for letting us go. They wanted somebody or something big. So ..."

Stein fell silent.

"You turned him in, didn't you?" I said.

"Yeah."

"Son-of-a-bitch!" shouted Max. "You gave up your Jewish brother. If I had known that, I would've never protected you."

"Look, Max. Since when are you so clean? Remember the camp and your kapo job?" Stein retorted.

"That's different. I never betrayed any of my Jewish brothers. And I never sent thousands a day to the camps like you did."

"No. You just delivered twenty a day to the SS. Tell me about it."

"Stein, you're alive today because I was a kapo and I protected you." Max was now consumed by anger.

"Don't make me laugh. You protected me because you couldn't handle the job alone. You needed help. And what about Bloom and Lucas? They survived and you didn't help them."

Max fell silent but continued to fume.

"Of course, you can't say anything," yelled Stein. I'll tell you why we survived. Because we were put into the camp late, in '44. That was the only reason we made it out. Not because of your so-called help. And, of course, there was the rivalry between the two German officials."

"Bullshit. I don't believe in that rivalry crap," Max cut his answer short.

"Look, Mr. Miller, I don't see any point in arguing with Max," said Stein. "But I'd like you to understand. I'm glad you're here. You see, our ghetto was created first, at the beginning of 1940. Of course, there were others under the occupation, but ours was isolated. We had nothing except what the Germans gave us."

"What were you doing then?" I asked.

"I was in the Jewish Police Force along with Bloom and Lucas."

"And you talk about me being a kapo," interrupted Max. "At least I never sent my brothers to the camps. I tried to save them, not kill them, you no-good sonofabitch!"

"Gentlemen, please. Harris and I aren't here to find out which one of you was the bigger sonofabitch," I tried to officiate. "You're both equal. You were both in the right place at the right time. Go on, Stein."

"Look, the only reason some of us survived was the fight between Speer, the Minister of Construction, who wanted the Jews to replace the German workers leaving for the Front, and Globocnik, head of WVHA[4] who wanted to take over the ghettos and exterminate them. Globocnik was under Himmler and he wanted the Jews destroyed. Speer resisted. He had influence with Hitler. Globocnik wanted to transfer us to the Lublin area, but Speer put his foot down. This mess went on for a couple of years. Finally, Globocnik won because on February 22, 1942 they started the liquidation of the unproductive people."

"Unproductive people?" Harris inquired.

"People who didn't work for the Germans. I was lucky being a Jewish policeman then. The particular 'action' begun Feb. 22 lasted until April 2, about six weeks later. At first, it was only those over sixty-five and under ten. Twenty thousand people had to go. All in all, they took about thirty thousand."

"And you helped Globocnik, didn't you?" Max shouted angrily.

"Of course I did. I had to save myself. But sometimes I can still see the mothers crying as their children were being taken. I can still feel their fingernails in my skin as they fought us. If we hadn't done what we were told, we would've died too.

"But we couldn't handle the job alone, so the Germans came inside the ghetto. They took sick people from hospitals. Anybody who couldn't walk was killed immediately. The action ended when everybody was told to assemble for selection on Zimmerstrasse. Everybody was scared to death. A German with one motion of his hand could spare your life ... until the next time.

"The next day, Bülow, the German who commanded the ghetto, announced that everyone who remained would work for Germany. There would be no more deportations. If everyone did as he was told, there would be no trouble. Everyone would be safe. So, Speer got his way too.

"In '44, when the Russian Front was coming closer, they decided to evacuate us to the west. By August there were no Jews left in the Lodz Ghetto. Eighty thousand went to either Auschwitz or Chelmno. Nobody was spared, not even the Jewish police.

"When we arrived at the camp, my friends and I were still in good shape. This was the only reason I survived, because I had gone there so late.

"You see, I suffered much more during the war than Max did ..."

"Oh Christ, let's not start that again," Harris snapped. "We were talking about Tadek, I believe, Mr. Stein."

"Okay, okay. In a way, Tadek's arrest was his own fault. All of us had done things during the war to save our skins, things we weren't proud of, which we wouldn't have done under other circumstances. But according to him, the war was still going on, so ... He was arrested. We told the authorities when the next shipment was due and where he would be and how to find him. They let us go.

"It was a convenient way to cut our ties and distance ourselves from all that business. We already had our visas to the States, but if we were sentenced to jail then everything would have been finished. We were worried about our future. There was nothing else for us to do. Look, we weren't saints. Without principles, maybe. But all we wanted to do was to have a normal life, marry, and have kids. Tadek didn't care about those things.

"I must admit that we didn't like him in the first place. He was always trying to prove that he was better than us. He always looked down on us, pushed us around."

"But Stein, he helped you make money, to be able to afford the life you wanted," I said.

"Yes, he did, but we could've done it without him. I don't know how to explain it. Maybe we would have liked him better if he had only talked about himself a little. He never told us anything although we suspected he came from a wealthy family. You see, my family was poor. We were seven in one room. I went to a cheder, a Jewish school. I knew nothing but misery and poverty. But I'm certain Tadek grew up very well.

"Anyway, he was caught and given three months. I didn't think about him anymore until I heard that Lucas had been stabbed by an Algerian while walking down the street. That sounded all wrong to me because I knew that Lucas had never had any run-ins with Algerians or any other Arabs. I suspected Tadek had manipulated the killing from jail. I knew he was capable of doing it. I packed everything I could take and went to New York posthaste. I wasn't sticking around to find out what that nut was going to do next.

"I never heard anything about him after that until today, when you came to my place and showed me his picture. That's why I asked Max for protection. He got Lucas, and I didn't intend for him to get me."

"And Bloom? What about him?" asked Harris.

"I never laid eyes on him again in Europe or in the States." Stein paused and looked at Max. Then he turned to me. "Are you satisfied, Mr. Miller?"

"Yes, but just a few more things. When you were with Tadek, did you meet or see or talk about any of his friends?"

"Well, I never met or talked to anyone. But I know that he has an uncle who used to live in Israel. Also, the Algerian hood or pimp. I think his name was Mustapha and he may be still in Paris. And the Pole he worked with after we split up."

"What's his name?" Harris asked.

"Don't know. But you can find out from the French Police. And Monty."

"Who's he?"

"I told you before. The black MP who gave us the uniforms and stuff. Are you finished with me now?"

"Not quite. One thing still bothers me. Why, when you turned in Tadek to the French Police, didn't you tell them about Nathan?"

"What!! I couldn't do that!"

"Why?"

"It would've been immoral."

"What?" snapped Harris.

"Look, betrayal can only go so far. I figured what I told the police was enough to get me free. I had no grudge against Tadek. I just didn't want to go to jail. Why should I tell them about Nathan?"

"Stein, you have a very strange conception of morality. Very strange." Harris frowned and glared at Stein.

"Perhaps, but that's the way it is."

"Go home, Stein," I said.

He looked relieved. "Thanks, Mr. Miller. Max, are you still going to protect me from Tadek?"

"Sure, sure. Now go. I'm sick of looking at you. Don't worry about a thing." Stein left.

There was a minute of silence. Harris and I were reading our notes. Max left the room and returned with some food. "That goddamn Stein. I don't like squealers."

"Forget it, Max. The next thing for us to do is to contact your friend, Monty, and see if he's the right one."

"That might be difficult for me," he said, handing me a pastrami sandwich. "You see, Monty's changed in the past few years. I think if Pasquale talked to him, it would be better. It would save a lot of trouble."

"Well, what are you waiting for?"

"Is it really necessary?"

"I wouldn't ask you if it wasn't."

Max picked up the receiver and dialed a number. "This is Max speaking. Pasquale there? ... Good. Let me talk to him." After a few minutes of silence, Max spoke again. "Hey, Pasquale ... It's me, Max. How are things? ... Good, that's good. Look, I've got a problem. I've got to contact Monty ... Well, you know how things are these days. He's a friend, but I don't want to put him out with his brothers. Look, can you get him to call me right away? It's very urgent. Thanks."

Max put down the receiver and picked up his sandwich. "He'll do it. You see, my Jewish accent on the phone and the way things have been going between the blacks and us ... Well, Monty and I are in the same business almost, and it wouldn't do to upset his operation that way."

We ate our sandwiches in silence. I hadn't realized how hungry I was. I hoped that he was going to invite me to stay for dinner. Then the phone rang.

"Hey, Monty. It's your Jewish soul brother, Max. How's by you? I'm still here. Same old shit. You know how it is ... Monty, been reading the papers? ... Yeah, not very kosher. Well, I've got a small problem. There's a couple of Feds at my place and ..."

Max turned to me and shrugged his shoulders. "Wait a minute, man. Let me clue you in. You had a call from Pasquale, right?... Wait a minute ... If you let me get a word in, I'll tell you what's happening ... Damn it! These cats only want to ask you some questions about someone you knew in Paris ... Well, it seems like it ... Yeah, the man who killed Berisov. I don't know how they know. I've already talked to them. Nothing will be held against you ... I know that, but if war starts, we've had it, Muslims, Zionists, Black Power, everybody ... Yeah, yeah, I know they're Feds, but they're okay." There was a pause and Max smiled. "In a half hour. I'll be waiting."

Max offered us another drink. Harris refused and took another sandwich instead. I looked at his solemn face. The more I looked at him, the more he looked like Elliot Ness on TV. "Elliot, have a drink with us?"

"Talking to me, Johnny?"

"Harris ... I won't call you that anymore. From now on, you're Elliot Ness. You don't drink and I'm sure you don't mess with women. You're like a chaperone."

Harris smiled. "Have a drink yourself, Johnny. One of us has to stay sober."

Max poured me another drink. I liked this old bastard, this old-time crook ... this patriotic American. He thought I was like Harris. If he only knew.

The phone rang again. Max grabbed the receiver. "Max here. Monty?... Okay." Max pointed to an extension, which I hadn't noticed before on the other side of the room. "He wants you to listen in."

"All right," I heard Monty say, "I'll talk to your Feds, but it's gotta be here in my place in Harlem. I don't want nothing I say on the record. Now there's one other thing. Remember Kabala Murat?"

"Yeah, one of your brothers. He's in Cuba now. Can't come back because they've got a warrant out for him," Max explained.

"Right. Well, I want the sedition charges dropped and an amnesty granted. Then I'll talk to your friends."

I signaled to Max and pointed at my watch. "Time. We're short of time."

"We're in a hurry, Monty," said Max.

"World War Three can wait another twelve hours. You've got my conditions. The charges dropped or no deal."

"Hold on a minute, will you?" Max turned to me, "What do you think?"

"I'll have to check."

"Johnny, what if the Monty we've got isn't the right guy?" asked Max.

"Don't say things like that. It hurts me to my heart to think about it. In case they give the okay, how shall we contact him?"

"Monty, suppose things go the way you want, how do they find your place?"

"I'll send a car to pick them up at your place. Okay?"

"Is that all right with you, Johnny? You and Harris can stay here. It's not much. It's filthy, but it's all I got. You're welcome to it."

I nodded in agreement. "I don't mind staying here, but if Mr. Ness doesn't like it, he can go home."

"I'd better go along to the office to see that things run smoothly," offered Harris.

"Good idea." I looked at Max and smiled.

"Okay, Monty. We'll speak to you later." Max hung up the phone, and I put the receiver into the cradle on my end.

"I have to make another call."

"Help yourself."

I rang the office. "This is Nick. Let me speak to Bobby."

"This is Bobby speaking." "Bobby" was Donaldson's cover as "Nick" was mine.

"My aunt just arrived."

"Yes, Miller. What's up?"

"We've run into a problem. We have to talk to a man in Harlem. But there's one condition. Kabala Murat, the black militant exiled in Cuba, has to be granted amnesty. Otherwise, no deal. He won't talk."

"Is it really necessary?"

"If it's the right man, very. What I thought you might do is run a check through Army records. His name is Montague Jefferson, called Monty. He's black and was stationed in Paris as an MP between '45 and '47 and also in Rheims. Evidently, he was a friend of 'Mr. H.' It might be useful to talk to him. But it's up to you."

"Okay, hang, on."

I grabbed another sandwich. Max was relaxing in his chair. Harris was reading a book he'd found somewhere.

"A long conversation, Johnny. Talking to your old lady?" Max laughed.

"Shut up and pour me another drink."

"I think you've had enough," said Harris, looking up.

"Go to hell. I'll drink when I feel like it. I'm doing this job. You're just sitting on your fat ass reading."

"I'm your chaperone, remember?"

"Go play with yourself, mother."

Harris was just about to answer when I heard Donaldson's voice. "Miller, they're processing your requests right now. I hope this works."

"Me too. I'm spending the night here and Harris is coming back to the office. We'll see our man tomorrow if everything goes okay. If you want to reach me, I'm at ...

"Max, what's the number here?"

"249-3280."

I repeated it and hung up.

"Well, it looks like I'm shacking up with you tonight, Max."

He laughed.

"Boy, I'm going to drink you out of house and home. Where's the Orzechowka? Hey, you're a big man around here. How about some action? Why don't you bring us some broads? We can have a good time tonight."

"Okay, I'm leaving. I'll see you in the morning. Johnny, mind your manners and don't do anything foolish," cautioned Harris with a goodnight to Max as he got up to go.

"We finally got rid of that schmuck," Max said after him. He went into the kitchen and started to prepare dinner. I poured myself another drink and turned on the TV. I tried to settle into a movie that had already started, but somehow, I couldn't help turning over the stories, characters, and events that had been thrown my way in the last twenty-four hours. They were mutant beings of the lowest order. On one branch sat the terrorists, the Newark gang, the Red Army Faction – all seemed to be connected with Donaldson's idea that oil money was trying to fuck up the world. Another was occupied by the Nazis, vile tree-dwellers who aped their demented leader. In fact, they weren't much different from the Communists on the next branch; their Party always rationalized violence in terms of proletarian justice. Like scavengers, the gangsters were everywhere, and since cops wouldn't have jobs without them, I liked to include myself with this bunch. As for types like Harris, well, I could almost imagine why terrorism exists.

What plagued me however was Tadek. This guy had always been in it to save his own ass, and now the idea that he was doing the dirty work for a bunch of Germans didn't jive. Donaldson was shrewd and would go to any lengths to exonerate his agency. Claiming that Berisov was eliminated as a part of a terrorist conspiracy was convenient. If the Russians bought that, then it would not only clear the CIA after all the shit from the Kennedy and Watergate scandals, but it would also promote a closer relationship with Soviet intelligence in the common struggle against international terrorism. So it goes with the logic of an outfit like the agency. On the brink of World War Three and they're already planning the next one. Still, I thought that Donaldson was in this game for personal reasons. Against the Machiavellian politics of the others, he had been all too willing to meet my conditions. I decided that knowing nothing about his motives was as good as knowing everything, and that from now on, I could play him for what I needed, come hell or high water, or even a nuclear war.

Chapter 6. Max's Tadek

I was right about one thing, the best way to get information from guys like Max and Stein was to let them reminisce. They were comfortable on those death-camp horror stories. They related to the rest of the world through them and in fact continued to act out the roles they had played there. What better proof than the lives they led here? Stein was still the simpleton who depended on the stronger types to save him, and Max, well, he was still a kapo. As much as the US was the promised land and the Mafia a nice kosher business, Max was still locked up in a Chelmno bunkhouse or in a little room in Warsaw. His house was evidence, an absolute dump in spite of his wealth. The one pleasure that these people allowed themselves, their children excepted, was food. I had seen many of them in the supermarkets in the years following the war. Wandering around with not one but two shopping carts, they would throw two or three packages of the same item into the cart as if they were picking fruit from the Garden of Eden. As for other pursuits, women were out of the question. The death camps had killed their sex drive and reduced them to starving animals. So now they consumed food to compensate for all those hungry winter nights. This was Max's paradise all right, and I could see his post-mortem coming into focus – diabetes, arterial sclerosis, a massive coronary or stroke caused by all that greasy fat. He was constantly eating and today was no exception. He strolled into the room with a sandwich in his hand.

"Johnny, the guy Tadek ..."

"What about him?"

"I knew him," he stated between bites.

"What? Why didn't you tell me that before?" I was furious.

"You didn't ask me." Max turned back into the kitchen.

When he came back, he laughed at me. "Well, you didn't ask, did you?"

I remained silent. Max put some food on his plate and continued to eat, ignoring me completely. "Well, are you going to tell me or not?"

"It's a long story. It all goes back to the Warsaw Ghetto."

"So?" I knew I was off on another fishing trip.

"I'm from a poor family, but I was a very strong kid. When the Polish boys attacked the Jewish boys in the Wola district, I defended them. Both Jews and Poles respected me. I worked as a porter in the railroad station. When the Nazis established the ghetto, I became a smuggler. I also helped build tunnels. People disliked me because they thought I was living it up. Though it wasn't entirely true, I had nothing to complain about. In the ghetto everything changed for me. I was somebody there, like in the camp. I took risks. I sold food and made money."

"What does that have to do with Ted?" I baited him a bit.

"He used to come to the café on Leszno Street where we had our headquarters. I noticed him because he was always staring at us and also because he had blond hair and blue eyes. One day I called him over. 'What's the matter, boy? Why are you always staring at us?'

"'I've heard you go on the other side ... ?'

"'That's right. We bring food back so you people can eat.'

"'And you're not scared?'

"'Naturally we're scared. We're scared all the time, but that's life. No risks, no money.'

"'I'd like to go with you some time.'

"The boy had a good face and didn't have a Yiddish accent. There'd be no problem on that score. I told him I'd think about it. Meanwhile, he continued to hang around the café. We became friends. I'm not boasting, but I became sort of an idol of his. One day I asked him what he wanted to do after the war.

"'I want to be a smuggler like you, Max.'

"Then, as you know, the situation got worse. In July 1942 the deportations started. In a few months there were only 50,000 left of the original 400,000 residents. I was one of those who remained. We were trying to organize a resistance group because we had no more illusions. The Germans were going to kill us all sooner or later.

"My group was called ZOB[5] As a smuggler, I had contacts on the other side, which made me very valuable to them. A few days after the liquidations started, we still were sitting in the café. The Jewish Police rarely bothered us and actually sanctioned our commerce. They even gave us their uniforms to wear in exchange for a piece of the action and our promise to stay out of their operations. It kept the SS from asking too many questions. That's how protection rackets work everywhere.

"Tadek walked in with a guy I had met before, Winarski. He was a well-known Communist. How that guy survived I'll never know, but now he is very high up in the Polish government."

"Did Tadek know this Winarski well?"

"Yeah, Winarski was his teacher. I didn't know that until the 'action' started. Tadek introduced us. I wanted to shake his hand because I was glad to meet someone who'd taken an interest in the boy like I did. But Winarski just looked at me.

"He started moralizing. 'I don't shake hands with hoodlums. You're living off the people in the ghetto.' From that moment on, I couldn't stand Communists. He was condescending, told me that I had no right to live in luxury while others were dying.

"He badgered me until I had taken as much as I could. 'You damn Communists and your high-blown ideals. Who the hell are you kidding? Maybe some people believe in all that equality crap, but I know better. I'm alive because I eat. They're alive because I give them food. They need food and that's what I'm giving them. What are you giving them?'

"He did not reply. Just as I thought. A bunch of hot air. 'Look, you, don't come around here with your damn ideals and moralizing because I don't want to hear them.'

"He left in a huff. Boy, was he hot! But I didn't give a damn. I was right. When I finally cooled down, I took the boy aside and gave him a police uniform. "'Listen, wear this during the action and they won't pick you up.'

"We really didn't have much to say to each other after that because I was too busy with the resistance."

"And you saw him again ..."

"It was in a very different circumstance. When the Germans moved against the ghetto for the final deportation in April 1943, we were ready to give them a run for their money. We had hand grenades and machine guns. But we knew that no one would survive. We were all going to die. But how were we were going to die? Like sheep or fighting? I had been fighting all my life and I wasn't going to stop then.

"On the morning of April 19, German, Ukrainian, and Lithuanian troops surrounded the ghetto. We took our positions according to plan. When the German column moved in toward Gensia Street, we started shooting and throwing hand grenades. We struck so hard that it surprised the Germans, who panicked and ran, leaving their dead and wounded. It was a victory, our first real victory although a short-lived one. We were enthusiastic.

"The Germans continued the counter-attack. SS Oberführer von Sammern-Frankenegg, the colonel who directed the 'action,' started another big move. The troops moved along the walls one by one, firing at the windows and using flame throwers. We shot back and repelled them again. Then we heard that von Sammern had been removed from the operation and that the general, SS Gruppenführer von Stroop, had taken over.

"In the meantime, they attacked for a third time. We threw more grenades and Molotov cocktails. It was hard to stay in one position; we moved from house to house through tunnels and attics. The Germans used planes to spot our movements and positions. We fought for about six hours and then set fire to the German supplies stockpiled on Nalewki Street as they pulled out. We had received orders not to leave anything the Germans could use against us.

"The Germans left the ghetto. I headed over to the Tobbens Shops to see a friend of mine. On the way I saw a hospital on Gensia that had been gutted by fire. It was a horrible sight. To avenge their defeat, the Germans massacred everybody and burned the hospital. Nothing had happened around Tobbens yet. I found my friend who was with one of the armed groups that were supposed to defend the shops[6] in case of German attack. Tobbens was a big manufacturing firm working for German industry. That same day Tobbens himself announced that his workers and their families would be transferred to safety in Trawniki. Nothing would happen to them. 'Don't listen to the underground fighters,' he told them, 'because their way leads to death and destruction. With my protection you workers will survive.'

"I listened but didn't believe a word," he said.

"While I was still in the district, I ran into Michaelson, a German who worked for Globocnik. We were on good terms; we did business together. 'Listen, Max, it's just a question of days. The whole ghetto is going to be destroyed. Make your decision now. The first transport today is going to Trawniki, but not for extermination. If fighting breaks out in this area tomorrow, it'll be too late. Take the train today. It's safe.'

"Normally I didn't trust Germans, but Michaelson had one thing in his favor. He hated Brandt as much as I did. Untersturmführer Karl Brandt was in charge of Jewish Affairs in Warsaw. Naturally he took part in the action. A few days before, Brandt had tried to shoot all the people in the ghetto he'd worked with so nobody would talk. I was warned beforehand and was able to hide. 'What do you want, Michaelson?'

"'Some jewelry and gold, Max. Can you get it for me?'

"'Sure. In Trawniki and not before.'

"'You still don't trust me,' he laughed.

"'Why should I? You're German. How can I trust you after what's happened?'

"'Hurry up. You have a chance to make it today. Take some people with you.'

"Before I had to choose whether to be slaughtered like a lamb or to die fighting. Now, it was between fighting and dying in one day, or taking the train. I had been given a chance to live for a few months more, and it seemed senseless not to take it. I went with the transport.

"Michaelson had been right. The train went to Trawniki where we were put in a camp surrounded by barbed wire. At the beginning we were treated well. We manufactured coats with and without fur, hats, and gloves for German troops. Sometime later, we heard that the resistance fighters in the ghetto held out for a few more weeks, but I didn't want to think about it. I was safe. Still, I wished I'd been there to help.

"As to be expected, things got worse eventually. In the middle of October, the Jewish inmates at Sobibor revolted. In response, Globocnik gave the order to liquidate all the Jewish camps in Poland.

"Our turn came on November 3. I remember that day all too well. The Einsatz troops moved in and separated the women and children from the men. First the men were supposed to be sent west and the women and children were to follow. But I knew better. I knew that they were going to be exterminated right there in Trawniki.

"On the evening before the liquidation, an SS officer had come along and selected about two hundred men including me. We spent the next twelve hours engaged in 'special work,' their term for digging graves. From dusk to dawn and into the next morning, we chopped the earth and shoveled dirt. It was exhausting. They had given us water, nothing else. I could hardly stand but kept going. I had no choice.

"That day, a German officer ordered the work detail to group ourselves in threes. They made an inspection. Who knows what they expected to find? I noticed a young German in a strange uniform, wearing an interpreter's badge. Although I saw him in three-quarter profile, I thought it was Tadek. I kept peering and squinting at him because I couldn't believe my eyes. He whispered something to the SS Sturmbannführer who was standing next to him. A few minutes later, they pulled me out of the ranks and put me on the train. Thanks to him I was spared the fate of those other two hundred men on 'special duty.' They were killed after they burned and buried the bodies."

"Was that the last time you saw him?"

"No. I saw him in Germany after the liberation. Remember I told you about my job with the rabbinical court? Well, one day some guys came to see me. They said that a load of cigarettes had been stolen from them and that one of their partners had done it. I found the partner in question and beat him into a confession. He had hired two guys dressed as American MPs to do the job, and he had sold the cigarettes on the black market. I managed to recover all the money except for the three thousand dollars he paid the Americans. He told me later that one of the GIs was not American, but a Polish Jew like us. 'Perhaps you can get the money back?'

"'Right. You tell me when he's in Salzheim refugee camp.'

"The next night the man came to the camp and I went to see him. 'You pulled a job on my friends. Give me back the three thousand dollars!' I stared at him. He had blond hair and blue eyes.

"He smiled at me. 'If I don't give you the money, what are you going to do about it, Max?'

"'You know me?'

"'Of course. Don't you remember me? You're Max, the smuggler who used to work in the ghetto in Warsaw ...'

"'And you're the Jewish boy with the good face.'

"'Yep. That's me.' I embraced the boy. I was happy to see him.

"'Listen, didn't you get me put back on the train at Trawniki? Weren't you the interpreter?'

"'Yes, I was.'

"'You saved my life. I'm grateful.'

"'Max,' he smiled. 'I saved so many lives and killed so many people that I don't know how my account stands now ... in the red or in the black.'

"'Listen. Forget about that money.'

"I told the other guys that it was impossible to get the rest of the money and that was that."

Now it was my turn. I told Max about how Tadek had saved my life when the Russians had appeared. We figured that he was a real hero. An unsung hero who had never found his paradise and wouldn't recognize it if he stepped into it.

"I saw him a couple more times at Salzheim before I immigrated," Max added. "We were still friends, but I never saw or heard from him until last week. Then this stuff in the papers and you show his picture to me."

"What!? You saw him last week?" My heart skipped a beat.

"Well, he came by here Saturday night. He called before coming. Said he was in New York on a business trip and wanted to drop over."

"You didn't think that it was unusual? For him to know your address and number after so many years?"

"Naturally I was shocked to hear his voice. He spoke to me in Polish, but his voice sounded very distant, as if he were speaking from another world. I tell you, Johnny, in my business the only way we survive is to be on guard for the unexpected. But when it concerns someone who has saved your life, you just don't think about it. " Max was becoming aggressive. I had crossed the frontier into the world of his real friends, and he didn't like that.

"What the hell did he have to say to you after so long?" I was trying to get back into Max's favor, but we were jousting now. Max was coming out of his dream world and into the reality of one whose history was now being counted in terms of hours.

"He asked a lot of questions about the UN building in Manhattan. He wanted to know who controlled security there."

"And what exactly did you tell him, Max? This is vital," I insisted.

"I told him what I knew. I told him about the security headquarters in the apartment building across the street. The hourly passages of the police boats on the river and the closed-circuit TV surveillance system. For some time now, we've had a contract with the Jewish

Defense League to protect Israeli officials as well as any other Jewish employees at the UN. It's very cloak-and-dagger. Sometimes the Palestinians hire other organizations to do their work for them."

Max, the kapo. It wouldn't have done any good to ask him why he told Tadek all those things. He owed him, and it was obviously nothing that was a direct threat to him or his operation. I decided to stop there since this was itself enough to dangle in front of Donaldson. Max began to clean up in the kitchen.

"I'll be finished soon. Want anything?" he waddled in and out of the room.

"I'll watch this movie and then go to sleep," I told him.

When he emerged from the kitchen, I was just dropping off for the third time. "Come on, Johnny. I have an extra room upstairs."

We went up and he showed me a tiny room, which was filthy like the rest of the house. It didn't make a difference. I was too tired to care and fell onto the bed saying goodnight to Max and quickly lapsed into a deep sleep.

I saw their bodies, the Germans, Billy and Jimmy together. They weren't moving. There was blood everywhere. Blood flowing from their bellies, from their heads. Blood all over. Then two hundred yards on toward the bridge, I saw Frankie's body. His brain was oozing slowly from his smashed skull. He was dead too. Nevertheless, he turned to me. "Johnny. Johnny. Come. Please, join us. Join me, Billy and Jimmy. We're waiting, for you. Come. Join us.

Chapter 7. Monty's Tadek

Thursday, October 6, 1983 – "The American President and his counselors have fabricated lie after lie in trying to excuse themselves for their deeds. The most recent assertion that the murder of our Premier was part of a terrorist plot is the most unfounded manipulation of the facts ever presented in the imperialist press. It is an insult not only to the heroic Soviet people who held so much esteem for their fallen leader but also an outrageous accusation against our Palestinian allies. The real blame must be sought in the treachery of the Zionists and their American puppets." – *Pravda*

I was awakened by a pounding on the bedroom door and Harris' voice. "Johnny, Miami called. Things are looking bad. We're on the brink of war. The President has issued a red alert. Military reserves in the US and Europe have been called up."

"What about Miami?" I demanded.

"Kabala Murat arrived from Havana at 6:00 this morning. He could have come back anytime he wanted. The statute of limitations on his case had expired."

"What a load of crap," interrupted Max, listening behind Harris at the open door. "They'll do anything not to appear as if they gave in to a bunch of niggers."

The phone rang, and Max stumbled downstairs to answer it. "Morning, Monty ... What? Murat in Miami? Your boys met him ... He wasn't too happy? That's not our fault," Max offered bluntly.

"What about them?" he asked. "Yeah, they're here ... Only one?"

Max put his hand over the receiver and spoke from the hallway, "Who'll it be, Johnny?" Then he talked to Monty again. "Okay. One it is. Make it snappy though. See you."

For the first time, Harris didn't object to my being the one to go. I couldn't see that chickenshit traveling to Harlem by himself. Max fixed us some breakfast. Just as we finished, a big Mercedes sedan pulled up in front of the house. Five neatly dressed young black men came up to the door. One of the boys let them in and showed them into the room. "Hey, Max. How's by you?"

"Hello, Feemi. How's things over your way? Wife and kids okay?"

Feemi started to answer when one of his companions interrupted. "Hey, man. We're not here to rap with some Jewboy. Let's get what we came here for and make it."

"Cool it, Rashid. Max is an old friend." Feemi raised his palm like a traffic cop and returned to Max. "Sorry, but you know how it is. Where's the man?"

"That's him," Max said, pointing to me. "The other one's his partner."

"Just one of them, remember! You," he motioned toward me and extended his arms to pat me down for weapons and wires. "Come with us. Rashid, you stay here and keep his friend company." Rashid narrowed his eyes angrily but said nothing. He stayed as we drove away.

During the trip nobody spoke. I tried to make friendly conversation, but nobody was interested. "Hey, you guys. I know you hate me because I'm a honky. Okay, I accept that. But you could say something since we're in here together."

Still nobody opened their mouth. I tried again. "Come on, fellas. You're too serious. You're too young to be like that."

"We're taking you to Monty. That's all we've been ordered to do."

"Okay, but why so many?"

"Man, when was the last time you were in Harlem?"

"I don't know. About twelve years ago, I guess."

"Well, things have changed since then. Because Monty don't want nothing bad to happen to you, he sent us to get you. Don't ask any more questions, okay?"

"Have it your way." I sat back and enjoyed the ride.

We stopped up on Morningside Drive. It was a 19th-century granite-clad townhouse in a hell of a lot better condition than Max's dump. We got out of the car and the boys walked me up the steep brownstone stairway to the front door. Someone rang the bell. A tall, attractive black girl opened the door. She wore a dashiki, and her hair was a big Afro. "Come in. Let me take your things and make yourself at home," she said, pointing to the sofa. "Monty, he's here," she called out and disappeared.

Monty was living in style. I was standing in the middle of my dream home, or at least one room of it. Very comfortable Scandinavian furniture. A couple of modern paintings, one of them unmistakably a Mondrian. Lots of museum-quality African sculpture, one of them an imposing wood-carved male figure with details of copper, brass, leather, fur, feathers, and mud. And a high-end stereo system with McIntosh amps. I went around the room looking and touching things. Then I found the vinyl records. I wanted to put one on but didn't dare mess around with his stuff. When the girl came back, I gave her a classical album and asked her to play it. She smiled at me. "I know it's rather early in the morning, but would you like a drink?"

I refused politely and watched her hips as she put the record on the turntable and carefully placed the needle onto it. "The Ride of the Valkyries" began. "On second thought, I think I'll have a whiskey, if you don't mind," I called after her. Picking up a magazine, I sank down into the sofa nearest me. I was in heaven.

"Wagner. The only thing Hitler and I had in common." Monty startled me. I hadn't heard him come in. "You like my system?" Monty was tall and dark brown with a good physique. He reminded me of Jim Brown, the great running back. I could imagine the girls going wild over him, lucky bastard. He stood there in the door holding two glasses. One was my whiskey and the other was milk. "I'm Monty. You wanted to talk to me? Taiwo said you wanted whiskey. Well, here's your drink." We sat down. "Taiwo also told me that you admire my crib."

"Yeah. I want to live somewhere like this someday."

"I know what you mean. When I was little, I used to dream of having things like this. But we couldn't afford it. There were twelve kids in my family. I promised myself that one day I'd have it all. The first time I ever had anything of my own, not hand-me-downs, was when I joined the Army and now ..."

"That's what I want to know, Monty," I interjected, "about your time in the Army."

"Oh? What's your name?" He looked at me strangely.

"Johnny Miller."

"I asked you to do something for me, Johnny. You came through. What do you want?"

"Mind if I call you Monty?" I started.

"That's my name. Have another drink." He got up and walked to the marquetry dry bar near the entrance to the room.

"You were an MP in Paris during the war. I wondered if you might have known this guy." I showed him the picture. "Do you know him?"

"No."

"Well, I didn't think you'd remember him straight off. But did you ever meet a Polish guy by the name of Ted, or Per, or Tadek, soon after the war? In '45 or maybe '46?"

I watched Monty's face. He seemed to be trying to reach into the back of his mind for something. "A guy who showed you how to make a bit of extra money while you were stationed in Paris, then in Germany when you were with the Military Police."

Then Monty grinned. "I remember now. How did you know?"

"Beginner's luck, you might say." I grinned back.

"Look, you're here in my place with no mikes, no bugs, so nothing can be taken down against me. If I tell you anything, it's because I want to help. But I'm not sure if what I'm going to tell you will help at all."

"That's for me to decide."

"Rheims, '45 ... I think it was sometime in June. I was on a train heading for Paris with a bunch of GIs. We were all going to have a good time. I had a few things to sell, whiskey and cigarettes and silk stockings. My compartment was almost empty but across from me sat a Polish guard. One of those guys we had assigned to play warden to the German prisoners. Man, those guards were pretty tough customers. You didn't mess with them cats. And did they hate the Germans!

"This one was an interpreter. I recognized him from the Provost Marshal's office. He spoke French, German, English, and Polish. I looked at him and he smiled. 'Your first time to Paris?' he asked.

"'No. I was there once before.'

"'I go up at least three times a week.'

"'What's your name?'

"'Ted. And yours?'

"'Monty. Glad to meet you Ted.' We shook hands.

"'Got a lot of stuff?'

"'A little bit, like everybody else,' I admitted.

"'How much you get for the smokes?'

"'Eighty cents a pack.'

"'That's all?' He laughed. 'Come with me. I'll get you a dollar-fifty.'

"He knew Paris pretty well. We arrived at the Gare de l'Est and he immediately took me to places I never dreamed existed. All I knew was Pigalle. It was always, get off the train and go to Pigalle. This time we went to the St. Paul district and sold our cigarettes for one-fifty like he said.

"'Okay, Monty?' he was asking for approval.

"'Yeah. Sure.'

"'How 'bout you and me doing business together?'

"'Why not? If you can double the profits like that, why not?'

"'Monty, we'll more than double them, we'll triple them. Listen, we've got a little money. Let's get into something.' I thought it was odd, this white boy wanting to work with me and all. But I figured, this guy wasn't white, only a Polak and they were different. 'Let's get wasted,' he suggested.

"I went along with the program, although I usually didn't drink much. But this guy could drink an Irishman under the table. Every place we went, three or four vodkas straight up. And then he started to speak German. I was embarrassed. It embarrassed everybody. He annoyed everyone, talking loud like those SS dudes you see in the movies. You know what I mean, the ones who give the little pep talks about the Führer and killing Jews. Everybody wanted to do him in. He was with me, so I felt that I had to defend him. Then suddenly he'd smile. 'Calm down, everybody. It's only a joke! It happened to me during the war. I got you all excited, didn't I?'"

"You say he spoke German? What did he say?"

"I don't know. I don't speak German."

"Did you consider him crazy?"

"No. He just had a thing about Germans. I didn't dig it either. I asked him why he came on like a German after what they did to him.

"'Monty, I don't know. I try to explain it to myself. I play German sometimes when I'm drunk. Maybe because I wasn't born a German. Maybe because I'd like to change my skin. Wouldn't you like to do the same thing?'

"I answered, 'Man, I'd give anything to be white like you.'"

"Johnny, remember, that was thirty-five years ago. Today, I wouldn't be white for nothing. Not for money. Not for power. Not for nothing. You asked me what happened just after the war and I'm telling you," he added defensively and continued.

"We became good buddies and went around together. I was afraid to pick up a white girl, though. I had a friend during the war who got done in by a white bitch. See, when we came to Germany, like any of the Allied soldiers, when we could get a piece, we took it. Some of the women were excited by heroes in uniforms. They gave themselves freely. We took anyone that came our way, especially the guys who had been in the field for a long time.

"There was this homeboy of mine. We had known each other in grade school but lost contact with each other for a few years and then ended up in the same platoon. We became running buddies again. I don't know if the whole story is true, but a Kraut bitch told an officer that my boy raped her. I don't know, maybe he did. Maybe she let him, or maybe she was disappointed or angry. But you know how honky cats are about your bitches and black studs. You folks created that myth, and now you believe it. Anyway, they hanged him on her testimony. That's why I was afraid, because of what I'd seen in Germany.

"When I finally told that story to Ted, he grinned. 'This is France. It's not like Germany. It makes no difference who you are. As long as they like you, it's okay.'

"'This must be a Garden of Eden,' I remarked.

"'Not really. But as far as fucking is concerned, it's a little better than other countries. That's all. This place is just as lousy as the rest. If you don't make money now, you'll be treated like all the rest. And now is the time. Monty, we're going to make some money. You just listen to me. We're not coming to Paris with penny-ante stuff to sell. We're gonna do it up right. Is it a deal?'

"'Sure.'

"He asked me to get ID's, official passes and travel documents. Under other circumstances, maybe I wouldn't have done it, but after what happened to my buddy, I figured, well, I wanted to avenge my homeboy. Maybe Ted saw it that way too. Maybe that's why he chose me. Anyway, I gave him everything he asked for. After he fixed them up, you couldn't tell them from the real thing.

"We took trucks from the motor pool and, with phony orders, drove to the PX, loaded up cases of cigarettes, took them to Paris, and sold them to gangsters that Ted knew well. They couldn't trace us, and I'd never had so much money in my life. I'd never seen that much money. 'Ted, how am I going to get this back to the States?'

"'Don't worry,' he explained. 'You don't take the money with you. On your next leave, we'll go to Switzerland. I'll show you what to do.'

"We went to Geneva. He opened accounts for both of us, and we deposited all our money there.

"Of course, we couldn't pull all those jobs at the same depot. We went all over the place using different fake orders. And we made a lot of money. One day, Ted came to see me. 'A truck is going to Paris ... a truck full of cigarettes. Here's the plan. We arrest the driver and take the stuff.'

"'Okay.'

"As you know, I was an MP, but of course, he wasn't. So, I got him a uniform. Man, we laid back in the cut and waited for that mother. I was really excited, since I'd heard about how they used to hijack trucks ... Al Capone and all those people. Now I was out there with them.

"We stopped the truck as planned. Ted took the driver's papers. 'What're you gonna do?' the driver asked.

"'This stuff is stolen. You're going to the police. Move over,' I ordered him and got behind the wheel.

"'Have a heart. I know the load is stolen. Don't turn me in. If you wanted to, you could overlook it. I'll make it worth your while.'

"'I'd like that, but if I did,' Ted answered, 'you might decide to turn me in for not doing my duty.'

"'No, I swear. I wouldn't do nothing like that,' he pleaded.

"I wondered what Ted would do as he pulled the driver out of the truck. I quickly understood his intentions but didn't like the idea. He motioned me to drive away. I turned on the motor and started to drive off. Then I heard a shot. Ted came back to the truck and got in. He'd just killed him. It was first-degree murder.

"'Monty, you don't know me very well,' was his only comment. That was the understatement of the year. But I was learning fast. 'Millions of people were killed in the war. One more or less doesn't make any difference,' he said. 'Our main thing is to make money because this is our time. And this truckload is worth a lot of money. We'll sell it. Nobody is going to know what happened here. Anyway, they won't connect us with it.'

"We pulled a few more jobs together. Then I was transferred to Germany. I kept in touch and continued to supply him with IDs and stuff. Once when he came, I asked him where had learned to forge things.

"'I was two years in the underground. They taught me a lot.'

"'What are you going to do when I leave?'

"He looked a little worried. 'Are you really leaving?'

"'Yeah, I'll be discharged soon.'

"'Don't worry, Monty. I'll find somebody.' He looked a little sad. 'Tell me something. Are you glad you met me?'

"'Man, you're crazy. I know a lot of crazy guys, but you're the only one who's helped me make some money. I'll need it when I go back home. I don't want to be a bum like the rest of those guys. I'm gonna be somebody.'

"That was in '46. I came back to Harlem and bought some hotels and bars. I sold the bars and bought laundromats. That was more than thirty-five years ago. I'm okay now. There's nothing more I can add. If there's anything there that can help you, Johnny ..."

"Sure. You say that Ted was crazy?"

"No, not like insane. An individualist. I liked him because he liked me as a man."

"But why you? He could have chosen anybody to help him."

"He said he was Jewish and, because I was black, we had the same problems. I told him I didn't know anything about a Jewish problem. Most of us knew nothing about the Nazis' gassing millions of Jews until we returned to the States. That's why he chose me. Things have changed. We're not friends of the Jews anymore. In a way, it's a pity, because our Civil Rights Movement was partially financed by liberal

Jews. They're caught in the crossfire. You see, many of us became Muslim. Look what's happening in Israel. The Jews are the aggressors. We have to stick by our Muslim brothers. Who owns the slums here in Harlem? Jews. Who's exploiting the blacks in those ghetto stores? Jews. I'll tell you something. Before I didn't have any feelings towards them one way or another. But now ... Anyway, this Jew was different. One of the few I really liked. If I could meet him again, I'd shake his hand and call him brother because that's just what he is for me, a brother."

"Like your Muslim brothers?" I suggested. "Level with me, Monty. I know you contributed to building that new mosque up here in Harlem. But Arab oil money backed the better part of it. What do you know about these people? Surely you met them?"

"Listen, cop! They came here and paid me good money. I don't play politics. They ask for women, and we supply them. We're the black pimps, not the Black Panthers. And don't moralize with me. For years you people had us believing that Southern Baptist horseshit and voting for white Baptists and shining their shoes. What did it get us? Someone comes along with a proposition and money to back it up. They help us to help ourselves. When this is over, we'll have our own Garden of Eden."

"Or Garden of Allah," I stated calmly. He was beginning to sound like poor Ellie back in Newark, but his junk was money, and he didn't have to wait for any connections.

"You stink, Miller. I've nothing more to say."

Chapter 8. Tadek's Johnny

Monty's boys drove me back to Brooklyn. When I got to Max's place, Harris was waiting impatiently but I didn't give him any of the details of my interview. Between what Max had told me about Ted's recent visit and Monty's hesitancy to talk about the Muslim operation in Harlem, he didn't know anything and didn't need to. The man I had to speak to was Donaldson, and for some curious reason I had the premonition that Donaldson wanted to see me. The theory of an Arab-backed terrorist attempt was tenable but not with Ted as its principal actor. From what I had learned, Ted was certainly no Zionist. Indeed, he had a certain morbid fascination for the German war machine and its Nazis. Yet I didn't think it came from anti-Semitic feeling on his part. He had been persecuted during the war and had shown too much determination for me to conclude he would now fall prey to blatant racism.

His connection with the Communists was another story. From Max I knew that this Winarski held a high post in his pantheon of idols. IIe was with the Polish underground during the war, but there were at least ten different brands of Polish freedom fighters. The principal groups were the Communist Peoples Army, the Polish Home Army, and the National Armed Forces. The Peoples Army (AK) were backed by the Soviets; the Home Army, the largest faction, was the military wing of the Polish exile government in London; the National Armed Forces (NSZ) were ultra-fascists who hated Germans and Jews equally. Furthermore, Ted had a complex personality and the detective's usual method of following one lead to the next could have put me into a dead-end. I had to talk to Donaldson.

"Harris, we have to contact the brass on this. I've got a couple of hunches, nothing solid. It seems our suspect has quite a complicated past, politically speaking, that is."

Max was there, eating as usual, and naturally put in his two cents. "Politics! For the past twenty-four hours, you've been dealing with gangsters. Some detective you are."

"Stay out of this, Max, and maybe we'll both live long enough to have that kishke. Harris, you'd better check in with your mother and set up a meeting."

"I'm one step ahead of you, Johnny. We've already been invited to lunch this afternoon. Joe's Shanghai on Pell Street. In fact, if we want to get through the traffic, we'd better move on."

We drove to Chinatown. On the way, Harris asked many questions. I had to give him something because I knew he'd talk to Haverson. If Haverson became suspicious from lack of information, he'd put the screws on Donaldson and force us out into the open where it would be impossible to operate.

"Look, Harris. This stuff about a plot seems bigger than anybody imagined. I think they might be controlling things up there in Harlem. If they have that much punch, then it would have been a cinch for them to get someone into the UN without suspicions. What do your people know about this?"

"Frankly, we don't have anything. Ever since the '73 War, the Bureau has been taken off internal surveillance of Arab operations in the US. The President reclassified it under national security, and the DIA or National Security Agency has been in charge ever since. They just give us what we need to know to follow through with prosecution of our own citizens."

Just like the Elliot Ness character he played. Never crossed the frontier of his bureau's jurisdiction. I didn't know if he was telling the truth but dropped the subject to avoid giving him anything more.

"If you ask me," he added, "I think that the CIA has its head up its ass and can't see any light. They've done nothing but fuck up for the past twenty years."

"Harris, just because your boy and Donaldson have a thing going between them, you don't have to follow suit. I'm in this because they wanted me. I didn't need any of them. Are you going to cooperate with me or not? If not, well, I can probably get you back to whatever you were doing before this. As a matter of fact, what were you working on before?"

"I was attached to inter-agency security. We watch other agencies to see that they're not violating federal laws. I'm speaking from experience when I say that the CIA is covered with shit."

"Finally, the Gestapo's come home," was my only comment, and Harris didn't take it well.

We pulled into a parking garage and past the guardian who was standing, arms akimbo, a Doberman at his side. He gave me a sharp wink. I didn't think anything, relieved however not to be stuck alone with Harris for the rest of the afternoon. I wanted this hound off my back, but having worked the miracle once in Wilson's case, I thought that my influence had probably gone far enough in those kinds of conflicts. Besides, if things got rough and anybody decided to abruptly end our investigation, well, there was a fifty-fifty chance that it would be Harris that they'd drop. I rather liked the idea of having a human flak-jacket.

We parked the car on the basement level and walked up to the street. Entering the restaurant adjacent to the garage, I spotted a table in the back where Donaldson and Haverson were engaged in animated conversation. They were in love, I decided. That's the only way they can express themselves in public. But at their age, they should've known better. Tarnovksy was sitting there too but pretending to ignore them.

The grouping was reduced. Gone were Berlinger, Goldman, and McClellan. When we appeared, the two lovers had the sense to stop this time.

"How's it going, Miller?" asked Donaldson as I sat down.

"So far, so good. But what have you got?"

"Some new stuff has come through our field offices. For the last ten years, our man hasn't been seen in public. He tends to be withdrawn, but in 1950 he testified at the trial of an ex-Nazi officer named Schlaube. For the defense! Made quite a flap in the Jewish community."

"Yeah, I'll bet it did. Is that all? What about his travels?" I wanted to see if they knew anything more about his recent activities in New York.

"Belgium, Germany, Israel. Israel must have been that uncle."

"And this Schlaube?"

"Jurgen Schlaube. Owner of an electronics firm in Frankfurt. Nothing unusual. Ex-Nazi, successful businessman. The same type of political affiliations as the rest. Nothing about any connection with the neo-Nazis. Just a regular post-war success story. He's kept his nose clean ever since."

"Now suppose you tell us what you've learned, Mr. Miller," demanded Tarnovsky as he sipped jasmine tea.

"Well, sir, Harris here can fill you in on the details, where we've been and to whom we've spoken. In general, I'd say that Mr. Donaldson's conspiracy merits a closer look. From what I've heard, the Arabs are in deep with the black community in this country. I think that whole affair about liberating Kabala Murat was just a smokescreen. When I pursued the topic with Jefferson, he shut up. I won't say Murat is connected to criminal activity and have no idea where he stands with the Arabs, maybe the terrorists, but something else is going on. A black nationalist living in Cuban exile becomes a gangster's pawn in the middle of a national security crisis. It makes no sense. Why hasn't Murat been on our radar? What has he been doing in Cuba all these years? Has he even been there? The agency ought to keep him in its sights."

"So, where does Shipansky come into all of this?" Haverson was as skeptical as ever.

"That's just the point, sir. Our man is no Zionist patriot and your information about this Schlaube trial seems to confirm that. But just the same, he fought against the Nazi extermination policies and helped smuggle weapons to the Jewish resistance in the Warsaw Ghetto. My background information portrays him as quite friendly with a former teacher in Warsaw. Abram Winarski, a Communist, now a big shot in the Polish government. Now, if the Arabs laid the Berisov assassination at our door and worked with Tadek, Winarski may be the one valuable lead for details on Tadek's political affiliations."

Donaldson's eyes glimmered with delight. "You see. That confirms it. It's a well-known fact that just as the Russians arrived in Poland, the Zionists recruited among the foreign resistance groups. This became even more important when the Iron Curtain fell, and the remaining Jews wanted to get out. Shipansky may have been one of them, and somewhere along the line, he became a double agent for the Palestinians. It would have been a perfect cover, and I don't think any of you gentlemen would deny that there are Jews who work for Arab intelligence. Would you?" Donaldson continued. "It would be helpful to send these men to Poland and see what else they could find out."

"I don't think any further investigation is needed, said Haverson. "I don't think that knowing more about Mr. Shipansky will do any good. If he wants to talk to Johnny, he'll talk."

"Of course, you don't," argued Donaldson. "Your agency isn't implicated. On the one hand, you could go home and forget about this whole thing. I need to clear my agency's reputation, on the other hand. We're innocent this time, and I'm sure of it. I want to retrace this job back to the minute when our suspect was born, if necessary. I want to clear our name. I want to be able to inform the President of our country's position in this affair."

Tarnovsky had been listening attentively. Donaldson's monologue finished, he began, "Two points, gentlemen. The first is that, regardless of what this Winarski has to do with our suspect, the situation in Poland at the moment is critical. If the Soviets decide to invade Western Europe, there will be massive resistance in Warsaw ... from the top down and from the bottom up. For years, the Poles have been waiting for any excuse to get the Soviets off their backs. The Poles are probably the toughest fighters in the Warsaw Pact and could give the Russians a lot of trouble. I wouldn't want to endanger that rather advantageous situation at the moment by giving the Communists any excuse to launch a wide-scale purge. My second point is that Poland is not the only example of internal dissension in the Soviet camp today. It's common knowledge in the Pentagon that the Soviet government has been involved in actively repressing Islamic rebellions in its so-called republics in Central Asia. This situation has been aggravated in the past three months, although very little news has leaked to the West. Moscow fears that Berisov's death might trigger a general uprising. Some people in the Kremlin believe the assassination is part of a wider conspiracy to destroy the Soviet Union. Such a development would considerably weaken their bargaining position in crises like this one. To summarize, we feel that the Soviet's open aggression is a function of its brittle domestic power.

"What you were saying earlier, Miller, about the Arab involvement with some blacks in this country could be just as true for the status of their operations among Soviet minorities. That makes it doubly important for us to know for whom and why Shipansky acted. If Winarski can help us, then I would be in favor of making contact with him, providing that it can be done discreetly."

"I can guarantee the utmost discretion in the matter, Mr. Adviser," responded Donaldson. He prevailed over the objections of Haverson, who remained silent for the rest of the meeting.

They ordered Harris and me to Paris that very evening. Our entry visas for Poland would be arranged in Germany. The time it took to clear us could be spent pursuing other possible leads in Paris and Germany. From Poland, we would return to Paris with whatever Winarski had told us. A contact there would put us back in touch with Tarnovsky. These details were decided over what I considered one of the finest Chinese meals this side of Hong Kong. The lazy-susan at the center of the table made it easy for me to keep pulling it around to my favorite stuff, the extraordinary pepper and salt prawns, lo mein, and the calamari in black bean sauce.

The lunch broke up when Harris and Haverson peeled off together. Knowing that Harris would eventually find me, I took advantage of this momentary freedom and left the restaurant alone. I walked quickly to the parking garage where the old guard and his Doberman were still on duty.

"Wait here!" he ordered in an Eastern European accent.

As I turned around, Donaldson appeared. "You know that in Poland you have to buy coupons to pay for everything. They don't want you taking their zlotys out of the country or changing dollars on the black market. The coupons are used for everything by the tourists – hotels, food, everything. Ten dollars a day you have to spend."

I was not surprised that Donaldson, who had been so eager for my trip, would approach me in private. Yet the conversation seemed senseless.

"Sir, you didn't corner me here to chat about Polish tourism."

"No, I didn't. Listen, I've got to make this fast. Neither of us can be off the scene for very long without being noticed. The conspiracy was a figment of my imagination. Whether it proves true or not, I couldn't care less. I know you and what kind of services you'll provide if the price is right."

"Look, whatever it is, I'm not interested in being involved in the looking-glass war."

"I'm not involving you in anything. Just bring back a piece of paper for me."

"Get Harris to do it. At least he's with the FBI. That's their line, not my thing."

"You and I both know what Harris' real job is."

"Why can't an embassy employee do it?"

"Our man in Warsaw would compromise himself if he were seen with anyone working in an official or semi-official capacity with us. Besides, you heard Tarnovsky in there. We have to be discreet."

I tried to argue my way out of doing it, but it was just to play stupid. I realized from the beginning that Donaldson was up to bigger things. "How will I get it?"

"Someone will shake your hand. That's all."

"Not quite," I said. Now I could raise the ante. "It's going to cost you. I'm not in the habit of going to Poland to pick up take-out orders for kielbasa."

"This is government work, Miller, and you work for the government!" he commanded sharply.

"Listen, Donaldson," I retorted. "If this is worth more than the end of the world to you, then I think you should cut me in for a piece of the action."

"I know that idea has been in your head from the beginning of this affair, Johnny. We're on the same wavelength but you'd better adjust your frequency. In this business everyone has a gun pointed at his head. Just do your share if you want to survive." Donaldson was in no mood to be blackmailed. He thought for a moment, just shook his head, and then disappeared with the old guard and the dog.

We had just taken off from JFK. I was about to order a drink when Harris asked, "Johnny, why do you have a grudge against me?"

"You tell me," I answered.

"They made me your chaperone?"

"What about the investigation?"

"What investigation?"

"The one you made when I filed for transfer to the Treasury Department."

"Look, you've seen the report. I did the best I could. I checked you from the day you got the Medal of Honor to your time in CID[7]. You were clean, straight. I never investigated anyone like you. And I said so. If they didn't accept you, it wasn't my fault."

"I know, Dave. You're a career man and even went to law school." He exuded pride in his educational background. "Harris, old buddy, I'll be friends with you on one condition. When we arrive in Paris, relax and enjoy yourself. Be like me."

His face fell. "I'll try." We shook hands on it.

The first time I was in France was in '42, almost a year after my father's death. He was German and my mother French. He was in the invasion of France in 1914 when he met and married my mother. Since both France and Germany were in ruins, they decided to immigrate to the United States. My parents made me learn their mother tongues, and I learned English in school.

I was nearly twenty, a junior in college, when my father died. It was Thanksgiving holiday 1941, and he wanted to discuss my future. When I entered his office, I was surprised to see a Nazi swastika flag and Hitler's portrait. My father smiled. "John, you're an American. I'm German and my duty is to help Germany. I do that by trying to keep America out of the war. Why? To save American youth, and you too, from dying for foreigners, for foreign interests, that's why. This flag and picture may shock you but trust me. I'm doing what's best."

He explained that he was a Bund leader, the German-American organization that was trying to keep the US neutral. But less than a month later, his attitude changed after Pearl Harbor and the declaration of war. He had serious talks with all his relatives and close friends. Then he talked to me alone. "Johnny, I helped organize the American Nazi Party to keep America neutral. That's all over. America has declared war, and we must fight with her. Now she's in it, there's no stopping her. I know American military potential. Germany will be crushed. We have to look to the future and help America because later on, she will help Germany. I'm sure of that."

The next day he went to the FBI and gave them the names of the Nazi spies he knew in the States. Two days later, he was shot. While he was in the hospital, I spent most of my time at his side. The doctors told me he was going to die and there was no possibility of saving him. When he finally regained consciousness, he again tried to explain his actions to me. "You're a man now. You have your own life to lead. Do what your instinct tells you is right." He lost consciousness again and didn't regain it until a day later. "It isn't easy, life. It gets more difficult day by day. To draw the line between right and wrong is very complicated. You were born American, so you won't have the same problems I had. So be an American but don't forget your German father." He died on Christmas Eve, 1941.

I volunteered for the Army in January and went through basic training. They posted me to Morocco. One day, we were returning from a Jeep patrol going toward Casablanca when we ran into some French troops. I told them not to fire because we were Allies. The officer in my Jeep suddenly became very interested in me. "You speak French?" he exclaimed.

"Yes sir, fluently. My mother was French."

About two weeks afterwards I received an order to report to Colonel Johnson. When I entered the office, I found the stereotype of a little old man waiting for me. "Corporal John Miller?"

"Yes sir." I saluted.

"Sit down, Miller."

"Thank you, sir."

"Your father was a hero, young man."

"I don't know anything about that, sir."

"Yes. He turned in all the Nazi spies in the States. You're the son of a hero." He was very excited and enthusiastic. "Wouldn't you like to be like your father?"

"Yes, sir. I would."

"You speak German, in addition to French. How would you like to work for the OSS?"

"Yes sir, but ..."

"'Why did you choose me?' I think you were going to say. Miller, we have a lot of boys ready to fight, but few of them speak foreign languages like you do. You realize that it's going to be very dangerous. You'll probably be parachuted into France or Germany in civilian clothes. There'll be no Geneva Convention to protect you. You can be shot by the enemy without trial."

"Sir, in war we expect to die."

"That's what I like to hear. Well, Miller, I ..."

"Fasten your seat belts please, we are landing at Orly airport.

Please extinguish your cigarettes and remain seated until the engines have been turned off. Captain McLean and the crew hope that you have had a pleasant journey."

After clearing customs, we walked through the hall and found a cab outside. "Where we going?" asked Harris.

"To the Lutetia Concorde hotel and then for lunch with a great French wine."

"Remember, we have work to do," he cautioned.

"Yes, Dave." Same old Harris. He'll never change. He wasn't even trying.

We checked into the Lutetia Concorde. During the Occupation, the German SS made their headquarters there. Now it was renovated and became a chic address once again. I washed up, shaved, and lay down for an hour.

Part II - Good People, Old World

"In a class society, every man occupies a determined position in his class and there is no thought that does not carry the imprint of his class." – Mao Zedong

Chapter 9. Juraski's Tadek

Friday, October 7, 1983 – "The United States bears no responsibility in this appalling murder. Our nation mourns the death of Premier Berisov and extends its condolences to his family and the courageous Soviet people. We are shocked nonetheless by the belligerent attitude of the Soviet leadership that leaves me as Commander-in-Chief no alternative but to put our armed forces on full alert. As of this morning, I have notified the offices of the Strategic Air Command of the current situation. They will respond cautiously but firmly to any provocation. I have also submitted a special request to the Congress for enhanced authority to protect our national security. My fellow Americans, this is the most serious threat to world peace since World War II. In an effort to avoid the risk of nuclear destruction, I am ready to go at any time and any place to talk to Premier Kuslov to resolve the situation." – *Television address by the President of the United States*

We needed twelve hours in Paris before proceeding to Germany to pick up the Polish visas. At breakfast, I suggested that Harris investigate the internal political situation as much as possible. I was concerned about the French Communist Party's knowledge of any terrorist activity that was spawned on the Continent. At the same time, I would contact my former associates in the French government and try to see Juraski, the Pole who'd been arrested with Shipansky back in '49, when Stein had ratted him out to the French police. I explained that we needed an exterior view of the events as much as an interior profile of our man.

Naturally Harris refused to leave me alone. His childish sense of bureaucratic dignity left no room for such a rational plan. It would be useless to argue with him. I did the next best thing and reconciled myself to his constant tagging along. Since there were two of us listening to a third person's view of Shipansky, that made three different opinions for each interview. Every time we added another person who had known Ted, there would be an exponential increase in what we gleaned about his motivations. In other words, thousands of ideas as to why he assassinated Berisov. It takes a lot of ideas to push a bullet through a guy's skull, and this would be the only way left to keep track of them. Maybe there would be a payoff and maybe not. At least I wasn't going to look stupid with a lone-bullet single-assassin theory which would be ridiculed by the press.

Harris followed through the hotel's revolving doors out onto Boulevard Raspail where I hailed a taxi. "Trente-six Quai des Orfèvres," I told the driver.

"Where is that?" inquired Harris.

"It's the French Ministry of Justice. We're going to see André Jouvert, my liaison officer when I was with the CID in Paris. But you already know that, don't you?"

"Okay. I forgot. Is that a crime? I thought we settled all that," he stated gently.

Harris was making great strides toward conciliation, but I resented his apologetic tone even more than his antagonisms.

We reached our destination in record time, considering the traffic. On the fourth floor, we knocked on one of the doors. A tall dark-haired man in his fifties opened the door.

"Hello, André."

He didn't seem to recognize me and then, suddenly, he threw open his arms. "Mon cher Johnneee! How are you? I haven't seen you in a long time."

"I'm fine, André. Yes, it's been a long time, but it's not my fault. It's your damn president who kicked us out."

"Yeah. Yeah, we all feel the same way as you. I enjoyed the time when we worked together. I miss these things from the PX. Look at me now. Criminal Division - hoods, Algerians, Portuguese, and Africans. When we worked together, it was great."

"Jouvert, we'll reminisce some other time over one of those fantastic French dinners. Right now, I need your help on a case." I showed him my credentials and told him about the assignment.

"That's too big for me. *Non!* Bereesov, I don't think I can help you, Johnnee," he intoned as only an embarrassed Frenchman could.

"Yes, you can. We want to find Franek Juraski, a Pole who did time with our suspect. You've got him in prison again, right here in Paris. He was arrested last week," I reported.

Jouvert sat down on the edge of his desk and recited several numbers into the phone. He leaned over and with a Bic pen scribbled something on his pad. He waited a few minutes and wrote something else. He said, *"Merci, bien,"* and hung up. Still sitting on the edge of his desk, he leaned his French nose toward my ear. "You're right. He's incarcerated at La Santé. Maybe I can help you after all," he whispered.

"It'll have to be soon," piped in Harris, who had been listening intently, "there'll be no time for formalities because the word may come from Germany any minute."

"Harris, you're green. Understand that the rest of the world doesn't necessarily work like we do in Washington. Sometimes cooperation happens over a bottle of nice wine here. Business and pleasure are included in the same transaction – just like with hookers." I winked at Jouvert.

"Of course, Johnnee. Let's have that meal first. I'm sure Monsieur Harris would love to see a little bit of Paris." Jouvert was always exuberant when it came to showing off his Paris. Together we had seen a lot. I remembered when I was at CID, he was attached to the Provost Marshal's Office as a liaison for the French Police Judiciaire. My job was to scout the bars in Pigalle for AWOLs and stolen goods. Usually, the girls told me what I needed to know, and Jouvert always covered me. When one of our informants got arrested by the vice squad, André managed to get her off. We worked as a team. Sometimes there was some extraordinary little deal involved. We made good money and kept our records clean at the same time. It was a perfect arrangement until that goddamn de Gaulle ordered the U.S. Army out of France.

For a long moment we sat silently in the office. Then Jouvert lifted himself from the desk and glided toward the door. He beckoned us to follow. I shut the door once we were in the hall. All the way down the stairs and out of the building, other super cops stopped to greet Jouvert. "*Salut*, André" was accompanied by the traditional French handshake. Harris was a little bewildered by all the pomp and ceremony, and in this case, I couldn't really blame him. The French must waste thousands of hours a day just shaking hands. Small wonder that their economy is always staggering.

Jouvert led us to a little restaurant on rue Dauphine. He claimed that it was one of the few Left Bank establishments that still had an all French staff. "Even the dishwasher is one of us," he noted. The rest of the places, he explained, had all replaced the expensive native labor with cheaper immigrants. They learned stock recipes and repeated automatically. Consequently, the owners never changed the menus to accommodate the fresh vegetables or seasonal game that were available at the vast wholesale market in suburban Rungis.

Jouvert ordered for all of us and the waiter arrived not long afterwards with a plate of fresh vegetables smothered in an aromatic vinaigrette. Later we were served a ragout that Harris seemed to appreciate more than anybody in the place.

"Have you ever eaten rabbit, Monsieur Harris?" queried André.

"I can't say I have, sir," he replied.

"Ah, *mais si*," laughed André, pointing to Harris's now empty plate.

Jouvert and I laughed. We let Harris digest his lunch while we got down to serious business. Leaning in, I whispered, "I must talk to Juraski. Today if possible. What's he in for?"

"Nothing serious, Johnnee. He came to recruit mercenaries, that's all. But it is against French law. We don't allow that sort of thing here … on our territory that is. He won't be in jail long."

"I'm looking for a full-blown profile of this Shipansky. Will you release Juraski if he agrees to give me some information?"

"I don't know. I'll see, but it would mean a lot of red tape." Jouvert left the table to phone his office.

A half-hour later he returned saying that things had been arranged. He would accompany us to La Santé prison and handle the warden. He sat down to finish the meal with us but said nothing until we were finishing our espressos. Angrily, he blurted out that it was the fault of the Americans that the world situation had deteriorated to this sort of dangerous impasse. He assured us that his beloved Charles de Gaulle had predicted East-West tension over a generation ago. He was indignant that his family should risk their lives in another war because of an incompetent U.S. foreign policy.

I returned fire saying that the American generals wanted to push toward the East after the German surrender but gave up the project when De Gaulle, who had to collaborate with the French Communists to hold power, backed down and refused to support a new offensive. He calmed down a bit and returned to the subject of Juraski.

"How do you expect this man to help you with Shipansky? Is he connected to Berisov's assassination?"

"I can't talk about that with you, André. Let's just say that politics in a big democracy like the U.S. is getting more complicated every day. Remember the Kennedy assassination? It still has repercussions on local elections. I've been assigned to follow this thing right through to the time our suspect was in the camps. I can't say I like it. This watchdog won't let me have fun!" I nodded at Harris, who smiled dutifully.

After lunch we went back to the Justice Ministry to get an official car and the papers necessary to secure Juraski's eventual release. We then headed back to the Left Bank. La Santé prison sits behind Montparnasse, near the Place Denfert-Rochereau. To get there we wound through St. Germain des Près, and I was pleased to see some of my old haunts. Even Harris seemed to enjoy watching the fashionable women.

We stopped in front of the medieval-looking prison. While Jouvert entered the gate, we stepped out of the car and walked across the street to a café, appropriately named "It's Better Here Than Over There." An hour later, Jouvert returned with the Pole and introduced us. I had met Juraski briefly during the war but was confident he wouldn't recognize me. We had both changed. He was about my age, tall and well built, but his hair, which had been strawberry blond, had now fallen out.

"Juraski?" I offered him my hand.

"That's me," he stated flatly in English. You're Americans, aren't you? I can always count on you to spring an old Polak, huh?" His eyes twinkled.

"Look, freebies went out with the war," I started. "We got you off a very serious rap because we want some information. Don't try to bullshit us, or you'll go right back into the slammer. That's the bottom line on our little deal, okay? Once we're gone, you never talked to anybody, never saw anyone. Naturally you must leave France too. Find a nice African war and settle down."

Juraski stared at me for a moment. He acted as if he owed us nothing for his release yet was willing to meet his end of the bargain. We parted company with Jouvert and took Juraski back to the hotel. I offered whiskey while Harris set up the tape recorder. I handed him some pictures of Shipansky. "Remember him?" I demanded.

Juraski gazed for a long time. "Yeah. Very well," he smiled.

"Where did you meet him? When?" Harris spoke into the microphone instead of looking at our subject.

"It's a long story ..." Juraski began.

"If it's another Holocaust tale, then I don't care to hear anything but the main theme. Shipansky."

I already had a good idea of the direction we would take ...

"It was back in the middle of January '43," he began again. "I went as usual to the movie theater on Marszalkowska in Warsaw to see if there was a message for me. That's the way we were organized in the underground. The movie theater was the mailbox.

"The girl selling tickets handed me a little piece of paper which read, '3:00. Usual place.' The rendezvous was a tram stop. When I arrived, I saw my underground contact, code name Krol, and with him was a blond guy, whom I had never seen before. He was a bit younger than me, but he looked seasoned. I still remember the strange glint in his eyes. The three of us got on the tram and took it to Saski Gardens, where we could talk without being followed.

"'Hello, Krol,'" I greeted my comrade.

"'Hello, Grat,' he returned the favor."

"What kind of weird names are those?" interjected Harris.

"They're not strange," replied Juraski indignantly. "They're real Polish words, which we used as cover names for underground security. I was Grat," he added. "This is the way my group, the Broom Squad[8], operated. Each squad had its own way of doing things."

"How many were in a squad?" asked Harris.

"Five at a maximum, a leader and four men. The leader knew all the names and mailboxes. Then there were six squads in a platoon, but we only consolidated forces for special assignments."

Juraski continued his story without interruptions for a half hour. He related how the boy wanted to be nicknamed "Trigger." The others wanted to give him a Polish pseudonym, "Cyngiel," but he insisted that he would use "Trigger," adding that he was a fan of American western movies. Krol had brought the boy with them in order to integrate him into the underground. He introduced him as his nephew and requested that Juraski (Grat) look after him.

Juraski was impressed by the boy's affability and told him to go to the mailbox the following day to find his orders. After the meeting, Juraski had proceeded to a scheduled conference with his chief, Slavek. Something special was up because he had never before met Slavek in three years with the underground. Slavek was one of the chiefs of KEDYW[9] operations in Warsaw.

"When I reached my destination, I looked for the sign. It was there, a potted flower was sitting in the window. If it wasn't there, I wasn't supposed to go in. I entered the building, climbed to the second floor and knocked on the door. A voice called to enter. The apartment was sparsely furnished with only a table and a few chairs. Slavek impressed me. Even though he wore no uniform, he had an authoritative, military air. His reputation as a peasant freedom fighter suggested a much different appearance, but he had worked his way up the chain of command by following orders, and this was the result. It was not entirely uncomfortable to be in his presence. 'Sit down, Grat.' He offered me a chair.

"'Krol, as you know, is a highly trusted man in our organization. Now he has introduced his nephew to us. I believe you have met the boy.'

"'Yes, I have,' I told him.

"'The problem is, Grat, that this boy comes from nowhere.'

"'A Jew or perhaps Gestapo,' I ventured.

"'That's what I thought too, but Krol has been with the organization for a long time. He has committed himself as well as his conscience to us – a pact sealed with a solemn oath to the Lord.'

"'Which eliminates the possibility of a Jew, so he must be a Gestapo agent,' I deduced.

"'Precisely. Krol told me that his nephew had just come from Germany. It seems that Krol's sister married a German and the boy, who has Polish patriotic leanings, or so he claims, fled from Germany without papers. He didn't want to join the German army.'

"'Without papers, these days?'

"'Yes, very unusual. And there's another thing. The boy had papers under the name, Tadeusz Szczepanski . Krol requested that I find some new ones.'

"'How did he get the papers?'

"'From the real Szczepanski when they were caught in a German raid.'

"'But why should Szczepanski do that?'

"'Well, according to Krol, the real Szczepanski and his nephew were friends. When they got caught in the raid, Krol's nephew didn't have any identification but persuaded the other boy to help him escape by giving him his papers.'

"'It doesn't make much sense. Why should a young man with perfectly legal papers give them to Krol's nephew? Wouldn't the Germans demand to see his papers? They could have executed him on the spot.'

"'Well, anyway, he got the papers and escaped. No one knows how. Krol himself is very obtuse. The whole thing is too much.'

"'Well, I don't think that a Jew would have the wherewithal to try and join the organization in such a way.'

"'Let's assume for the moment that he's a German agent. The whole story he told Krol could have been pure fiction. The Germans may have blackmailed the boy into using his uncle in order to infiltrate the organization. Krol is the type of person who would never suspect blood relatives.'

"'We should get rid of the kid,' I concluded.

"'No. We can't kill or remove anyone without unshakeable evidence or orders from London. Anyway, there is a possibility that however fantastic it may seem to us, the story is true. Maybe the boy does feel loyalty to Poland. After all, the western part of Poland was gobbled up by Germany. It's possible that he hates Germans for that. Maybe he's telling the truth. We have to give him a chance to prove himself.'

"'What are you going to do?'

"'Have him kill a known Gestapo agent.'

"Slavek left the room and returned a short while later with Sergeant Lech, the leader of my squad. They entered the room talking. They agreed that the time had come to put their plot into action. The target was an agent called Weber who frequented a café on Nowy Swiat. The KWC[10] had ordered his execution because he had informed on too many of our best fighters. I was surprised to find out that this was the first time Lech had heard about Krol's nephew and the dilemma that he posed. Slavek explained the connection between the assignment from KWC and the little test we had devised for Trigger. Lech quickly agreed to handle the logistics of the plan. He added that he hoped everything would turn out all right, for Krol's sake.

"Lech and I left Slavek's place separately. The organization took no chances. It especially never risked its men for stupid everyday-type slip-ups.

"That night I put a letter in the mailbox telling Trigger to meet me the next day. I explained his assignment when he arrived. I also received a message from Slavek telling me to proceed with the plan, but cautiously.

"On the day of the execution, I went to the mailbox as usual. There was one message. It said, 'Proceed with cleaning.' I made my way to Bednarska Street. Lech was already there with the rest of the Broom Squad – Byk, Stal, and Plug. They all debated whether the new boy would show and if he would be on time. Unpunctuality was the worst defect a person could have as far as Lech was concerned. Plug had been assigned to follow him during the interval. He reported that nothing suspicious had occurred. No phone calls, no contacts. Just an encounter with a lonely girl in Saski Gardens. She too was clean.

"It was still early, but tension was written on everyone's face. Nobody wanted to risk their lives for a punk. It would have been difficult to learn whether he believed that we suspected him of something. We had a contingency plan in case anything backfired. Stal had volunteered to kill him.

"Before any mission, there were tense moments, but this was the worst. Byk's fat body was drenched with sweat. Lech himself smoked constantly, even though cigarettes were in short supply. As he passed a smoke over to Byk, the door opened, and Trigger came in.

"He asked if he was on time. Lech replied that indeed he was. He introduced Trigger to the rest of the Broom Squad. Everyone made quite a thing over the name 'Trigger.'

"'I'll try to live up to it,' he joked as we shook hands all around.

"'I hope so,' agreed Lech, 'but I'm sorry to cut short the formalities. We have to hurry. I must explain what you have to do. There's a curfew. It's 4:00 now and that doesn't give us much time. The target is Weber. You are all aware of who this dog is. Gestapo like him can't go on liquidating all our good men. London has ordered us to kill him. The best place to do it is the Erica, a café at 21 Nowy Świat, his favorite place.'

"He pulled out a photograph and handed it to Trigger. He ordered him to study it very carefully, to memorize every feature.

"'You're going to kill this man, kid,' stated Lech flatly.

'Plug and Stal, you'll go into the café at 6:00 or just before. Wait until Weber enters. Find out where and with whom he is sitting and come back out. Trigger, when they come out, that's your signal to enter. Plug and Stal will tell you where Weber is. Byk, you take the Schmeisser and go in with Trigger. While you two are inside the rest of us will cover you from the street. Everybody, take it easy. This may be our only chance to get him. Trigger, can you use a vis[11]?'

"'Of course. I grew up in the countryside where every boy learns to hunt.'

"'Okay. Here. And study that picture carefully.' Lech handed him the gun and pushed the picture back into his face. 'We don't want any mistakes. We don't want to kill someone else, at least not until we're ordered to. Understand? And don't forget his ID papers. It may cost precious time, but it's as necessary as pulling the trigger. We must have proof that it was the right person. After the operation, withdraw through Foksal and Kopernica, come back here and deposit your weapons.'

"At 5:15 we left the base and headed down Bednarska for the Erica. When we reached Krakowskie Przedmiescie, we could see the café. Plug and Stal crossed the street and went inside. We waited ... for a long time. Lech became uneasy. It was dangerous to stand about for a long time, especially if you were armed. I looked across the street at Byk. Everything seemed quiet on his side. Trigger was standing motionless. Suddenly, Lech signaled at Byk.

"I never saw Weber's face, only the back of his head. But it must have been him because Plug and Stal came out ten minutes later.

Trigger crossed the street, stopped for a few minutes with them, and then proceeded inside. Then Byk crossed the street and entered the café. He later recounted what had happened in there.

"Byk had followed Trigger into the café and stayed by the coat-check, talking to the girl inside and telling her that he was waiting for a date and didn't want to check his coat for the moment. Out of the corner of his eye, he'd watched Trigger.

"Trigger had recognized Weber immediately. He was sitting with a good-looking blonde and didn't notice Trigger. His attention was divided between Vogel, one of our greatest singers, and the girl. Trigger went past the table and into the men's room. When he disappeared, Byk started to have second thoughts.

"But Trigger had emerged five minutes later and passed the table again. It seemed as if he stumbled. He fell dead on the table, knocking over glasses and bottles and creating havoc. Simultaneously, Byk heard three shots and saw Trigger reach inside Weber's jacket and pull something out. Pandemonium broke loose. People were screaming and running for shelter under the tables behind the bar and to the side of the stage. The blonde had Weber's head in her hands, it was covered with blood, as was the tablecloth. She'd recoiled in horror, screamed and dropped the lifeless, hairy mess. By that time Byk had drawn his Schmeisser. Vogel was no longer singing. He stared at the scene in disbelief. Some German officers stood up to see what was going on and then started to move toward Weber. Then one of them noticed Byk with the gun. They returned to their seats. A wise move under the circumstances.

"Lech entered the café and just after that, Trigger ran out into the street where we were waiting for him. Lech and Byk followed on his heels. No one had dared to follow us, and we made our way back according to plan.

"Once back in the Bednarska base, we opened a bottle of vodka to celebrate. We were pleased that Trigger had passed the test. We toasted him. Then Byk said, 'How does it feel to kill a man for the first time?'

"Trigger just smiled. A very strange smile like a snarling dog who bares its teeth. 'It was a pleasure,' he said softly.

"The next day I took Weber's papers to Slavek. 'Let's keep him on the execution squad,' I advised. 'He likes the job and seems quite able.'

"'Right. Take care of him. People in that line tend to become very lonely and sometimes dangerous. Good luck. Oh, yes,' added Slavek, 'bring him to me tomorrow afternoon. He has to take the oath, and I'd like to chat with him.'

"I left a message for Trigger with the time of the appointment for the next day.

"'What's up,' he asked when we met again the next afternoon. 'Another job?' He seemed gleeful.

"'You're going to meet Slavek, the commander. He was very impressed and wants to meet you. You've got to take the oath too.'

"Slavek was standing in front of the window with his back to the door as we entered. When the door closed, he turned around and smiled. 'So, you're Trigger! Glad to meet you.' They shook hands.

"'Same here, sir,' replied Trigger.

"'Slavek, not sir...'

"'Yes, Slavek.'

"'Good show, that Weber business. Welcome to the fold. Now, although you were recommended to us, I'd like to know a little more about you. First of all, what's your real name?'

"'Hans Bauer.'

"'Your relation to Krol?'

"'He's my uncle. My mother's brother. She married a German, Kurt Bauer, in Poland. As you know, three hundred thousand Germans lived in western Poland.'

"'And your mother?'

"'She died just this year. Cancer. I stayed with her to the last. I promised her to be a good Pole. Anyway, I always felt more Polish than German, especially after they annexed the area where I lived and made it a part of the Reich. As soon as my mother was buried, I crossed the border and threw away my German passport[12]. I went to see my uncle and asked for his help to join up with you.'

"Slavek accepted what Trigger recounted in good faith. He began to administer the oath by giving Trigger the text and a crucifix. Trigger raised the crucifix with his right hand.

"'In the name of Almighty God and Holy Mary, the Queen of the Polish Crown, I place my hand on this Holy Cross, sign of suffering and salvation and swear to be faithful to my country, Poland, to guard her honor and to liberate her by all means within my power, even to sacrifice my life if necessary. I will obey all orders of the President of Poland and the Chief of the Home Army and keep all their secrets whatever the consequences may be for me.'

"Slavek took the crucifix and the text. 'I take you as a soldier of the Polish Army fighting in the underground for the liberation of our country. Your duty is to fight with a weapon. Victory will be your reward. For treachery and treason, the punishment is death.' Slavek put the paraphernalia away and asked Trigger, 'What kind of job would you like in the organization?'

"'Anything you give me is fine.'

"'How did you feel after the killing?'

"'I can do it again,' Trigger smiled.

"'Would you like to stay with the Broom Squad on executions?'

"'Why not?'

"Slavek looked a little uneasy. 'Any questions?' he asked.

"'No,' replied Trigger.

"'I presume Krol mentioned something about the setup of the organization. Allow me to clarify a few things. The resistance is divided into three main groups. In the first, members lead normal lives. They follow their professions. But from time to time, they receive orders to perform certain duties and help prepare for a general uprising. The second are the partisans who live in the forest, wear a uniform, and use guerilla tactics to fight Germans. Eventually, you'll train with them. The third is the KEDYW, the professionals. They're on call round the clock. Grat and I are part of KEDYW ... and so are you now. I must warn you about the danger from two groups – those who take orders from Moscow and the NSZ[13]. They both want to take over after the war. The NSZ fights the Communists; we don't. Not because we like them, but London's orders are to concentrate our efforts on getting rid of the Germans.

"'As for your behavior, dress inconspicuously. Whatever you do, don't wear boots. The Germans think that all members of the underground wear boots. Don't try to look pretty. You'll live longer. Act naturally. If you see a German guard in the street, never act mysteriously. Don't hesitate. Check your mailbox by noon every day. Be on time for your appointments. A minute late may cost someone his life and it could be you. Don't forget that.'

"'I'd like to add something,' I offered. 'There are some armed people that are neither Communists, NSZ or Home Army. Some are Jews, others may be bandits or just ordinary citizens who want to protect themselves. So be alert. I think that's all.'

"Slavek fell silent. He meandered about the room, deep in thought. Then he slowly lifted his head toward us. 'I've said all I have to say for the moment. You lads may go now. Trigger, good luck. And I hope to see you again.'

"We left Slavek and went our separate ways.

"The next morning, the Grey Scouts[14] had been at work. Everywhere, there were red posters on the walls announcing the execution of Weber by the Home Army. I went to the mailbox and found a message requesting another execution. Normally, each man on the execution squad did one killing, in rotation. The big chief never wanted us to do more than three at one time. On moral grounds. Personally, killing people unnerved me, and that was true for most of my squad. But we were soldiers.

"As the instructions circulated around the Broom Squad network, everyone found out about the next mission. Trigger was the only one who volunteered for the job of executioner.

"Two weeks later we received another order. A man named

Gutowski was to be hit. He was a Polish collaborator, working for the Gestapo in the water plant in Praga, the eastern quarter of Warsaw. Two German soldiers were assigned to guard the plant from sabotage. Their presence added to the danger of the mission. Trigger proposed a solution. 'Grat, could you get an SS uniform?'

"We finally tracked down an SS uniform. He tried it on, and to everyone's surprise he looked and acted like the real thing. He was very pleased with himself in that uniform. He smiled and strutted about, mimicking the Nazis. 'Now I can carry my gun legally,' he kidded us.

"According to the plan, Trigger was to fool Gutowski into thinking he was secure with him alone. Once he was away from the guards, we were to execute him and disappear. But things didn't exactly work out that way.

"We arrived at the water plant and took up our positions. Trigger approached Gutowski and saluted him. We waited as they talked, but then the two of them disappeared. The German guards remained in their original positions near the gate. We waited several minutes but still no Trigger, no Gutowski. The plan went awry. We were dumbfounded and, since things had not run smoothly, decided to scratch the mission. The protocol in such cases was to disengage quietly even if it meant leaving a comrade behind. We returned to Bednarska Street and waited an hour for Trigger, but he didn't show. We figured that he had gotten into some complications in that SS uniform, so we gave him up for lost and went home.

"The next day I received a message from Trigger. When we arrived at the base, he was waiting for us, still in the uniform and grinning from ear to ear. 'What the hell happened?' I blurted out.

"'Don't look so upset. It went okay. Here are his papers. He's dead.'

"'Things didn't go according to schedule. We left. We gave you up for dead.' I kind of accused him of disobeying orders, although the whole plan was his and his alone.

"'It couldn't be helped. Gutowski had to give some instructions to his workers. I had no choice but to go with him. I shot him through head. He died immediately. I ran to the gate and told the guards there had been an accident inside. They rushed toward the commotion and I just walked out.'

"'So why are you still wearing that goddamn uniform?' I demanded.

"'I like it. It makes me feel safe.' He smiled and caressed the outfit. 'Listen Grat, I could do a lot of jobs in a German uniform. What do you think?'

"He was right, perhaps. He'd fooled Gutowski and we needed operatives to do dangerous and important work, like transporting arms and rescuing prisoners from jail.

"'Well, Grat?'

"'Perhaps.' I actually had no authority to grant such an unusual request.

"'I could use some training,' he continued. 'If I could use a silencer and hand grenades, I'd be of more use. Couldn't you speak to Slavek?'

"I had to see Slavek to submit my report anyway, so I agreed to make the request.

"'He wants to be trained?' asked Slavek. 'That's unusual. You say he also fooled Gutowski? Well, take him to Kampinos and see how he does.'

"Soon afterwards, Trigger and I left Warsaw for Kampinos forest, which is about 30 kilometers outside Warsaw. We received uniforms and three weeks of intensive training – SK[15], guns, explosives, and so forth. We had a few run-ins but nothing serious. Upon returning to Warsaw, we had more cleaning orders."

"Was he in uniform again?" I asked.

"Yes, first the SS uniform that we had stolen. Then the forest camouflage outfits worn by the partisans."

"Wait a minute," interjected Harris. "You've been saying 'cleaning.' What exactly does that mean?"

"Killing, executing somebody."

"That's what I thought, but I wasn't quite sure." Harris delayed the conversation in order to change the tape. Meanwhile, I offered Juraski some more to drink and we talked about life in Paris.

As we coasted back toward the subject of Ted, or Trigger, as he was known in the Polish underground, Juraski seemed more concerned with confiding his own opinions. True, he was more relaxed. A few drinks and a sudden liberation from a jail sentence would have the same effect on anyone. Yet, at the same time, I got the distinct impression that this was the first time in many years that he had even thought about Ted or the underground. He certainly had a captive audience. Neither Harris nor I had ever heard the hidden history of the Polish resistance. Like all good Americans, we had read books and seen movies about the "glorious" French Resistance, which wasn't as honorable as portrayed, and the stubbornness of the British during the Blitz. But never had we read about what went on in those countries that fell on the other side of the Iron Curtain after the war. Juraski had no trouble recalling the details, places, names, and dates, but now he began to emphasize his feelings.

"After the sixth killing, I became worried about Trigger. Not only had he gone over the limit, but murder didn't seem to bother him. It was a case of 'service with a smile,' if you know what I mean. He was anxious to kill, always volunteering. The squad didn't care, but we had our rules. I didn't know how to handle the situation and, realizing that more executions were on the way, I went to see Slavek.

"'What's the problem?' he asked, somewhat annoyed at my request for a special meeting.

"'Trigger,' I told him.

"'What's he been up to lately?' Slavek took a personal interest in the kid.

"'He's over the maximum and he wants to do more killing.'

"'All right. We'll discuss that later, but something more important has come up.'

"This was in April 1943. Sometime around the 18th. Lech and four other lieutenants whom I did not know came into the room. Then Slavek took the floor. 'I've just received word from Intelligence. The

Germans are planning to liquidate the ghetto tomorrow morning.'

"'What! Final destruction?' gasped Lech, incredulously.

"'Tomorrow morning,' repeated Slavek. 'But what's more, the Guard is going to counterattack to help the Jews.'

"'You mean the Jews are going to fight?' asked one of the other lieutenants.

"'They did last January. That's why the Germans stopped the action. Now they've reinforced themselves with the Rheinhardt Kommandos and the Lithuanian and Ukrainian mercenaries. They've moved them into Warsaw surreptitiously, but we've had someone watching and counting all along. They're massing these cutthroats in Warsaw, which means that the ghetto will be destroyed. If the Communists are helping the Jews, then so shall we. Like it or not, orders from London.'

"'London! I never heard anything about helping the Jews,' objected Lech.

"Helping the Jews, no one had ever mentioned anything about that to us before. We were all slightly amazed. Slavek just ignored Lech's remark and continued. 'I want to make a coordinated move on the ghetto walls from all sides tomorrow.'

"Everybody protested. Most of us were fervent anti-Semites. We complained that it would be impossible to assemble all our operatives on such short notice. It would take at least 24 hours, better 48, just to coordinate the different sections.

"'All right! All right! Who can do it tomorrow?' Slavek insisted.

"'I can,' murmured Lech, unenthusiastically.

"'Jolly good. That's settled. What about the rest of you?' Slavek stared into everyone's eyes.

"'Forty-eight hours!' they responded in unison. Not only were they loathe to obey Slavek's command, but they had a legitimate reason. The oath. It said nothing about defending the Jews, and in fact many had already argued that the Jews were the principal enemies of the Holy Crown.

"Slavek tried a different approach. 'Look,' he reasoned, 'we don't want people to think that the Communists help the Jews more than true Poles do. We have to show that if Moscow helps the Jews, London can and will do even more. Contact your men and come to see me tomorrow at the same time. Lech, Grat, I want to talk to you. The rest are free to leave.'

"After the others had left, Slavek took out a map and spread it on the table. 'Here's how you'll do it,' he explained. 'Tomorrow, six platoons will hit the area along Bonifraterska. You'll mine the wall to make a hole for the Jews to escape if they can.' He reviewed the plan in detail and told us to report back as soon as it was over. I left Slavek and contacted my men, giving them the necessary information.

"On April 19th at 5:30 in the morning, two battalions surrounded the ghetto. They were composed of Rheinhardt Kommandos, SS men, German and Polish police, and Lithuanian and Ukrainian mercenaries – about five thousand men in all. They were poised for the final liquidation, to round up the remaining Jews and deport them to the death camps. When we took up positions, Bonifraterska was already crowded with spectators. On one hand, this was good because nobody paid any special attention to us. On the other hand, the distance between the squads was too great. We couldn't see each other and that always made things a bit sticky.

"At 6:00, everyone was or should have been in position. My squad was near Jan Bozy hospital. To our left was Sergeant Tygrys. At the corner of Bonifraterska and Sapiezynska was Sergeant Las. They were our best sharpshooters, assigned to cover the 'engineers' waiting a few yards down Sapiezynska. The 'engineers' were not attached to any particular platoon. They were an independent unit used for demolitions or other technical operations. This time they were supposed to blow a hole in the wall under Lech's supervision. Behind them were two other squads waiting to cover their retreat. As we waited for Lech and the 'engineers,' I overheard people talking. At first, I paid them no attention, but soon it began to unnerve me. I admit that I never liked Jews. Nevertheless, I was furious to see all these bloodsuckers standing about, expecting a big show. How could so-called civilized individuals crowd around like that and wait to see other people die? This is something I could never understand. I will never understand that!

"Of course, what was about to take place had never been seen in a civilized country before. But still ... the Jews had a choice. They could be shot or burned alive, or they could commit suicide by jumping from the fourth story of a building."

I asked him what Ted's attitude had been in this case.

"I have no idea, Mr. Miller. He never said anything. He just stood there on the corner behind us, staring at the wall and waiting like the rest of us.

"According to the plan, Lech was to fire a signal shot, which would begin the operation. But a police car was situated in our vicinity. The Polish police were collaborators for the most part. Evidently, they had been tipped off by someone in the group that was unwilling to defend the Jews. Maybe it was the NSZ, I don't really know. Anyhow, a shot was fired. Not Lech's, but this excited people all around us. Soon there was gunfire in all directions. Germans fired machine-gun salvos from the rooftops surrounding the ghetto. Slavek had forgotten to remind us of that possibility, probably because he was too preoccupied with outdoing the Communists. I saw the 'engineers' run toward the wall. They had misunderstood the gunshot and took it to be Lech's signal. Halfway across Bonifraterska, they were cut down. Two men ran out and pulled the wounded to safety. The mine was left in the middle of the street.

"Our group started to pull back, with Trigger giving us cover. In his uniform, he confused the Germans and they stopped shooting, thinking he was one of them. Then the mine exploded. In the confusion that followed, Trigger managed to slip away. Two of our men were killed, another two wounded. The operation was a dismal failure.

"Meanwhile the Jews had attacked the Kommandos when they rolled into the ghetto in armored cars and tanks. Personally, I'd always thought they were cowards. But they had known what was coming and were prepared to resist until the end. A fury of bombs and grenades rained down from the rooftops, killing hundreds of Germans. Every wave of Kommandos was cut to shreds in a murderous ambush.

"The next day, I reported to Slavek. He appeared unaffected by the previous day's fiasco.

"'So, it failed. Don't worry, Grat. Tomorrow, we'll coordinate the operation. Lech will have the east, Bonifraterska again. Tygrys will be south on Leszno. Kastor on Okopowa in the west. This time we'll attack the Germans and blow the wall.'

"The lieutenants were not very happy. Slavek noticed it. 'Men, you have your orders. Whether you like the people or not, it doesn't matter. Like me, you have to obey London. Last night I spoke to the Commander-in-Chief. He wanted to know what kind of plan I had to help the ZOB. I told him the same thing I told you. I also said we'd take any Jewish escapees to Kampinos. Is anybody dissatisfied or want out? If so, speak up! You're free to do so ... Now you have the plan. Dismissed.'

"After the rest had gone, Slavek turned to me. 'I know my officers. They're good men. They always follow orders.'

"By the next day, however, the situation had changed drastically. The Jewish uprising shocked the Nazis into a massive retaliation. Military reinforcements and emergency medical teams flooded the streets surrounding the ghetto. Absolute mayhem prevailed. This time it was Slavek who decided, albeit reluctantly, to abandon London's plans.

"On the 23rd, Von Stroop, the German commander in charge of the action, ordered the burning of the ghetto. The heavy artillery on Krasinski Platz began to batter them. We didn't participate because Slavek decided that we'd done enough for the moment. Two days later, I heard that all our operations on the ghetto walls had failed. Although we bit the enemy, we didn't achieve our objective to breach the walls.

"After about four weeks of fighting with heavy artillery, flame throwers, and aircraft, the Germans announced that the ghetto had been destroyed. We went back to 'cleaning.'

"We received two more jobs, one of which was to get rid of a Gestapo agent, Szucki. And the other ... KCW ordered us to protect Jews from blackmailers. The directive read: *Whoever causes the death or imprisonment of Polish citizens, or blackmails or denounces Polish citizens who have been forced into hiding by the present events, shall be sentenced to death.*

"There could be no dissension on this. The orders were handwritten at the top because, ironically, the Commander-in-Chief had himself been mistaken for a Jew and narrowly escaped capture.

"The last operation was against two Poles who were blackmailers. We were standing in the living room of their flat. They were kneeling in front of us, begging for their lives. I was on the point of releasing one of them when Trigger pulled out his pistol and fired. He merely wounded them. But their shrieking was so hideous that I had to finish them off. Trigger just smiled that bizarre grin of his, that snarl. It was irritating me now.

"I went to see Slavek later on that week.

"'What's the matter this time?'

"'Trigger again. He's over the maximum. He wants to do more! He even kills when he's not supposed to!'

"'But he's good, isn't he,' insisted Slavek.

"'That's just the point. He's too good.'

"'What do you mean by that?'

"'He likes killing. He can't get enough. He volunteers for it.' I described the operations we'd done and said, 'If he goes on like that, he'll never adjust to a normal life after the war. He may become a professional killer.'

"'After the war! If there is an after-the-war, he'll straighten out,' Slavek asserted. 'Stop worrying. After all, he's human, he might be killed.'

"'And if he isn't?'

"'All right, you've made your point. Bring him to me. He's done enough in the city anyway. You could take him to the special group near Lublin. That ought to sort him out.'

"I said nothing to Trigger about my report but brought him to Slavek as instructed.

"'You've done quite a job in Warsaw, Trigger. But according to our rules, we can't keep you on the 'cleaning' operations indefinitely. We've decided to transfer the Broom Squad operations to the Lublin area. A lot of things to do out there.'

"'A partisan unit?' Trigger asked.

"'Not exactly, you're going to settle in a village and meet only when there's an operation to be carried out.'

"'But you're putting me out to pasture,' he protested. 'That's a high penalty to pay for eliminating more than my share of Gestapo men.'

"'I'm sorry you feel that way, Trigger. But orders are given to be followed. You've gone over the limit, and that's the reason. Anyway, the massacres and fires have convinced the citizens that the Germans are worse than butchers. They know the Germans for what they are, but in the countryside, the peasants forget ...'

"'As you wish, Slavek.'

"It was around the end of May when we left for the village. Upon our arrival, a Captain Marek greeted us. He was in charge of the KEDYW in the region and he impressed me. Tall, dark-haired, with piercing eyes, his spirit and vitality made you forget that he was over fifty. He earned his reputation with the partisans after two years of clandestine activity. The rugged life seemed to prevent him from aging.

"After all the formalities, we got down to business. 'What's our first job?' I asked.

"'To liberate an underground fighter who's been arrested by the Gestapo.' Marek pointed to the map lying on the table. 'He's in the Lublin hospital. In his condition, he might talk. If he does, he may ruin the whole setup here. I haven't quite decided how to organize it. I've got two or three things in mind.'

"'Organize what? We just move in and take him.' Trigger was both impatient and naïve.

"'City boys!' Marek's eyes flashed. 'Listen, it's not that easy. First the plan must be made with split-second timing. Then we have to transport the man, and he's critically wounded. This won't be like it was in Warsaw, kid. You must learn to expect the unexpected. You'll have to be trained just like I was. Understand? No one is unique in this war. Heroes die while the rest of us survive for another life. You'll follow orders here!'

"His eyes cut straight through me. That's what I remember most vividly. You couldn't read anything in them, but when he looked directly at you, you felt lower than a worm's belly. I never knew why. He had a pleasant personality and wasn't overbearing like some military men who'd ascended the ranks. When he was right, he was right, and he knew it. If you contradicted him or made some banal remark, he just stared at you. A man of few words but very decisive and very firm. I really enjoyed my stay with him.

"But Trigger started to have difficulties from minute one. I tried to caution him. 'With your attitude, Trigger, we'll never get anywhere. He's right. He knows the score out here. We don't.'

"Marek smiled as he watched us argue. 'Are you the one who fooled Gutowski?'

"'Yes. That's me,' answered Trigger.

"'We can use you. Don't worry, you'll see plenty action here. Go now but be here tomorrow at the same time. I'll have my plan sorted out by then. One more thing. Shoot Germans only when it's absolutely necessary or when you have been given an order to do so. We aren't here to vent our anger. Besides, for every one of them killed, it means the lives of hundreds of Poles, innocent countrymen.'

"The next night, we came as he requested and received instructions. I must admit that if it hadn't been for Marek and Trigger's imaginations, we could never have pulled it off.

"When I first listened to the plan, I couldn't believe that it would work, but it did. It never ceased to astonish me how Marek secured German military vehicles and papers and such accurate information. I mean, it was fairly easy in the city, one could always find a way, but in the country, you're just a fish in the water and can never tell the difference between a lure and live bait.

"When the day finally arrived, the operation went smoothly. We penetrated the hospital without any trouble. Trigger in SS uniform, as usual, was shouting about the hygienic conditions and giving orders right and left. Neatly stuffed in the barrage of commands he shouted was the demand that a certain patient be released immediately. That was the man we were after.

"Byk and Plug ran around and found a wheelchair. Two frightened Poles led them to the ward where the wounded patriot was being held. About five minutes later, five men exited the ward. Trigger pulled out the phony papers Marek had supplied him and began to joust with one of the SS men in charge of the hospital's security. They bickered and signed papers back and forth. Trigger 'outranked' the man, so naturally he had his way.

"While the wounded soldier was being put into our car, Trigger lingered inside with the Germans and then came out. He was yelling at them at the top of his lungs. He even frightened me. The three Germans stood paralyzed. Trigger got into the car, slammed the door, and told me to drive away quickly. Whatever he said must have really put the fear of God into them because it was a week before the Germans began to search for the missing prisoner. That was the only time I can remember we pulled off an operation without any shooting.

"A few days later, we received another order. British planes were to drop weapons destined for Warsaw in a predetermined area. Dressed in German uniforms, we took the arms to the capital. Along the way, we were stopped by German MPs, who asked us for some special orders. While I was pretending to search for the papers, Trigger opened fire and killed all three of them. We got out of there quickly, fearing that reinforcements would come. I can't condemn that shooting because it was necessary.

"But soon after that, we ran into a lot of trouble. In connection with a plan called 'Operation Wooden Board,' we were assigned to burn certain papers in the town halls of the region. The papers showed the quota of men to be taken from each village and sent to Germany as slave-labor. Whenever we moved into these small towns, German civil servants would see us coming and scatter. German uniforms or not, they knew who we were, knew we outnumbered their handful of military guards, and didn't want trouble.

"But this time, the Germans didn't have time to move out. I told Trigger to keep them occupied while I destroyed the records. I was upstairs in a clerk's office when I heard shots ring out from the gallery below. I didn't even have to guess! When I saw the dead bodies, I asked Trigger why he'd shot them. He claimed that they had jumped him, yet I doubted that he was telling the truth.

"In a two-week period, we did six town halls. We took every precaution to avoid bloodshed. I had to keep a close watch on Trigger and was always careful to leave another guy with him. This worked quite well until we did our last job. I left Byk with Trigger. Stal and another man were standing at the main entrance. Plug and I went to destroy the papers. Two German soldiers who had been hiding inside the office opened fire. Plug was hit. I returned the fire and called for help. Byk came to our rescue, shooting. When the Germans saw him, they dropped their weapons and surrendered. I told Byk to take them downstairs and then return to help us finish the mission as soon as possible. In the heat of the affair, I completely forgot that I was leaving them alone with Trigger. I put a handkerchief around Plug's arm to stop the bleeding and set fire to the documents. By that time Byk had returned. In my haste, I must have missed hearing the shots because when we came down, there was Trigger smiling over the bodies of five dead soldiers. This time I was angry at him. 'Don't you realize that what you've just done will cost the lives of at least 500 Poles, maybe more!'

"'Don't YOU realize that I just saved my own ass!' he yelled back. 'I didn't have time to think about what I was doing,' he insisted.

"'Next time try and find time!' I was really fed up his with his antics. Trigger really lived up to his nickname.

"The next day the Germans moved against the village where the operation had taken place. They burned everything in sight and shot all the men. The women and children were locked inside a burning schoolhouse. After that, I decided to return to Warsaw. I left Trigger in the village with instructions not to do anything until I returned.

"In Warsaw I made a report to Slavek about our activities and naturally about Trigger's 'achievements.' Slavek listened in silence. After I finished, he got up and strolled to the window. He stared outside awhile. When his reflections were over, he informed me that I had been promoted to lieutenant. I thanked him but persisted in my case concerning Trigger. 'Will you bring him back to Warsaw?' I asked.

"'No. I have other plans for him. More good news for you, though. KCW has just ordered a temporary halt to the village activities because of the extent of the German retaliations. As far as Trigger is concerned, we'll just have to transfer him to the partisans. Out there he can do all the shooting he wants.'

"'But he doesn't like the forest life,' I suggested.

"'I'm not here to cater to anyone's likes and dislikes. This is war. He's in the Army. And he'll go where he's told to go. He asked for it.'

"At the end of June, I returned to the village. Things were as normal as one would expect until one night during a meeting at my house, there was a knock on the door. Everyone had his gun drawn. 'Who's there?'

"'Ostry unit.' The old Polish lady who took care of the house opened the door. Three men entered. 'Lieutenant Grat. KEDYW.'

"Ostry was a legendary figure, especially in the cities. There were all sorts of stories about his exploits. There was even a saying, 'The Germans run the country during the day; Ostry runs it at night.'

"After the defeat in 1939, Ostry took to the forest. He now had virtual control of a part of the region we were in. At first, KCW had a hard time getting Ostry to follow Home Army orders. He always asserted his independence. Also, our own officers looked upon him as an outsider and disregarded his authority. In turn he disregarded KCW. A compromise was finally reached because none of the military men could run a partisan unit the way Ostry could. KCW recognized Ostry, and he reciprocated by following the Home Army command.

"The two men with Ostry were around my age but seemed older

and more mature than any of my own men. This was something you kind of expected from partisans nestled in the forest. It was no life of luxury. All three were dressed in semi-Polish, semi-German uniforms and hats with a crowned eagle.

"Eventually I ordered my men to collect their gear and we set out for the forest camp. It was the first time I had seen a forest camp. Most of the men were dressed like our escorts. Their weapons were an assortment of German, English and Polish rifles. There were hunting rifles and even some World War I vintage guns.

"When we had installed ourselves in a small shack which served as Ostry's headquarters, he pulled out some papers and began to speak, his back to us. 'I received a message from Slavek that you're to join us. As you know, here in the forest we live freely and are able to move about as we like, more or less. We have men working outside the forest watching German troop movements. They inform us of any unusual maneuvers.'

"'How many men in the group?' demanded Byk.

"'About 150 peasants, escapees, unskilled laborers, even some escaped POWs ... they've all managed to elude the enemy. We take care of them and train them well. But you blokes are professionals.' For the first time since he began addressing us, he turned around and scanned our faces. 'Is this the one who does SS men?' he motioned toward Trigger.

"'Yes, he's the one,' I confirmed.

"'Good. We need someone like him. Good.'

"Ostry had nothing more to say at that particular moment. Instead he ordered one of his sergeants to show us around the camp.

"What he showed us was the latest in prehistoric luxury. It was an underground cave, more like a wild animal's lair, cold and damp, camouflaged at the entrance with branches, twigs and leaves. It was a far cry from this hotel room, but that was the price paid for joining the partisans. Despite the accommodations, we felt secure.

"One of our first skirmishes was with two members of a group of roving bandits who referred to themselves as partisans. Ostry sentenced them to death, and as might be expected, Trigger volunteered. I tried to stop him, yet unsuccessfully. Ostry ordered Trigger to take the two men outside. Although obscured somewhat by the rustling noises of the forest, their pleas for mercy drifted to our ears. Four consecutive shots echoed through the forest. Then Trigger came in smiling the bizarre executioner's smile which had become his trademark.

"After that I called Ostry aside and advised him not to give Trigger any more assignments like that. He enjoyed killing and was in fact dangerous.

"'That the type of man I like,' came the reply from Ostry. 'Our fighting demands it. Listen, here in the forest, we don't go by the book. No prisoners. If the Germans catch us, we're dead, it doesn't matter how. They choose the most convenient method. Sometimes, you know, we have to shoot our own wounded.'

"I wasn't a coward, but I didn't like the thought of having to shoot one of my own men or being shot by someone in the Broom Squad if I was wounded.

"It was rough out there and, in the middle of July, I decided to take everyone back to Warsaw, except for Trigger. He had been ordered to remain with Ostry. We were both a little sad on the day of my departure. I told Trigger to take it easy and kidded him that I'd like to see him after the war. It was kind of ironic. Trigger was the one most likely to survive, and there I was, cautioning him to be careful.

"About a month later, I heard through the underground network that Trigger hadn't returned to his unit. A day later it was confirmed that he had been arrested by the Germans when he left the forest to buy food in the village. KCW had a policy based on the belief that any captured Home Army soldier would under torture surrender information about covert activities. Accordingly, we burned the Bednarska base, Slavek's temporary headquarters, the movie theater, and anything else we could think of that Trigger knew about. We also sent a warning to Krol. We heard that Ostry's unit had moved too.

"Out of curiosity, we left people to watch the old places. There was still no news about Trigger, but at least we were sure that he hadn't talked. I was glad. He had always been a tough customer, and I reckoned that if in those two weeks he hadn't said anything, he never would. Yet we didn't use those places again.

"Sometime in January '44 I received a message from Krol. This was odd because his group was not connected with mine. I was suspicious but went to his apartment anyway. When I knocked on the door and it swung open, there was Trigger. I was really surprised. 'How did you get here?' I questioned him in disbelief.

"'It's a long story.'

"'What happened?'

"'I was captured by the Germans. They beat me for nearly a week. I told them I was Tadeuz Szczepanski, a smuggler from Warsaw, and had come to the village to buy food. After a week they stopped trying. One of the officers came to see me and asked why I shouted in German during the beatings. I told him I had learned it in school. He offered me a job. I had no choice. It was either work for him or a one-way trip to the camps. I knew that the camps meant a long, slow death. Even then, I thought I'd prefer the camps to working for the Germans. But I reconsidered afterwards and figured I could be of use to the organization by infiltrating the Germans.

"'The officer came to my cell the next day,' Trigger continued. 'It turned out that he was convinced all along that I would finish by cooperating. His name was Sturmbannführer Schlaube. I accompanied him to the outskirts of Lublin where he shared an apartment with a couple of other SS officers. I was given a room of my own and worked in his office during the day. It was a routine job. I did translations from German to Polish and vice versa. One day I read what I was translating and realized that a lot of confidential material was passing through my hands. Some of it would have been very useful to you,' he said. 'Only trouble was that I had no way of passing it on.'

"'What about Ostry,' I asked.

"'You know damn well he moved!'

"'And you couldn't find anyone in Lublin?'

"'Would you trust a Pole working for the enemy? I asked Schlaube to give me a leave during Christmas, but he refused. After New Year's, he finally authorized me to come to Warsaw. So here I am,' he said. 'Grat, if you could send a man to Lublin, I can pass on information about troop movements. Especially where Einsatz Kommandos are moving against the local population.'

"I told him I'd see what I could do. I wasn't quite sure if he was sincere or not. Perhaps he was still with us and then again, he could have been working for Schlaube. I tended to trust him though because no one from our squad had been arrested since his disappearance.

"Fortunately, I was able to see Slavek the same day. He was happy to know that Trigger was alive. 'His story seems plausible,' he observed. 'If we don't take chances, we'll never get anywhere. Perhaps we should accept his offer.'

"'He's been living with the Germans for five months,' I warned.

"Slavek was confused by my reaction. 'What gives with you?' he asked. 'First, you're all excited about his offer, now you start casting doubts on it. No one's cover was blown. I'm sending a man to Lublin. You choose him, preferably someone Trigger knows.'

"I'd already called a meeting for that evening. Back at the base, I explained to the squad what had happened. Byk volunteered to go to Lublin and went there a week later to anticipate Trigger's return. Because of the extraordinary nature of the assignment, Byk was transferred to Counterintelligence. But as a friend and former commander, I was kept informed of what was going on.

"For a few months we received occasional messages from Lublin. In April, however, Byk returned to Warsaw unexpectedly. 'I couldn't trust a courier with this message,' he announced.

"'Well, what is it?'

"'It's Trigger's SS commander.'

"'Explain yourself, man!'

"He searched for the right words. 'Cooperate. Schlaube wants to cooperate with us ... to a certain extent.'

"I contacted Slavek and 48 hours later, Byk and I met with Rowny, head of Counterintelligence, Colonel Targ of KWC, and Slavek of course. I introduced Byk and let him have the floor.

"'One day Trigger walked into my room and said that his CO, Schlaube, wanted to meet someone from the organization. I thought he had flipped his lid,' Byk said. 'But Trigger was serious. He was serious and said that Schlaube wanted to call a truce because the Russian Front was moving closer. Schlaube was ready to curb all anti-Polish activities in his region if the organization would leave him alone.'

"We stared at Byk, then Slavek spoke. 'Byk, we can't do that. A deal like that would go against explicit orders from London.'

"'Wait, I haven't finished,' continued Byk. 'Trigger also said that Schlaube would give us schedules of trains passing through his district on the condition that we bomb them somewhere outside his jurisdiction.'

"Colonel Targ smiled sarcastically. 'The war must be coming to an end. Right, we'll think about this proposition.'

"Two days later we received a message. KWC obeyed the truce. It held up until the Russians arrived. The next time I saw Trigger was a few days before the Warsaw uprising against the Germans. That was the end of July. He was at Krol's flat again. This time he wore a weird uniform and a Dolmetscher badge.[16] He swaggered about the room shouting that the uniform was legal.

"Legal or not, it made him a sitting duck for any anti-German fanatic. I warned him to be careful and advised him to take it off. 'Still playing errand-boy for Schlaube?' I taunted him.

"'Schlaube? He left as soon as the Russians moved too close. He was recalled to Berlin. But before he left, he told me to look up a friend of his here in Warsaw, a man named Reinefarth. I've just come from seeing him. I was very well received at Avenue Szucha, I must say.'

"'Avenue Szucha? The Gestapo prison! Trigger, I believe you've gone off the deep end. While everybody in the organization is trying like hell to stay out of there, you walk in for a tête-à-tête with them! What were you planning?'

"'Schlaube told me to go there. He even gave me a letter of recommendation. They hired me immediately.'

"'Doing what? Interpreting?'

"'No, I'm an agent. I'm supposed to join the Home Army, find out the date and time of the uprising, and of course anything else that might be important to the Germans – plans, location of munitions, contact spots. At least that's what he said.' Trigger recited his orders solemnly.

"'German Counterintelligence. I don't believe it!' I started to laugh. 'I'll be damned!'

"'Laugh if you wish, but just remember I still work for you, not for them.'

"'HQ will never believe it. Never. I ... I don't know, though. After that Schlaube thing, they're likely to buy anything you say.'

"'My regards to Slavek,' he added. 'How's he getting along?'

"'Arrested and shot a week ago.'

Trigger's face dropped. He looked sad and disturbed. I apologized for breaking the news to him that way.

"I sent Trigger's story to Rowny and he in turn sent for me. I'd never liked the man, ever since that meeting with Byk. It was nothing personal. I simply didn't like him. He was small, dark and ugly. His beady eyes and thin face made him look like a weasel. His most annoying habit was rubbing his hands together constantly. He asked my opinion and I replied that my trust in Trigger was unshakeable.

"'Hmmmm.' He shrugged his shoulders and rubbed his hands together. 'Tell him to relay a message to the Germans that the uprising is set for the end of August, but the precise date is still uncertain. That should give us some time.'

"He looked at me, 'You like this Trigger, don't you?'

"'An acquired taste, a bit overzealous, but yes,' I answered.

"'And he's still wearing that damn uniform, I suppose? Well, tell him to take it off, for his own sake. He's liable to get shot by one of our own patrols. And don't let him go off on his own.'

"I relayed Rowny's message in my next meeting with Trigger. He delivered the message to a German contact and added that our organization had ordered him to remain with us to fight.

"'Grat, I want a Schmeisser,' he said as he undressed.

"'Well, you'll get a weapon. Don't worry.'

"'But I don't have any other clothes, Grat.'

"I gave him some of mine. He folded the German uniform very carefully as if he planned to use it again.

"Between July 29 and August 1, Warsaw was teeming with activity. The Russians were within several miles of the city. I watched the Germans scurrying back and forth across the Vistula. The majority of them were heading west in order to flee the advancing Red Army.

"The night Trigger returned; Russian artillery pounded heavily on the outskirts of town. The Russians had begun to make Polish language radio broadcasts to the population, urging them to insurrection. Their little performance always began and ended with the playing of the Polish National Anthem.

"As planned, the uprising began all over the city at 5:00 PM, August 1. Our KEDYW unit took up positions in the Wola District. The citizens were enthusiastic. As you know, we fought for two months, but something happened for which I shall never forgive the Communists. As soon as we started fighting the Germans, the Russians halted their advance with neither warning nor reason. They just stopped and stayed right where they were, seven miles west of Praga and watched while the Germans crushed us almost to the last man, trampling down the uprising they had encouraged us to lead!

"Our group fought for eleven days. During the battle, the Germans adopted new tactics. I saw three, perhaps four hundred soldiers and five tanks with Polish civilians in front of them, heading straight for us. It startled me and I lost my voice momentarily.

"'Open fire!' Trigger shouted to the men. 'Grat, if we let them get away with it now, they'll use these tactics right down the line ...' I couldn't argue with logic like that despite the fact that, coming from Trigger, I suspected a darker motive.

"We killed Poles and Germans alike. A few people started to run toward our barricades. Most of them were cut down by German machine-gun fire, but one man made it. He scrambled over the bricks and wood and collapsed. Someone brought him some water and forced the semi-conscious man to drink. He was covered in blood and filthy. You couldn't even tell what color his shirt was. There were pieces of human flesh and brains clinging to his clothes. Some people became sick when they saw him. Finally, he regained consciousness.

"German counterattacks became heavier. At one point, when the Germans were pushing through Wolska and Chlodna, we received orders to retreat, but they came too late. We succeeded in getting to a pile of debris which had once been a brick house on Zyntia. Between the German machine guns and the Nebelwerfer mortars, we were trapped and pinned so low we could hardly turn our heads to look at one another. I tried to count how many fighters were left. 'The rest of the unit must have pulled back to Okopowa,' I said to Trigger.

"'There's only about fifty of us with weapons. The rest have nothing. The unit must try to get through the enemy lines tonight. The people must surrender. That's the only way out. Pass the word!' I shouted.

"'Surrender! I don't think so. Look at the uniforms. Look who's attacking!' shouted our newest arrival, the wounded man.

"I found some field glasses and took a clearer look. Sure enough, it was Dirlewanger and Kaminski. Dirty no-good bastards, the two of them! Killers in soldiers' uniforms. No one, but no one surrendered to them."

"Who the hell were Kaminski and Dirlewanger?" inquired Harris.

Juraski flicked his tongue and wrestled with his seat. "Kaminski was a Russian. In Byelorussia, he organized his own army to fight the partisans. Dirlewanger was the Kommandant of the Strafbataillon, the punishment brigade. The men they commanded were all sadists and bloody killers. They threatened their own men with death if each one didn't fulfill a quota of ten dead per day. They were just stimulated by killing."

"What happened to them?" Harris himself seemed stimulated by the cruelty of a real war.

"We don't really know about Kaminski. After the war, there were rumors that he had been executed by Himmler when he discovered the atrocities that had been committed. Dirlewanger was lynched by the population when the Russians arrived. The people hung him up in the middle of town and cut chunks out of his body with knives."

"Let him continue with the story, Harris. There's no sense dwelling on two names that have no connection with Shipansky. Besides, it's bad for your mental health to hear all these Holocaust tales." I didn't want Harris to get our man off on a sidetrack. He already had had enough to drink, and his consciousness was becoming fogged by the vodka fumes and the smoke rising from the ruins of Warsaw.

"Yes. Better to stick to the story," agreed Juraski. "Where was I? Dirlewanger, Kaminski ... They were advancing rapidly, and we were low on ammunition. I didn't think we could fight them. To surrender to them, to stand and fight, to stand period, to try and fall back ... those were all variations of suicide.

"'How did you know it was Dirlewanger?' I asked the new man.

"'My block was raided at the beginning of the uprising. I hid until two days before. We were taken to Ursus factory with the rest of the population in the area. The grounds were cordoned off by barbed wire. People were being executed there. We were led into the factory yard in groups of twenty, and then in groups of four through a passage to a smaller yard where I saw a huge pile of dead bodies. As each group approached it, they were shot. Some tried to bribe the guards, but the German in charge of the executions interfered,' he said.

"'My group moved forward. I heard shots and fell. The bullet passed through my neck without hitting anything vital. Others fell on top of me. Soldiers took anything they could get their hands on and tried to finish off those who were still alive. Most of the job was done by Ukrainians from the Kaminski Division.

"'That night I was able to escape by crawling back to the outer courtyard where the rest of the Poles were standing about, probably waiting to be executed,' the new man continued. 'I saw the Ukrainians raping our women, right out in the open. Others were standing in a circle, watching and urging their comrades on. I was able to join the other Poles unnoticed. Then someone gave orders for us to burn the dead bodies. The Germans didn't want any telltale evidence left.

"'Most of yesterday and today, I spent burning our dead countrymen. The few hundred of us who were left didn't think we had any chance, but some Germans came. They told us that we were bandits. Then someone asked why they'd killed women and children? A German soldier shot him. About an hour later, a new group of Germans came and blamed everything on the Ukrainians. "We don't kill women and children – only men! The Ukrainians killed them. They're barbarians. They don't have our German culture. But you have risen against us. The Ukrainians have finished. Now we take over." Some of us were to be kidnapped to Germany. The rest were herded in front of the tanks and told to walk. We had to keep walking, no matter what. You people opened fire and I made it here. It's certain death if you surrender to them.'

"I tried to calm the man. 'I thought those stories about Kaminski and Dirlewanger were just talk. The Germans would not do such a thing to the Poles.'

"A voice in the crowd corrected me. 'They did it to the Jews, don't forget. Now, the Jews can be satisfied that they're not alone. We Poles will learn how they suffered.'

"'We've got to get through the lines tonight,' Trigger said.

"'We can't do that. We can't leave these people to Dirlewanger's mercy. We have to do something.'

"'What, for instance? These people are going to die anyway,' Trigger said. 'We're low on ammo, but we are trained soldiers. If a few of us can get through, we can bring back weapons to defend the area.'

"Trigger's reasoning was sound, although somewhat inhuman. I stood up on a pile of bricks and told the crowd to fall back toward the center of the city. They would have to cross German gunfire, but it was a fate better than facing Dirlewanger.

"There were screams, shouts and curses from the crowd. Trigger smiled, 'See how grateful they are!' The mass started to run toward Okopowa where other Home Army units had started to organize a defense.

"On the 9th, we lost Okopowa and from then to the 24th, we defended and ultimately lost Mirowski and Stare Miasto districts back to the former Jewish Ghetto. From August 26th to September 2nd, we evacuated the population of Stare Miasto through the sewers. As usual, my unit was the rearguard. The Germans didn't realize that most of the district had been evacuated. On August 30th, we learned that our allies – England and America – considered the Polish Home Army as a part of the Allied forces. That made it so the Germans had to treat us as POWs according to the terms of the Geneva convention. It was some consolation. Nevertheless, the Polish people and the Home Army held out for sixty-three days, which was longer than the French, Belgian and Dutch armies.

"On September 2nd, a German officer came to our lines carrying a white flag. While Byk and the other men covered me, I went out to talk to him. He spoke in Polish.

"'Gruppenführer Reinefarth recognizes you and your men as soldiers of the Allied Forces. If you surrender, you will come under the protection of the Geneva Convention.'

"'Come back in an hour,' I told him.

"Ten minutes after the German's departure, the artillery fire stopped. There were not many of us left, just twenty soldiers and a handful of civilians who had been injured and could not be evacuated through the sewers. As for arms, we had only a few grenades. I asked my men what they preferred to do.

"'Fight!' some shouted.

"'Surrender,' murmured others in despair.

"Trigger just smiled. 'I have my uniform, my German uniform.' He started to pull it out of his bag. 'You call a truce, surrender, and take me out as your prisoner. I'll tell them how fairly you've treated me.

That may be our only chance.'

"'Well, men, you've heard his offer.'

"Trigger didn't wait for the discussion. He changed immediately.

"'Right, Trigger, the men are with you. They say that if the Germans find out you're a double agent, you'll suffer more than they will. All right. In five minutes, the hour will be up. Prepare yourselves.'

"We raised a white flag and the German officer returned. 'Push me out in front of you,' Trigger whispered to me. 'I'll talk to him.'

"When the German officer was five yards away, we stopped. Trigger raised his arm in salute. 'Heil Hitler! I was their prisoner, they treated me well. They want to surrender ... if you keep your word.'

"'We Germans always keep our word. Let them surrender,' came the response.

"'I told them, but they've heard so much about German atrocities ...' Trigger shrugged his shoulders.

"The officer appeared upset. 'We're regular Wehrmacht troops, not SS.'

"'I can see that, but they don't know the difference,' explained Trigger. 'Please contact my CO, Gruppenführer Reinefarth.'

"The officer frowned and looked quizzically at Trigger. 'Who shall I tell him is calling?'

"'Tadeuz Szcepanksi from SD. Just tell him the translator.'

"'SD?' The officer just stared at Trigger, then called an orderly and gave him the necessary instructions. The orderly looked at Trigger and then walked away.

"I thought that Trigger had overacted, and about fifteen minutes later, the orderly returned and hurriedly whispered into the officer's ear. He slowly inspected Trigger from his feet to the top of his hat. I was sure now that they had identified him as a traitor. The officer still faced Trigger but sidestepped closer to me. 'We've talked to your Herr Gruppenführer.' Then he turned to me and said, 'Please start your evacuation. Your Schmeisser first.'

"I gave him the gun. Then the rest of the people started to walk through the ruins of the area. Germans and Poles alike helped the wounded. Everything was peaceful. The Germans conducted themselves properly. No robbery. No rioting. No raping. Trigger, the German officer, and I were watching the evacuation. Our group joined other Poles from the surrounding district. Another officer came up and whispered something to Trigger. He did not look happy afterwards. He glanced back at the officer and then shouted in Polish, 'You are suffering because of the Jews. What has happened to Warsaw is the fault of the Jews. Anyone who knows of a Jew among you is advised to push them out of the ranks, so they can receive their just punishment. It's your duty to point them out. For they, and they alone, are responsible for the destruction of your beautiful city and all your sufferings.'

"People began shouting and pushing. 'Here. Here's one.' A tremor rippled through the crowd like a spasm through a snake's body. Out popped a man here and there. As those unfortunate people were being ejected from the society of would-be survivors, the Germans grabbed them. Some of them who were taken weren't Jews and were allowed to rejoin their comrades. One young woman and two men were detained and shot. After that the crowd seemed satisfied. 'You see,' shouted a Pole, 'the Germans don't want to harm us. They only want to kill Jews.' He was jubilant.

"Once the shooting stopped, I noticed that the officer was again talking to Trigger, but all I could understand was a '*Vielen Dank.*' A German staff car pulled up. 'Tadeusz Szczepanski ?' asked the driver.

"'Yes,' replied Trigger.

"'Get in and bring that man with you,' pointing to me.

"We drove west out of the city for a couple of miles and stopped in front of a heavily guarded villa. We were taken inside the building and into a large hall. Soldiers and orderlies ran back and forth. We stood there five minutes observing the activity and were then escorted into a room. The moment we entered, Trigger recognized the fat smiling officer behind the desk.

"'I'm so happy to see you again,' he greeted us, getting up and coming to shake Trigger's hand.

"'Herr Gruppenführer, I would not be here if not for this man,' said Trigger.

"Reinefarth stepped in front of me and shook my hand. 'Well, you're the one I have to thank for saving this young man's life! Honored to meet you. The Poles fought bravely, and it's too bad there was a misunderstanding between them and the Reich. Now I hope that you realize where your future lies. By now you must be aware of what it means to collaborate with the Russians. They provoked you to rise up, but did they help you? Certainly not! We Germans have made errors in our treatment of the Poles, but from now on everything will be different. I'll tell you something that even most of the Germans here don't know yet. A new man is taking over in Warsaw. Obergruppenführer Erich von dem Beck. He's Polish, Zelewski was his name. He's a good friend of mine. You can trust him. Now things will go smoothly for Warsaw.'

"'What will happen to the people who were captured? What will happen to me?' I inquired.

"'The civilians, or most of them, will be transferred to neighboring villages. You, as a soldier, will be transferred to a prisoner-of-war camp. I'm sorry, but the car is waiting for you.'

"I turned to Trigger. 'After the war?'

"'Yes, after the war ... in Warsaw,' he replied.

"The Germans took me to a camp in Pruszkow, three miles from Warsaw, for people who had been taken from the capital during and after the uprising. Certain individuals were sent to concentration camps. Others went to POW camps. A handful were released. Naturally, if any of them were revealed as Jews, they were executed on the spot. I didn't hang around for them to decide what they were going to do with me. At the first opportunity, I escaped and hid in the Radom area for nearly four months. In January, when the Russians launched a new offensive and swept through Radom, they took me back to Warsaw with them.

"I arrived in the capital with the rearguard about three days after the actual liberation. Warsaw was in ruins since the Germans destroyed all the remaining buildings before they capitulated. Oddly enough, Praga was practically untouched. All the DPs went there. I wanted to get in touch with members of the underground and form a new group to resist the Russian occupation. But I heard through the old networks that the Russians had called our leaders together on the pretext of Russo-Polish cooperation and arrested them instead. I was warned to be very careful, not because there were so many Communists, but because people were beginning to collaborate with the Russians and Communists. They were anxious to curry favor in advance, since they weren't really sure what type of society awaited them at the other end of the long war-tunnel. It was the same spirit that had led to collaboration with the Nazis but more open this time.

"Toward the end of January, I ran into Trigger. He was walking down Targowa, oblivious to what was happening around him, hands stuffed into his pockets and head facing the street. 'Trigger!' I called.

"He stopped and looked up, perused the horizon and then saw me. 'Grat!'

"We approached and hugged each other. He looked very sad. 'We won, but the fight isn't over yet,' I said. 'Now we have to get rid of the Russians. Come on Trigger, cheer up! There's a lot more killing to do.' His response was very slow and un-Trigger-like. He had changed, or something had happened.

"'You really think so? It's going to be difficult. We had a small number of traitors during the German occupation, but now ... look, everybody is going to collaborate with the Reds. They can use ideology as an excuse now. They will expose their countrymen with a clean conscience.' He was dejected. The Home Army spirit was gone.

"'What are you going to do now?' I asked him.

"'Don't know yet. I might go west. But I have a few things to take care of first.'

"'Aren't you going to join the unit again?'

"'No. We've done enough fighting. Now's the time to do some living. We can't live forever under the repression and occupation.' He pointed to the passing Russian soldiers and the Red Polish militia. 'Is that the victory we were praying for?' he observed sarcastically.

"'No. Not really. I don't think so.' It broke my spirit too to see the Reds parading around and us still in hiding or under detention after having struggled for so long.

"'Grat, do me a favor. Get me a gun,' he said.

"'I'll try. Are you sure you won't join us?'

"'No, Grat. I'm going west, and I advise you to do the same.'

"We met a couple of times later and I gave him a gun. He didn't have much to say, but just before he left, I asked him what had happened with the Gruppenführer. I was curious to know how he got away.

"But he dismissed my question. 'I'll tell you one day. Take care. The Reds are looking for Home Army everywhere.' Then he disappeared.

"Three days later, I learned that he killed two Red Polish cops who had come to arrest him. That was the last I saw or heard of him in Poland.

"I ran into him again in Paris, in Pigalle, nearly four years later. I was standing in a bar drinking. There was someone shouting and singing Nazi songs at the top of his lungs. I was furious. What kind of nitwit could have the nerve to do that so soon after the war! His back was toward me and, as I turned him around to belt him, I saw it was Trigger.

"'What the devil are you doing here, Grat! Glad to see you.'

"I told him that I had almost killed him for singing those fucking Nazi anthems. He explained that he was joking with the locals. He was loaded to the gills.

"I sat down with him and we ordered a bottle of vodka. He paid for it. Cash. He peeled it off a big wad of bills.

"'What have you been doing, Trigger?'

"'A little smuggling, a little black market. By the way, everyone here knows me as Tadek,' he confessed. 'And what about you?'

"'After your little incident with the two Poles, I left. Have you been doing any cleaning lately?' One never knew with Trigger.

"'No. Not anymore,' came his surprising answer. 'Those days are over.'

"I told him that I had gone to England to join the Second Armored Division of Poland but that as soon as I had arrived, the corps was demobilized. After that the British felt guilty over the sell-out at Yalta, so they gave us the opportunity to settle there. I lived in London but came to Paris from time to time.

"'Hey, are you still thinking about fighting the Reds?'

"'Always. And you?'

"'I don't think about it anymore. Right now, I'm drinking. Have some more.'

"'What are you celebrating tonight?' I baited him.

"He laughed. 'Celebrating? You might call it that. My business partners just walked out on me. My fucking partners. The little bastards. I hope they get what they deserve.'

"Abruptly, he stopped talking and just stared at me. After a moment of silence and another swallow of vodka, he opened his mouth. 'Grat, how would you like to join me?'

"'Doing what?'

"'Smuggling. Black market. Look, it's just like the war. Instead of dressing like Nazis, we dress as American MPs. U.S. troops are all over Europe. I have all the papers, uniforms, orders, commissions – everything we need. We simply wear the uniform and travel as Military Police couriers.'

"'But if we're caught ...?'

"'Jail. Three months, maybe six. What's that?' he laughed. 'Remember what we risked with Ostry? What we're doing here I don't even consider work, just a pastime.'

"'Why not? But I don't even speak English.'

"'No matter. I'll do all the talking. If anyone says anything, act dumb, drunk, anything.'

"We traveled to Germany, Austria and Italy, bringing all kinds of commodities back to France. We made good money at it for three years."

"Didn't you have any trouble crossing the borders?" asked Harris.

"Never on the border, sir."

"Well, how many times did you cross?"

I couldn't understand what Harris was getting at.

"Well, we averaged three times a month for three years ... over a hundred times."

"And were you ever caught?"

"No. Although once we were arrested. It wasn't Trigger's fault. It was one of his old partners who turned us in. The French cops were waiting for us when we entered Paris. We were convicted for not having the proper commission for the goods we were carrying."

"How long did they give you?" Harris was really getting a chance to demonstrate his gumshoe technique.

"Three months. But you know all that. It's in the file."

"And afterwards?"

"We started again. Naturally."

"Who gave you the papers? How did you get the travel orders?"

"I don't know, Mr. Harris. Trigger never told me."

"Didn't you ever ask him?"

"Once or twice. But, like in the Home Army, you can't tell what you don't know. In fact, he called our business the second underground. Before, we were fighting for our lives, he used to say, now we're fighting for our existence."

"Tell us about your trips."

"A normal one or a special one?"

"What's the difference?"

"Well a normal one, there's nothing much to tell. We dressed in MP uniforms, went to Germany or wherever. Most of the time it was

Salzheim to the Jewish refugee camp. We purchased photographic and electronic equipment and brought it back to Paris. That's it."

"What about the special trips?" pursued Harris.

"There were different kinds."

"Such as?"

"On one of our trips to Salzheim, we met a young Pole. He was probably Jewish. 'I've got a problem,' he said to Trigger.

"'Haven't we all?' was his response.

"'No, listen. I was stopped at the border in my UNRRA uniform.'

"'What's UNRRA?'

"'United Nations Relief and Rehabilitation Agency.'

"'You can't speak English ...'

"'So what? Nobody in UNRRA can. Well, practically nobody. But they had never checked us before.'

"'What happened?' asked Trigger impatiently.

"'They asked me to open my suitcase and I was carrying four thousand dollars' worth of camera equipment,' he said, grinning sheepishly.

"'And they let you go?'

"'They were lenient because I was wearing the uniform. They just took the stuff and let me go. Now they're waiting for an explanation. Forty-eight hours they told me. What kind of explanation can I give them? See, that's why I was looking for you. Maybe you can do something.'

"'Why me?' Trigger seemed puzzled.

"'I've heard that you can do those things,' suggested the kid.

"'Oh?' Trigger smiled. 'What's my cut, if I pull you out of this shit?'

"'Fifty-fifty.'

"'I'll talk to you tonight. Where do you live? And what's your name?' The young man gave Trigger his name and address and left. We returned to our hotel. I fell asleep immediately. When I woke up it was early evening. Trigger had left, but a few minutes later, he re-entered the room.

"'What are you up to?' I demanded to know.

"'Things. I don't need you tonight. I have to go with a real American MP. We're going to the border to pick up stuff.'

"'If you think you're leaving me here, you're mistaken,' I snapped back.

"'Why take unnecessary risks?' he reasoned.

"'Bullshit! When do we leave?'

"Without answering my question, he left again and didn't come back until morning.

"That's when he burst in, saying, 'I've got an MP downstairs. The Jeep's running. Hurry up!'

"Trigger, the American, and I were in MP uniforms and the Pole in his UNRRA uniform. We piled into the Jeep and headed for the border. On the way, Trigger explained the plan. He told the Pole that he had a summons for his arrest from the Provost Marshal's office. We would pick up some contraband as evidence and handcuff the kid to make it look real.

"'But it's too risky. They may arrest us all,' whined the Pole. He was trying to back out.

"'What are you bitching about? All we risk is three months in jail. The driver ought to have his head examined. If they catch up with him, he's up for at least twenty years. Just shut up!'

"Trigger had calculated the time to see the man who picked up the young Pole. Luckily it wasn't his day off. We stopped in front of the office, and the three of us got out. The driver stayed with the Jeep. As we walked toward the main office, a French officer came out. He threw up his hands and shook his head in surprise. 'Ooo-la-la! Him again!'

"'Anyone speak English?' shouted Trigger.

"'I do,' responded the French officer.

"'I see you know this man,' said Trigger in an authoritative tone.

"'Yes. He was here yesterday. We take two valises from him. Camera, lights, other camera things.'

"'Well, then, why the hell did you release him?' Trigger was almost screaming at the officer, who was becoming intimidated.

"'He said he was American. We have nothing to do with Americans from the German zone,' the Frenchman protested.

"'Well, you should have kept him and called us,' barked Trigger sternly. 'He's no more American than you are. He's a Polish refugee.'

"'Oo-la-la! A Polish refugee.'

"'He's dealing on the black market. We arrested him at the Hauptbahnhof in Frankfurt.'

"The Frenchman made the appropriate gesticulations and sounds. Trigger pulled out the phony orders which were written in French, German and English.

"'Look!'

"The officer read them carefully. 'I see. I see. You want the valises for the trial.'

"'If you please ...'

"'*Eh bien. Voilà.*' He motioned towards another building. 'Come this way. Afterwards, you drink with us, maybe?' the Frenchman grinned.

"'Not while on duty. But come to visit us in Frankfurt. Provost Marshal's Office.'

"We got the suitcases and brought them back to the Jeep. Just as we were getting in, the officer ran out waving some papers and shouting madly in French. We just looked at him. He ran up to Trigger. '*Signez les papiers, s'il vous plaît. Les papiers!*'

"'What?'

"'Oh. Pardon. The papers. Please sign the papers.'

"Trigger signed them. 'Is that all?'

"'*Oui.* Yes. *Au revoir.* Bye-bye.'

"'So long,' Trigger smirked.

"'We drove back to Frankfurt. The Pole was still frightened, but while Trigger would usually be happy and smiling after a caper like this, instead he was quiet and sullen. 'You feel okay?' I said to him.

"'Sure.'

"'You know, I haven't seen you this serious since the war. Something's bothering you, isn't it? ... I know what's bugging me. I want to go home to Poland. Is that why you're so upset?'

"'Not exactly. Let's change the subject.'

"'I know what you need.'

"'What?' he snapped.

"I leaned over and whispered to him. 'A cleaning.'

"'Shut up!'

"When we got to Frankfurt the kid directed us to an address in Westend, a neighborhood that had survived the Allied bombing. We waited while he took the camera equipment inside. Twenty minutes later, he emerged and turned over half the cash as agreed, with half of that to the American and half for Trigger, who then gave me half of his take. I didn't want to accept it. I had invited myself along, yet he insisted. 'Here, take it. I didn't do this trip for money. It was a special trip.'"

All through the story I felt somewhat uncomfortable when he mentioned the MP. I hoped that he had not recognized me after all those years. Evidently, he didn't. If so, he didn't let on. Not even with all that vodka in him. It had started to take effect, however. Even in that Polish blood there was a saturation level. He turned his head away as if he were sick.

"Anything wrong, Juraski?"

"No, nothing. I think I drank too much."

"Just a few more details, Mr. Juraski." It was Harris pumping him for details that could only fascinate a criminologist's mind. "On the whole, this smuggling operation, did he do it for kicks or money?"

Without hesitating, Juraski answered. "For kicks and adventure. He really didn't care about money, but he was always drawn to danger or kicks, as he called it."

"Why did you split up?"

"I fell in love with an English girl and wanted to settle down. I went back to London and got married. The money I made with him helped me to get organized. I worked in a factory where the salary was adequate. Then my wife started running around. It happens sooner or later with most of those bitches. I sued for a divorce. Trigger had been right as usual. He warned me. 'It'll finish in a mess. You'll get hurt, Grat. Mark my words.'

"At the time I tried to defend my choice. 'I want to have a normal life, someday. Don't you?'

"'Now you sound like Stein,' he declared reproachfully.

"'Who's he?' I asked.

"'He is the one who gave us to the French police. He too wanted to have a normal life. I bet he's married now to a fat mama with five kids. Is that what you want, Grat?'

"That wasn't what I wanted, but I did love the girl. Trigger was never able to understand that. He never loved anybody. He changed women like a kaleidoscope changes its images. 'Never the same one twice' was his motto.

"London was boring in those days. I used to go to the Polish Military Club, which was like any other men's club. We talked about the good old days in the underground, dreamed about Poland free from Communist rule, of going home, of starting another underground movement. It was a load of bullshit, but it occupied my time.

"I even tried to stay in touch with Trigger. I came to Paris a few times. Nothing. I continued working in the factory until the beginning of the '60s when I heard they wanted mercenaries for Katanga. I had the experience of the Home Army days and was still in good shape physically. I applied, was accepted and went to the Congo. Sure, the money wasn't much, but I was happy. I was happy because I was fighting Commies, which was something I wanted to do but couldn't do in Poland. Every six months, we were flown out on leave to Brussels. London sometimes. Even once I went to Paris. That was when I saw Trigger again.

"He was walking down the Champs-Elysées. He hadn't changed much, just a little heavier. All of us tend to spread as we age. 'Trigger!' I shouted. He turned around. There was a weird look in his eyes.

"'Grat, what are you doing here?'

"We hugged each other as Slavs usually do.

"'I'm just passing through Paris. I've been trying to get in touch with you for ages, but I couldn't.'

"'Well, now that you've found me, let's have dinner together.'

"'I'm game.'

"There were a few places on the Left Bank that I always wanted to try. We found an interesting cellar-restaurant over near the Pantheon. It had lots of atmosphere, candlelight and a small bar. I liked it. I'll try and find it again before I leave Paris. We settled ourselves at a table for four. They had those benches like the church pews. We ordered a Chateaubriand for two and a bottle of Bordeaux.

"'I'm fighting in Katanga now,' I told him. 'I'm happier than I've been for years. I'm making a little money and fighting Reds. It's better than working in a factory, let me tell you.'

"The waiter arrived with the bottle, uncorked it, poured a drop for me to taste, and filled our glasses. We toasted to old times. Eventually I got to talking with Trigger about his women. I reminded him about his motto, 'Never the same one twice.'

"'I've finished with women,' he said decisively.

"'Come off it, Trigger,' I looked at him. Something in his face told me that he was serious. I changed the subject. 'What kind of business are you in now?'

"'I bought some nightclubs with the money we made together. But they don't really need me. They run themselves. I check them once a week.'

"'What do you do the rest of the time?'

"'Nothing. I go to the movies or stay home.'

"'Come on man, wake up. That's not living. Listen, Trigger, remember when we met after the war, you said that we'd start a second underground – no risks, no torture, three months in jail at the worst. We'd make lots of money. Remember?' His faced brightened. 'And it worked, just the way you said it would. The travel, the adventure. Everything worked. Now I'm offering you something. Come with me to Katanga. We'll make money. We'll fight Communism. It'll be just like in the old days.'

"The waiter brought a large wooden platter with a tremendous piece of filet mignon, garnished with tomatoes, fries and béarnaise sauce. Trigger smiled faintly. 'Grat, I don't need the money.'

"'I know people who are richer than you are!'

"'So what! Even money has its limits. I can't drive more than one car, live in more than one house, or wear more than one suit at the same time. Anyway, I don't think that by fighting in Africa we're going to solve the Communist problem in the world.'

"'But you've got to do something. What do you want to do?'

"I was really worried about him. He had turned in upon himself a thousand times. He would be so hard to unwrap. Then something occurred to me. 'Listen, if you don't want the money ... remember in the Home Army when we used to call you "trigger-happy" Trigger? Remember how you loved to kill? Well in Katanga, you can kill as many people as you want.' I stopped talking. I wanted to say more, but decided to let what I had just said sink in. Anyway, the food was getting cold. 'Do you realize that when we pass through a village, we shoot everyone we see?'

"'Even women and kids?' He was obviously not charmed by my description.

"'Yeah, we have to. Not because they are inferior, not the way the Germans did it, but for military reasons, security. Understand that the Reds use everyone, even little children, for information. And they outnumber us. But you can kill as many as you like. It'll be a good deal for you.'

"'How many men did you kill?' Trigger was sullen.

"'Oh, I don't know exactly. Perhaps a hundred. I don't know. When you shoot into the bushes and use the flamethrower, you really don't know how many you kill. But quite a few ...'

"'That's not enough.' The weird, mad-dog look drifted back into his eyes.

"'What's not enough?'

"'Your offer's no good to me. Even if I kill two or three hundred or even a thousand, it won't make a dent in the score. It'll never balance the account I have with humanity. Thanks, anyway, Grat, but it doesn't appeal to me.'

"'It doesn't appeal to you? So what? Come along anyway. You're just vegetating here. What'll you do for the rest of your life?'

"'No! I'm not vegetating. I'm in the underground, the third underground.'

"'The third what?'

"'I don't like to talk about it. It's a conspiracy. I keep my mouth shut. I don't say anything. I don't do anything. I don't go anywhere. One day I'm coming out of this underground with such a bang that it'll surprise everybody, even you!'

"'Suit yourself. I only tried to help ...'"

Third underground. A conspiracy. It made no sense. I turned these words over again and again. It did no use to grill Juraski as Harris was now doing. Shipansky had been closed-mouth about whatever was going on.

"Did he mention to you that he belonged to any movements, political groups, or something like that?" I asked.

"No, he just said that he was in the third underground and that eventually, everyone would sit up and take notice."

"What about the name, Qaddafi? Does it mean anything to you?"

"You mean that crazy Arab bastard? No, Trigger never mentioned him, nor anyone like that. As for myself, I'd like to get my hand on Qaddafi's neck. The Soviets are behind him. He's funding all the terrorist gangs in Africa and the Middle East. We're having trouble in North Yemen now. That's why I came to Paris this time, to recruit for the war on the Arabian Peninsula."

"Was that the last time you saw Trigger?" queried Harris.

"Yes. That was the last time I saw him. That's all I can tell you. Now suppose you answer one of my questions. Why are you so interested in Trigger? To get a guy out of a French jail is not very easy. It must be something big, very big ... like the Berisov case, maybe?"

"Why that?" asked Harris. His embarrassed look was a dead giveaway.

"So, it is the Berisov thing. So that was it," Juraski smiled. "That was the conspiracy and his underground. His third underground."

"Do you think he would be capable of something like that?"

"He was capable of anything. He cooperated with the SS during the war, then he pretended to be an American MP who had the French, Belgian, and German officials under his thumb. Why couldn't he kill Berisov? After what we did during the war, the UN building would have been child's play."

"You like Trigger, don't you?"

"Of course. I didn't always agree with the unnecessary killing that he did, but he was sort of an idol in a very strange way."

"Did you ever think that he might be a Jew?" I studied his face.

"No. Why should I think that?"

"A minute ago, you said that he was capable of anything. Why couldn't he be a Jew?"

"You don't understand. In Poland, the Jews look and talk differently. Even if they have a good face, the accent gives them away. We're experts. It's something like light-skinned blacks in the United States. I mean the ones who are white enough to pass. Other blacks can spot them fairly easily, but many whites can't."

"Are you anti-Semitic?" I asked him.

"No. Never have been, but if he's Jewish, I would know it. Everybody would have known it in the underground. Counterintelligence would have found out. We were living together, almost like brothers. I knew him better than I knew myself. But sometimes I felt that he did too much killing and that I could never understand."

"Did you ever wonder why he kept killing Germans although he knew it would cost the lives of so many innocent Poles?"

"No."

"Look at it this way. The Germans were anti-Semites, so were the Poles. Don't you think that if he were a Jew, he could kill two birds with one stone, so to speak, by killing Germans? Isn't that possible?"

"It might have been possible if he were a Jew, but he isn't."

"Where did you come from, and why did you join the underground?"

"I was in an orphanage. I never knew my parents. I supported myself by selling newspapers. The underground approached me because they felt I would make a good contact man. But I was a ..."

"Hoodlum," I ventured.

"Yeah. In a way. But you see, in Poland, hoods were gentlemen ... Always."

"You joined the underground voluntarily, more or less?"

"Yeah."

"Imagine a man who joins your type of organization. Imagine that the man has been condemned to death. He has nothing to lose. Doesn't it make sense that he would have a surplus of courage? More guts than anyone else? After all, how many times can a man lose his life? If Trigger is a Jew, then he had nothing to risk and with every German he shot, he took hundreds of Poles whom he probably hated even more. It could have been his way of getting revenge."

"Why are you trying to turn me against him? It's not going to work, you know. If he is a Jew, I would know." Juraski was highly annoyed.

"Okay. Let's drop it. What are you going to do now, Juraski?"

He paused a moment. Then he became very self-righteous. "If that French cop keeps his word and lets me out, then I'm going to go anywhere they need me to fight the Communists."

Still an idealist. I was tired of listening to Juraski's rather unsound logic. It smacked of honor codes of the type they claim exist among thieves. His mercenary exploits bored me even more than his body, a flabby reminder of the cynical Green Beret courage that went no deeper than a film script.

"Always. I shall fight Communism till I die. May I go now?"

I called Jouvert at his office and let him know that the interview was over. We were finished with Juraski, and as far as I cared, they could throw him back in the hole. Yet André had seemed pleased to be able to deliver the goods to an important American intelligence team. I had no doubt that he would honor the promise that we had made.

Harris escorted Juraski to the lobby. As they went out the door, I could still hear the Pole muttering to himself, "Crazy Americans. What will they come up with next? Trigger, a Jew? Impossible ..."

Chapter 10. Johnny's Lucini

I took advantage of Harris' absence to telephone an old acquaintance, Lucini Spaggiari. He was a French Corsican whom I met during the war. He was fighting in the French Resistance ...

My third parachute mission came in August 1944. I was dropped with a "piano," a new code, instructions, and a few explosives into the midst of a small zone in southern France. It was controlled by an underground unit.

My feet touched the countryside as smoothly as they had done in all those practice jumps. I had time to detach the parachute when two civilians came running toward me. "*Vite! Viens vite!*" They buried my parachute and uniform and hurriedly dressed me in peasant attire. As they collected my deliveries, a big man appeared.

"I'm called Lucini. Lucini Spaggiari." His English was far from perfect, but the accent had a familiar ring. Not exactly French and not exactly Italian, it reminded me of Sicilian. Sicilian English from New York City.

We went to a village and entered one of the tile-roofed houses. The people in the room greeted me and gave me some food. Lucini later told me that my hosts were very poor, but they always guaranteed a warm welcome to anyone who had come to help France. Most of the village was wiped out by the Germans three days after we left.

As I was finishing my meal that day, a skinny guy with glasses came in. He glanced at me and went over to talk to Lucini. He began to shout orders. They rummaged through the equipment which I had carried and began to assemble the pieces. As they were working, Lucini leaned toward me. "Most of the people here can't speak English. He doesn't understand us." He motioned toward the skinny guy.

"Who the hell is he?" I asked.

"The section leader. He's a Communist," replied Lucini.

"A real Communist!"

"Yes. Most of the underground is under Communist influence. They took me because I know how to fight." He emphasized the word fight. It was pronounced with a particular relish. "I am a Corsican, like Napoleon!"

"Of course," I responded, "Corsica is a part of France."

Lucini became very angry, took a deep breath, and started to lecture. "You've got it backwards, you Americans. France is a part of Corsica," he stated fiercely. We conquered France and went to Moscow. We were more powerful than the German Reich. The name Spaggiari was pronounced with respect all over the continent."

"Do you have relatives in the States? I know a family named Spaggiari." I had heard the name in connection with the underworld but did not want to let him know that.

"To my knowledge, Miller, I have no relatives in America. But Spaggiari is a very common name for Corsicans. We arrived upon the island from Italy quite early ..."

We didn't have a chance to finish because there was an explosion outside. We doused the lights and crawled out of the house. After running about two hundred yards toward the village periphery, I heard a blast and a scream. Somebody had either been shot or hit by a mine. More shots broke through the hushed, frightened atmosphere. After the screaming had stopped, Lucini lost his patience. He moved away from us. Watching him hustle along a grove of palm trees, I looked up and saw something move in a tree just above him. Quickly I fired into the leaves and a soldier fell to the ground. Lucini glanced back and waved a thanks. In the ensuing skirmish, two more snipers were killed.

"Let's get out of here," said Lucini, "they've found the setup."

That night we travelled to another village about ten miles to the east. We stopped at a house similar to the original "headquarters."

Lucini made himself at home and struck up a conversation with a redheaded woman who apparently was another member of the Resistance. Either that, or his wife, by the way she had greeted him upon our arrival. I was still staring at her when Lucini slipped over to my side and asked, "You like her?"

"Not bad." I was lying through my teeth. She was beautiful, and I hadn't had a woman in months.

"You saved my life back there. I owe you. Do you want her?"

"Maybe she won't like me." I couldn't understand why I was so coy, but in retrospect I think that I was afraid of insulting some Corsican code of honor.

Lucini laughed. "Go on. I don't mind. Take her if you please, you crazy American. She'll go with you. Just ask her."

"Is she related to you?" I wanted to know.

"She works with our unit. She sleeps with everyone. Me, my men and the Germans. That's how we keep track of enemy activities in the area. She gets inside information. She's a damn good soldier. No, she isn't my relative. I don't believe in incest. Don't be shy. Ask her."

I was still very reticent. "Introduce us."

Lucini burst out laughing. "I'm her CO, not her pimp! Quit staring at the broad and get your ass over there. Tell her to come to your room tonight."

That wasn't very American, I thought. I went upstairs by myself, undressed as much as I dared and went to bed. A few minutes later there was a knock at the door. The redhead opened it and entered the room saying, "Hello, Yankee. Lucini says you want to see me."

I remained silent.

"What's wrong? Shy?" She laughed. "You Americans. You're like babies. Don't think about anything. Try to relax."

She moved over to the bed, leaned down and kissed me on the mouth. I felt her tongue. Her moist caresses roamed all over my body. She paused but only to remove another piece of clothing. Then she returned to kissing me. She sucked me. That was the first time I had ever been sucked. That night I learned the difference between American women and real women. Making love to American women was like masturbating with a hole in the mattress. Red was different. I wanted to satisfy her but didn't know how until she taught me. She taught me all kinds of positions and caresses. From that night on, I became a real lover.

In the morning, we got ready to move out. The Germans were after us and moving fast. Lucini announced that I would have to re-unite with my unit. I protested and Lucini cracked a smile. "Hey, how do you like Maria?"

"She's good." I wanted to act cool.

"She's not just good, Johnny. She's an expert."

"Sorry, but I can't be particular. I haven't had much experience."

Lucini howled. "What do you Americans do in your spare time? Listen, if you want to marry her, she'll wait for you. And if you're in Paris, come see me. Here's my address."

That night I made love with Maria again. I had never realized the power of sex. It was a total removal from the events around me. Nothing mattered except the woman. The harder I tried to satisfy her, the more pleasure I felt.

The next morning, I received the message I'd been waiting for. Within ten days' time, my unit would land in the area ... ten more days. We moved from village to village, accompanied by Maria. I fucked her every night, never realizing that I needed to rest. I fucked her every night, all night.

The Krauts had already begun to retreat. They were uneasy and fired upon every occasion. We didn't have much trouble ferreting them out. For the most part, we were idle.

"If you don't like that skinny guy, why is he here?" I commented to Lucini one day. He had become edgy, and I thought it was the Communist who was responsible.

"He and his comrades have the upper hand now, but when De Gaulle comes to power, we'll get rid of them. Their time is limited.

Soon it will be over for them." He was quite convinced and from then on, he seemed more relaxed. Lucini, Maria and I spent much time together. It was the type of friendship which develops only in wartime, with intimacy of such intensity that our personalities merged into one another. War breeds such relations because people disappear so quickly.

The tenth day was August 15. Paratroopers were dropped into our zone. Amphibious units landed at St. Tropez, and they were advancing north toward Grenoble. In a few days I would rejoin my unit. Lucini was very excited.

I reported to my CO in the company of my underground unit. We were debriefed and supplied information as to which railroads and bridges had been destroyed. The captain greeted us warmly and thanked the Resistance for their help. They were showered with all sorts of gifts – personal items and goods for them to take back to their families, even silk stockings for Maria.

Lucini told me to visit him when we reached Paris. "By the way, Johnny. Maria is in love with you; she'll be sorry to see you leave."

"Sometimes we have to do things we don't like, Lucini."

"Perhaps," he replied. "Last night ... well, now that we're sure that De Gaulle is on the way, I shot the section leader. I'm boss now."

"You what!" I reacted with surprise. It was shocking to think that a Resistance fighter could murder his section leader as if it were a mob hit. I paused a few seconds and let it slide when Lucini responded wordlessly, glowering at me. Better to change the subject, I reasoned.

"Lucini, I never asked you, but why are you in this game?"

"I was a gangster in Marseille. I pimped three women. One night I killed another pimp in a knife fight. I had to get out fast, so I joined the Foreign Legion and went to North Africa. When the war broke out, I came back to France. I felt that I had to do something good. I knew how to fight. These Communists don't. They need people like me. They give the orders, and I do the fighting. Now I give the orders and do the fighting too. Much less complicated that way. I'll never go back to the old style."

We shook hands. "Bye, Lucini Spaggiari. Keep yourself in one piece."

"Come join me in Paris, Johnny. Maria will be there. Come join us ... join us ..."

It had been a long time since I'd spoken to Lucini, but now I had government business and thought he could give me a lead on Szczepanski . I shut my eyes and fell into a deep slumber.

I saw the dead bodies of Frankie, Billy and Jimmy. There was blood everywhere. Blood flowing from their bellies, from their heads. All over ... blood all over ...

"What's all over? What is it, Miller?" Harris had returned to the room and shook me awake.

"Nothing, Dave. I think that the booze and Juraski's story just put me out of touch. But that's not important. Look, I've just called an old acquaintance of mine who wants us to have dinner with him. What do you say, Dave?"

Harris turned sour. He suspected that I had made some kind of clandestine liaison with a CIA operative. He trained his professional stare on me and began. "Miller, we've been sent here for a specific mission. Now that we've interviewed Juraski, we should be trying to make sense out of his story. You're trying to accomplish something else over here in Europe. Just what it is, I'm not sure, but you'd better wise up. Nothing can be more important than our assignment ..."

"Our assignment!" I shot back. "Our assignment is so important that your goddamn agency has to check up on me every time I wipe my ass."

Harris tried to interrupt me, but I continued to shout. I really wanted to hit him. "You're not here to cooperate. I attempted to divide the work like any reasonable operative would proceed. But you've only been sent to keep an eye on me. Watch for my contacts, make notes on what we say, and report back the first chance you have. You've got me pretty uptight about being alone. You're by my side constantly and when you're gone, you try to make me think that somehow, I've managed to rid myself of you for a few moments. It's a convenient way of operating when there's information to report back."

"I'm assigned to you. You're assigned to a job. My job is to see that you do your job." Harris was very calm. He tried to hide the embarrassment of being discovered.

I was still hot and fired salvo after salvo, attacking not only him but his agency too. "Your goddamn office politics monopolize so much of your action that there's no time or space for being a cop. A cop spying on another cop when we're supposed to be tracking down a fool or criminal or whatever. Political police are the same everywhere. No emotion, all racism and visceral suspicion.

"For the record or off the record, as you like, yes, these people are underworld figures," I went on. "You don't have to be too bright to figure that out. I'm not so pure-bred myself, as I imagine you've already guessed, but that's not important either. After the war, I was with CID. The people in these countries loved us and, by association, loved all Americans. Not because we gave out cigarettes, nylons, and chewing gum, but because we were genuine. Sometimes we took things too. They knew we were real people.

"Your kind stinks! You come to these places and act like you're still in Kansas City or wherever. You come on like gorillas, pushing the locals around like they were criminals for the simple reason that they're not Americans. Is it any wonder that they hate us now? Christ, it's worse than when the Germans occupied these countries. You don't even have the decency to sit with these people over a bottle of wine."

"We're supposed to remain straight. That's the only way to do a job, Miller." Harris was trying to fight back but kept sinking deeper into the morass of bureaucratic lingo that is taught to the lowest order of primates if they show any potential for following orders.

"Straight is just a word. It is just an excuse for not having a state of mind. It reflects a bad conscience. As far as I'm concerned, it's another form of racism, which is worse than the old-style fascist variety. It describes the kind of logic where if someone is different, then you stay away from him. You isolate him for his difference and the more you can isolate him, the more superior you are. The Nazis couldn't have existed without the Jews, the Poles, the Gypsies, and the Russians. They needed them because their reflection, albeit distorted, served to mark a superiority. The exterminations were a part of these reflections. At first, the killing was done gradually. Artisanal extermination. As the minorities were done away with, the German people saw themselves grow taller and braver. They sucked the courage out of those who resisted.

"Then came the war machines: the Hitlerian war machine, the American war machine, and Stalin's war machine. Killing 500 people a day was nothing; it was replaced by the gas chambers on one side and incendiary bombs on the other. Nobody saw the Jews and Russians dying. There was no longer any courage to be sucked out of a brave resister. The individuality of fascism was replaced by mass totalitarianism, and the people began to die like cowards and kill like cowards. The whole issue of life and death was banalized. Then of course came the A-bomb, the epitome of a banal end to a banal existence."

My tirade against Harris had no effect; it only served to make me even angrier than I originally was. "Look, you goddamn gorilla, look at this scarred face! It's covered with dirt! Clean dirt, compared to the kind of slop that you'll never wipe off yourself!"

He wouldn't respond and I had no more energy to waste on trying to make the bastard think about his work intelligently. I grabbed my jacket and left for the rendezvous I'd set up with Lucini. Perhaps Harris would follow me and even if he did, I would not care. All I knew was that he would be there, waiting to leave for Germany when the time came.

The time it took to finish two gin-and-tonics was about how long I waited in the hotel bar until Lucini showed. When he saw me, a big grin spread across his face, he opened his arms and walked toward me. We exchanged greetings, kissing each other on the cheek, just like the Latins. I hated this custom, but it was Lucini's and he was more than a good friend. He was like a brother.

He hadn't changed much. He was tall with dark hair and looked like a French bourgeois businessman.

"Lucini, I think I'd like to celebrate. A tribute to Paris is what we need." I wanted to get loaded and forget about Harris and the whole Berisov thing.

"What about the Crazy Horse, Johnny?" Where else would Lucini choose to impress an old war buddy but the Crazy Horse? High-end showgirls, uniformly sized and performing modern burlesque. I wondered if this was one of his rackets.

As Lucini paid my bill, Harris appeared in the lobby. He was silent and just followed us into the taxi. I introduced him to Lucini as we were on our way to Alma Marceau. When we approached the club, Harris gasped. "Look, mounties, Royal Canadian Mounties. Are they here on holiday?"

"No, Dave," I said, "Those are the doormen. And if you look at the two big pictures in the entrance, you'll see Chief Crazy Horse and Buffalo Bill."

Once inside, Harris stood before the pictures. "Hey, that's wild!"

We walked down the red corridor into the main room. As usual, it was crowded, but after Lucini slipped a five-hundred franc note to the maître d', he conducted us to one of the best tables in the place. It was to the left of the stage, and dinner was served with a bottle of champagne. For dessert, Lucini ordered another magnum of champagne. Throughout the evening, he peeled off five-hundreds like Monopoly money.

When the show began, we had a hard time keeping Harris from jumping onto the stage. He followed the gyrations of the girls' hips for the entire spectacle. I was still suspicious, however, and could say nothing to Lucini. He in turn seemed to understand my predicament and was silent. We had a good time just being together.

Noticing Harris' apparent interest in the girls, Lucini proposed a liaison. The "gorilla," as I now thought of him, had long since stopped sulking and eagerly accepted the offer. Lucini left our table and then returned with one of the girls who had appeared on stage in the previous act. She smiled at Harris. "Hello," she purred.

"Hi. Would you like a drink?" he offered clumsily.

"Sure, buy her a drink, Dave. It's only the government's money," I said, half sarcastically.

"You like her, Mr. Harris?" asked Lucini.

"Sure," replied Harris. "Do you think she'd be willing to spend the night with me?"

"Why, certainly." Lucini looked at me and winked.

I leaned over to Harris and whispered, "Harris, forget about the money. It's on Lucini."

Harris was enchanted by the girl. They excused themselves and moved to another table. I expected to see him in the morning when the plane would take us to Germany.

"What's up?" I addressed Lucini when we were alone.

"When are you going back to the States?" he inquired.

"In a few days. I have a couple of stops to make. Germany, Poland and perhaps Israel. If possible, I'd like to stop here on my way back. What can I do for you?"

"The same thing as before. In the present French economic situation, money is hard to come by."

"Lucini, don't give me that crap. You've got plenty of money. Look at the way you've thrown it around here tonight. You're not broke."

"All right, so I'm not broke. But I still like to make money. just like the Americans. Money is power, and it's always good to have your hand on the source. With the contacts I have and you, Johnny, why not? Come on, will you take a package for me?"

"I'm not sure I can shake this FBI man, Lucini. It might be the wrong time. It could ruin the entire operation." I hesitated but realized that it was a flimsy excuse.

"Remember the trips you made for me? Your positions gave you many special privileges. I gave you tips in order to eliminate my competition and advance your career at the same time. I made money, you made money, we both came out on top. Come on, will you take this package for me?" He was pleading.

"But you've got a good business, Lucini. You supply liquor and women to most of the big clubs. You export those overrated wines to the States where they're sold at sky-high prices. What more do you want?"

"But this is special, and I don't want to take any chances. You're the only one who can do."

My assignment was special too. I didn't want to take an unnecessary chance despite what I had said to Harris. On the other hand, I didn't want to disappoint Lucini either. I did need him. "Okay. I'll do it for you on one condition."

"What?"

Without warning I played a card Stein had given me back in Brooklyn. "I want to meet Mustapha." I was betting that Parisian mobsters all knew each other.

Lucini stared at me. He didn't like the idea. I could see it in his face. "What do you want with him?"

"Never mind."

"He'll never talk to you."

"That's my worry. You just introduce us."

"Okay, but you know that he and I aren't very close friends. I'm from Corsica and he's Algerian. That's probably the worst possible chemistry in the entire French-speaking world. We don't belong to the same clan. Sometimes I even wonder how we in France are so civilized."

"Except when you're shooting at each other."

We both laughed.

"Johnny, you haven't changed a bit, still full of jokes. When do you want to meet him?"

"Now."

Chapter 11. Mustapha's Ted

We left the Crazy Horse and hailed a cab. There was no sense waiting around to see Mustapha. Lucini had agreed to the deal, and I wanted to cash in on this opportunity to check out another lead on Shipansky. Lucini was evidently on the spot. Otherwise, even he would never have pleaded so hard to make the kind of pact we had just concluded. I was on the spot too. Not that much of what Harris had said during the afternoon's discussion made any difference, but I really was becoming obsessed with Ted Szczepanski and his "third underground." Lucini and I talked on the way to find Mustapha.

"What are you doing politically these days, Lucini?"

"No more politics. I did the full circle: Gaullist, anti-Gaullist. Now I go where the money is; I stick to Unione Corse."

"Sounds like the Mafia to me, Lucini."

"We don't call it a Mafia, we call it the Corsican Union because we have OUR men everywhere – the police, the ministries and all the political parties. But the only alliance we have is our fidelity to the Union."

"Okay, but it still seems like a Mafia to me."

"Johnny, we have our own country, France. We also have our ideas on how to run it. Think what you want, but we are not the Mafia."

What I did think was that perhaps Lucini had some connection with the Corsican separatist movement that was creating problems in Paris. I didn't want to provoke him though, since I felt that Mustapha was a much more important contact. There would be time later.

The cab stopped at a club in Pigalle. Lucini paid the driver and we entered the bar. There were about a dozen girls sitting there, mostly

Algerians and Africans. They stared at us lasciviously.

"I warn you, it's not going to be easy," Lucini whispered as we strode past the attractive hookers.

"Don't worry. I've got confidence in you. Remember the deal?"

Lucini nodded to a heavyset Algerian behind the cash register. We found a table and ordered some drinks. "He's your man, Johnny," said Lucini with a business-like tone.

I stared at Mustapha. I think that Mustapha must have recognized Lucini. He swaggered over to our table.

"Bonsoir, Monsieur Lucini Spaggiari," he practically spit the name onto Lucini's lapels.

"I've brought you a customer, Monsieur Mustapha. He's American. May I present Mr. Johnny Miller, Mustapha."

Lucini was probably doing his best not to stand up and punch the Algerian. Two things stopped him. Our deal, and the four hoodlums hanging around the interior of the place with a handful outside ready to enter on a moment's notice.

Pigalle had changed since I was here as the war drew to an end. The war in a commercial sense continued until De Gaulle kicked the American troops out of his country. But until then, the GIs had practically supported all the night spots in Pigalle. Now it was different. The black GIs were gone. The honkytonks had folded or been replaced by movie theaters and cheap apparel stores. Everything else was strictly the casbah. The movies were in Arabic, as were most of the wall posters. Even the beggars in this part of Paris were Arabs. Lucini had explained how the French tried to run the Arabs back to North Africa several years ago. The National Assembly had been forced by the Communists to push through legislation barring immigrant workers from staying in the country in order to preserve jobs for native French workers. Debates followed, but except for a few diehard liberals, the consensus was that France could no longer afford to be the land of liberty and political refuge. Riots resulted, and the North Africans barricaded themselves in Pigalle. The Algerian government broke diplomatic relations with Paris and financed the immigrants' resistance movement. At this particular moment, the situation was at a stalemate. Recent immigrants who were still in the country were classified as illegal aliens, but the police could not muster the strength to enforce the expulsion laws. Suspicion reigned in all affairs transacted between the Algerians and the French.

"Have a drink with us," I suggested, trying to cut through the fog of hostility and suspicion.

Mustapha accepted my invitation and ordered a type of mint julep, without alcohol of course.

"I don't drink alcohol, especially on the job." Mustapha looked at me inquisitively.

I understood. The Qur'an and alcohol do not mix. If the Poles like Juraski could drink and drink without letting it affect them, then it was just the opposite for the Arabs. They can't hold it, and when they're drunk, they begin to fight among themselves, not such a good idea if the casbah is surrounded, indeed infiltrated, by cops.

"I know you're wondering what brings me here. Johnny will tell you. He speaks some French." Lucini made his contribution to breaking the stony atmosphere.

"Oh?" replied Mustapha. "I speak English fluently." He was quite proud but also defiant.

"Really? Where did you learn it?" I asked in pursuit of friendly conversation.

"In Algeria. You see, Americans brought a new spirit of national independence to Algeria. We Algerians had been in almost the same situation as the blacks in your country, with one exception – the French were foreign invaders and were finally kicked out. The administration, beaches, good housing, money – everything belonged to the French. We were given the ghettos and the casbah. They were the masters. They told us we were equal like you tell the blacks ... 'all men are created equal.' I didn't feel equal. But in November 1942, when the Americans landed, there was a big change in Algeria. The French were pushed aside. They no longer counted. The atmosphere was relaxed.

"Once an American soldier protected me from a French policeman and from that moment on, I adored Americans. My friends and I would do anything for our new friends – shine their shoes, bring them presents and food, even Arab women. Naturally, they paid ten times what the French paid, but they didn't care. I felt guilty, though, treating my friends like that. To compensate, I gave them girls free of charge. My idol was a sergeant named Smitty. He was the guy who really taught me English. I wanted to go to the States with him when he left. I was heartbroken when he shipped out. I begged him to take me with him, but of course he couldn't.

"When most of the Americans left, things returned to pre-war ways. The French went to their private clubs and we went back to the casbah. I didn't want to live in Algeria anymore, and one night during the summer, I took the boat to Marseille. I wanted to see how the colonialists lived in their own country. I also had it in my head that Smitty might be there. I never found him, but I did meet up with another American sergeant and followed him and his company to Grenoble.

"In Grenoble, the French were gracious enough to offer me the opportunity to join the French First Army. I was furious. In Algeria, my homeland, I wasn't good enough to sit next to them. But now that I was in France, well, I could do the honor of defending the mother country."

I wanted to sound sympathetic to his position, so I added what I had remembered about the Arabs in the French Army. "Yes, I remember very well a propaganda film made by the Nazis. It showed how the French had been too cowardly to defend their own borders. Instead of resisting the German onslaught, they sent immigrants and colonial subjects to the front lines. The Nazis' point was to impugn the racial integrity of the French, but to a certain extent, the propaganda was true. The French did not fight valiantly. How the hell could they expect others to spearhead the national defense? It wasn't even their own country."

"We understand each other, Mr. Miller. I was thinking the same thing when I was invited to join the French regiments, but my language was, shall we say, less refined and more descriptive.

"When the war ended, I came to Paris and did a little smuggling with the Americans. I bought cigarettes and exotic foods. I enjoyed myself. But what pleased me the most was that the Americans took the French down a notch or two. They showed the French that they were nothing but shit." Mustapha paused on the word shit, and then apologetically turned to Lucini. "I didn't mean to insult you, Monsieur Spaggiari."

"That is quite all right. I'm not insulted because I am not French. I am a Corsican! I must be going. I am sure that you two will be able to talk more freely without me. Au revoir, Monsieur Mustapha. Bye bye, Johnny, see you on the way back."

"So long, Lucini." I waved as Lucini got up and left the table. He bowed toward Mustapha and me and then made the appropriate gestures as he passed the hookers on his way to the street.

When he had gone, I turned to Mustapha. "Do you know a Pole who masqueraded as an American GI in Paris after the war?" I pulled out the picture of Shipansky and shoved it under his eyes.

Immediately Mustapha shook his head. "No. I've never seen him before." He was lying and I knew it.

"Look, I'm American, and you say that you like us."

"In some ways, the Americans remind me of the French sometimes. Especially the younger generation, they act like they always have something to lose. They aren't adventurous like before."

He caught me off guard with that answer. I thought of Harris and what I had said this afternoon. It was coming true.

I decided to try another line of attack. "Quit lying, Mustapha. You know Ted. I know you know him. Now he's involved in a very serious matter. I'm here to investigate him. I need your cooperation. I have to know everything you know about him. If not ..."

"Don't threaten me."

"Do you want to see the world destroyed?"

"No."

"Then cooperate."

"Why should I?"

"If you want to stay in the country."

He laughed but stopped when I showed him my credentials.

"I met Ted in La Santé," he began. "I was doing a two-year stretch. It was at the end of '49 when he came into my cell. I thought he was an American at first – the haircut, the suit. I knew Americans when I saw them, or so I thought. I greeted him in English, and he answered me in English. Nobody else in the cell understood us. We became friends as the days passed. He finally told me that he was a Polish refugee. He was in for three months on a smuggling rap. I told him my story and added that I'd be out in a few months too.

"'For what?' he asked.

"'Armed robbery,' I confessed. The whole thing must have appealed to him, because he kept asking me different things. I told him everything.

"'Stupid, stupid,' he said.

"'What's so stupid about armed robbery?' I objected.

"'Nothing, but you didn't do it right.'

"'You think you can do it better?'

"'When we get out of jail, I'll get in touch with you. I've pulled a few jobs myself ... for the underground. I'd like to do it again for the kicks.'

"'What! Are you crazy? Nobody commits armed robbery just for kicks!'

"'Well, call it what you want. I'll show you how to make money without taking chances, without risking two, five or ten years in jail.'

"Why not?

"When I was released, he had one more month to serve. I saw him three months later, walking in Pigalle in an American sergeant's uniform. I didn't recognize him until he came over to me. 'Ted, why are you parading around in that get-up?' I asked him in astonishment.

"'For kicks.' That's what he answered, for kicks!"

"What kind of impression did you have of Ted back then?"

"He was different. He wasn't like our boys. He wasn't even a hood. Yet he didn't act bourgeois either. He was easygoing. When he offered somebody a drink, it was easy. When he talked to people, it was easy. He was at ease everywhere. In uniform, out of uniform. In jail, out of jail. Once I took him to a hoodlum café. He was perfectly relaxed. That's what struck me the most about him. He was always at ease."

"I don't quite understand. Aren't you at ease?"

"Yes, but I still feel I'm Algerian, no matter where I am. But he was able to fit into any crowd and be like the people he was with. There was no difference between them and him. He was generous, smiling, altogether charming. He never put pressure on anybody. Although once you were under his influence, you felt a certain type of pressure. I don't know how to explain it. But you had a feeling that you were sitting on top of a volcano. I don't know, maybe I'm wrong. I just had this feeling."

"Please continue, Mustapha." I found his characterization intriguing. Juraski was evidently not close enough to Ted to have picked up sensations of that order.

Mustapha stretched out his arms and then twitched his moustache. The hookers in the bar had exited one by one and there was only one left. It must have been very late.

"That day in Pigalle, he came close to me on the sidewalk. 'Mustapha, remember what we talked about in prison?'

"'Sure,' I responded.

"'I've got the robbery all planned.'

"'You mean it?' I was flabbergasted.

"I wouldn't say it if I didn't. But I'm running the show. This you must understand.'

"Again, I must emphasize that he was at ease.

"'What is it?'

"'A jewelry store.'

"'How many do we need?'

"'You and me, that's all.'

"'My cut?'

"'A million francs.'

"'You're joking!'

"'Take it or leave it,' was his only comment. There was something about this man which fascinated me.

"'Are you going to go on the job with me?' I asked him.

"'Of course.'

"I figured that if he was going to stick his neck out, I could too.

"'When?' I wanted to know.

"'I'll let you know. Maybe in a couple of weeks. Maybe in a month.'

"I didn't see him for a while. Then one Wednesday morning I received a phone call. 'Friday at noon, we'll do the job. I'll see you tomorrow. I want you to see the place.'

"He picked me up the next day and we drove to Avenue Victor Hugo, parking nearly opposite a small jewelry store. 'That's it. Only two people working in the shop. An old man and a girl. Friday, there's going to be a lot of jewels in the place. The girl goes off for lunch at noon. As soon as she leaves, you go in. You ask the guy to open the safe and grab everything in the drawers and the safe, but not the stuff in the window. It's phony.'

"'Are you sure the guy will cooperate?' was my only question.

"'Yeah. I'm sure. Take my word for it. If you can't, the deal's off.' He was so calm, so sure of himself. 'You go in without me. I'll be here in the car. I don't want the girl to see me. But one other thing. When you take the jewelry, slug the guy and tie him up. Remember, hit him, but don't kill him. That's very important.'

"'Don't kill him? Why's he so special? From what you told me in jail, you don't care too much about human life.'

"'If you kill him, we'll have no one to fence the jewels!'

"That remark hit me like a bullet. And I began to realize his genius. I was so stunned by the plan, that I too didn't really care about the money. I just wanted to see the job through to the end, for kicks.

"Friday morning, he picked me up as arranged. We drove to Victor Hugo and waited until the girl left. The man was at the door. I thought he was waiting for too long. According to Ted, he was supposed to close the door immediately. Finally, he disappeared. I got out of the car, crossed the street and entered. The action was as coordinated as the Swiss watch mechanisms we were stealing. When I returned to the car, Ted just sat there briefly and then drove off.

"'Did everything go okay?' he started to debrief me.

"'Just like you said. What do we do now?'

"'Give me the stuff. We'll have the money in two or three days.'

"Three days later, we had the money. It was extraordinary. I asked him how he had accomplished it.

"'It was very simple. I know the jeweler. You see, I'm half-Jewish and know most of the Hebes around here. This guy has a lot of jewelry, all insured. I went to see him and made a deal for one-third the real value of the stones and the rest. He would get the insurance money. All he was worried about was getting hurt. It seems that he doesn't like pain. Anyway, I returned the stones to him on Friday, and on Monday he gave me the money. Naturally the police are investigating, but the old man won't say anything. He was in a camp; that means he's tough as nails.'"

"Can you help me get in touch with this jeweler, Mustapha?" I asked.

"I heard that he died several years ago."

"Something else, Mustapha," I was interested to see his reaction. "Did Ted's being Jewish ever get you into any complications?"

"Ted showed me how to make money without taking risks. Perhaps all Jews know that. I'm not sure. He also worked with Poles. I guess they were Jews too. I even knew the Pole he worked with on a regular basis. When they came into Paris, he sold part of the things to the Jews and part to me. Sometimes we used to laugh because of what was happening on the political scene. We didn't give a damn about politics. We were cut from the same cloth. We were for money. The only thing we cared about was money. That's what we learned from you Americans.

"Later things got a little difficult for me. The FLN[17] started to push all Algerians into clandestine activities. I didn't know what to do. I asked around for advice, but no one could tell me anything intelligent, so I got up the nerve and went directly to Ted. 'The FLN wants money from me. Okay, I can do that. But they want me to work for them too. What can I do?'

"'Listen,' he said authoritatively, 'I was in the Polish underground for a long time. I'll help you. Give them some money. Pull a couple of jobs. Don't take chances. They'll leave you alone.'

"It worked for me temporarily. In 1956 the Suez crisis exploded when Israel invaded Egypt. Things got pretty bad, yet curiously our friendship grew stronger. Once when the police were after me, I called Ted. He hid me for two weeks at the end of which I made a wisecrack. 'You're a funny guy,' I told him. 'I never expected a Jew would do this for an Arab.'

"'Who's a Jew? And who's an Arab?' he replied.

"Then another time I needed a place to hold an underground meeting. He agreed to let me use his place. 'Sure. What time?'

"'About ten.'

"'Well, don't come in a big group. It'll arouse suspicion, especially since you have such bad faces.' Then he started to laugh. I don't know why. I couldn't see anything wrong with our faces. They were the ones we were born with.

"We held the meeting there. He sat in the corner reading. We conversed in Arabic. Sometimes the word Yehudi came out. I told the others to watch their tongues since the owner of the apartment was Jewish. They stared at him in disbelief. They couldn't believe that a Jew would be capable of helping Arabs. I described some of the jobs we had pulled together, and they were really impressed. They even invited him to drink Buka, Algerian vodka.

"Ted always did me little favors, like hiding our guns in his apartment. He never complained.

"'Aren't you offended because Arabs hate Jews?' I asked him one day.

"'Not all of them hate Jews.' He looked at me and smiled. 'Anyway, I did it for you, not for the others. One day I might need your help. We're friends, that's all.'"

"Anything else you can tell me?" I asked.

"I've told you the most important stuff. We saw each other quite often over the years. Even though we didn't do much business together. There was a little café on St. Germain where we used to go for a drink. Everybody went there – hoods, writers, philosophers, punks, hustlers, queers. We drank and talked. And this may be of interest to you, Miller. He met a man who was a well-known philosopher at the time. 'The Professor.' Ted would talk to him for hours."

"What did they talk about?"

"I don't know. I wasn't interested. I was there to pick up girls. But they just sat there and talked."

"Didn't you ever ask him about those conversations?"

"Yeah. He told me, 'A whole lot of shit, but you wouldn't understand.' I never bothered him again about it."

"Can you find this 'Professor' for me?"

"I'm sure I can. Easy. He hangs out at La Coupole now."

"Try to arrange a meeting between us?"

"No problem, Miller."

"One more thing, Mustapha. I've heard that Ted changed somewhat in recent years. It had something to do with women. Know anything about that?"

Mustapha began to reflect. I already knew that Arabs, especially Arabs who lived in Europe, had a peculiar type of attitude toward women. I couldn't help thinking that maybe it was this line of machismo thinking that might have drawn Ted closer than would be expected to the Muslim fundamentalist movement.

"When I first met him, women didn't mean anything to him. He changed them every night until he met one particular girl. This must have been around 1960. When he started to see her, he just dropped out of sight. They said he spent most of his time with her. I talked to him when we ran into each other, but he stayed very cool. As far as I could see, he was pussy-whipped, as you Americans say. Then one day, I ran into him and he appeared quite upset.

"'Mustapha, do me a favor,' he proposed.

"'Of course,' I agreed. Nothing and no one can come between my friendship. A woman is the lowest piece of shit when I am concerned with friendship. Even the Jews have a saying, 'Look up to pick your friends, look down to pick a wife.' I didn't have to guess that it was this bitch that was causing him problems.

"'My girlfriend went to Nice,' he said. 'I hear she's met an American sailor and fallen in love with him. Now she doesn't want to come back. I want you to bring her back here to Paris.' He was embarrassed to confess that a woman had caused him heartache. That a slut had drawn him away from his friendships. 'This is her name and there's her picture. She's in Villefranche-sur-Mer working in a bar called the Montana as a hustler. Her lover is a swabby on the USS Saratoga.'

"'Okay Ted, I'll bring her back.'

That was Ted's problem with women, I recalled, needy to the point of suffocating them in a relationship, yet vindictive when they exercised their freedom. It was less a matter of jealousy than suspiciousness about where they went, what they might be doing in his absence. Emotionally, he was a mess and and often used extreme measures trying to resolve such conflicts. It never ended well.

"I took the picture," Mustapha continued, "and went with a friend to Villefranche-sur-Mer and waited until the Saratoga shipped out. We had been watching her constantly and knew her routine. One night we grabbed her and loaded her into the car. We took off immediately for Paris. With a little help from a bottle of chloroform, she went to sleep. She was out of it for the entire trip. We stopped and phoned Ted to tell him we were on our way. When the girl awoke, I put a knife to her throat. 'Bitch, if you open your mouth, it'll be the last words you ever say.'

"'Why? What have I done?' She was pleading with me as if she was really innocent. I knew better and realized at that moment that women are treacherous. The more they stay locked up, the better off we are. And I'm saying that as a man who is as westernized as possible. Not from an Arab point of view, Mr. Miller. From a pragmatic point of view.

"'Ted wants to see you,' I pronounced his name menacingly.

"'Ted? Leave me alone. I can't stand him.'

"'But he's in love with you.'

"'What does he know about love?' she protested. 'He doesn't know about love. He doesn't love anybody.'

"'It would be so easy to cut your throat and dump your body somewhere,' I threatened. I had had enough of this white woman's middle-class bullshit.

"'He's a strange man. You don't know him,' she kept insisting despite my threats.

"'Oh? If I didn't, I probably wouldn't be doing this.'

"Then she turned to me very seriously. She was really frightened and for the first time began to make an impression on my skull.

"'He's moody. He's weird. I think that he's insane sometimes. He's got Bogart's pictures in every corner of his apartment. He watches them and thinks. He doesn't even talk to me. I don't know why he wants me back. And the music, always Sinatra songs. I can't get interested in that music. I'm young. I like lively music, soul and jazz. I don't want to waste my life with him. Why do you force me to go back to him? I'm just going to leave him again.'

"'Do what you like,' I told her, 'but we promised to bring you back. That's all.'

"When we arrived in Paris, we went directly to Ted's apartment building. He was standing in the doorway. We didn't have to force the girl anymore. She got out of the car and went with him. Then they disappeared. Sure, we took some risks, but it was for a friend. We were happy that everything on our end went smoothly.

"I saw Ted two days later. I asked him how things had worked out.

"'She's gone.'

"'What! Did she escape again?'

"'Nobody escapes me,' he asserted with conviction. 'No, I sent her away.'

"'After all the trouble I went to? What's your problem!'

"'Nothing. I just sent her away. You see, I hate to be deserted by anybody. But she came back. When I realized that there was nothing more between us, I told her to go back to Villefranche and marry the American. I wished her happiness.'

"Ted was such a strange guy. I could never figure him out. After that affair ended, he was never the same. He started running around with prostitutes. He was ruining his reputation as a lady-killer. I even reproached him for paying to get laid.

"'You think it's wrong if I give them money?' he asked.

"'Of course.' I was sure. We were the ones who were supposed to take money from them. 'I can't understand how you can act like that.'

"He repeated his question.

"'Sure,' I insisted. 'It's wrong. You're a sucker. Take the money. Don't give it. Take everything. They give your money to the pimps.'

"'I see what you mean,' he conceded finally. 'I don't want to be made a fool and I'm no pimp.'

"'What's wrong with being a pimp?'

"'In Poland we dislike pimps. Like you told me in jail that you didn't like bicycle thieves and men who raped little girls. They both break the law, and so do you. But in your eyes, they were not equal crimes. What they did was not at all on the same level as what you did.

Were they?'

"'Of course not.'

"'The Polish code of honor simply doesn't allow us to live off women. We consider women so inferior to us that we feel they should be protected. To accept money from our inferiors is like being dishonored. It's hard to adjust because every country has a different code. I prefer to follow my own.' He stopped and looked up at the ceiling.

"'I don't want to be a sucker,' he mused. 'I don't want to be a pimp either.' Suddenly his tone became lively. 'I don't want to adjust. I want to be a man. It's so easy and yet so hard to live by one's own rules.' He got up and started to pace the floor.

"It was a shame that he felt that way because, with his hatred of women, he would have made a wonderful pimp.

"'But Ted,' I pleaded, 'you left Poland years ago. You're living in France now. You have to adapt. You'll have to change your way of thinking or else you won't survive.'

"'Please, Mustapha, don't ever tell me that I have to change the way I think.'

"From that day on, he stayed away from us. In a way, Ted was a bourgeois kid who thought the underworld was right because the middle-class world was wrong. Even then he lacked consistency and found fault with everything and everybody. He liked me as a person but didn't like our system. That's what he told me one day, subtly of course. There was a kind of aristocratic flavor in his opinions that you don't see today. He withdrew after that episode with the girl. I'd run into him now and then but never again saw him with a woman."

"You really believe he stopped seeing women?" I was amazed.

"Yes, I even asked him why. He replied that if there was no other way to live except by being a sucker or a pimp, he would rather withdraw and terminate his relations with women, with people in general. He kept his word."

"That's very strange." I thought to myself. Strange? It was

outlandish, downright weird.

"Look, Mustapha, let's change the topic a bit. You claim you liked Ted. He helped you with the FLN and was able to bridge the gap between Jews and Arabs. Mustapha, what's your attitude toward the Palestinian problem?"

"The Palestinian problem," said Mustapha, "is not my problem. I live in France and I'm a Frenchman."

"Well, do they come to you for money?"

"A man has to be reasonable, diplomatic. But their goals are not my goals. I have nothing to do with them. I don't participate in their movements."

Chapter 12. Sturmbannführer[18] Schlaube's Hans

Saturday, October 8, 1983 – "The Federal Bureau of Investigation reported yesterday that the man who assassinated Soviet Premier Dimitri Berisov last Wednesday has been positively identified as Tadeusz Szczepanski . The assassin is being held under close surveillance by federal officials in an undisclosed location. The only details that have been released concerning Szczepanski 's biography are that he is a Polish refugee who had been living in Paris since the end of the Second World War. Szczepanski has been associated with known underworld figures and also with members of international terrorist organizations. International law-enforcement organizations are still trying to determine if Szczepanski acted alone or in accordance with a premeditated terrorist plot. The State Department has entered into contact with Russian authorities to try and clarify the subject's motives." – *International Herald Tribune*

Blood was running in streams. There was Frankie again. His brain was oozing slowly from his skull. He turned to me and said, "Johnny, Johnny. Come. Please. Join us ... Billy, Jimmy, and me are waiting for you. Come join us."

"Hey Johnny, wake up. We're going to miss the plane." It was Harris. "You talk in your sleep, you know."

"What did I say?"

"Pretty gory stuff, a lot of talk about blood. You screamed. I thought someone attacked you."

"Did I say anything else?" I worried.

"No. I really didn't understand what you were saying, Just a word or two here and there. Listen, are we or are we not taking a plane this morning?"

I was glad he woke me. Those dreams were becoming too real. They were really beginning to get to me. And with Harris staying in the adjoining room, it could be a bit difficult to explain. It's hard to control yourself and your thoughts when you sleep. You're liable to say anything. I looked at Harris who was waiting patiently.

We checked out of the hotel and took a cab to Orly Airport. We just made the plane, but finally we were on our way to Frankfurt.

During the flight I didn't talk much. I didn't have anything to say. As we crossed the Rhine, it took me back nearly forty years to the bridge and Frankie, Billy, and Jimmy.

"Fasten your seat belt," said Harris, waking me from my daydreams. "We're going to land in a few minutes."

After the usual customs formalities, we took a bus into the center of town. I was amazed to see how much the city had changed since I had been there with CID. The last time I visited Frankfurt, it was in ruins. Now it looked like an American city had sprouted out of place.

We checked into the Victoria Hotel near Kaiserplatz. I remembered the hotel but was thrown off by all the new construction. It seemed as if they had shifted the blocks around, and the area was no longer familiar. We got lost almost immediately.

"Does Schlaube know we're coming?" asked Harris.

"No. And the way we're going, we may never get to pay him our surprise visit."

Finally, in desperation, we asked a cop who pointed out that the sign behind us to the right read, Kaiserstrasse.

We found the number and entered the building. At the reception desk, we spoke English to a young woman. She picked up the phone and dialed Schlaube's office. Then turning to me, she asked in perfect English, "Do you have an appointment to see Herr Schlaube, sir?"

"No, we don't. But tell Herr Schlaube that a friend of his from

Trawniki wants to see him." She relayed the message. I looked at Harris, who was lost and angry. He didn't understand the reference to Trawniki.

"What's your name, sir?" she repeated as if I hadn't heard her first question.

"Johnny Miller."

She listened again to the voice on the other end and then asked, "Are you sure you know Herr Schlaube from Trawniki?"

"Quite positive."

"All right. You may go up. The lift is over there to your right, sixth floor."

We followed her instructions. When the doors opened, a secretary was waiting for us. She showed us through an American-style reception room into a large office. There was a big, fat German around seventy-five years old standing behind a large mahogany desk. He wore a permanent smile and reminded me of Orson Welles. He greeted me in German.

"Herr Schlaube, we'd better speak in English, so that my comrade, Mr. Harris, can understand. Otherwise he's liable to get very nasty."

Harris glanced at me like I'd lost my mind.

"Oh?" Schlaube studied Harris very carefully. "Please sit down. You're Americans, aren't you?"

I thanked him for the seat as Harris and I sat down.

"Yes, we're Americans."

"What can I do for you?"

"We need some information."

"My secretary said that you knew me from Trawniki. Americans in Trawniki. That's very strange."

"We've never been in Trawniki, Major." His smile faded at the word "Major." Perhaps I should have said, "S.S. Sturmbannführer Schlaube?"

"Gentlemen, I've dealt with your type before," he cautioned.

"There is no need to interrogate me. I was an SS man and I was tried for it and acquitted by the Allied and the German de-Nazification Courts. I was rehabilitated. I don't think I should be subjected to this type of greeting. You Americans have a Constitutional amendment prohibiting double jeopardy, if I am not mistaken."

"My apologies, Herr Schlaube. We do need your help. We have a few stories on you. Neither the Americans nor the Germans can touch you, but we have friends with the Mossad. We could tell them certain things about you.

"Couldn't we, Harris?" I turned to Dave, who smiled. This was his sort of work.

Schlaube became anxious. "What do you want? Why do you threaten me? What information can I possess that is so important?"

"We know that you met a man in Trawniki. I showed him the picture of Shipansky. "That man was involved in a crime, and we would like to know everything you know about him. We can start by his name when you met him."

Schlaube stared at the picture.

"He testified in your defense at Nuremberg," I added.

"Tadeusz Szczepanski," Schlaube smiled. "Tadek."

Pleasant memories of the past, I thought to myself.

"What else do you want to know?" he added.

"Everything about your relationship with this Tadek, during and after the war," I continued.

"Would you like a drink?" he asked himself as much as us.

Harris refused. I asked for a schnapps. Schlaube graciously poured two drinks and then ordered his secretary on the intercom not to disturb him under any circumstances. Then he sat quietly for several minutes trying to recollect his thoughts.

"I was a member of the Waffen SS, which was in no way concerned with the general SS extermination program. I was in charge of the police and SS activities in the Trawniki area between Radom and

Lublin. There were heavy partisan operations in the area. They were camped in the nearby forest and gave me a hell of a time. I directed security in the town and operations against those bandits, who called themselves underground fighters. Although we kept a close watch on the forest, they still managed to get out and commit acts of aggression in the villages and town halls in the region. One night in August '43, my men brought a young Pole to my office. I stepped into the adjacent room while my sergeant, Obersharführer Weinz, was interrogating him. 'Why?' he kept repeating as he beat the boy.

"'Because I don't know anyone in Trawniki. This is my first trip.'

"'Where did you buy the food?'

"'At the market.'

"'What were you doing between the village and the forest?'

"'Walking. I didn't know it was illegal.'

"'Which organization do you belong to?'

"'None!'

"Weinz hit the boy again. I heard him swallow the punch and then he gasped as another blow hit him unexpectedly before he had a chance to breathe. 'What's your code name?'

"'Most of my friends call me Tadek.'

"'Where's your weapon?'

"'What weapon?' cried the boy indignantly.

"'Look, you goddamn Pole, I know all about you. Tell me what I want to know. Otherwise I'll beat it out of you.'

"Weinz was our expert interrogator. Often his methods were so brutal that I could not bear to listen in on the sessions. This boy was different from the other Poles, however. He spoke perfect German and seemed almost believable under interrogation.

"'What are you talking about?' came the response.

"'Don't play games with me, boy. When I get angry, I find many methods to do my job. Some of them I never realized I knew, but they often prove effective. Now what's your name?'

"'Tadeusz Szczepanski .'

"'Place of birth?'

"'Warsaw.'

"'Education?'

"I left the office and came back about an hour later," Schlaube now recalled. "They were still at it. 'Political affiliations?'

"The Pole was tired. 'All right, all right. I'm a food smuggler. I came here to buy eggs, butter and flour.'

"'Who sold them to you? What are their names?'

"'I told you. This is my first time here. I don't know anybody, but if you come with me to the market, I'll show you the people.'

"'What do you think I do here, run a guided tour of the market? I have more important things to take care of. Like renegades and bandits.'

"'I came here from Warsaw to buy food. I'll go back and sell it at triple price. That's how I make my living. And in Warsaw there's no fresh air. I like to walk in the country. That's why you found me near the forest.'

"'Don't expect me to believe that, you filthy Pole! You were walking toward the forest. You know that's illegal.'

"'No, I didn't.'

"'Don't lie. You know there are bandits there. YOU were going to join them because you are one of them.'

"'No. I am not a bandit.'

"'Stop lying!!' Weinz slapped him hard and kept it up for about twenty minutes. The boy must have fallen to the floor because I heard a thud. 'What were you doing in the forest?' Weinz shouted now.

"Tadek repeated his smuggler's story.

"'Schweinhund! You work for the bandits. You'd better admit that you work for the bandits.' Weinz started beating him again. Then something unexpected happened.

"'Please don't hit me anymore. I'm one of them. I work for the underground,' he admitted.

"'Ha!' Weinz laughed triumphantly. 'So, you confess!'

"'Yes, I'm one of them.'

"'That's all for the moment.'

"Weinz went to the door and called a guard. 'Take him to the cell.' The prisoner was escorted out of the room, and Weinz turned to me as I crossed the partition. 'What shall we do? Shoot him?'

"'Keep him in jail for now. I want to think it over.'

"It was very unusual for the underground men to confess like that. They usually offered much more resistance ... and especially since we didn't have any proof. His papers were in order. No arms. I wondered why he did it. To confess being a member of the underground risked death. Suddenly I remembered Weinz was still awaiting my decision. 'He stays in jail for now, and don't let your men kill him.'

"I went to my house, which I shared with two other officers. I had a young Polish girlfriend living with me. She greeted me at the door and had already prepared my usual drink. I still couldn't stop thinking about the Pole. I couldn't figure out why he confessed so readily. Then it occurred to me that only one type of man would say that – a Jew. Such a confession wouldn't necessarily mean death, but a Jew would surely die as soon as he was discovered.

"Next morning, I decided to question the man myself. I had Weinz bring him to my office. Curiously, he didn't look like a Jew. He was blond and around seventeen. Now that I think about it, I remember that I felt a pang of friendship as he stood there facing me. You must understand that I am not an anti-Semite. I wasn't even a Nazi at heart, but the party was necessary to any successful career. As a youngster, I chose to be a police officer. I wanted to be a police officer no matter what. When Hitler came to power, they advised me to join the SS if I had any ambitions. Another thing was that I didn't want to be sent to the Front. I'll tell you, Mr. Miller, if there had been a Communist government, I would have become a police officer too.

"We had a camp about two miles from Trawniki where six thousand

Jews had been transferred after the liquidation of the Warsaw Ghetto. They worked there for the German fur industry. Conditions were uncommonly humane, but they didn't get much food. My dilemma was whether to feed these people and alleviate their suffering or do the patriotic thing and re-expedite all our surplus to the Front where soldiers were dying from hunger.

"I looked at the young man again. He really didn't appear to be a Jew. 'Do you know what's going to happen to you?' I asked. 'We're going to shoot you.' We can do it if we choose. On the other hand, perhaps you would prefer slow death in a concentration camp?'

"He gave no response, but then there wasn't much he could say in such a position. I clicked my tongue and made him a different kind of proposition. 'With your cooperation, we could capture those bandits in the forest. In return we won't shoot you. Will you cooperate?'

"'That's fine with me, sir,' he said without hesitation.

"I was surprised. He was the weakest guy I'd ever arrested.

"'How should we do it?' I asked.

"'You let me go back to the forest and I'll send you a message where the group is located.'

"'If I let you go, we'd never see you again. Take off your clothes,' I ordered.

"He jumped when I said that, but I wanted to make sure that he was indeed a Jew without his knowing. 'I want to check everything you're wearing.' While going through his pockets, I glanced at him to see if his prick was circumcised. It was. I gave him back his clothes. 'Okay, I want you to shoot two men.'

"He didn't protest. For me it would be proof that I could trust him. I handed him my pistol and called for Weinz to bring in two Jews captured the previous evening. When they were standing before us, I ordered him to shoot. He pulled the trigger, but the gun didn't fire because it wasn't loaded. He was confused, but I was satisfied. I stared at him. He was ready to shoot his own people in order to stay alive.

"Many things ran through my head at that moment. In retrospect I am a better judge of the situation, but then I was really unsure of my motives. Maybe I felt that Germany would lose the war and I would need someone to help me. Or perhaps his self-effacement appealed to my perversions. I saw so many murders but had never killed anybody. I watched and never did anything to stop them. I had no choice. It was preferable to being sent to the East. In a way I was performing a job that was just as degrading as the one he had just accepted. I felt very close to him at that instant. I don't know if you will comprehend that ... Ever."

"Herr Schlaube, I was in combat." I tried to ease his conscience.

"Yes, but I don't think that you ever experienced having to do abhorrent things, driven only by the desire to live and survive."

To live and survive. To live and survive. I understood him all right.

At the end of March '45, we had a secret meeting at our headquarters not far from the Rhine. Frankie, Billy, Jimmy and two other guys were with me there. Colonel Washburn was briefing us on the mission. "Tonight, you're going to be parachuted across the Rhine. There is a bridge crossing the river, right about here." He pointed to the map. "We'd like to take it if possible. Artillery will start at 0600 hours. You'll be dropped at 0300 with radio equipment. We want as much information about the area and the enemy as possible. The Germans aren't stupid. They'll blow it up if they suspect we're making a move. Any questions?"

"Sir?"

"Yes, Miller."

"I'd like to wear a German uniform."

"All right, but if the Germans capture you, you won't be covered by the Geneva Convention."

"I don't trust them whatever I'm wearing. Maybe with one of us in German uniform, we can prevent them from blowing the bridge. My father was a German, and I speak the language fluently. I can protect myself."

"Perhaps. Anyone else want a German uniform?"

Nobody wanted to risk it. They felt safer in American uniforms.

I put the uniform on immediately. About 0245 we boarded the plane; at 0300 we hit the silk. It was a quiet night. We rendezvoused and buried our chutes about a half mile from the bridge. Frankie was the team leader. I was the radio man. Billy, Jimmy and the two others were sent to scout the area.

About an hour later, we heard hideous screams. Frankie went pale. Neither of us had the courage to guess what was happening, or at least neither of us wanted to admit we knew. Cautiously, we moved toward the sound. One of the two guys was dead, the other wasn't in view. Billy and Jimmy, however, were hanging by their hands from a tree. And the Germans were cutting their bodies with knives. They shouted, "American swine! Where are the rest of your men?"

Blood was streaming down from their bodies. I was terrified they would crack under the torture. I crawled up. It happened so fast. I threw a grenade and started shooting my machine gun. Everybody was dead, Krauts, my friends, Jimmy and Billy. Frankie was staring at me in shock. "How could you!"

"Frankie, they were going to talk."

He didn't say anything.

"I wanted to put them out of their misery."

"You're just the one to do it! Like your father, you, Nazi bastard!"

I wanted to kill him. "Yes, I'm just like my father," I stammered. "I'm proud of my father and what he did. He helped America just like I'm doing."

"We'll see what a court martial will say."

I stopped listening. All my thoughts were on the bridge. There was an hour left before the artillery would begin. The army would cross the Rhine if we could keep the bridge in one piece. I started to move in the direction of the bridge with Frankie behind me. We spotted the Germans on the right. I threw hand grenades and fired on a machine gun nest. Two soldiers started to run towards the bridge; they were carrying charges. I tried to get a clear shot at them but couldn't. Germans were now running at us from all directions. Then Frankie, who was two hundred yards to my right, opened fire. With him keeping the others busy, I could concentrate on the men heading toward the bridge. As I looked in that direction, I could just make out the two of them feverishly planting explosives. I wiped my hands, took careful aim, praying that I wouldn't hit the detonators, fired twice and killed them.

Then a sound of German soldiers came up behind me and mistook me for one of them. "What's going on here?"

"Americans. They're trying to take the bridge. We have to blow it up. Do you have any engineers?"

"Yes. That's what we came for," shouted one.

"Are you coming with us?" asked the captain.

"No. I'll cover you." I watched them run to the bridge and I kept shooting, cutting them down one after the other. So did Frankie. They were caught in a crossfire and didn't have a chance. I kept looking at my watch but still no artillery. I kept playing and firing. Every time a few Krauts would advance, I hailed them, smiled hello and threw a grenade at them. I continued this until the bombardment started.

The motherfuckers on the other side didn't give two shits about Frankie and me. I couldn't blame them. I just kept on shooting, shooting at anything that moved. Suddenly I remembered Frankie and his court-martial threat. There was no sense in taking any chances, so I shot him in the back of the head. I could see the brain oozing from his smashed skull. Safe! I turned around just in time to see three or four Germans running toward me. I cut them down. Then I heard the jeeps on the bridge. Why don't you bastards hurry up, I thought. You're so damn slow. I kept shooting. Then there was an explosion about ten yards away from me.

When I awoke, I was in a field hospital. Colonel Washburn was standing beside my bed. "You're the only survivor, Miller. Thanks to you, we're over the Rhine. I've recommended you for a medal, but I think the President has something else in mind for you. You're a hero now. Look at the papers, THE MAN FROM THE BRIDGE." I could barely read the hazy title.

My injury wasn't serious. I asked for permission to rejoin my unit. A couple of weeks later, I was riding in a jeep as part of the advance troops. Heading toward the East, I was taken prisoner by the Germans and then by the Russians. I met Ted and he saved my life.

"I understand, Herr Schlaube. I do understand the tragedy of survival and what it means to live by clinging to a human raft."

I could hear the words leave my mouth and with a pained chill in my brain, I shut up. Heroes were for history books; scum is the stuff of which real persons are made. During combat, I had often reasoned that only I and perhaps a few companions had a will to survive. The enemy to my mind was a faceless, senseless beast, devoid of all morality and bored with killing. The torture of a concentration camp was wrong, while the torture that occurred in a field commander's tent was right. The Americans had won, and the Germans had lost, but now as I sat in Schlaube's modest yet comfortable office it became evident that there were winners on both sides, and their common obsession was guilt for perpetrating the atrocities in which others had perished. Life after combat was a dirty, lonely cell, an executive office, the corridors of an airplane, or even the dunes of a tropical beach. Had Ted's underground been designed by the same architect?

Schlaube was confessing his past without much resistance. The threats about Mossad were meaningless and even he knew that. The interrogation chamber had moved from a house in Trawniki to a tribunal in Nuremberg and now to a skyscraper in Frankfurt. Despite the nightmarish details, Schlaube was comfortable. He had relived the events a thousand times in his head, the conversations spoken by figures who appeared in the transparent reflection of his own face.

Brushing aside the cobwebs of our collective wartime memories, I guided Schlaube back to Ted. "Once convinced of the boy's reliability, how did you use him?"

"I sent him back to his underground unit with instructions to report their position back to me," he answered.

"'They won't trust me if you just let me go,' the boy reasoned.

"'Don't worry about that. Is it a deal?'"

"'Okay, but it will have to look like I escaped. Your men will have to shoot at me. Tell them not to be too accurate.'"

"We waited until nightfall and around 10 PM, Weinz brought Tadek back to my office. In order to provide further authenticity to his 'escape,' I ordered Weinz to work him over some more. Weinz responded to the task with pleasure and beat the boy for about twenty minutes. 'Now it looks much better, doesn't it?' observed Weinz with an air of satisfaction.

"'Right. Now take him out and release him.'"

"'What? We can't do that.' Weinz protested the loss of such a good customer.

"'It's all right. He is going to work for us, or have you forgotten? Let him escape and have the men fire above his head.'"

"'Yes, Herr Sturmbannführer.'"

"'Well, young man, would you like to have one for the road?'"

"'Another beating?' inquired Tadek, trying to make a joke.

"I laughed and handed him a glass of schnapps.

"About six weeks later Weinz came into my house around midnight. I looked behind him and saw the Pole with a couple of my soldiers.

"'Oh, it's you. What's happened?'"

"'We picked him up as he was coming out of the forest. He wanted to see you personally.'"

"Weinz and the other men left the boy in the room with me and returned to their barracks. As soon as we were alone, the boy revealed his plan. 'Tonight,' he explained, 'you can capture them tonight.'"

"'Do you know what time it is?' I barked.

"'Yes sir, but ...'"

"'Well, what's your plan?'"

"'I'll go back to my post and take one of your soldiers who speaks Polish without an accent. That is not terribly important, but he must know SK[15]. We'll destroy the other outpost.'

"I sent for a middle-aged blond named Straffer and assigned him to accompany the boy, giving him orders to do as he was told. Later Straffer recounted what had happened. They went to the forest, found the dead body of the boy's mate, walked on until they were in sight of the next outpost. They stopped. The Pole advanced, branches cracking under his steps and warning the two guards that someone was approaching. A call came from the shadows and the boy gave the password. He was told to come forward. 'The captain sent me,' he announced. 'There's movement in the village ... German troops.'

"Straffer began to wonder just who the boy was betraying, them or us? What he said was true. Our troops could be seen advancing slowly from the village toward the forest.

"'We have to alert headquarters,' deduced one of the guards.

"'I'll do it for you,' volunteered Tadek. The guards turned around to watch the troops, and suddenly Tadek stabbed one of them with his knife while Straffer jumped out and broke the other's neck. The way was cleared, and the advance signal was hailed. We took the camp by surprise. Nobody escaped. We shot all of them and by 4 AM the operation was completed. Tadek returned here with Straffer and the next morning I requested that he report to my house.

"'To tell the truth, Szczepanski, I didn't think you'd return. Why did you do it?'

"'Well, I had no choice,' he stated flatly.

"'What do you mean? You could have kept going.'

"'I told you I would cooperate, but in reality, I just wanted to save my life. To tell you the truth, I hadn't planned to come back at all. But something changed my mind.'

"I didn't ask him what influenced his decision. All I cared about was that the operation had been a success. The command was very pleased and promoted me."

Now I was really perplexed. I looked over at Harris who was thinking the same thing. According to Juraski, Ted had never betrayed the underground. He was a hero for the Home Army and even a confidante of Ostry, the legendary Polish freedom fighter. From Schlaube's story, however, we learned that he had been loyal to the Germans all along too. It was unbelievable. He had delivered an entire unit of resistance fighters to Schlaube near Trawniki, yet Slavek, Juraski, and the rest were totally ignorant of what he did.

Schlaube stared into space as we grappled with this information. In retrospect he was almost as cold-blooded as Ted.

"The destruction of the underground was a very good mark for me," resumed Schlaube, breaking our uneasy silence. "And in anticipation of similar exercises I asked the Pole to stay on. He accepted. I remarked that he was right to remain with us because if we won the war, he would have a good chance of being integrated into our society. I even went as far as to propose that he join the German army.

"'Too risky,' he declined. 'I would, but I couldn't pass the physical examination.'

"'I forgot about that. Sorry.'

"As an alternative, I made him my interpreter. Soon we became very friendly. I heard disparaging remarks about our friendship, especially from Weinz.

"'Sir, your friendship with that Pole ... well, it's ...'

"This was the first time I had heard Weinz stammer.

"'Well, sir, it doesn't look good. Some of the men are beginning to think ...'

"'Beginning to think, are they? Who gave them permission?' I snapped. 'Without him we would have never gotten that nest of bandits in the forest.' I left the room, slamming the door. After that there were no longer any objections to my choice of friends.

"On November 2, 1943, I heard a knock at my door and a tall, slim blond SS man entered and saluted. 'Hauptsturmführer Lencke reporting, sir. I'm the commander of the Einsatz Truppen of the Rheinhardt Kommando. We have orders to liquidate the Jewish camp here. Tomorrow morning. We ask you to allow your men to work with us on security.' Lencke was a rank lower than me, but his assignment was such that I had no choice but to help him.

"'Very well, Herr Hauptsturmführer. I'll give you what you ask for.'

"He saluted and left the office.

"Later I invited him and his aide, an ugly man named Sturmscharführer Slyceny to dinner. Ted and my Polish girl joined us. Lencke, Slyceny and I talked about the political situation in general. Then Lencke started to talk about the 'action' that was planned for the next day. 'Herr Sturmbannführer, there are only three thousand places on the train. You have a total of six thousand here, is that not correct?'

"'That is correct.'

"'We'll have to do the rest of the job right here.'

"'There is no other way, I suppose.' The thought of having to watch that made my flesh crawl. I think he realized my distaste for the idea.

"'The train is going to Chelmno.' Lencke paused. 'I'll need a couple of hundred men to prepare the graves and a lot of wood. I'd like to get them started immediately.'

"'Anything you say.'

"'We don't want to leave any bodies lying around for the Russians to see.' He smiled weakly. 'They're advancing rapidly.'

"We ate the rest of the dinner in relative silence. About twenty minutes later, I heard a car pull up outside. Weinz came in and made his apologies for having interrupted our meal. We stepped aside to discuss an important local matter, then I gave him Lencke's orders. 'Go to the camp and take two hundred inmates.'

"'Slyceny, you'd better go with him and show him where you want him to dig the graves,' said Lencke.

"Weinz smiled, 'The graves?'

"'Yes, and be discreet, dammit,' I added. 'We don't want to alarm the people unnecessarily. Those graves have to be ready by ...' I turned to Lencke.

"'As early as possible, but no later than 7 AM,' he said.

"Slyceny and Weinz left to supervise the ghoulish task. Their hunched backs disappeared through the door frame and into the street. I was glad to get rid of them both and evidently so was Lencke.

"'Horrible man, that Slyceny,' Lencke said as he screwed up his face in disgust.

"'Really?'

"'A sadist. No culture. Can you imagine? He really enjoys killing people. I'm a soldier and so are you, but I don't believe you take pleasure in those kinds of instructions from Berlin.'

"'Of course not.' It was true. I didn't.

"'I don't either, but I believe in the cause. The Führer gave us a mission. Do you think that it's easy for us to exterminate women and children?' He addressed the question to no one in particular. 'Don't you think that we suffer horribly afterwards? It's necessary to make this kind of sacrifice for the next generations. In the future, we shall be spoken of in praise for the pure world we've created according to the Führer's directives.'

"We all rose and lifted our glasses. 'To the Führer!' Then we sat down again.

"Lencke was the first to break a rather ridiculous silence which followed that ritual. 'The difference is that you, Schlaube – you and I – we understand this horrible job we have to do. We don't enjoy it. But Slyceny enjoys it without the least comprehension. You think he likes music or literature? He was a criminal before he joined us. A common thief.'

"'But why do you bother to listen to him? You outrank him.'

"'He has much influence with Herr Himmler. We go fifty-fifty.'

"'What!'

"'When we have an operation to do, half the people are killed my way and the other half his way. I think my way is more humane and efficient because they go to their deaths believing that they will live. When Slyceny does it, it's sadistic and cruel. He's just wasting his time. Terribly inefficient. Simply satisfying his sadistic proclivities.'

"I wanted to make Lencke feel at ease. I put on a Wagner record and passed around some cigars. I was glad that Tadek had heard the conversation and hoped he'd understood that there was nothing I could do to prevent the slaughter. It was sort of a silent effort to assuage my conscience. But it didn't work very well.

"Suddenly the telephone was ringing. I picked it up. 'Sturmbannführer Schlaube speaking. Heil Hitler!'

"'Heil Hitler,' the voice answered. 'Is Hauptsturmführer Lencke in your office?'

"'Yes,' I responded.

"'I would like to talk with him for a moment,' said the voice.

"I passed the phone to Lencke and with a motion let him know it was for him.

"'Hauptsturmführer Lencke speaking. Heil Hitler!'

"Lencke was silent during his conversation, but he turned pale and began to act nervously. After a few minutes he said, 'Jawohl, Herr Obergruppenführer. Heil Hitler!' He hung up the phone.

"'I have a surprise for you,' said Lencke after a pause of several minutes.

"'I hope it's a pleasant one, Herr Hauptsturmführer.'

"'It all depends on our action tomorrow. Some very important people are coming here to assist us.'

"'You mean Reichsführer Himmler, himself?'

"'No, it's Herr Obergruppenführer Globocnik.'

"'But he's in Trieste now.'

"'He's supposed to be, but he's coming tonight to see part of Operation Erntefest. Although he's only been away a month, he asked to return to finish what he started, and Herr Himmler gave him permission.'

"Until August '43, Globocnik had been head of the Rheinhardt Kommando. Under Himmler's orders he killed all the Jews in Poland.

"'What time is he coming?' I asked.

"'In a couple of hours, by plane. He's coming with Herr Gruppenführer Sporenberg. Sporenberg was named to be Globocnik's successor. Not to worry, Herr Sturmbannführer, you've done a good job here. I think your visitors will be extremely pleased. But we'd better get busy arranging things for their arrival,' he added as an afterthought.

"Precisely two hours later, the plane landed. Two men extracted themselves from the small cabin. Lencke and I were standing at attention. 'Heil Hitler!' we saluted.

"'Heil Hitler!' shouted the taller of the two men. 'Sorry for the sudden intrusion but we come on the orders of Reichsführer Himmler.'

"'You'd be more comfortable in my house, Herr Obergruppenführer,' I proposed. We walked slowly into the house. Once we had gathered in the salon, I offered them drinks. They did not turn down the offer, and I felt a little easier at that moment.

"'To the Führer,' toasted Globocnik. He smiled that half-cracked smile of his. I can remember it to this day. He exuded an uneasy presence wherever he went. Anybody who committed the act of trying to hide something from him eventually paid for it. He had the quick darting eyes of an eagle and the memory of an elephant. We all followed suit with his toast, stood up facing the Führer's portrait, and clicked our heels in salute.

"When the ritual was completed, Globocnik turned to me. 'Herr Sturmbannführer,' he addressed me, 'I hope you have plenty of vodka on hand. I'm bringing Einheit 7, a Ukrainian unit specially trained for these exterminations. There'll be some Latvians too,' he added. 'We need vodka for them. It's not easy to kill women and children, so they get drunk. If you don't have enough, how soon can you have it here?'

"I ordered at least two liters of vodka per person for a total of two hundred men. 'It's too bad, Herr Obergruppenführer, I didn't know that you and Herr Gruppenführer Sporenberg were coming. I might have had the opportunity to prepare better lodging for you.'

"'It came as a surprise for me too.' Globocnik had a rather sick look on his face. 'I thought Governor Frank's view held. That's why I was sent to Trieste and Jacob here replaced me. You can't imagine how astonished I was to hear about this change. You see I had just written a letter to Herr Himmler supporting Frank's view. In my first report I did mention the danger of another Sobibor in the remaining camps. But Germany is suffering from a labor shortage and the extermination policy should be relaxed for the time being. Let's face it, the Jews are good workers and we don't have to pay them. So financially, having them work is a viable proposition.'

"'Didn't Herr Reichsführer take your views into consideration?'

"'I'm not sure. Herr Obergruppenführer Krüger received a letter yesterday. It ordered him to destroy all the camps. Maybe my letter arrived too late to change his way of thinking, but on the other hand, I'm inclined to think that he was quite upset by the Sobibor revolt. You know, people think I'm pretty powerful.' he confided to me, 'but I certainly can't countermand an order from Herr Himmler.'

"'Would you like another drink?'

"He accepted and I refilled everyone's glasses.

"'I'd like to ask you a question,' I said quite candidly. 'Herr Obergruppenführer, do you think that the new generation in Germany will think that we were right to perform these tasks?'

"'If the new generation is so unintelligent, so un-German as to think that this great service we have rendered to society by ridding it of the Jewish cancer, if they believe that it is in any way wrong, then all our efforts are in vain and our names should be buried with our coffins. No matter what the new generation thinks, there are some who will follow us. They will use our system in other ways. But they will use it. I think it would be a pity if our sons and our daughters didn't understand what we are doing for them. The world shall praise us for having the courage to undertake such a great enterprise.' He paused and reflected for a few moments.

"'The job is very hard,' he continued. 'Very few do it and very few are able to do it. Therefore, I've asked Herr Himmler to give everyone who participated in Operation Rheinhardt the Iron Cross because I want to show how grateful the commanders are, especially the Führer, to those who do such an ungracious job. Don't look so gloomy, Herr Sturmbannführer. I'll put your name on the list. You shall receive an Iron Cross and what's more, I'll promote you to Standartenführer.'

"'That pleases me, Herr Obergruppenführer. But I still don't understand why you are with us tonight.'

"'Herr Himmler reasoned that since the Rheinardt Operation was originally under my command, I ought to be the one to see it through to completion. In three days' time, there will be no more Jews in the General Government[20] and I shall return to Trieste. I must go now. Thank you very much, Herr Sturmbannführer. Thank you for your hospitality. I am confident that I can depend on you.'

"'Natürlich, Herr Obergruppenführer Globocnik, Herr Gruppenführer Sporenberg,' I addressed both of them. 'You can depend on me.'

"But at that moment I realized I had been a little too hospitable. Globocnik swung his head around to Sporenberg and suggested, 'Jacob, why don't we stay and observe this operation?'

"'Good idea,' answered Sporenberg.

"As you can guess, I wasn't pleased at all. I didn't want them to stay. They made me nervous. Unfortunately, there was nothing I could do.

"They stayed in my place and asked to be roused an hour before the operation was to start. I imagine that they rested well after such a long journey. I didn't sleep at all that night.

"In the morning, Einheit 7 and Einsatz Kommandos surrounded the camp. None of my men participated, they just acted as security guards. Lencke was on stage first. He called a meeting of community leaders, the same group the Nazis used to run the workshops. 'You have nothing to fear,' he counseled them. 'I give you my word as a German officer that nothing will happen to you. The Russian front is moving closer, so we want to send you to a safer area. Trains are now ready to take you west to Germany. Nothing will happen to you as long as you follow my orders. I'm your friend.'"

"I was standing next to Lencke. Slyceny was behaving fairly

civilized, but you could see how tightly he held himself in check. After all, it was Lencke's party. His turn would come soon enough. Some people protested, but most of them were like sheep. As the men were climbing onto the wagons, one of the elders approached me. 'What happened to the two hundred men who were taken away last night?'

"I was embarrassed, but Weinz came to my rescue. 'They'll join you soon.'

"The answer seemed to satisfy him, and he slowly walked away to regroup with the others.

"'What will happen to those two hundred? Will they be sent to Germany?' asked Tadek who was just in back of me.

"'No, they'll stay right here to bury the corpses. Afterwards they'll be shot themselves.'

"'Where are they now?'

"'I'm not sure,' I confessed. 'But they were digging graves all night long. They know what's going to happen.'

"Some minutes later the gravediggers emerged. They were in a frightful condition. Exhausted, thirsty and starving, some were leaning on each other for support. They were caked in mud from head to toe, making it nearly impossible to distinguish their faces. Tadek scrutinized this haggard crew. He seemed overly interested as if looking for a long-lost brother. He turned to me. 'See that big man over there?'

"'Yes,' I strained to look where he was pointing.

"'He might make a good kapo. Why don't you send him to Chelmno?'

"'Perhaps.' I motioned to the big man to join the train. He was very surprised, but I could see how grateful he was. I wondered if he'd be so grateful when he arrived at Chelmno. Anyway, he got on the train. I felt a little better. Maybe I had contributed to something good in the midst of all the carnage.

"I felt better until I saw Globocnik staring at me, that is. The man had eagle eyes, as I told you. Not a single detail escaped his scrutiny. 'Doing your good deed for the day?' he asked sarcastically. He demanded to know why I sent that man to the wagon.

"'Well, Herr Obergruppenführer, my interpreter suggested that the man might make a good kapo in Chelmno.'

"'Where is this interpreter?'

"Tadek stepped forward. 'Here I am, Herr Obergruppenführer.'

"'Do you always take the liberty of suggesting what we should do with these people?' Globocnik glared at both of us.

"During this confrontation between myself, Globocnik, and Tadek, the train began to pull away. Lencke's work was finished. There was actually no longer any point in debating the matter. Globocnik realized that. He turned on his heels and strode away. He was angry. I knew his reputation and I could tell. Several minutes later he turned around and looked at Tadek yet made no further comment.

"Then all hell broke loose. Slyceny ordered our men to move into the camp and begin rounding up the three thousand or so people who remained. Slyceny himself went on the hunt for any who had been hiding. He looked like a madman running all over the place, shouting and yelling, satisfied only when he found a poor creature cowering in a corner. There was one woman with her two children. For some impulsive reason, he grabbed the children by the legs and smashed their heads against the wall. The mother became hysterical. Next, he took a knife and slit her belly like hari-kari. He shouted, 'Now you have something to cry about!' He grabbed a pistol from one of the soldiers and charged at the compound, shooting in every direction.

"I was almost tempted to take cover. Lencke came over to me. 'You see? When they put somebody with no culture in charge of an extermination, it's horrible. It could have been done so quietly, so nicely, so cleanly, but that's Slyceny.'

"The people were marched in groups of fifty toward the graves where they took off their clothes and died under a hail of machine-gun bullets, or from the blast of hand grenades which were occasionally chucked at them. The living and the dead fell into the same hole. It was a pile of mutilated flesh and blood. The bodies looked like giant earthworms writhing about in hyper-acidic soil. The shooting continued. Each group of executioners alternated so the others could rest. Killing three thousand people is grueling work. There were ten or twelve men in each execution squad. About fifteen squads worked round the clock in shifts. Everybody was drunk, cases of empty vodka bottles strewn all over the ground. It was disgusting.

"It was Globocnik who spoke first. 'Herr Sturmbannführer, don't you participate?'

"'I thought my men were assigned to the security detail ...'

"'And your little Pole,' he interrupted my excuse. 'The one you protect. He just saved one of them.' Globocnik had an eerie expression on his face.

"'But he did it for Germany,' I replied.

"'Oh, did he now? Well I think he ought to shoot a few Jews. For the good of Germany.'

"Globocnik handed Tadek a Schmeisser. I was never so frightened in my life. Tadek could have shot all of us on the spot. There would have been no way to stop him.

"Tadek pivoted himself toward the death-pit and emptied the magazine. He turned around and asked for a reload. He was in a frenzy. I'd never seen anything like it. Slyceny had a habit of smiling when he was shooting, but not Tadek. He took it very seriously. 'More, more!' he shouted whenever the cartridge was finished. Globocnik was quite surprised.

"'This boy can't be Polish. He must be German!' Globocnik offered Tadek some vodka.

"'Sir, I don't like vodka, but I like killing,' was the way he declined the offer. He turned away and began shooting again. His action surpassed my understanding.

"After nearly twelve hours, it was over. Lencke, for all his crocodile tears, was satisfied with the results. It made him look good. It goes without saying that Slyceny was as happy as a pig in shit. The small group of officers crowded around Tadek – Slyceny, Lencke, Sporenberg, and Globocnik. Globocnik eyed Tadek like he was a fine specimen. To see the look on his face you would have thought he was the Reichsführer himself passing judgment on the fine upstanding character of the Aryan race.

"'Your interpreter has performed heroically,' remarked Globocnik. 'Don't you think he should be given a chance to join the German army?' He turned to face Tadek. 'Would you like that, young man?'

"'Of course, Herr Obergruppenführer.'

"'Choose yourself a German name.'

"'Well, I had a friend whose name was Hans Bauer.'

"'Globocnik turned to Sporenberg. 'Jacob, make this boy a *Volksdeutsche* with the name Hans Bauer.'

"'Herr Obergruppenführer,' I interrupted, 'that partisan unit I destroyed ... it wouldn't have been possible without his help.' I felt a tinge of pride since Tadek was almost my protégé.

"'Is that so? Well done. Perhaps you might add a weapons permit and anything else you dream feasible, Jacob.'

"Before they left, Globocnik and Sporenberg filled out all the necessary papers for Tadek, including a gun permit and territorial passes. I was relieved when they had finally gone.

"Later that evening I spoke to Tadek. 'I don't understand,' I began. 'They were your people. How could you do it?'

"'Some of them were alive when they fell into the pit. Being burned alive or suffocating ... that's a horrible way to die. I merely saved them from suffering. I helped them.'

"In a way, I understood him.

"Things went well after that. Globocnik kept his word. Tadek received his official papers and I was promoted. He was registered under the name 'Hans Bauer.' On the back of the ID card was a citation: FOR THE DESTRUCTION OF A PARTISAN UNIT AND KILLING JEWS NOMINATED FOR THE IRON CROSS. I started laughing.

"'What's so funny?' asked Tadek, now officially Hans.

"'You're going to be the first Jew to receive the Iron Cross from the Nazis. Listen, the Russians are moving closer and those damn partisans are about to drive me crazy.'

"'I hope you're not thinking of sending me back to the forest?'

"'No, I was planning something more subtle. Can you get in touch with the Home Army?'

"'Why?'

"'To call a truce. If they don't operate in my territory, I won't bother them. What do you think?'

"'I'll give it a try. I need a vacation anyway.'

"When he returned from this mission, he reported that his comrades had agreed to my proposal. I would supply them with the schedules of the supply trains, and in exchange they would promise not to destroy them until they had passed through my zone. Things went smoothly until July 20, 1944.

"I was having breakfast with 'Hans' for the last time. 'Well, Hans, I am leaving for Berlin.'

"'Can't I go with you?'

"'No. You go to Warsaw. I have a good friend there, Herr Gruppenführer Reinefarth. I'll give you a letter for him and the recommendation from Berlin. Everything will go smoothly at least with the Germans. But beware of the Poles.' I was sorry to have to leave him, but my transfer orders had come and would not wait for personal reasons."

"Was that the last time you saw him, Herr Schlaube?"

I had already seen the importance of this interview. It checked out in many ways with both Juraski's and Max's stories. It was a much different perspective. Coming from the German side there were different details and unanswered questions. But I had no reason to doubt them, as fantastic as they sounded. Besides the psychological profile of Ted, I was searching for more immediate links. A better understanding of the second and third undergrounds which occupied his life after the war. If he had grown bitter during the war, those organizations were ready outlets for his misanthropy. But they were not passive outlets. He still held certain values, but institutions have a power of their own which they impose on individuals. His tragic life was a string of inconsistencies, acting on his personality and compelling him to commit irrational acts in the eyes of the world. I needed to find the thread which made his actions consistent.

Schlaube told me about the next time he saw Ted at the Nuremberg trials in the war's aftermath. Ted had indeed kept his sense of loyalty in testifying in favor of this deposed tyrant who had saved his life and even stood uncritically by his side as he rescued another from certain death. Thanks to his testimony, Schlaube was released and sitting in front of us today, a successful businessman.

"Did you meet with him right after the trial?" asked Harris.

"If you mean immediately after I was acquitted, no. I didn't see him until some ten years later."

"What were the circumstances?"

"It was either '63 or '65. I was with some friends attending a party at a nightclub here in Frankfurt. We were singing and drinking when someone put his arm around my shoulder and whispered, 'Herr Sturmbannführer Schlaube?'

"I felt as though a needle had been thrust through my clothes and into my back. I stared into the stranger's face. 'Hans?'

"'Yeah, it's me,' he laughed.

"'What are you doing here?' I excused myself from my company and sat down with him in a secluded corner of the bar. 'I must thank you,' I began. 'I never expected you to come and testify. I hope it didn't cause you much trouble among your friends.' I was very grateful and almost apologetic.

"Hans, on the other hand, was unmoved. He seemed almost embarrassed at my insinuation that he had acted graciously. 'Well, they didn't understand,' he stated.

"'But you didn't have to come all the way to Germany just to testify. I'm grateful to you. Why did you do it?'

"'I felt very close to you,' he stated bluntly, trying to hide any emotion. 'See, back in the fifties, people of my own race betrayed me. You had saved me, and I was your enemy.'

"'What are you doing now?' I inquired.

"'Buying a few things. Prices are much cheaper now in Germany than in France where I've set up headquarters.'

"'What is your business in France? Perhaps I can aid you.'

"'I'm nearly finished with my business, almost retired.'

"'Already? But you're younger than me ...'"

I interrupted Schlaube. A word had caught my attention, "headquarters." It was just a figure of speech to say one had set up headquarters, but it was rather perplexing coming from Tadek who was so enthralled by all that was military. "He used the word, 'headquarters,' did he not? What did he mean by that expression?"

"I'm not really sure at all, Herr Miller."

"But do you think that he enunciated the word with conviction, as if he were really involved in some sort of military or paramilitary organization?"

"Not exactly, Herr Miller."

"What do you mean, 'not exactly?'" cried Harris.

"Please calm yourself, Herr Harris. Realize that I am not on trial here. You have no reason to subject me to a formal interrogation. We are familiar with police methods here in Germany. They only serve to harden criminals and provoke honest people to lie. If you please, I will continue and try to explain what I mean."

Harris just sat there. He looked over at me for some reinforcement, but I showed him no sympathy. "You've got a lot to learn, Harris. Schlaube here is a hardened man. He won't submit to your textbook methods of questioning."

Schlaube refilled my glass and, with a comradely smile, returned to my original question.

"During our conversation, Hans asked me about the others who were at Trawniki. Lencke, I told him, had died in Berlin defending the Führer. He blinked and pretended he was sorry but was careful not to show any true remorse. When I told him that Slyceny was still alive and I came across him working in Frankfurt, however, his reaction was totally different.

"'You mean that butcher got off scot-free?' He seemed amazed, and I noticed that something had sparked inside his head. He stared at his drink. 'He never stood trial for war crimes, I guess.'

"'That's right,' I said, regretfully.

"'Then I'll try him and sentence him too.' He suddenly became calm again.

"'Why?' I asked.

"'You know what for. You saw what he did during the war.'

"'Why take unnecessary chances?' I counseled him. 'If you kill Slyceny, you'll go to jail. You're too young for that. There are thousands of Slycenys alive in Germany and all over the world today. What about the waiter who served our drinks, the cab driver who brought you here, or some of the men we pass on the streets? Perhaps they committed worse crimes than he. How do we know? You can't kill everybody. You knew the Poles were even worse than the Germans. Do you go around shooting Poles? And even if you killed one or two, it can't bring justice. For those who died, two or three more deaths won't solve anything.'

"He stayed silent but there was a fanatical expression on his face. 'Listen!' I said, trying to break his misguided logic. 'You know all about the Germans and the Poles. What about your friends, the Americans? What about the British?'

"'What about them?'

"'In August '42 a report went to America about the exterminations. Do you think they did anything? Not one damn thing, not even a moral, public condemnation. Did you hear about Cable 354?'

"'No. What was it?' He seemed interested by this information. I suspect that he had such high esteem for the Allies that he never guessed that they were part of the complicity which permitted the Holocaust to take place.

"'It was the cable that American authorities sent to their European diplomats and officials, especially those in Switzerland. The cable contained a directive to block all diplomatic channels from being used for personal messages. Those messages were about the extermination. The Americans didn't want anybody to know because the immigration authorities didn't want to accept any refugees.'

He looked at me in disbelief.

"'Did you know that in November 1938, eighteen months before the exterminations started, German newspapers stated that all the Jews were going to be exterminated and in September 1939, Hitler repeated it, saying that if this war starts because of the Jews, not one of the Aryan race will die because of them? America wasn't concerned. She didn't want to know. The British didn't want to accept any refugees either because they were afraid they'd have an Arab-Jewish conflict on their hands. They lost Palestine anyway. The British and the Americans could have saved many Jews. But they were all full of the hypocrisy of Cordell Hull, Roosevelt and even the President of the American Jewish Congress, who decided that mass demonstrations in the United States would have a bad effect on the war effort. Consequently, the whole world turned a blind eye and a deaf ear and didn't do anything to aid you – a bunch of hypocrites. At least we stated our intentions publicly. They said they liked Jews, but they never lifted their hand to help until their own interests were directly concerned.'

"Hans was staring at the table. He didn't say a word. 'Look, all I'm trying to say is that everybody, everybody, was responsible. Not only the Nazis. What does the murder of one man like Slyceny prove? If you want justice, you should kill them all.'

"At that point, he looked up. 'Just for an appetizer, I'll kill Slyceny. I'll take care of the rest later.'

"I tried to reason with him. I suggested that he'd never get to Slyceny, who was a wretched man and trusted no one, probably not even his business associates.

"'But he trusts you. You said that you do business with him from time to time.'

"'Naturally he'd trust me. We were accomplices in the same crime.'

"'You'll call him then. He'll open the door for you.'

"I'm not sure whether it was his persuasion or my own weakness, but I finally agreed to go along with his plan. I gave him Slyceny's address. He told me to be there in a half hour in a taxi.

"When I arrived at the address, I saw Hans standing in the shadows, a short distance from the building. As I got out of the cab, he walked toward the entrance. I approached the threshold and pushed the buzzer to Slyceny's place. The same creepy voice, which had haunted me for so many nights since the war, answered. I identified myself and told him I was downstairs with a friend who wanted to talk to him about an urgent business deal. He agreed to see us. By the time the buzzer rang to unlock the door, Hans, who was by my side, slipped in. As for me, I returned to the waiting taxi and left for my home.

"The next morning the police found Slyceny's body in the apartment. It was horribly mutilated. Blood stains everywhere. During the investigation, I was questioned as an associate of his. I told the police that I had gone to the building around midnight, but he wasn't home. I took a cab home, the same one which had brought me. The cab driver confirmed my alibi.

"You see, gentlemen, in a way, 'Hans Bauer' was conducting clandestine paramilitary activities, but I don't believe that he was working for anybody in particular. At least I don't think so. The tactics he used were the same as during the war. Does the Polish Home Army still exist? I doubt it. If he worked for neo-Nazis, then why would they want to murder Slyceny?"

Schlaube's assumptions were accurate. A right-wing paramilitary organization would have no reason to kill off one of the few remaining heroes of the Reich. If a secret Polish organization did exist, they would be more concerned with eliminating the Communist powers in the East than with taking revenge on Slyceny. Besides, from what Juraski had confessed, the likelihood of such an organization was next to zero.

The only remaining hypothesis that connected Slyceny's killing to an organized, premeditated attack was Mossad. The Mossad was known for its executions of fugitive Nazi war criminals, and Ted may have formed a de facto alliance with them in order to take revenge on Slyceny. If this were the case, though, then why had he been so surprised to learn that the Americans and British had also participated, albeit indirectly, in the extermination? Certainly, a member of the Mossad would be aware of the distribution of guilt. It would be a professional necessity to know that even the Allies had connections with the Germans who were being sought. That's how so many of them had landed in South America and even in the U.S. I remained completely baffled on this point and consequently filed it away in my memory. Perhaps Ted was working for Mossad ... it would be a question to ask Donaldson.

On the other hand, the political atmosphere in Germany was such that I couldn't help thinking about terrorists like the Red Army Faction. The motivation of these groups was a mystery. Rebellious children reacting against the crimes of the past generation? They could have hired a marginal figure like Ted to do their dirty work. I was also suspicious about the fleeting explanation which Schlaube had given for his sudden change of heart when Ted proposed the plan to him. In a way, he felt responsible for having worked him up with those comments about everybody's guilt. Personal motive or secret contact? I couldn't tell but would have to proceed gingerly; otherwise this fish would never bite.

"Did you see him after that?" I asked, trying to pretend that I was interested only in hearing the chronology of the story.

"Three years later he came to see me. I asked him if he was in a better mood.

"'I'm always in the same mood, Schlaube.'

"'Want to kill somebody else?' I asked him jokingly. 'Seriously, Hans, what happened with Slyceny?'

"'It was easy,' he stated with a smile. 'Slyceny opened the door. He didn't recognize me and was a little surprised that you weren't there. I told him you were paying the taxi. He let me in and offered me a drink. As he turned to get the glasses, I knocked him out. Then I tied his hands and feet with his neckties and stuffed a sock in his mouth. Once he was immobilized, I found some spirits of ammonia in his medicine cabinet and brought him around. I wanted him to know that I was going to kill him and to repay him with the pleasure of watching.

"'I asked him if he remembered me but could see that he didn't. I mentioned Trawniki, which brought fear into his eyes. I talked to him about you, Lencke, Weinz, the Einsatz, and the Ukrainians who fired themselves up with vodka as a means of executing his orders. I recalled the mother who had hid under the barracks with her two children. Schlaube, you should have seen him!' Hans had a confident look in his eyes. 'The beads of sweat on his face and the quivering lips. I told him that he was too heavy for me to smash his head against the wall but that I could slit his belly like he did to that woman. He wriggled to get away from me, shaking his head in terror and disbelief.

"'I left him there struggling to free himself and searched his kitchen for the dullest knife in the drawer. When I returned to the study, he hadn't moved very far. I bent over him and slowly cut his belly open. I could see the agony on his face and could just make out the muffled screams. Then I poured myself a drink and gazed into his bulging eyes as he died. I admit that I really enjoyed his suffering. You know I think that in every one of us, there's a little bit of Weinz, Lencke, and Slyceny. I could be every one of them at the same time, but unfortunately, I'm nobody. This is the problem.'

"'Are you still driving yourself crazy over that problem?' I was becoming progressively concerned about my own life. Although he had saved me once, I couldn't be sure about his mental condition. He scared me. Still, I didn't want to show my fear. I used the opposite strategy and attacked him. 'You know, Hans Bauer, if you had been a Nazi, I think you would have been worse than Slyceny.'

"'I didn't choose to be born a Jew. Perhaps if you were born Jewish, you would have been worse than me. Schlaube, you're lucky. You enjoy life. I don't. I don't feel Polish. I don't feel Jewish. I don't belong anywhere. After the war, I tried to lead a clean life. I'm still trying.'

"'By killing Slyceny! That's how you lead a clean life?'

"'Yes. Doing that was a part of the cleaning. But the problem is still there.'

"'I'll try to help but you must look for a better way to express yourself. A psychiatrist might not be a bad idea.'

"Hans was not angry that I suggested he needed professional help. He was merely resigned to live with his anxiety, and I realized that not even drugs would bring him relief.

"'If I talk about it to anybody, it'll be to you,' he confided to me. 'We have something in common. Look at these young people today. What are they so bitter about? Remember the concentration camps? Remember people dying from hunger? From wounds? Schlaube, when I look at these people, I have the impression they're playing games. They're wearing masks. They say, "hello" and "good morning." They're nice or try to be, but every time I see them, I see the faces of people about to die. And when I look at them, I say to myself, if they knew they were going to die in a half-hour, would they act the same way? Would they say the same things? Would anything be more important to them than survival?'

"'Hans,' I pleaded, 'the war was over long ago. I don't think like that anymore.'

"'Yeah, that's why I can't discuss the problem with you. In some ways, you won't understand. Anyway, I don't belong any place. People I meet, I see how phony they are. I don't want to have anything to do with them. I can only be friends with an old motherfucker like you because you were in the war with me. My Jewish friends wouldn't even understand. A Jew, friends with a former SS officer. Ha!'

"Suddenly his manner became contradictory. He was laughing and drinking. At his request, we went to a nightclub, which was filled with young adults. There was a band playing soul music. Sooner or later the inevitable happened, and someone insulted us. Hans started to fight back, and I had no choice but to help him. There were six or seven kids beating us up before the police came and took us to the precinct. We didn't file a complaint. The cops didn't seem to mind, and we left the precinct with a word of advice to stay away from places not meant for respectable people. On the way home, I asked him why he had provoked a fight he couldn't possibly win.

"'It's good for the morale. When you have physical pain, you don't have low morale anymore.'

"'Your morale is low, Hans, and I'm concerned.' I thought that this would be a good time to straighten him out. In fact, all the while I had been thinking I had found his problem. It occurred to me that back there in Poland, when he had collaborated with me under the threat of certain death, I had forced him to betray the partisans he'd been fighting with. He had lived with that disgrace ever since."

Ted's behavior was unfathomable. Absent any moral compass, how could he have calculated his chances from one predicament to the next? Only one conclusion seemed possible. His instinct for survival implied murder as the sole response to every situation.

"How do you think he betrayed his comrades, Herr Schlaube?" Harris asked the question which might have just as well come from my mouth. Neither of us could reconcile how, according to Schlaube, Ted had delivered an entire unit of resistance fighters to their deaths near Trawniki, yet according to Juraski, he had remained entirely loyal to those same resistance fighters.

"That night after the fight, as I told you, I became convinced that Hans was living with the knowledge that he had sent his fellow Poles to their deaths. I even felt somewhat guilty about it. Still, I didn't understand the details. Until then he had never told me what happened when he entered the forest.

"When we returned to my place, he was sufficiently calm for me to ask him. 'By the way, you never did explain what happened in the forest near Trawniki. All I know is Straffer's sketchy story.'

"He thought for a moment and admitted that he had once promised to tell me. At the time, he said, he was still worried that I might have him killed anyway. 'I went into the forest,' he began. 'I was stopped. I identified myself with the password and asked to see my CO, Captain

Ostry. They told me that his unit had moved, that when he removed from the area, they had replaced him. They weren't Home Army. They were NSZ and their CO was Captain Bogdan.

"'I'd heard of NSZ and Bogdan. A Jew had more chances with the Germans than with that band of cutthroats. At least the Germans could sometimes be understanding, but NSZ hated Jews more than Germans, Russians, or the worst enemy they ever had. The NSZ didn't want to unite with the Home Army because they were critical of our association with the Communists. NSZ liquidated Communists. They were responsible for the shooting of the head of our Information Service, Malicki. NSZ published their own newspapers, which I read every so often, *Szaniec* and *Barykada*. When the Jews were fighting in the Warsaw Ghetto, there was an editorial stating that the Jews wanted the Poles to revolt in order to distract the Germans and prevent the ghetto's destruction. The editorial concluded that the Polish nation should liquidate all those Jew-bastards. Real Poles should have no pity on the Jews, they deserved what they were getting and after the war, Poland would be a pure country.

"'For some reason Bogdan had heard of my exploits as Trigger. He invited me to stay with his unit and I obeyed. Most of the time we fought Communist partisan groups. Otherwise, life with the NSZ was like it had been with the Home Army units in the forest. Almost the same, that is, with the exception of a constant dose of anti-Semitism. It was a phobia. Everyone suspected the other guy of either having Jewish blood or sympathizing with the Jews.

"'One day, things finally cracked. A few Jews escaped from a ghetto and came to the forest. They wanted to join the underground. After being picked up like I had been by one of our patrols, they were brought before the captain. The admitted that they were Jews and the captain told them not to worry. He called his adjutant officer and in front of the Jews ordered their execution. On the spot. When the shooting was over, the captain turned to his adjutant and expressed his concern that there might be other Jews who had already infiltrated the NSZ. They planned to have an inspection the next morning.

"'When I heard that, I knew what would happen to me. As soon as

Bogdan looked between my legs, he would know I was a Jew. It was then that I made up my mind to work for you, Schlaube. I volunteered for night patrol and took my position on the edge of the forest with another man, Zdzicho. Zdzicho had been my only real friend with the NSZ, but I had to kill him. If he found out I was Jewish, he too would have turned against me. I hated to do it, it hurt me. Later I crawled toward the village. The rest you must know from what Straffer told you.'"

Schlaube looked up at Harris and me. Poor Schlaube was now more confused than ever, or so it appeared. He suspected that Tadek punished people as a way of punishing himself, but in the end the Poles were as bad if not worse than the Germans. "He really had no choice, you see. He had to choose between the Polish fascists and me, and I guess he trusted me more than them. It was his logical choice and it turned out that it enabled him to survive."

"You were both professional survivors, the only two I know," I said. I was lying by not counting Max, Stein, and myself. The problem was that Ted's behavior confounded all logical explanations. He never married. He no longer had any girlfriends. Who would want to live with a guy so wrapped up in tragedy? The most concrete evidence of his involvement with the terrorist underground now was Schleyer's disappearance. Even if he did act for some organization, I don't think it could have governed all his actions. Schlaube was a real friend if he had any at all. Schlaube had tried to understand what drove him to murder and thought he had it figured out, but in the end, it didn't add up. Would my investigation turn out the same way?

We had been sitting in Schlaube's office for two hours. Harris was handling the tape recorder and listening attentively. From what was said I knew that Harris's conclusion would reaffirm Haverson's lunatic-assassin theory. I hoped that it would be a mistaken conclusion because I now felt close to Ted in a very bizarre way. He was too much of a hero to wind up in an asylum. Asylums aren't for professional survivors anyway. They exist for those who need help to survive, or those who don't really want to survive and are forced to. Ted's life was too large. It encompassed several different armies and many uniforms. It crosscut ten or twelve different ideologies. Nobody could pin him down and yet he readily worked for anybody as long as their business could provide him with the "kicks" so necessary to his survival.

"Did you see him again?" I asked Schlaube. I wanted to revive the old German from his pensive trance.

"He came back about two months ago. He was very moody. I asked why.

"'Look at our society today,' he droned. 'The Red Army Faction and all those terrorist murders in our proper society. Even Ulrike Meinhof said that the liquidation of Jews meant the beginning of the end of capitalist society. Today there are no more Jews in Germany and the killing still goes on. The young generation is no better than the old one.'

"I tried to explain that the political processes still worked. That even the extreme left politicians deplored those terrorists, and that the Germans had not yet absolved themselves of war crimes. He didn't seem to hear me.

"'War crimes!' he shouted. 'These aren't war crimes. It's the moral conduct of prosperous society. Even the vocabulary is one and the same. Don't businessmen talk about liquidating their stock and wiping out competitors?'

"'By the way,' I asked him, 'do you know who is behind all those fucking terrorist organizations?'

"Hans looked at me and licked his lips. 'I think it's that crazy Qaddafi and all his oil money. You stop Qaddafi and you'll put an end to terrorism. But there can still be another solution.'"

The name, Qaddafi, went through Harris and me like a bolt of electricity. There was finally a connection with Qaddafi and Ted's thoughts.

"What happened afterwards?" I asked Schlaube.

"Well, he asked me a question. 'Do you have any connection with the Red Army or the neo-Nazis?'

"'Yes,' I answered, although hesitantly. 'I have to have those connections in order to survive. Survival, remember?'

"He remembered."

Me too, I thought.

"He asked me another favor. He wanted me to get in touch with the Red Army Faction. I was astounded. 'Let me get this straight,' I stared into his eyes. 'You think that Baader, Meinhof, and their Red Army are the barbarians out to destroy our civilization, and now you want to work with them! I would have thought that the neo-Nazis are more your line.'

"'You are wrong, Schlaube,' he said. 'The Red Army, that's who I'm for.'"

I poured myself another schnapps and looked at Harris. I was quite thrilled. Donaldson's imaginary plot was materializing in reality.

Schlaube continued. "It took me several days to present his case to a contact for the Red Army. I explained to the guy that in spite of his age, Tadek was one of the most anarchistic men I ever met. The meeting was agreed to, without me of course. They probably talked for hours. The next day, when I arrived at my office, Tadek was waiting for me. He was sitting in that chair, Herr Miller. He thanked me for the risk I took and assured me that I would not be implicated by their actions. My address and phone number would not be recorded. 'But what did you talk about?' I was curious.

"'I just took some steps toward the final solution,' he said.

"'Hitler had one for the Jews and you see where that got him.'

"'I've got one for humanity,' he announced. 'I'm going to beat the game.'

"'Hitler failed,' I reminded him.

"'I had a good teacher. Where Hitler failed, I won't. With my final solution, I'll take all those bastards together, everybody. You were right, you know. I checked the books. The Americans and British were just as responsible as anybody else. There are no innocents in this world. Everybody's a bastard, including me.'

"'You, goddamn ... you're more a Slav than a Jew. Stop thinking.

Forget the final solution. Make some temporary resolutions. Make money, get drunk, get laid. Forget it.'

"'Okay, you're right for the moment. Tonight, we're going to have a good time, but the final solution will come anyway. Don't forget that.'

"That's all I can tell you about him, *meine Herren*." And with that, Schlaube paused as if to conclude our interview.

Chapter 13. RAF

Shipansky had entered into contact with the Red Army Faction, and together they probably engineered the Schleyer kidnapping. Schlaube hadn't make the connection and neither had the German police. Had Ted evaded the West German counterterrorism dragnet? Or had the RAF infiltrated the police and covered his tracks from inside?

I wanted a favor from Schlaube, but I needed to get rid of Harris. He was getting drunk slowly and not really used to it. This would be a good excuse.

"Herr Schlaube, I don't think my associate feels well. I'd like to send him back to the hotel with someone to take care of him. You know what I mean."

Schlaube smiled. "And you too ... ?"

"Yes, but much later on. It's Mr. Harris that we should take care of right now."

Schlaube pulled out an address book and leafed through it. "Just a minute. I have an idea." He picked up the receiver and punched a number. There was no answer. He hung up and, after searching methodically through his book, punched out another number. This time someone answered. "Hello, Uta? Herr Schlaube here. Are you and Hannah busy tonight?" He put his hand over the mouthpiece and smiled at me. "From one German to another ... Yes, good. I have two business acquaintances here. I'd like you girls to entertain them. Take very good care of them, they're important American clients. Victoria Hotel. Kaiserplatz. Quite all right. *Danke*."

He put down the receiver. He rubbed his hands together like a little boy. The three of us sat there with shit-eating grins on our faces. "How much is this going to cost the U.S. government?" I asked.

"No, no, *meine Herren*, you've misunderstood. This is a gift from one German to you. What you might call an offering, a sign of belief in future American-German cooperation." Schlaube stood up and escorted Harris to the door.

"You handle the tape-recorder, Johnny," Harris slurred his words.

"Don't worry, Dave. I'll get everything down. You can listen to it on our way to Poland. We'll take care of the visas in the morning. Just relax for now and have a good time. I'm sure that Herr Schlaube has offered us some extraordinary entertainment. I'll join you at the hotel as soon as we're finished."

Schlaube took Harris to the elevator. He really seemed like a gentle old man. I wondered if I would be like that in a few years. A retired, successful survivor.

While he was gone, I concentrated on how I would approach Schlaube with the special request which made Harris's absence absolutely necessary.

When he returned to his chair and made himself comfortable, I took the direct line. "Herr Schlaube, I'd like to ask you a favor."

"What kind of favor?"

"It may surprise you, but do you think you can do the same for me as you did for Tadek?"

"Slyceny ... or Trawniki?" Schlaube smirked at his own joke.

"Get me in touch with the Red Army Faction."

"I knew that was coming, Herr Miller. But that's impossible."

"You did it for Tadek. As a sign of German-American cooperation, do it for me."

Schlaube became nervous. He fidgeted with the objects on his desk. Several times he opened his mouth in an apparent protest which he never articulated. He posed his chin on his clenched fist like Rodin's "Thinker" and stared off into space. For an old warhorse like him, I didn't think this would be such a complicated matter. But then there was his business. He almost reminded me of Max, the man whose life he had saved, at Ted's suggestion. The German-Jewish-Capitalist, an amalgamated corporation. Take apart the components, send them through time and reassemble them in the future in a different world, and they'd still be stuck in the same dilemma – sucker or pimp, with or without the kishke. I thought about Gary. He had been a Red Army Faction fan. One day in that stinking Newark tenement, he too had recited Ulrike Meinhof's words, "six million Jews were killed and thrown into the fires of Europe, for what they were, the Jews of money."

I was standing next to that poor twisted guy when he got his "final solution." Like the rest of that Newark gang, he was a loser. I wondered if the RAF and other terrorists were similar and, if so, why would Ted affiliate with such a band of losers?

Finally, Schlaube made his decision. I perceived it by the way his posture suddenly collapsed, as if relieved from the pressure of making a choice. He lifted the telephone and punched numbers. He knew their code all right and had been no liar when he said that he had connections with everybody as a necessary step for survival.

When the other end answered, Schlaube conversed in a Bavarian slang which I did not understand. The speech he made was short and business-like. The responses from the other end must have been short, one-word questions. As he was talking, Schlaube opened one of his desk drawers and reached into it. Instinctively, I made a motion to my left shoulder holster ... but it was unnecessary. He pulled out what looked like an ordinary pair of polarized sunglasses, the kind painted silver on the outside. The lenses were reversed on this pair, though, the silver coating turned inside out so that the wearer couldn't see out.

Schlaube exchanged greetings and hung up. He turned to me. "You'll have to wear this mask. That's the only condition they have demanded."

"I don't mind. I'm very grateful, Herr Schlaube," I said.

Schlaube stood up. I followed him out of the office into the hall, which was now empty. His receptionist and the other office workers had gone home. I didn't even see any maintenance people as we waited for the elevator.

When the button lit up, he handed me the sunglasses and I put them on. The doors opened, and he took my hand.

I was flabbergasted by what happened next. The elevator lifted up under my feet instead of descending. At first, I thought that it was a mechanical error or that the elevator had been called to another floor. It would stop, others would get on and we would go down to the lobby or garage. However, the elevator kept rising. Disoriented by the sunglasses and the unexpected itinerary, I was unable to estimate the number of floors we mounted until the compartment stopped and the doors opened.

Schlaube led me out. He grabbed my arm tightly as we marched down a carpeted hall. I did not comment to him that it was strange we hadn't left the building, but he sensed my surprise. "The world has indeed changed since we fought battles in jungles and deserts, Herr Miller, but we must all learn to survive. I did this because I believe you can help all of us."

We walked down a main corridor and then turned right, right again, and entered a type of reception room where he deposited me in a soft chair. He told me to wait and then left but through a different door than the one we entered. As I heard the door close behind him, a voice greeted me.

"Good evening, Mr. Miller. What can I do for your agency?"

I count on my eyes to orient the world for me. Without my sense of view, nothing else is organized. My eyes are a center of mental gravity and, when they are closed, the other senses do not function at the superior efficiency they were trained for. Although I was not drugged, I felt as though I were hallucinating. The voice repeated its question. It sounded like Frankie talking. I almost slipped into that nightmare again but fought the temptation and responded. "We would like to know your relation to the man who assassinated Berisov. We are somewhat perplexed that you did not claim responsibility for this crime."

"It is a reasonable question, Johnny Miller," Frankie's voice said. "To begin with, there was no crime for us to own. Secondly, the man you are investigating, Shipansky, he double-crossed us."

"But I don't understand!" Many things I didn't understand. The setting, the building, Schlaube, Frankie's voice. "Double-cross?"

"I'll explain," said the voice. "He was convinced he could fulfill our demand for an almost suicidal mission. Seldom have I met a man with such a narcissistic attitude."

"What went wrong?"

"He did not complete his mission. He was supposed to blow open the roof of the General Assembly Building during the meeting. Our contacts in the United States supplied him with the semtex. He had devised his own plan, which we concurred with. Instead, he killed Berisov, and that was not a part of the original plan.

"We had a most difficult time abducting Herr Schleyer and forging his diplomatic papers. We risked the security of many different people in our organization. But, you see, this Shipansky did something completely different. What he did was not what we had instructed him to do. For this reason, we claimed neither the assassination nor the kidnapping of Schleyer. Does this answer your question, Agent Miller?"

Things were more complicated than I suspected. Ted was as usual unpredictable. The words had an additional emotional impact because of my disoriented psychological state. It was becoming a grand effort just to register the things that were being said and the thoughts running through my mind. I could not ask my interlocutor for a few minutes to collect my thoughts. With the utmost energy, I managed to strike a bargain between my brain and ears. I did not want to forget what had been said during this transaction. To do so would have meant that the trip had been wasted and that I could bring nothing new to my envisioned encounter with Ted. I answered slowly and deliberately. "Yes, that answers my question, but it does not solve my problem."

"We must seek solutions to our problems as individuals, Johnny Miller."

"One more thing I would like to know, if you please. Who finances your movement? The money from kidnapping and bank robberies would not be enough to maintain such activities as yours."

"As you know, we receive support from organizations that are better equipped than we. Certainly, we possess a certain expertise and technical sophistication that they don't ... it is like the way your government transforms the resources of the developing nations into useful products and services. Your agency is already familiar with our Palestinian contacts. We also import resources from Colonel Qaddafi. He's crazy and most willing to back any revolutionary movement. He's got an exceptional amount of oil for such an underpopulated country. Are you satisfied, Mr. Miller?"

"You have taken an enormous risk by revealing your financial sources to me. Suppose I told Qaddafi what you have just told me?"

Frankie's voice howled with laughter. "He would not believe you. Don't you realize that this discussion we are having never took place? If you told him that he was responsible for our activities, he would respond by saying it was a figment of your imagination. Perhaps he would tell you to consult the Qur'an, if you were interested in pursuing riddles. Are you entirely satisfied now?"

I said yes, but I wasn't. "Are you people satisfied?" I returned the question to see what would happen.

"Not exactly. The presence of Herr Schleyer is most embarrassing to us. We cannot ask for ransom. The German government no longer strikes deals of that particular nature. Alternatively, if we set him free, we'll appear to be fools."

"Why don't you kill him," I said seriously. "He is not important."

"An interesting solution coming from you, Johnny Miller. We shall consider it. Thank you. I hope we shall never meet again."

I heard the man move away and listened for the door to shut. One door shut and simultaneously the other one opened. I felt Schlaube's hand grab my arm. It was a soothing and familiar point of reference. We followed the same path back to the elevator, which descended this time and deposited us in the garage.

Schlaube was silent as we drove to Kaiserplatz. He left me in the hands of the doorman and said goodnight. I thanked him for all the cooperation he had provided. His parting words had something to do with sex or a comment about the girl I was to meet in the hotel room. He spoke again in that Bavarian dialect that I did not completely understand.

Before venturing into the elevator, I collected my senses in the Victoria Hotel bar. As my powers of reasoning returned, I easily recalled what had happened with the RAF operative. I resolved to call Langley before I forgot anything.

I found a secluded phone booth in back of the bellhop's desk and punched out Donaldson's hotline number at Langley. He answered and recited the poetic code. My patterned response contained a signal for him to switch to an encrypted line. I hung up and waited five minutes in the booth before the phone rang again. "Yes? What do you have?"

"Shipansky's connection with the Red Army Faction."

A long silence on the other end. "It can't be!" The excitement in Donaldson's voice was not obscured by the four thousand miles that separated us.

"It is," I reassured him. "Are we to continue our mission to Poland as planned?"

"Yes," said Donaldson. "Have you not forgotten about our agreement? Find out more about the subject. It's surprising how reality confirms my initial suspicions. They were based on pure fantasy, you see."

"Schleyer," I pronounced the name with a German accent, "I told them to kill him since he was becoming an embarrassment. I think that it will make your story more credible."

"Well done!" shot back Donaldson's voice. "I made no mistake in choosing you. I would gladly have you employed full time with our agency."

"How do you plan to handle this?"

"A simple matter. I shall call Weschsell at BND[21]. If and when Schleyer's body turns up, the papers will print an acknowledgement by the RAF. We have enough power to make the claim stick. Schleyer will become a martyr like Aldo Moro."

The conversation ended there. I hung up and slipped out of the booth. The Polish journey was still one which meant that, war or no war, I would have the opportunity to squeeze Donaldson for running his special assignment. The other benefits of my work were more immediate. I entered the hotel room and felt a warm, naked body rub against me.

Chapter 14. Johnny's Ted

Sunday, October 9, 1983 – "By approving the President's emergency power to reinstitute military conscription, the Congress has sent a clear message to the nations of the world that inexplicable acts provide no justification for the threat of military aggression. Contrary to the sentiment of certain Americans who have grown lax over the problem of defense, the President's decision is not only right but long overdue. In the face of unjustified aggression, the U.S. and its allies are ready to move." – *Editorial, Washington Post*

"In response to growing tensions between the world's two superpowers, the European Parliament in Strasbourg has approved a common defense plan. Under the conditions of the accord, the ten member countries will share the same political and military leadership. After more than twenty years' absence, France has decided to reintegrate itself into NATO. In exchange for this concession, the Parliament designated the President of the Republic of France to serve as the first President of United Europe for a period of five years." – *Agence France Presse*

"The corpse of missing UN delegate, Rudolf Schleyer, was found this morning in the trunk of an abandoned car in Trier near the French border." – *Frankfurter Allgemeine Zeitung*

The following morning, Harris and I had to stop at the Polish consulate before boarding the airplane to Warsaw. When we came downstairs, Schlaube was waiting for us in the hotel lobby. He drove us to the consulate, faithfully waited in his car, and then took us to the airport. He was always willing to serve us. I think his ex-Nazi bad conscience must have worked in our favor. As we were about to go through passport control, Schlaube embraced me and said, "You, Hans Bauer, and I, we're all scum. We have to stick together."

"We will," I promised as Harris hurried me toward the gate.

We boarded a Lufthansa 727 past the plastic smiles of the stewardesses and installed ourselves in first-class seats. Harris was wearing one of his reproachful looks.

"Something wrong, Dave?" I asked without much interest.

"No."

"Out with it. We're in for a big change once we get to Poland. So, tell me what's bugging you," I needled him.

"It's the money … the government's money."

"Don't start that again, pal. Anyway, you're mistaken. Last night it was Schlaube who paid. The night before it was Spaggiari. Don't complain. You've had two nights of free fucking."

During the 90-minute flight I found myself unable to sleep despite the fatigue of the night's activities. Something about Ted was nagging at me. All kinds of theories concerning genocide raced through my thoughts. Not all racism is the same. There are all kinds of racisms. Nazi racism was based on so-called scientific principles. The exterminations that took place in the gas chambers and before the firing squads were only part of eugenics. For years, psychologists have experimented with laboratory animals to prove the tenets of natural selection and artificial breeding. Xenophobes refer to eugenics when they talk about immigrants and the darker races. In the camps and ghettos, the same twisted pseudo-science was at work. Put a crowd of people together in subhuman conditions and only the fittest will survive. This sort of logic worked on the turnkeys as well as the inmates. People like Max, Stein, and Ted managed to survive, but so did the Schlaubes and Slycenys. Ted, of course, had solved the problem as far as Slyceny was concerned. Evidently, the Nazi wasn't as fit as one would have thought just after the war. Chance plays a role in all human destiny and is always corrected by actions.

As for the other survivors, however, they now formed a type of social group that transcended nations and ideologies. Schlaube was right, we were all scum but evolutionarily adaptable scum. Our survival disproved the logic of the Final Solution. The Jews had been exterminated but not eliminated. After the war, they bounced back stronger than ever, stronger than anyone else with the possible exception of the Japanese, who were also the target of the ultimate weapon of extermination. The sense of survival was so strong that it appealed to those who had once subscribed to the racist genetic theories. It was no wonder that the Jews were always being persecuted in history. The first time, whenever it happened, was inexplicable, but each time after that their strength was the continuous source for the next inquisition and so forth. The strongest survived and bounced back, strengthened by the experience, more capable than ever before to survive. They created the problem for the next generation of racists to solve. I wondered what kind of final solution Ted had conceived in his meeting with the RAF. Did I know him well enough to guess what this solution would be?

I had met him for the second time at the beginning of '46. I was in Frankfurt working with the CID. I was one of the lucky Americans in the Army who didn't have to wear a uniform, not even during office hours. I had just left the office for the day and was heading for my favorite restaurant. I saw an American sergeant coming toward me but didn't pay any particular attention to him. There were twice as many American soldiers in Germany then. I heard someone calling me. I looked around and then I realized that it was that sergeant. I stared at him but couldn't recall the face. But then, they do say "a uniform changes a man." It was Ted, and I was very happy to see him. "Hey, man, what are you doing here?"

"Let's have a beer and I'll tell you," he answered cheerfully.

We entered the nearest bar. "Ted, you look good. That uniform really suits you. I'm pleased to see that you finally joined our Army."

"I'm not in your Army," he stated with a deadpan grin. "These are my work clothes. I smuggle from Germany to Paris. Dressed as an American MP, they don't bother me."

"Oh!" I stared at him in surprise. "You know, I'm with CID. I should arrest you."

Ted smiled. "I don't think you'd do that."

"No. I don't think so either," I concurred with a warm smile. "Making any money on these deals?" I wanted to change the subject a bit.

"Around a thousand a trip with my friends. And you?"

"Nothing. Not a bean. But I got a medal."

"No kidding?"

"Yeah. Congressional Medal of Honor." I was quite proud of it at the time. Frankie and Jimmy hadn't started their nocturnal visits yet.

"From the President?" inquired Ted mockingly.

"Himself."

"That's great. Congratulations." He really meant it.

"What's so great about it? There's nothing you can buy with a medal."

"That's bad. Money problems, huh? Listen, I've got a proposition for you." He looked around the bar.

"I'm listening."

"Let's go eat."

That proposition caught me off guard. I was expecting a little more.

"How about the American Club?"

"Too many Americans," pooh-poohed Ted. "I know a place where we can talk without anybody accidentally overhearing us."

Ted knew Frankfurt much better than I did. We found the place which was tucked away in an alley. It reminded me of the Prohibition days at home. We knocked on the door and a little window slid open. Two beady eyes peered out at us. After a few minutes' deliberation, the door opened. We were taken down a long corridor and into a sort of living room. Ted greeted some of the men and then we went through another door into the restaurant. All this just to get a decent meal with some privacy! But I admit it was better than the ration restaurant I used to frequent. We ordered wiener rostbraten and kartoffelkloesse.

"Listen, Johnny. The guy who gives me the passes was discharged. Now I need someone to supply me. Otherwise, I'll be circulating on bad papers."

"Let's see them," I requested.

He took them out and handed them to me. They were certainly the real McCoys. "They're all right," I told him.

"Sure, but for how long?"

"Okay," I consented without much reflection. "Keep in touch and I'll see you straight."

"I'll pay you, of course," he added.

"If it was wartime, I wouldn't take the money. But right now, I have no choice."

"Okay, Johnny, it's a deal."

He came to Germany almost every week. I furnished him with all the papers and ID cards he needed. Every trip, he paid me a couple of hundred dollars. Then he mysteriously disappeared for three months. He contacted me from France later.

"What happened?" I asked.

"Somebody turned me in," he stated somberly. "I was in jail."

"Do you know who it was?" I asked, eager to help my friend with revenge.

"Don't worry, I already took care of it. I knew what to do. I never rat out my friends. It doesn't matter now anyway. I'm back in business again."

The racket continued as usual. Ted kept me in supply of ready cash, and I reciprocated with the necessary papers. Then, in the middle of '49, he came to me with a big job. "If you're not chicken," he began, "we can make four thousand bucks."

"It all depends." I was hesitant.

"One of my friends, a Polish DP, was arrested by American police for handling stolen American property. Although he's in a German prison, he'll be taken to the American DA's office for investigation and trial."

"What do we do?"

"Spring him. His family is willing to pay four grand if we succeed. This is my plan. You find out the procedure for picking up military prisoners and taking them to the DA's. Then get all the necessary papers. I'll fix them up."

"I don't know whether it'll work, but I'll go along with the program."

The next morning, I brought him the papers. I watched Ted as he filled them out. The man's name was Liebermann. Ted noticed I was getting nervous. "It's worth two grand," he said without looking up. "And by the way, you'll have to get a Jeep from the motor pool. Don't worry. It'll be easy. Nothing like this has ever been pulled off before. They won't get wise until it's too late. It'll be easy, I assure you. Just bring the Jeep."

"What time should I pick you up?"

"What time do they usually pick up prisoners?"

"9 AM."

"Then come for me at 8."

The following morning, he was waiting for me in an MP's uniform. I was wearing one too. We drove to the jail and rang the bell. German guards opened the gate and we drove into the yard and parked the Jeep. Ted climbed out and ambled into the reception office. I kind of hid since I didn't want my face to be seen. About ten minutes later, he emerged and flashed an OK sign. He climbed back into the Jeep, and we waited until Liebermann came out, accompanied by two guards.

The prisoner did not act surprised. I figured that his family had already alerted him. I slapped a pair of handcuffs on him while Ted signed the receipt. We left the prison and drove straight to the Salzheim DP camp where we delivered the prisoner to his family.

His wife was ecstatic. "Oh, Jacob, you're free! Won't you please take off his handcuffs?" she implored.

"Four thousand dollars first." Under the circumstances, Ted's tone of voice and manner were a little cold.

She searched in her handbag and took out the wad of money. She handed it to Ted, who counted it and shoved half into my pocket. That was my signal to remove the handcuffs.

The next morning it seemed as if the idiots' carnival had come to town. Everybody was looking for the two MPs who had sprung Liebermann. They went to Salzheim to search for the prisoner himself, but he and his entire family had disappeared. The Jeep was never identified nor were the two MPs. I was put in charge of the investigation. Ted and I laughed over that assignment for days.

We did some more special jobs. One of them involved Juraski, and also involved springing a young Pole from police custody. Thank God Juraski hadn't recognized me thirty-some years later when I came to Paris to question him for this case. If he had, then he concealed it very well.

At the end of '49, NATO was founded. My knowledge of French and German enabled me to get a transfer to CID in Paris. Some of my assignments were linked to NATO bureaucracy. I had Ted's Paris address and tried to contact him, but I didn't hear from him for about two months. It was only in the beginning of 1950 that I discovered he had been in jail again.

But one day, I was in Pigalle and saw him walking on the other side of the street. He was much skinnier than I remembered him. "Don't they feed you in French jails?" I shouted, making my way through the traffic.

"Nope. And I don't think that French jail food is as good as the U.S. Army's commissary," he chuckled.

After we caught up a bit, I asked him, "What are you planning now?"

"Same as before. If you can still help me, that is."

"I'll help you, but I don't want to be cut in on any deals from now on." I was working some other angles by then and thought it was safer to keep business associates apart.

"Have you heard anything about Stein?" he asked matter-of-factly.

"No. Why?"

"It's just that I'd like to talk to him."

I checked up on that character Stein. He had left for the U.S. on short notice. He was most likely afraid of Ted's vengeance. Stein had emigrated, and I felt that things would be better for everyone if I didn't tell Ted about it.

A few weeks later, Ted came to me with another proposition. He was in civvies this time. "I've stopped playing GI. That was only a part of my job. Now it's over."

"You should have done that a long time ago. I always wondered why you wore that fucking uniform all the time."

"Two reasons, Johnny, but I don't think you'd understand."

"Try me."

"First thing. Girls like GIs. I had much more success with them in uniform. Secondly, I didn't like being looked down upon as a DP. People considered us as inferior. It's the same attitude the French hold toward all immigrants. No papers, no rights. That uniform made me equal. That's why I did it."

"So why the sudden change?" I baited him.

"I feel equal now. I've got money. Besides I don't feature going to jail anymore. Twice is enough."

"What about your new deal?"

"It's a new kind of racket for me," he revealed. "Doesn't involve goods."

"How the hell can you do that here?"

"Well, you know all the bars that cater to the GIs?"

"Sure. What about them?"

"If they're put off-limits, they lose a lot of business, don't they? The Provost Marshal's office can slap a ban on any one of them, anytime, can't they?"

"If there's trouble," I conceded.

"Precisely. Look, how well known are you in these bars?"

"Very well known. They also know that I work for CID."

"Okay. One night I'll make the rounds with you. You'll just tell them that I'm a friend of yours. That's all."

"Seems okay with me. But what are you up to, exactly?"

"You'll see," he grinned.

We made the rounds together one night. I was greeted by the managers and owners as usual. During the ritual, I presented them to Ted. Wherever we went, they offered us drinks. Of course, we always accepted.

"What about this deal? Or is it your plan to get drunk every night for free?"

"Patience, Johnny, patience. We'll make another round."

I finally began to discern the plot. They thought Ted was a cop because he was always with me. Every place we went, the ritual repeated itself. Barmen never forget faces. I was getting impatient.

"What are you trying to do, Ted?"

"The next trip, I'll go it alone. All I want from you is to tell me in which bars they had fights."

In the morning I went through the files and found the information he wanted. I gave it to him the next day. He looked over the list. "I have three customers. Johnny, would you like to go with me?"

I couldn't risk my job. "No, you do it alone as you said."

"Well, I guess you have enough money. As for me, I'll have to practice this racket until I've got enough money to go legitimate. You see, Johnny, after this stinking war, I lost everything. I have to get it back, and I don't want to be a gangster forever."

A few days later, he brought me three hundred dollars. I took the money and asked him to explain. "Tell me what you did. I'm curious."

"Are you sure you want to know?" he asked seriously.

"I think I'd better."

"Easy. I went to the first bar and had a drink with the owner. Then I told him, 'I heard there was a fight in your place last night. I also hear through the grapevine that they're considering putting your place off-limits.' Then the guy started to get nervous."

"'Can you fix it?' he begged me. 'Can you keep them from closing me down?'

"'I'll try, but I can't guarantee anything.'

"I repeated the same act in the other two bars. The next day I made my rounds again, telling each one of them that I could probably do something. I told them that I was friendly with the sergeant in their district, but that it would cost them two hundred dollars apiece. You know, Johnny, they gave it to me. Suckers, but at least they're happy now."

It was a very easy racket for Ted. A man just had to use his head and imagination. He always used to say, "I just stick to the old American saying, 'There's money laying in the streets. You just have to know how to pick it up.'"

The racket didn't bring in too much money because you couldn't do it in every bar every week. Once a month was about the average. But for me, this was side money since I was making a good profit with Lucini. It could not have meant much money for Ted either. I liked to think he was doing it for kicks. Yes, he was unpredictable and contradictory. He was a life saver and a ruthless killer. He was a womanizer who despised women. He hated the Nazis but collaborated with them when it was convenient. He was cunning yet child-like. He liked danger for money but more for kicks. He was an enterprising criminal, then wanted to become a legitimate businessman. Then turning mad and killing Berisov, was that for kicks or money? I never knew who he really was.

In 1958, he quit racketeering and gave a party to celebrate. I thought a lot of people would be there.

"Nope, just you and me. I've left the black market. It doesn't pay anymore. It's finished. I'm legit now."

Ted had his nightclub business. We met each other now and then for a drink. He was completely different with me than the people I investigated. Once I asked him, "The racket and that thing you did with Juraski, it really was worth more than you got paid? Why did you do it?"

"Johnny," he confided, "I don't do everything for money. I do it for kicks. I need them. Don't you?"

"No, I don't."

"Look, I never told you about my life," he tried to explain.

But I cut him off. "I didn't tell you about mine. It doesn't matter."

"Johnny, you know that after you do something for a very long time, it becomes second nature. You don't even notice that you do it. That's what happened to me during the war. I faced death so many times, had it as my shadow in the background for so long that I thought it would always be there. I couldn't even remember a time when it wasn't there. When the war ended, the shadow disappeared and well ... what I expected to happen after war just didn't happen."

"It didn't happen to me either."

"But the shadow, did you have the shadow?" he persisted in his metaphor.

"No," I lied.

"When the war was over, I missed that shadow. That's why every time I did something against the law, I felt pleasure, like I had the shadow back with me."

"I can't understand, Ted. I wouldn't want to be in the same situation I was in during the war."

"I don't blame you, Johnny. Nobody would, not even me. Not really. It's absurd, isn't it? I'd like to be like you, but I still miss the shadow, and I can't explain why."

As he fell into the routine of his business, I saw him less and less frequently. On each occasion, however, I realized that he'd told me the truth. For he was becoming sad and solemn. He didn't enjoy life the way he had before. He wasn't like he used to be. I once asked him about the change.

"It's nothing in particular."

"How are your girls?" I attempted to steer him toward a favorite subject.

"As usual," he said modestly, "about two or three a week."

"I remember in the old days when you had one every night."

"I'm getting old," he sighed.

I thought he was joking for a split second, but I saw he was dead serious. It was unusual. He was younger than I, and I was still doing all right.

"Haven't you found one special woman; someone you were really in love with?" I doubted it but felt compelled to explore his sentimental life.

"I don't know." His face was long, his eyes sadder than sad. "There was one. My concierge and some other friends used to tease me about her. But I don't think so. She left me for an American sailor in Nice, and then all I could think about was punishing her. I persuaded a friend to kidnap her and bring her back to me. Then I realized it was hopeless and let her go.

"I don't know," he reflected. "You see, I don't particularly like people. There are a few exceptions though. People who've proved to me that they're my friends. I tend to hate women in general. No, not in general. It's closer to the truth to say that I'm a complete misogynist. So, I can't say I was in love. I just don't like being deserted. I know that I'm better than any of those punks that she ran around with."

I understood that smuggling was just another word for commerce to him. He enjoyed the risk the same way traders go wild on Wall Street. But kidnapping made no sense at all. No one ever wins.

If there was a common denominator to Ted's actions, it always seemed to elude my reach. Even criminals always act according to a certain pattern. Did Ted have a pattern? At first, I thought I almost had it, but like Juraski, I was mistaken. I thought I could discover the key if I learned more about his lifelong behavior. But I couldn't think anymore.

The stewardess announced that we would be landing momentarily at Okecie Airport in Warsaw.

Chapter 15. Ted's Communist

We descended from the plane by means of a portable staircase like in the old days at home. Walking toward customs, I noticed Polish militiamen everywhere. Airport workers performed their labor mechanically. They did not stop to converse with each other. Their gestures seemed fluid and yet automatic, as if they were programmed robots. The atmosphere was not stultifying, but it did not reek of the luxury we usually associate with air travel. It reminded me of LaGuardia Airport in the early sixties.

As we approached customs, an officer greeted us in English. "Good afternoon, gentlemen. Anything to declare?"

"No, sir. And good afternoon to you," recited Harris.

A well-dressed man came over to us as we moved away from customs and glided past the families and military personnel patiently waiting in the terminal. "Excuse me, John Miller and Dave Harris?"

I was a little startled. "Yes, we are. How did you know?"

He showed me his embassy ID card. "Glad to meet you, Mr. James," I said, looking up from the document.

I disliked James immediately. He struck me as officious, a true factotum. "Where do you gentlemen prefer to stay, on the embassy grounds or in a hotel?"

"I'm for the embassy compound," said Harris.

"Sure, you are," I smiled. "But we'll stay in a hotel, thank you."

"The Hilton?" asked Harris in a childish tone.

"You ass! There's no Hilton in Poland."

"There are," laughed Mr. James as he escorted us toward a little black car. "The only thing is that they're not called Hiltons. The hotel in Warsaw is named the Victoria. It belongs to the Hilton chain, but that wouldn't be very Marxist to have it known that an international capitalist chain has set up headquarters in a Communist country."

"What a bunch of hypocrites!" exclaimed Harris. "They won't have a capitalist name but don't think anything about accepting our luxury or even the greenbacks that pay for it."

"I cannot condone the government's policy," commented James. "Yet those of us capitalists do find the accommodations quite satisfactory here. We even manage to have a good time. I was previously stationed at the Paris office, but I am much more comfortable here than in gay Paris."

I paid no attention to their clucking. I was too busy comparing modern Warsaw to the remnants of the city I had passed through with Ted during the war. I knew nothing of the prewar capital but admitted to myself that despite the bad press given to socialist systems, Warsaw was a magnificently beautiful town. I even preferred it to the imitation American architecture of Frankfurt and other Western cities which had been reconstructed under the Marshall Plan. As we passed shops, I noticed well-dressed urbanites waiting in line for their turn to purchase state commodities. The lines were long. The numbers and quality of merchandise, however, were extraordinary by all the accounts I had heard from returning tourists. Along with the East Germans, the Poles were among the best fed and best clothed of all East European nationals. The workers' revolt of the seventies, combined with the installation of an aggressively Slavic pope in Rome, had worked wonders to soften the outward appearances of the austerity-minded regime. I began to wonder what my dollars would buy.

"What about our currency coupons?" I asked James.

"Oh, the coupons. You can exchange dollars for them, even in the hotel. Thirty-three zlotys to the dollar, but I wouldn't advise you to change more than the minimum in the hotel or the state banks."

"Why not?" asked Harris.

"It would be foolish," James began to explain. "The official government rate is thirty-three zlotys to the dollar. But the black-market rate is about four times as high. It ranges from one hundred twenty to one hundred thirty zlotys."

"Who can change them for us?"

"Anybody. I can do it if you wish."

Even this guy was on the lookout to make a buck, just like everybody – embassy officials, tour guides, pilots and stewardesses.

There were all kinds of merchants at the entry to the Victoria, waiting to sell their wares to us and any other foreigners who passed by. They wanted to exchange them for dollars. It was strange to witness the villainous capitalist middlemen working in the midst of a society that claimed to have eliminated the fetish of materialism.

"I'll give you one hundred twenty-two," I heard James saying. He was hustling us, and it almost made me angry until I recalled my own black-market activities. I thought about the old American Polaks taking their retirements in the homeland. With this exchange rate, they would be able to live like kings. It did look comfortable. Maybe someday I would retire here.

I handed James a crisp hundred-dollar bill, and he pulled out a wad of dirty, worn zlotys. He waved them in my face. A symbolic exchange – the mass-produced "clean" dollar for a bunch of dirty zlotys, worn thin by the sweat of toiling laborers in a Workers Republic. Dirty workers whose heroic fathers marched thousands of Jews to their self-dug graves. Here was their redemption. A clean slate where everyone or no one is a criminal, no need to be particular. The Jews are gone.

"In case you need some more, just call the embassy. Do you have the number?" James was making the best sales pitch this side of Wall Street.

"We've got the number," I replied. "Maybe I'll need you soon in fact."

"Sounds like a prediction," said James in a stupid Midwestern accent, and grinned.

"Why should I be making predictions?" I was annoyed by his presumption, his job, his face, his similarity to me.

"In this country, one never knows," he smiled.

The hotel director approached us and greeted us in perfect English. "Good afternoon. Welcome to the Victoria. How are you, Mr. James? Are these the two gentlemen?" He took us over to the desk and leafed through the ledger. "Messieurs Harris and Miller, we hope you enjoy your stay here." He called a bellboy to take our bags up. We remained in the lobby for another fifteen minutes, engaged in small talk with whoever happened by. I tried to look over the girls very discreetly. But to my surprise, all I saw were drunks. Practically all the local population was drunk. I wondered whether the other tourists in the lobby were aware of this. "Is it always like this?" I asked the director.

"Unfortunately, yes. In Poland we don't have much entertainment, so everybody drinks. It makes them happy, or at least anesthetizes them. Besides, it doesn't bother the government."

Leaving the lobby, I stopped to admire two stunning blondes emerging from the elevator banks. I felt Harris push me. "Come on. Business first, pleasure later."

I shrugged. We took the elevator to the fifth floor. A woman showed us to our rooms. I settled in and washed, shaved and changed clothes. Then there was a knock at my door. I responded by inviting them to come in.

I expected Harris, but two men entered my room. They both looked very morose.

"John Miller. Come with us."

"Why?"

"You want to see Comrade Winarski? We shall take you to him."

"Right." I hurried into my jacket, checked my papers and money and left with the men.

In the hall I found Harris waiting with two similarly dressed men.

"Hey Johnny, what's going on?" he shouted. He seemed worried.

"We're going to see Comrade Winarski, Ted's Communist teacher back in the Warsaw ghetto," I reassured him.

A black Russian Zil was waiting for us outside the hotel. We drove for twenty minutes and stopped in front of a large drab building. It looked like every great hall of Communist bureaucracy. Three entrances and military guards everywhere were its only distinguishing features. My stomach began to act strangely. It does that sometimes when things aren't strictly kosher. It was that street name, Rakowiecka. Although I couldn't place it right off-hand, it seemed like it was among the top five on my places-to-avoid list.

"This Winarski is rather well-protected," Dave remarked as we exited the car.

"You can say that again." There was nothing I could do to reassure him now. The anxiety had struck me too.

We were escorted through the middle entrance into a big lobby with a thick, red carpet. The escorts motioned for us to sit down in a couple of overstuffed chairs.

There were lots of well-dressed, morose-looking people milling around. In fact, it seemed that the place was in mourning for someone. Soon after we were seated, a Polish major approached me. "Mr. John Miller? Come with me, please."

"What about Mr. Harris? We're together."

"You'll see him later. We have something very important to tell you."

I followed him through a maze of corridors. We finally came to a spacious, well-decorated room. "Please sit down. Comrade Winarski will be with you in a moment."

As the major was about to leave, I asked, "Who died?"

"Why do you ask such a question?" he replied.

"Everybody is so morose. I can't understand it."

He said nothing and left the room.

In the middle of the room was a table on which I saw a bottle of whiskey and a bottle of vodka. There were two glasses. I poured myself a whiskey and toasted my imaginary host. I sipped the alcohol and looked around the room. There were a lot of books, mostly in Russian and Polish. One or two American magazines littered a newspaper rack. Fear began to take hold of my senses. "Funny," I mused, "Harris was always tagging along behind me, and now, when I really want him here, what happens …"

My drink was two-thirds finished when a dour-looking captain entered. "Please follow me." He ushered me through another door, and we entered a bigger room where two male secretaries sat on either side of an imitation oak desk. There was an empty chair in front of it. The captain motioned for me to sit down.

"Before you see Comrade Winarski, we'd like to ask you a few questions."

"Sure. Shoot."

"Do you work for the CIA?"

"No. Why do you ask that? I thought you knew why we were coming and approved."

"You are right. But there are a few things that bother us. If you give us your complete cooperation, you'll be able to carry on here and still have time to see our beautiful city," the captain smiled.

"You better get a move on. World War Three won't wait," I commented sarcastically.

He ignored my statement. "Mr. Miller, we know that you were once an agent for the OSS."

"That's right. During the war."

"You were captured and then rescued by the Russians."

"Right again."

"After the war, you were transferred to CID."

"Yes, CID … not CIA," I emphasized.

"Now, Mr. Miller, you are as aware as we that OSS became the CIA. Do you still deny that you work for the CIA?"

"Dammit! I worked for the OSS before it was the CIA. Now I work for the Narcotics Bureau. I'm here on a special case. I've come to talk to Winarski about a man he knew, someone involved in the Berisov affair. Winarski's testimony might help us discover something about the murderer's intentions."

"Yes, I know all that. But in addition, we received a message that you've come to spy in Poland," the captain said bluntly.

I tried to laugh but it wasn't natural. The looking-glass war is about to begin, I thought to myself. "I did not come here to spy. I came to see Comrade Winarski."

"Do you deny that you are a CIA agent?"

"Of course."

"Mr. Miller, you are in Eastern Europe, in a civilized country. Have a cigarette. And another drink."

I accepted both.

"We know a lot about you. An awful lot about you. For instance, we know you came here on a job for the CIA and that your meeting with Comrade Winarski is altogether secondary – a pretense as you call it. You'd better tell me what your real mission is or otherwise ... I don't have to draw a picture for you, do I?" The captain paused and drew a long whiff of his own cigarette. "Your anti-Communist propaganda should have told you something of our methods. Did you know that we can make a man confess to anything we want? I don't like brutality, though, especially when it concerns a man of your ability and reputation."

"I have nothing to say."

"Thank you, Mr. Miller." He turned and whispered something in Polish to one of the other men. The man took his cue and left. He returned shortly thereafter with two armed guards. They muscled me out of the room and into a cell.

I sat there three hours until the captain came back with two thugs. This time he wasn't smiling. "Miller, we don't have much time."

"You're right. Wars don't wait for this type of nonsense."

"That doesn't matter. I want you to tell me that you came to our country to spy. I want to know what you're after," he shouted.

"How many times do I have to say it? I did not come here to spy."

One of the thugs cocked his arm and punched me in the stomach. The other gave me a judo chop on the back of the neck. I fell to the floor. "Stop that!" shouted the captain. "The chief doesn't want any marks on his body."

"Very thoughtful of the chief," I remarked as I picked myself up. My stomach was cramped, and my head felt like it didn't belong to me.

"We can keep you here for a very long time. Nobody will know. No one will ever question. Ten, twenty years perhaps. It's a long time. So why not cooperate?"

"I can't tell you any more than I've told you already. But I'd like to get in touch with the American Embassy."

The two men moved toward me threateningly.

"No marks on his body," commanded the captain. "He has to die a natural death." One gorilla grabbed me and pulled me off the cot. The captain said something to him, and he tightened his grip. As I turned my attention to the captain, he opened his pants and pissed in my face.

"You see," he laughed, "one can humiliate a man without leaving marks on his body. You will receive the same treatment every half hour or as often as one of my men has to relieve himself." They left the cell.

I was furious. Somebody had fucked up. But where? And who?

In another twenty minutes the captain opened the door. I braced myself for what I thought would be round two.

"Your friend, Harris," he announced, is just as tough as you are, but we know that he isn't involved." The captain and the two guards led me to the basement and finally pushed me against a door with a small window in it. I saw three men, their hands tied behind their backs. They were standing in front of two executioners who held pistols. One of these prisoners was Harris.

"Well, Miller?" came the inevitable proposition.

"I can't tell you more than I already have."

The shooting started and the first man went down. Then the second man fell to his knees, blood gushing from his chest.

"If you don't tell us what we want to know, we'll shoot your friend next. Perhaps he's innocent but it will remind you of what will be your fate if you refuse to cooperate."

"My friend!" I laughed. "Shoot the fucking bastard. I can't tell you what I don't know."

I heard the shot and watched Harris fall. My ambivalence aside, there was no time to mourn for him. My turn was next. They didn't give me much time to think about it. I was dragged back to the cell by my feet. Once there, they held me down while another guard came in and pissed in my face.

About a half hour later, the captain arrived with two new guards. "On your feet," he ordered.

"Come on," echoed one of the others in an accent.

"Where are you taking me?"

"To be shot," the other said matter-of-factly.

"I thought you were going to keep me in jail for twenty years," I snarled at him.

"No jokes please," he said dryly. They took me back to the same basement room and I found myself standing where Harris had faced the executioners. The same trigger-happy vanguards of the proletariat were still there. I felt the bullet as if it were already in my neck.

After all that had happened to me, I thought this was a foolish, stupid way to die. After all the situations I had squirmed my way out of with words or cunning. Something told me to keep my mouth shut this time. The guards approached me. Then someone shouted an order in Polish.

I tried to believe they were bluffing. I remembered the captain's orders that I was to die a natural death, and one never knows what kind of tactics they'll use to get a man to make a false confession.

They aimed at me. My thoughts waved goodbye to life, saluted all the girls I had ever fucked, kissed off that fat bank account I had never touched.

A voice interrupted my personal last rites, saying, "You're lucky. I received orders not to kill you today." It was the captain. I still wasn't sure whether he was taunting me or not until they took me back to another interrogation room. The major who had originally greeted me in this dungeon was there.

"I must congratulate you, Mr. Miller. You are a very tough bourgeois. Had you been here longer we would have taken the opportunity to demonstrate our more radical methods employed to break people. It's a shame." He moved closer to my face. His breath stunk from dark tobacco. "There's no use in denying it. We know everything about you. OSS service ..."

"You said that before," I sniped at him.

"CID," he continued mechanically.

"It's all in the records. You know, I know. What's the point?"

"And is Monsieur Lucini Spaggiari in the records?"

My heart jumped. "No. I don't think so."

"Is your deal with him in the records? The deal concerning the housing construction contracts for the American NATO staff. Or the American officer you blackmailed?"

How did these bastards know about that?

"This Spaggiari was very helpful, wasn't he? The names of AWOLs. Location of stolen goods. That was very nice of you to procure Army surplus contracts for him."

These gorillas were smart. They were aware that even the Americans knew nothing about such deals.

"Years later when you began your new career with the Narcotics Bureau, Monsieur Lucini came to you with another proposition ..."

"You know so much. Tell me about it."

"You smuggled heroin to the United States for him. As a narcotics agent, it was a child's game, wasn't it?"

It was true, but how did they know?

"The Credit Suisse Bank in Geneva has a balance of three million dollars in account number 1256-8YZ-917. That's your account, isn't it, Mr. Miller? We're no longer asking you to confess."

"That's a relief. I hate to repeat myself."

"Taking heroin back to the United States for him now will be trouble for you. If you refuse to cooperate, we'll inform the Americans. I'm quite sure that will not please you."

"What do you want?"

"We'll let you know later."

Turning to two guards, he commanded them to return me to my cell.

I sat down on the cot and stared at the wall like a convict in a B-movie. Everything they had said was true. After the war, my Presidential Medal in hand, my uncle had offered me a position in his factory. I had refused, I couldn't picture myself as a businessman in a three-piece suit. Neither could I continue with my family, who had become distant and lacked the capacity to soothe the wounds I had suffered in Europe. America itself was an indifferent heap of faceless people.

I ended up in New York and made the rounds of the bars in Times Square. In one crowded place, I stayed for too long one night. I was hanging onto the edge of the bar, lost in an alcoholic daze when someone had said, "Hey fella, watch it. I didn't pay for my drink to have you spill it."

I looked at the man. He was about six-four and two hundred fifty pounds, a side of beef right off the hook of a packing plant.

"I didn't spill your fucking drink," I screamed belligerently.

He pushed me.

"Look," I tried to cope with his anger, "all I want to do is stay here quietly and have a few more drinks. So why don't you just go back and sit with your friend."

I turned away and started to make light of the incident with a guy on the other side of me. Suddenly the big guy's elbow shot out, hitting my arm and spilling my drink. I pushed back. He swung around, hit me and almost knocked me down. I picked up a beer bottle and hit him over the shoulder. Just as he was about to land a right hook to my nose, a man grabbed his arm, pulled him back and whispered something into his ear. My assailant's eyes narrowed, and his face grew taut. He bared his teeth and breathed heavily. I braced myself for the blow that was sure to follow.

"I don't fucking give a goddamn if he is a hero. I'm gonna show him that just because the President pins a medal on him, he can't throw his weight around."

The next punch missed my head by inches, and then he lunged forward. We grappled in a wrestling hold and fell to the floor, dragging four other bystanders with us. His arms wrapped around my neck and flipped me onto my back, pinning my shoulders to the ground. I gasped for breath and heard the faint whine of police sirens.

We were arrested and taken to the precinct. Most of the detectives recognized me and took me to see the captain. He shook my hand and congratulated me. "Miller, we're going to keep you in a cell overnight. Just until you sober up. I wouldn't like to see you in more serious trouble."

"But I didn't do anything," I protested. "I was standing in the bar drinking and this big punk came over and started in on me. Everybody wants to take a swing at a hero. God knows why!"

"Why don't you go to another town?" suggested the captain.

"I'd like to, but where? My face is known all over the country. I can run into assholes like him anywhere I go."

"Perhaps you should reenlist and return to Europe. You did a lot of good over there. They'll pay you more respect." He tried to be genuinely helpful.

"I never thought of that." I hadn't, in fact.

The next day, my face was plastered all over the newspapers: WAR HERO IN BARROOM BRAWL. It got so bad I couldn't even eat quietly in a restaurant. I sank into a depression. I didn't want to return to my family. I simply wanted out of all that mess. I didn't even want to be a hero anymore. I wanted to be Johnny Miller ... myself. I wanted a normal life, whatever that was.

Following the captain's advice, I contacted my old unit. Unfortunately, they told me that they were creating a new task force and if they needed me, they'd get in touch. The only thing left was to reenlist. I was sent to CID in Frankfurt.

Germany was a vacation. I did as little as possible. Now and then I arrested a few black marketeers. In 1949, when NATO was formed, I was transferred to Paris. A month after installing myself there, I ran into Lucini at one of our old haunts that still operated.

"Hey, Johnny! What are you doing here? Back in the service?" he guessed right.

"Yeah. By the way, where's Maria?" I asked hopefully.

"She died during the last days of the war." His voice quavered. "Germans."

We mourned Maria for several moments. My face and eyes burned as if I were crying, but no tears fell. We downed a few more shots in silence, afraid that words would break the shimmering portrait of a woman, superlative to others by her exquisite beauty. Her image flickered in my mind's eye. It was not the alcohol playing tricks of sentimentality. I felt true remorse. A friend had disappeared.

"What are you doing these days? Still pimping?" I shifted the topic.

"On the side," admitted Lucini. He wanted to tell me about what had been happening since I had last seen him. At that moment, I had to return to my office. We planned to meet again for dinner.

By the time dinner was over, we knew everything that had happened to each other up to the present. Lucini let slip that he had a proposition for me. He hesitated to reveal any details because he wanted to work out the entire plan beforehand. We parted and arranged to see each other the following week.

Our business meeting fell on a Saturday. Lucini and I met in the Tuileries. After a quick stroll around the Orangerie, we found a free bench by one of the fountains. "Look, Johnny, NATO is going to give us a lot of scope in housing construction. The markets in Paris, Evreux, and Châteauroux are going to be thrown wide open. To certain people, that is. I want to be one of those individuals. If you can arrange a contract for me, there'll be a percentage for you."

Suddenly, he switched the subject. We continued talking about everything under the sun except the proposition. Before we separated, I told him that I'd call him when I had thought it over.

All that night, I debated the pros and cons of his offer. The money part was particularly attractive. During the war, my relatives had made money. Everybody back in the States was rich. All I had to show was that stinking medal. It was worthless. My war profits came to a total of that stupid medal, which I didn't even deserve, and shitty nouveau riche relatives who couldn't do a damn thing for me. I needed more money. I realized I would not stay young forever, and I didn't enjoy the prospect of working like a dog for the rest of my life only to survive. Washed-up soldiers littered the social landscape everywhere. But if I could wrangle a contract ...

Twelve days later, I called Lucini and invited him to have an aperitif with me. We met in a little café on rue Jacob near the Ecole des Beaux Arts. The sun was shining but we went inside where it was empty except for a couple of fossilized alcoholics in the corner.

The waiter approached us. "What will you have?" he demanded in English with a German accent. We ordered two whiskeys and he returned almost instantaneously. He seemed like the nervous type. I paid him no further attention and turned to Lucini. "Listen, I may be able to help you."

"What do you have in mind?" he asked eagerly.

"I want them to remember me when I leave CID. I'd like to be known as the best investigator they've had. You can help by giving me tips – AWOLs, small-time hoods, hot stuff."

"It is done," Lucini smiled without even deliberating the counteroffer.

"Okay, now I can't say that I can get you a contract tomorrow," I began slowly, "but you'll get it." I just needed a little time to contrive a watertight plan.

Lucini made my work with CID easy. He spread the word that I was OK. I made the rounds at bars in Pigalle. I struck up acquaintances with the pimps and the whores who gave me information readily. I recovered a lot of stolen property, and after six months I had what I wanted, the reputation of being one of the best American agents. Now it was my turn to arrange the other half of the bargain.

An American captain named Johnson was chief of the Contracts and Development Section. I had been watching him closely since I had decided to play ball with Lucini. He lived in a nice home in Neuilly with his American wife. He also had a charming French mistress whom he had set up in an apartment on the Left Bank. I knew that he couldn't afford all that sexy activity on his Army pay. There was no concrete evidence, but I was sure he was getting kickbacks for the contracts.

I approached him and laid my cards on the table without revealing what I knew about his personal life. He was curious enough to invite me to his apartment the following day. I was greeted at the door and conducted into the living room. "Sit down, Miller. Have a drink?"

"No sir, not while I'm on duty," I pretended.

"You're on duty? Now?" he seemed surprised.

"Yes, sir."

"What can I do for you?" He was definitely uneasy.

"Like I told you yesterday, we have a file on you."

"What kind?" He grew nervous, gripping the arm of his chair.

"You get kickbacks on those contracts," I stated coolly.

"That's a lie," he insisted vehemently.

"Is it?" I looked at the picture of a woman in the mantlepiece. "Is that your wife?"

"Yes."

"Very pretty." Then I took a picture out of my pocket. "This is my girlfriend." I handed him a photo of his French babe. He took one look and turned pale. It almost looked like he was going to puke on the carpet. "Something wrong, Captain?"

"How? Where?" he stuttered.

"That sable coat that Lucienne's been wearing and her Jaguar, both must cost plenty of francs. And to keep that lavish apartment on rue de Tournon near the Senate. It must break your balls, Captain Johnson." I stared at the floor and acted somewhat embarrassed. "I don't want to cause any hard feelings between you two. Naturally, she isn't my girlfriend. I just acted like a tourist and asked her to pose for me one day. She wouldn't even remember me. Anyway, I couldn't afford Lucienne on my pay. And down at the office, they're wondering just how you manage to do it on your Army pay."

Johnson looked really worried.

"What do you want, Miller?"

"Sir, you've been indulging in some rather questionable activities. I know why. What I want to know is how?"

"Miller," he tried to act convincing, "what's wrong with trying to make an extra buck? I don't want you to think I'm confessing but try to put yourself in my place."

"I'm trying, sir," I stated truthfully.

"So, you do understand."

"I'm not sure."

"Miller, maybe we can reach an understanding," he said seriously.

"Sir?" I raised my eyebrow.

"You have a lot of contacts, a lot of friends. Perhaps some of them are in the construction business?"

"I have an old war acquaintance who does that kind of work," I tried to sound as innocent as possible.

"What's his name, if I may ask?"

"Lucini Spaggiari."

"Tell him to bring his dossier to my office. I'll see what I can do for him."

"That's very kind of you, sir. I'll tell him what you said."

"Now about your investigation?"

"What investigation?"

He laughed. "Miller, how about that drink now?"

"No. No thank you, sir. I'm very particular about the people I drink with."

I left Johnson and went to see Lucini immediately.

In another ten days, Lucini's bid was accepted. He invited me to celebrate at the restaurant in the George V Hotel.

"Well done, Johnny boy. We'll split everything fifty-fifty. There's plenty for both of us. We're going to be rich."

All the money I made with Lucini I invested in an account in Geneva. It gave high-yield dividends that I reinvested every six months. Lucini had warned me to be absolutely discreet. I played it straight and did not live extravagantly, sticking to my job and creating the impression that I was just an honest but poor worker.

In 1958, when De Gaulle came back to power, Lucini contacted me. "Johnny, things are going to change soon."

"What are you talking about?" I didn't really understand French politics at that time. I was complacent and getting rich.

"De Gaulle hates America. He'll kick you out the first chance he gets. No more contracts. No more bases. We'll have to find a new way to make money. It's about time you put in for a transfer," he counseled. "In two years, you'll be eligible for retirement and a pension."

"What do you suggest, Lucini?"

"If we ran dope, we'd make a fortune ..."

I wasn't against breaking a few laws, but I could not think of a guaranteed way to do it.

"Simple," proposed Lucini. "Try to get a job with the Bureau of Narcotics in the Treasury Department. I'll set you up, and they won't be able to refuse you a job. You'll be instrumental in nailing a big smuggler. You'll prove that you know a lot about the business and it's probable they'll hire you. From now on though, you'll have to watch your contacts because they'll do a very thorough investigation on you."

I requested a transfer for 1961. Then I went to some friends, asking to borrow money, telling them that a girlfriend was pregnant and wanted to have an abortion. This was to create an atmosphere, according to Lucini. I played the role, repaying the money in installments commensurate with my salary and what I could spare. The report was excellent, but I didn't get a job at Treasury.

On my leave I went to Washington. I discussed the transfer with the head of Personnel at Treasury. "I'm sorry, Mr. Miller. We would love to have you with us, but ..."

"I understand. Listen, I've run across a few things while I was in Paris. Maybe I could help you just the same."

"Such as?"

"I know one of the routes used for dope smuggling."

"Oh? I'm going to send you upstairs to Nickerson at the Bureau of Narcotics."

I made my report to Nickerson and the follow-up was successful. A bust was made at the harbor in Red Hook. But still no job at Treasury. I was sent back to Paris with CID. Lucini wasn't upset. "We can wait. This is a long-term deal with a big pot of gold at the end. You'll be with them eventually. They're just waiting and checking you out. Just keep your nose clean no matter how long it takes."

I continued to live off my salary and kept straight for several years. I didn't touch my Swiss money and even transferred it into a safety deposit so they couldn't trail me to Geneva when I would have had to renew the old investment. Everything went cool. I worked, I sweated and drank and fucked. Now and then, Lucini forwarded me a big tip. Sometimes they turned out to be real leads and a bust was made. Other times they were false. "You can't look too good," advised Lucini.

Finally, things clicked. In '66 they took me on at BN[22]. Almost immediately I used another one of Lucini's tips to score big just to show them that I was worth the effort.

There was only one man in the section who didn't like me. It was my boss Wilson. He watched me suspiciously.

"What bugs you about me, Wilson?" I asked one day.

"You're too good. You're too goddamn good," he replied nervously.

"Everyone can't be as inept as you," I joked. "Anyway, if there's a chink in the armor, Wilson, please show it to me."

"I will, Miller. One day I will."

After working in Washington for a year, I was sent back to Paris to work as the liaison man with INTERPOL. I made two or three arrests, some without any help from Lucini, who thought that the time had now come to move. I told him about my trouble with Wilson.

"He's bluffing, Johnny. Just a jealous character. If he's as inept as you say, he'll never have time to put someone on you. Any trouble and we'll take care of him. Don't fucking worry."

The next time I returned to the States, I imported twenty pounds of heroin. Everything went smoothly. My bank account grew steadily, but I still couldn't spend a penny of it.

Wilson was annoyed by my success. "You travel too much, Miller. You'd better stay home for now."

I agreed, but some big-timer upstairs thought otherwise and after a year countermanded Wilson's order. I got to go to France again. The same seesaw game continued until '78 when some politicians got the idea that terrorists were financing their activities with dope money. I was brought back to the States permanently and put on the anti-terrorist squad as the narcotics specialist. First, I conducted seminars at Quantico. Then I worked with the Oakland Police for a few months, and then they recalled me to Washington and assigned me to that job in Watertown, which led me to New York and New Jersey. The Berisov murder stopped everything.

I was walking back and forth in my cell, thinking about my past and about how efficient they were, the Polish agents. I wondered how they'd found out so much. Who told them? Captain Johnson? Lucini? It could have been anybody.

I was lapsing into boredom when the major came into my cell. His attitude had changed. He became affable and asked if there was anything I needed. I told him that I wanted to get in touch with the Embassy. He acted as if he had not heard that request. "Would you like to wash and change your clothes?" he suggested. "We brought your things from the hotel." He led me to a bathroom.

After I'd finished, I was taken to a very large office. "You will now meet the Director of Internal Security," announced the major.

A few minutes later, a general entered the room and introduced himself. "Mr. Miller, I apologize for what has happened. It was all a misunderstanding. Can you excuse our error?"

"Why did you shoot Harris?" I asked. "That misunderstanding won't protect you from the American authorities. You'll have to answer for that."

"Don't worry about Mr. Harris," said the general. "He'll be here in a moment. Alive. It was, unfortunately, one of the captain's favorite little games."

He fell silent, the door opened, and Harris was ushered in. He looked at me and went pale. I guess I went pale myself at seeing him alive. A torrent of questions rushed through my mind, but I couldn't talk to him in front of the others.

"Gentlemen," the general continued, "you must understand that a mistake sometimes happens in a profession like ours. But this one was really outrageous. Both the major and the captain will be reprimanded."

"Sir," I interrupted, "it isn't the treatment that bothers us at the moment. We have a job that must be completed as soon as possible. We would like to meet Comrade Winarski. That is the reason for our mission, the only reason, as we have insisted all along."

He bowed stiffly. "Don't worry. You'll see him. Is there anything else I can do for you?"

"That's all. Let us see Comrade Winarski."

"We'll make sure that reparations are made for the way you have been mistreated."

Was he really trying to excuse our beatings as an honest mistake? And now that it was over, they were going to make things right! I didn't believe it for a second. They had plenty of dirt on me and wanted to make a statement about the hypocrisy of America's much-hyped moral authority.

"We want to show you that we have justice in Socialist Poland." Then he said something to another aide in Polish. He left and returned with that son-of-a-bitch who had pissed in my face.

The general addressed him. "Captain, you have committed a grave error. Honor your debts according to the just, social laws of the Workers' Republic of Poland. Right the wrong you have rendered to these two American ambassadors who journeyed to our country without malicious intentions." He turned to me. "Do you want to see the execution?"

"No. It's not necessary. If you permit me, I'd like to handle it the way we do in the States." Then I turned to the captain and hit him with all my might in the stomach and followed that blow with a rabbit punch to his neck. Finally, I kicked him in the balls. He lay on the floor groaning with pain.

"Is that all?" asked the general incredulously.

"Well, if you want to shoot him, that's your affair. Can we leave now?" I suggested. Looking over at Harris, I knew damn well that nothing would happen to the captain after we left. All that "honor your debt" and "two American ambassadors" crap was strictly for show. It was right out of a cheap nineteenth-century novel. I almost laughed.

"Yes, you may leave. But you will stay in our country until tomorrow.

Why don't you have a look around our city. Warsaw is exceptionally beautiful this time of year. I'll give you one of my best lieutenants to act as a guide. He'll take you to see Comrade Winarski." He called in a young man. The lieutenant reminded me of Ted the first time we had met. "He will take you anywhere you desire. And you have my word that nothing unpleasant will happen to you again. Would you care for a drink before leaving? Cognac? Vodka?"

I accepted and so did Harris. "To the friendship of Poland and America. We haven't forgotten that you contributed to the destruction of our common enemy, the Third Reich."

I wasn't listening to any of his bullshit. I was enjoying my drink. I certainly needed it! When we were leaving, the general stopped me. "Oh, as a matter of record, in view of your illegal detention, the Polish government offers you an official apology. You will see that it carries my signature." He handed me a paper and extended his hand.

Apology, I thought? Communist governments never apologize for anything. They always rewrite the past so they look like they never made a mistake. This was strange. I was infuriated at this charade and wanted to punch his gut too, when suddenly Donaldson's words swept through my dry mind, "Somebody will shake your hand." I flashed back to the acidic exchange with Donaldson in the cavernous Chinatown parking garage. He had ambushed me there after the joint intelligence briefing about the assassination. He had refused to bargain over this mysterious errand and even threatened violence. An image of the old security guard lurking down there with his Doberman was etched in my mind like the deepest, darkest black hole.

I shook his hand firmly.

I began to wonder. Was the general our mole? Or was he unaware that there might be a microdot attached to that piece of paper? Had our arrest been real or simply a ruse? I thought about Donaldson's reaction when he would learn their methods of operation. I folded the paper and carefully placed it in my pocket.

"Oh, yes. One more thing," the general continued. "Your friend Harris, he confessed to all the crimes. It's very embarrassing, but you are familiar with our methods of interrogation by now. Here's the confession. You can tear it up."

Once outside I lit into Harris. "You big G-man," I sneered. "You confessed. Why the hell did you do that? And how come you're alive? I saw you shot with my own eyes. How do you explain that?"

Harris turned red and put on a big show of being a pal. "They put pressure on me in order to put pressure on you. They ordered me to simulate the execution by taking a dive when the shots were fired. And I honestly believed that maybe I was saving your life." He gave me a sickly smile. "But it was all a bluff. We weren't in danger of being killed at any time."

I laughed. "Harris, what I'm going to say may make you mad, but even when I saw you in front of the firing squad, I didn't confess."

"You bastard," he mumbled.

"Yes, I'm a mother-fucking bastard," I said. "You're so pure and clean. You're just Elliot Ness and you always will be."

Chapter 16. Winarski's Adam

We left the "Great Hall of the People" without any further difficulty and traversed Warsaw in a government car. We were finally on our way to see Winarski. We stopped in front of a small frame house in a Warsaw suburb. It was a very modest house for such an important Communist official. The lieutenant ushered us to the front door but bade us to knock on it ourselves. A man opened it, acknowledged the lieutenant, who saluted, turned and went back to the car.

The man escorted us into a study that was filled with books, stuffed with papers and overcrowded with empty cigarette packages. It reminded me of Max's place, but he was a congenital slob. In this case, I got the feeling of deliberate modesty, perhaps to inspire the "little people."

Winarski came in. He looked about seventy-five years old, even older. He spoke English. "I heard about what happened. I'm sorry," he apologized.

"You knew about it?" I ventured.

"Yes, I was aware of what was going on," he said.

"Why did it happen?" Harris demanded.

"I'm the only Jewish member of the Politburo. Because of the Israel situation, I'm in disgrace. I realized that you would be taken for Zionist spies if you approached me. Anyway, my disgrace was temporary. I assured them that I'm a better Communist than a Jew. On the other hand, they still need me. They need at least one Jew in the government to show that they aren't prejudiced. I apologize for the rude treatment you received. The Security Ministry operates independently of the Party with minimal oversight. Mistakes happen, but now that it's over, I'm at your service. If I can answer any questions, I shall. I want to cooperate because I want peace. Most of us in socialist countries want peace."

"Comrade Winarski," I addressed him respectfully, "you know of the Berisov assassination. I have been assigned to the affair. Sources we have in our possession indicate that you knew the murderer when he was a young man."

"Did I?" pondered Winarski.

"Yes. We have a declaration from an informant stating that the suspected murderer knew you. You were his teacher in school at Lodz and then in the Warsaw Ghetto. Do you remember this man?"

I pulled out the picture and passed it to him. "What name did you know him by?" I asked as he scrutinized the photo. He stared for several seconds and mumbled in Polish. By the tone it must have meant, "I'll be damned."

"Yes, I remember him. His name is Adam Polanski. I was his teacher from '36 to '38. I was in charge of a class in a Polish school. I remember him very well."

"Why?"

"Because he was different. He was the youngest boy in the class and an excellent student. His marks were the best. What always worried me was his antisocial behavior."

"What do you mean by 'antisocial'? Non-communist?" asked the ever-inquisitive Harris.

"No. Not at all. I have to admit that I was always a communist. I came from a poor Jewish family and the misery of the class differences around me shaped my mind from childhood. It made it much easier for me to accept Marxism because it seemed to be a path to social justice. Although I am Jewish, I managed to attend a Polish school and university. The Party helped me to do that. It displeased my parents who wanted to see me become a good Jew. They could never understand my ideas and dreams. I studied political science and sociology at the university and eventually became a professor at the Catholic gymnasium in Lodz. All the while, the Party concealed my Judaism for my own benefit.

"Adam, yes, back to Adam. He made a very bad impression on me because he was always against everyone in the class. I remember in '37 when we organized a dance party with boys and girls, he came to see me and declared, 'I'm not coming to the dance.'

"'Why not?' I asked him.

"'It's unclean. It's with boys and girls.'

"'Why is it unclean, Adam?'

"'My mother told me it is unclean.'

"'I'd like to talk to your mother. Have her come to see me.'

"I waited and kept an eye on him. He was between a year and eighteen months younger than the rest of the boys. I thought that he felt that way because around twelve years old, boys are becoming sexually mature. They start to notice girls. Perhaps he didn't feel anything yet. Understand, gentlemen, this is my personal opinion.

"I met his mother at the next parents' meeting. 'Countess Polanska, your son is very antisocial,' I explained.

"'What do you mean by antisocial?' she answered indignantly.

"'Well, he doesn't want to play with the other boys. He's always by himself. We are organizing a party. He is against it, the only one against it.'

"'I'm glad,' she said, and swept her head up in pride. 'He doesn't have to play with those dirty boys, and I don't want you to push him into it. My son is the image of his father. He is very clean, and I want him to stay clean.'

"'Tell me about his father,' I asked her.

"'His father was a Count and a Colonel in the army. Adam never knew him because he died of a heart attack when Adam was only four. Nevertheless, I always tried to develop his character the way my husband would have wanted it, noble. His father was a doctor. I'd like for Adam to become a doctor too. But I do not want him playing with those dirty boys in school. I don't want him to learn their bad habits.'

"I tried to defend the school, but it was hopeless. Adam was strange.

When he got involved in a fight, he would come crying to me, 'Teacher, those boys beat me.' He complained in an infantile manner that was strictly out of step with his level of intellectual maturity. Frankly it surprised me. No boy had ever registered a similar complaint before.

"'Adam, can't you defend yourself?'

"'Yes, I would if they were my equals, but they aren't. They're just dirty nasty boys.'

"'Why do you say that?'

"'My mother told me that everybody in the school is dirty and nasty.'

"'And you always believe what your mother says?'

"'Yes, sir.'

"'Why?' I asked.

"'Because she's always right,' he answered firmly.

"His attitude didn't change very much until '39, and then it changed for the worse. I tried to check her influence on him as best I could, but he was completely under his mother's thumb. There was nothing I could do.

"Then in '39 I left Lodz and went to Warsaw. When they closed off the ghetto, the Party decided it was important to continue teaching youngsters and sent me inside. I was surprised to see Adam in one of the little groups organized by the elders to continue the children's education. At that point, he was about fourteen.

"'Teacher! You're Jewish?' he questioned with an astonished look and a gaping jaw.

"'I didn't know you were Jewish either.' I turned his surprise into a friendly greeting.

"'My mother is Jewish.'

"'Oh? Is she here? Still following her advice?'

"'Yes, but I'll listen to you too, teacher.'

"I observed him in my small group of six boys. His grades were bad. He was indifferent to school. I asked him why he was not taking advantage of the opportunity to learn.

"'What for?' he replied. 'We're going to die.'

"When I think back to that young man's comment, I am still shocked by the lucidity of his premonition. During that year, even the adults in the ghetto had no inkling of the total death and destruction that was to come. Today it is easier to look back. While all the other boys were discussing the future, he was all alone and constantly daydreaming. I guess he had a feeling the others didn't.

"Hunger was the biggest plague in the ghetto. Every morning when you came down into the streets, there were more emaciated corpses. Every day, hundreds of bodies, dead or dying, were put into the street. The boy seemed fairly well fed. 'How do you and your mother manage?' I asked him one day after class.

"'My mother sells her jewelry to buy food,' he answered honestly.

"'What do you feel when you see all those dead bodies on the street?'

"'Nothing, sir.'

"'Nothing? You're indifferent to those poor souls and their suffering families? Would you share your food with someone who is dying and wants some food?'

"'No, sir.'

"'Why not?'

"'Why should I? They're going to die anyway. If I share my meal with someone, I'll have less. And it won't do him any good. Why should I? I have nothing to do with these people who are dying on the street.'

"'But they're your people.'

"'No sir, they are not. My mother is Jewish. I didn't know that until we moved to Warsaw. As soon as the war started, we had to move, so naturally I stayed with my mother. But I don't feel close to these people.'

"'But you are a part of them, and they are a part of you.' I tried to appeal to his logic rather than his moral code.

"'I realize that,' he conceded. 'If I weren't, I wouldn't be in this situation. But I still don't have any feeling for them.'

"Later, when things started to get really bad, I suggested to some of the boys that we organize a resistance group. All of them were excited.

"'Yes, defense is the only solution,' someone commented. 'But where do we get guns?'

"'There is a way. Would you like to fight and perhaps die in the ghetto defending the others?'

"'Yes. Why not?' came another response.

"'What about you, Adam? Why are you so silent?'

"'I was just thinking, teacher.'

"'Too late for that. Tomorrow you may be deported or dead. You must decide now.'

"'I'm going over the wall. I have nothing to do here.'

"'What? And leave your mother?'

"'Teacher, my family is going to die. If I stay here, I'll die with them. And I don't want to die. Everybody tells me I have a good face. You can see for yourself, my blond hair and blue eyes. I don't belong here. Why should I fight for people who are nothing to me? I'll go over the wall.'

"'You're really going to leave your mother?'

"After some hesitation, he said, 'Yes, I am.'

"'I remember when you were at school. Everything your mother said was holy to you. Why are you leaving her now?'

"'She lied to me, teacher. She lied to me. Can you help me?'

"'I'd like to, but I don't know how.'

"'I'll go to Max then. He's never failed me. I'll see you later.'

"By early 1943 the Germans' intention to destroy the ghetto was apparent. We Communists had organized an armed militia inside and were prepared to strike at a moment's notice. Naturally we coordinated our defenses with the non-Communist ghetto resistors and also the Party cells beyond the wall in greater Warsaw. On the 18th of January, we engaged the Germans for the first time. Skirmishes continued through the winter and early spring. We became adept at urban guerilla tactics such as picking off small SS patrols and then vanishing. With the April uprising, however, we detonated homemade grenades to destroy their vehicles and shot the bastards from the rooftops. Thereafter the conflict rapidly escalated into open warfare, house-to-house fighting, heavy artillery salvos from Nazi tanks, and sporadic sniper fire. After a couple weeks, the ammunitions stockpile was depleted, total annihilation was imminent. Despite the heroism of the united Jewish resistance, everyone realized that it would be a matter of days until we were crushed.

"At that point we received word from our Warsaw comrades that the Party had decided to exfiltrate the remaining Jewish Communists and hide them either in Warsaw or in the forest. Our mission was to defend our people and safeguard our ideals. We had slaughtered scores of Nazis. Our job there was done. I was among the lucky ones who escaped alive.

"I didn't see or hear of Adam until the end of the war. I didn't know what had happened to him. As a matter of fact, I really hadn't thought about him. By August 1944, you see, I was already integrated into a Soviet combat team, which began to advance on Warsaw. But we had been told not to help during the general uprising. The reasons were that the Polish fascists wished to establish a state that would be hostile to the Soviet Union. A pitiful excuse, but we positioned ourselves just beyond the range of German artillery and held back. At the time I felt no sympathy for the people in Warsaw. I was a Communist first, then a Pole, and a Jew. I remembered what they did to me because I was Jewish, and I didn't want to see a fascist government in my country. By January 1945, the entire Red Army advanced on the Eastern Front. That's when we went to Warsaw, which smoldered in ruins. As a well-known activist in the Party, I was given the job of organizing security in the city. The war was still going on.

"It was then that I ran across Adam. I hadn't liked the boy at school, but at this moment I had a warm feeling for someone whom I hadn't seen in a long time and who had survived the hard way like myself. 'Adam, what are you doing here?'

"'I was in the Home Army. Then I hid in one of the villages. Now I'm back in Warsaw. How did you make it?'

"'I came to Warsaw with the Soviet Army. I have a position with the Party now.'

"'Oh.' He seemed interested. 'Can I work with you?'

"I laughed. I couldn't believe it. 'But Adam, you forget that I am a Communist.'

"'So, I could be one too,' he smiled proudly.

"'You, a Communist! You were one of the most bourgeois boys I ever knew. The most selfish, the most hypocritical kid I ever met. How could you accept the rigors of a life as a Communist?'

"'Teacher, it's very simple. Germans hate Jews. Right? Poles hate Jews, right? Germans hate Russians, no?'

"'They do ...'

"'Poles hate Russians, too. Isn't that right? So mathematically speaking, Russians like Jews.'

"'Listen, Adam, things aren't quite that simple. Life isn't mathematics.'

"I don't know why I said that because I had reached the same conclusion in almost the same way when I was Adam's age. I felt I owed him a better explanation. At the time all I could think of was a story about something I'd experienced.

"'Adam, I was a partisan with the Red Army in the Wolna District. One night they parachuted a lot of weapons and advisers. We still depended for the essentials of life on the local population. We harassed the Germans and the Ukrainian Nationalists. One day a group of Jews tried to join us. I was glad. I reported their arrival to my chief, Captain Roczak. He wanted to talk to the men.

"""So, you've finally decided to fight. What have you people been doing until now? Hiding? Working with the Germans to buy a week's worth of life with money? Is this the kind of men you are? We don't need men like you in our unit. You're not Communists, just people who want to survive. I can take on anybody I like, but not your kind. Get out! You helped the Germans when you could. Then they turned against you. I have no reason to help you."

""Aren't you going to take them with us?"

""It's impossible!"

"Why?"

""We aren't fighting this war to save the Jews but to destroy the Nazis. The people in the villages, who give us food, hate Jews. The German propaganda tells them that if you fight for the Jews, you'll die for them. Winarski, you're the only Jew in my unit. We can't let the locals see that we like Jews or that we help and shelter them. As Communists, our first duty is to the Soviet Union and the Party. Our object is to survive and carry on the war against the Germans. We won't survive if they think we support Jewish escapees. It's very unwise for us to have too many Jews in the camp."

"'Adam, I'm a good Communist. There was nothing I could do. I had to agree with Roczak although it broke my heart.'

"'What did you do with them? Kill them?' Adam asked me.

"'No, we didn't, but it would have been better if we had. The Captain was generous. He gave them some food and sent them away. Evidently, they were captured by the Ukrainians because we heard their screams as they were tortured to death the next day. The captain consoled me, telling me it had been for the good of the Party.

"'You see, Adam, this equation of yours isn't as brilliant as you'd imagined. It doesn't apply in all cases. Sometimes two plus two doesn't equal four. Sometimes it equals five, six or something else.'

"He looked very confused. 'But now, what should I do?' he asked.

"'There's still hope if you do what we ask you to do and don't act like an opportunist.'

"'You mean that because you consider me bourgeois, I can never get a job with any responsibility?'

"'Correct, Adam. The Party gives those jobs to people who are known to them as longstanding members or workers or peasant stock. You don't fit the bill.'

"He still wasn't satisfied. 'You know,' he confided, 'the Nazis said I had to die because I was Jewish. Now you push me down because I'm bourgeois. It's not my fault. None of it.'

"'Adam, it's normal for a worker who is born into the proletarian class to be a Communist. The party is for him a means of liberation. But a boy from a bourgeois family could never completely integrate since he would always be welcomed back into the fold of the bourgeoisie. His commitment would lack weight. Communism is the path to freedom for a worker, but I don't think it would work in your case.'

"'But teacher,' he protested, 'I could become a good Communist if I tried. If you could give me a chance.'

"'I think you've talked yourself into an impossibility. You're too young to realize how difficult it would be for you.'

"'You lied to me, teacher. You told me that by serving the cause it would save our lives. But it's just not true. You serve only the cause and never the people.'

"'I didn't lie, Adam. You see, one cannot join the Party by choice. You have to be born into it. Certain people can't enter into it completely or sincerely, and you're one of them. There is one possibility. We seek allies everywhere, but revolutionary values can stem only from a certain type of movement – a social movement that challenges the march of history. This is rather essential to Marxism. This is the reason we tend to distrust intellectual and bourgeois elements like you, who pretend that they want revolution. You people look at revolution from a different angle. You view it abstractly. You can't adhere to our concrete values because they are foreign to you. Regardless of what you do, the ends we set in the Party will be different from those you have.'

"'That's just a different type of racism.'

"'I think we can do something for you, Adam. You stick with me.

Right now, the Party needs Jews. All the Poles hate Russians and Communists, so for the moment we can trust Jews. For how long we don't know. One day the Poles will realize that the Jews are at the top of the Party ladder. That will provoke a new wave of anti-Semitism worse than Hitler's.'

"'Are you predicting the future, teacher?'

"'No. But Marxism is a form of science. I can only think and talk in those terms. It might seem absurd to you at times, but you must understand that the Party is everything to me. The Party cannot make a mistake. During the war we were forced to kill loyal Polish Communists because it was in the interests of the Party. The Party is like the Church, if you understand me.'

"'Yes, sir.'

"'The Party is the new Church.'

"'Teacher, you speak like you believe what you are saying is false.'

"'You're wrong. I am one hundred percent Communist and always will be. But I'll try to do something for you.'

"'I'd like a job with responsibility,' he exclaimed.

"'Not for the moment. We have to watch you. I'll take you on as my office boy.'

"'Maybe you'll ask me to sweep the floor too,' he said sarcastically.

"'Why not?' I replied.

"'Thank you, teacher.' His tone was full of bitterness.

"But it didn't stop there. We received an order to arrest all former Home Army members because they posed a threat to the Soviet forces. I contacted Adam and told him about the new orders. Unfortunately, other workers in the office also knew he had been a member of the Home Army. One day some Party officials – two security guards – came to my office. They questioned me as to my reasons for keeping him.

"'I've known him for a long time,' I answered. 'He's Jewish. Even in the Home Army they didn't know that. You can't really consider him to be one of them.'

"'As far as we're concerned, he's a security risk. We have to arrest him.'

"I offered to accompany them to his small room. It was the beginning of February 1945. The security officer ordered him to open the door. We heard a noise in the room.

"The door opened. 'Hello, teacher,' he greeted me with a smile which faded quickly when he perceived the reason for my visit.

"'I'm sorry, Adam. But we have to clear up certain things about the Home Army. You know it was a fascist organization. I've spoken for you. Now I'm here to help make things easy for you. You have to come to the office with us.'

"'Okay.' He seemed resigned to whatever awaited him. The agents were satisfied. Everything was going along smoothly. 'Wait a minute, I just have to piss,' he said.

"In Poland we didn't have the luxury of toilets in the room. Most of them were on the landings. We waited for him in the hall. We heard the chain and the water flowing. He opened the door. All I remember of that moment is that the two security guards fell. I don't think I ever heard the shots because it happened so fast.

"'Sorry, teacher, your way doesn't sound so appealing after all.'

"He left me there with the two dead bodies."

"And you never saw him again?" I asked.

"How did you explain that one to the Party officials?" demanded Harris.

"Well, one man was dead and the other was rather badly wounded, but he lived. I was above suspicion and had an excellent record with the Party. They called it a fascist plot. Even now after all the anti-Semitic and anti-Zionist purges, I remain at my post."

"How?" I inquired.

"Thanks to my protector. Remember I mentioned a Captain Roczak? Well, you've met him. He's a very powerful man, the Director of Security.

"Now gentlemen, is there anything else I can do for you?"

"Adam was a very troubled individual," I said, "a mass of contradictions from everything I've learned. I understand that war does this to people more often than not, but his case seems extraordinary. Can you throw any further light on it?"

"In my opinion it was more of a psychological problem than anything else. Adam tried to be like his father who rejected him by dying. His mother tried to mold him into something that he couldn't be. She allowed him to grow up not knowing he was a Jew and, in that way, denied him an identity. The war had a devastating effect on him. It threw his whole system out the window. Adults became untrustworthy liars who could, in the end, only reject him. His mother's principles weren't appropriate to his survival during the war, so in a way she rejected him too. People like Max, the smuggler, the partisans, and myself became surrogates by default. Yet we were all enmeshed in a desperate struggle to survive. There was no time to consider his needs as a young man or help him grow up. Only his mother could have helped but she didn't. Perhaps I am wrong, but this is my only explanation."

"A personal question, if you don't mind, Comrade Winarski?" I interjected.

"Everything you've asked me is personal," he laughed.

"As a Communist and a Jew, how do you feel about the Middle East crisis today?"

He blinked and cleared his throat. "Gentlemen, I am a Jew, but I have never been a Zionist. Israel is the aggressor. Personally, I am only a Communist. This is the career that I chose for myself and I am now too old to question it."

"Could Adam have ultimately joined a left-wing terrorist outfit?" asked Harris.

"I don't think so. He was too bourgeois to want to suffer the rigors they put their members through," replied Winarski.

"Comrade Winarski, you have been very kind to receive us. I know that our unfortunate interrogation was not your fault. Before we leave, could you tell me one last thing? Are there any anarchistic movements in the Eastern Bloc countries?"

"This is our internal security business and not for outsiders. You have your own codes of secrecy in the United States. Even if I knew, I could not tell you the answer to that question."

We thanked Winarski and left. The guide was still waiting outside. We asked him to take us back to the hotel. We went upstairs and changed clothes. Harris came to my room. Then we went downstairs to the bar. It was a nice hotel, like some of the better class ones at home, except for the unusual number of drunks. I don't know why, but they bugged me.

The guide entered. "Would you like to see a little of Warsaw before it gets too dark? Afterwards, well, that will take care of itself."

"Sure. Why not?"

Then Dave had second thoughts. "No, we'd better stay here. We've had enough trouble already."

"Chickenshit," I laughed. "What could be any worse than what we've been through? Just keep your mouth shut if we do run into another unpleasant situation." At first Harris flushed, then I heard him swear under his breath.

The three of us left the hotel. Outside, the multitude was milling around. Noticing foreigners, they began to approach us. "Don't you want to change your dollars?"

"I'll give you the best rates."

"Have you anything to sell?"

They jostled us and were babbling all at the same time. I grabbed the guide by the jacket and demanded to know why such activities were allowed in a socialist city.

"They're our agents, informers as you call them. We get our information and they are allowed to keep the money they make," he explained.

I got the impression he was actually proud to tell us that fact. He probably expected to get into a conversation where we intelligence people could compare notes. I kept my mouth shut though. Harris for once was smart enough to do the same.

The guide took us around the city and told us a bit about its history. When it was dark, he took us to one of the caves. When we entered, it looked just like any disco one might find in New York or Paris. The décor was modest, and the kids were the same. Some girls wore blue jeans and the guys had long hair. Jeans were a luxury in Poland. The latest American music was blaring out of the most expensive amplifiers that could be imported from a capitalist country.

Our watchdog was a type of celebrity, and people greeted him with an easy familiarity. He introduced us as visiting Americans. Almost immediately we were surrounded by a core of Americanophiles. They seemed quite friendly except for a few characters, who asked questions like whether the blacks in the States are allowed to work and whether American Indians know how to speak English. Not only were these the embarrassing type of questions that Americans abroad would like to forget, they were stimulated by intentional ignorance on the part of the powerful Communist propaganda machine.

And the questions kept coming. "Are you really Americans?"

"Where do you come from?"

"My sister lives in New York."

"Yes, we're really Americans and we come from New York."

"Here's my address. Please send me some records," asked a rather aggressive young lady. Others requested pen pals, clothes, pictures of movie stars and even pornography.

"Okay, we'll try," I lied and took some addresses. The guide maneuvered us toward the bar where the only drinks were vodka or beer. The place began to get really crowded, and I just sat back and watched the dancers gyrate.

I noticed a little blond in very tight jeans. She and a redheaded friend shot Harris and me a wink and disappeared. Harris nudged the guide toward a table, and as we sat down the two girls popped out of the crowd again. This time the guide noticed them. He beckoned them to sit with us.

There was a liter of vodka on the table, and the guide went off to hunt down two more glasses. Harris wasn't drinking too much. He had a tendency to get sick from vodka. Poor guy. As for me, I continued to drink. Soon I was so blitzed that I fell off the chair. The guide and Harris had to help me back up. I slid off the chair again five minutes later. Evidently the guide and the blond helped me back to my hotel room. I remember hearing the guide say, "I'm no longer needed."

Through the haze I saw the girl standing above me. She stared into my eyes. I looked back at her.

"How old are you?" I asked.

"Seventeen," she replied in almost perfect English.

"You're old enough to be my daughter." I could feel her tugging at my clothes, but my eyelids were so heavy I couldn't open my eyes.

"I don't care. You're the first American I've ever met."

"Do you always go to hotel rooms with foreigners?"

"Please turn over. Yes, sometimes, if I like the guy." She struggled with my shirt, then busied herself with my trousers and underpants. Then she kissed me and stripped. She climbed into bed and began to suck me. Her lips ran all over my flaccid cock. I was so drunk that it wouldn't stand up. Then she shifted into second gear, caressing my entire body with her mouth. She nibbled at my ear and then deftly slipped her tongue into my mouth. I wanted to be aroused but the alcohol was too strong. The harder she tried to excite me, the hotter she got.

She fell back between my legs with her head upside down, buried in my ass. She began rimming me, first with her mouth, then with her fingers while she scampered up my perineum. Back and forth, back and forth until I was indeed starting to become hard. She opened her mouth and sucked in my balls while delicately shoving her finger expertly into my ass. No doubt most of the guys she fucked were in the same state I was. She didn't seem to mind and took complete liberty with my body. She flipped up, slipped down onto my cock and started to hump away. I felt her clawing my skin and moaning passionately. She became wilder and wilder, frantically shifting position, then shoving her ass over my pulsing prick, working more erratically but progressing steadily to an orgasm. Then I broke out in a profuse sweat that preceded a long, dreamlike orgasm of my own. I felt transported to another world.

I was standing alone in the dark. I could sense something moving. At first, I could see only a shadow that gradually increased in size. Suddenly I realized it was a grizzly bear. He was coming straight toward me. Inexplicably, there was a gun in my hand. I started to shoot but the bullets did not arrest the beast's advance. He came closer and closer. I wanted to run but my feet wouldn't move. In a minute he was on me. I felt his weight crushing me. I woke up screaming. I was in a hotel room. The girl was still there. I lay in bed trying to orient my senses, then turned over and attempted to fall back to sleep. In the morning I kissed the girl on the cheek. She opened her eyes, stretched her body like a kitten, and yawned. "Do you think I'm a whore?" I kissed her again.

"What?"

She repeated her question.

"No. You're not," I said tenderly.

"What are you thinking about?" she asked childishly.

"Nothing."

"I want to ask you something," she began rubbing my legs.

"Go ahead, but don't stop rubbing me."

"Please promise me," she stammered.

"I can't promise you anything until I know what it is, honey."

"Take me out of this country. Marry me and take me away from here. I'll give you a divorce. I promise. It's the only way I'll ever be able to leave. It's horrible to want to leave one's own country like this, but I want to have beautiful clothes and a house and a car. I want to live like the girls in the West. It's not much, is it, to want nice things? These are the only jeans I have," she complained as she pointed to the floor. "I wouldn't even have them if foreigners didn't smuggle them here. Please take me with you," she pleaded.

"I will. What's your name?"

"Wanda."

I promised to come back for her when my mission was completed. A promise is not very expensive. She wrote me her address and then fell back on top of me. We made love again.

A half hour later, I had to push her off of me and hurry her to get dressed. She was clinging to me as we heard a knock on the door.

Harris burst in, grinning from ear to ear. "Excuse me," he said to Wanda. He nearly knocked her down.

"Harris, this is the first time I've seen you smiling. What happened?"

"Guess what, John? I've met a girl and she asked me to marry her."

"Oh? Fine. It'll be a double wedding. You see, the little blond just asked me the same thing."

The girls were waiting in the hallway. We came out and they accompanied us in the car to the airport. I gave them twenty dollars apiece, which pleased them to the point of ecstasy. I realized that a dollar was more than just money. It was magic. As we descended from the car, we were smothered with hugs and kisses. They implored us to write in order to say when we would return for them. The guide got into the act too. "Could you gentlemen send me some jazz records? I like Miles Davis."

"Sure, we will. Give me your name and address and if the world is still here in two weeks, you'll have your records."

He scribbled his address and shoved the paper into my pocket. I handed him a twenty also. Maybe I would return.

Our plane was going to Rome since there were no direct flights from Eastern Europe to Israel.

Part III - The Promised Land

"In this world every man is responsible for everything to everybody." – Fyodor Dostoyevsky

Chapter 17. Sol's Adam

Wednesday, October 12, 1983 – "One hundred Soviet Divisions have moved into position in the republics of Azerbaijan, Kazakhstan, Kyrgyzstan, Uzbekistan and Tajikistan. The regular combat forces of the Red Army were accompanied by T-54 tanks and Mi-24 helicopters. The information was divulged by Pentagon officials who have been monitoring Soviet troop strength. The aforementioned republics border on the nations of Iran, Pakistan and Afghanistan. No other details were released but observers speculate that the recent Islamic Revolutions have triggered social unrest among the Soviet minorities. Terrorist activity has intensified in these areas. It is feared that the Soviets may pursue the rebels into neighboring countries where they enjoy sanctuary and support. The office of U.S. Secretary of Defense, Caspar Weinberger, has cautioned the Kremlin against violating the frontiers of these countries." – *The New York Times*

"It is obvious that the American imperialists and the Soviet revisionists will reach an understanding and form a coalition to prevent world peace and which will be to the detriment of the aspirations and self-determination of the People's Republic of China." – *People's Daily*

Rome. The airport at Fiumicino to be precise. We had a couple of hours to kill. I went to the English bookstand and bought *Lauren Bacall: By Myself*. I didn't know what compulsion pushed me to buy that book especially since I hate biographies.

We landed in Israel at 4:25 PM. It was a very dull trip and the atmosphere at Lod was oppressive. Hot, muggy weather complicated by an excessive military presence. But nobody shot at us and no bombs exploded.

We checked into the Tel Aviv Hilton and I called Ted's uncle. He was a local bigshot and worked with Histadrut, the powerful workers' union. I introduced myself and he acknowledged that he was expecting my arrival. Without further conversation, he told me to wait at the hotel for him.

We waited in the lobby. We ordered some wine which I didn't like. I guess I was spoiled by France. Harris, opposite me, was smoking a cigarette. We both watched the women. Nearly all were dark-complexioned with high cheekbones. A few wore military uniforms and carried Uzis. Then I heard myself being paged. At first, I was startled at hearing my own name. Then I walked up to the reception desk and Harris followed. There was an older man in his eighties, waiting. "You must be Johnny Miller. I'm Mr. David," he introduced himself.

I returned the greeting and introduced Harris. The wizened old man stared into his eyes. "Pleased to meet you."

"Would you like to come with us? It's not too private down here," I suggested.

We took the elevator up to the seventh floor and entered my room. The windows were open and the unmistakable scent of Mediterranean pollution wafted in. Mr. David was already in shirt sleeves. Harris and I took off our jackets and made ourselves comfortable.

"Would you like a drink?"

"No, thank you, I don't drink anymore," he sighed.

"You don't mind if we indulge, do you?"

"Go right ahead."

I ordered a bottle of Chivas Regal whiskey. When the bellhop had come and gone, I took a shot and gave one to Harris. I was very surprised that he took it. Something had happened to him in Poland. I wondered what.

"Mr. David," I began, "I have some very unpleasant news. Of course, you know about the Berisov assassination?"

He nodded.

"Well, I don't know if you're going to be happy about what I'm going to tell you." I watched the old man's face. "The man who killed Berisov is your nephew."

There was no sign of surprise, absolutely no emotion. "For the last few days we have been trying to trace people who knew him in order to establish some motive for his action. His statement about the CIA was false. We would like your cooperation. We're here to find out as much as you know about him."

"Of course, of course," he mumbled. "I understand. I'll tell you what I remember." He sat back and pulled out a linen handkerchief with which he patted his face and the back of his neck. "My sister Ann was his mother. As you know, we're Jews. Between 1918 and 1920, during the years of Polish independence and the war with the Soviets, she fell in love with Count Zbigniew Polanski, a Colonel in the Polish Army Medical Corps. He was a nobleman and a Christian."

"That must have created quite a scandal," I commented.

"Well you know, it's always half-and-half. Even now when it seems so common, the parents raise hell and then quiet down. When the children grow up and have their own kids, it's the same thing all over again. But you are correct in a sense. Although my family was very assimilated, I was already a committed Zionist. But Poland had a big Orthodox population, and they tend to impose their comments on everything that they learn about. They were very concerned with genealogy. When word got around, there was a scandal. Yet Ann was very much in love and nothing could have prevented the marriage.

"I asked her, 'Ann, in which religion will you bring up the children?' I thought by pointing out this difficulty, I could get her to reconsider her decision. But it didn't work.

"'If and when they're born, they'll have no designated religion. When they turn twenty-one, they can choose for themselves.'

"'That's all right in theory,' I agreed, 'but what if you have a boy, and he decides to become a Jew? It's painful to get circumcised at that age. And there's no other way for a man to be a Jew.'

"'We've discussed that already. Zbigniew said that we can have him circumcised as soon as he's born. He thinks that it will be better for the boy's health anyway. That's the way they do it in America.'

"When we realized that there was no way of coping with her stubbornness, the plans were accepted. Part of his family and part of our family attended the wedding. The atmosphere was very cold. We watched each other suspiciously. It was like we were saying, 'What are we doing here with the goyem?' while they were thinking, 'What are we doing here with these Jews?' Both sides made an effort to see that things went smoothly, in a very refined cultured environment. But when we drank vodka, all civility collapsed.

"I came to Palestine in 1927. I was one of the first pioneers in the kibbutz movement. I specialized in finance. When I returned to Poland it was on business. I was trying to recruit immigrants from the three-and-a-half million Jews there. Naturally, I went to see my sister. I knew that her husband had died from a heart attack. She was living alone with Adam who was only four years old then. She managed her estate with a very firm hand.

"'You're doing all right, Ann?' I asked.

"'Yes, Sol. Zbigniew taught me how to handle everything. The manager respects my orders. I don't think that they even suspect that I'm a Jewess.'

"'How's Adam?'

"'Come in and see him.' She opened the nursery door. I saw him sitting in his governess's lap. She was reading to him. They looked up. 'Adam, this is your Uncle Sol. Come and say hello,' she announced.

"'Hello, Uncle Sol,' he said, extending his hand.

"Ann told me that she named him Adam because it sounded both Jewish and Polish. She explained that it was the name of the first man and symbolized unity between Jews and Christians.

"Adam and I became friends immediately. 'Ann, I'd like to take him out.'

"'Yes, that's a good idea.' She seemed pleased to see Adam getting along with someone from her family.

"'We went walking through Lodz. I bought some ice cream and asked him if he'd like to go to the movies. We went to see an American Western. When we came out, I bought him some more ice cream. Walking home, we passed a Hasidic Jew wearing the traditional long, black robe with black hat, forelocks, and beard.

"'Look, Uncle. That's a Jew,' he pointed out with derision.

"I was shocked. 'Don't you like him?'

"'No, Jews are no good.'

"'Who told you that? Your mother?' I inquired suspiciously.

"'No. My playmates. Everybody. Nobody likes Jews. They're no good.'

"When we returned from the walk, I went to my sister immediately. She saw my agitated state and asked what was bothering me. She thought that perhaps Adam had misbehaved.

"'You've raised a little Jew-hater,' I said to her bitterly.

"'But Sol, I've always taught him that everybody's equal,' she answered defensively.

"'You say so, but what about the school he's attending? The people he meets?'

"'Please, Sol. Let's not discuss this anymore. He's young. Only four years old. I'll explain it to him when he's older. He always listens to me.'

"'I hope so, Ann. I hope so.' I left for the Zionist Congress in Geneva and then returned to Palestine.

"The next time I was in Poland, Adam was ten years old. I hardly recognized him, but we renewed our friendship easily. I asked him to come out for a walk with me. I felt there were too many women around him, his mother, his governess, the cook. They spoiled the boy.

"As we were walking into town, I once again asked him what he thought of Jews. 'Mother says they are good men like everybody else. But I don't think so,' he confided.

"'Why?' I asked.

"'Well,' he paused to reflect, 'a lot of them don't dress the way we do. They don't speak the way we do. They're different.'

"'What would you do if someone said that you were a Jew, Adam?'

"He became very angry and started to scream. 'I'd kill him. I'd kill him.'

"Ann was waiting for us as we reentered the house. 'Did you two have fun?' she inquired.

"'Oh, yes. We got along very well. Adam is quite a mature boy for his age. Aren't you, Adam?'

"'Adam, your homework.' His mother turned to him seriously. 'You'd better finish it. Uncle Sol will be here for a few days. You'll have plenty of time together. You know what I'm going to do if you don't finish your homework.'

"Adam was afraid. He hurried away to his room. 'Poor kid. Ann, why did you threaten him like that?'

"'I tell him that if he doesn't do his work properly, I'm going to send him off to a kibbutz in Palestine,' she remarked off-handedly. 'And believe me, he does it well. So well, in fact, that he's the best student in his class.'

"'Ann, maybe I haven't the right to advise you about the boy's education and upbringing. On the other hand, I'm your brother and I'm warning you. The way things are going, he'll be anti-Semitic. Remember what you said about his right to choose his own religion when he comes of age? He'll never choose to be a Jew if you employ those tactics on him.'

"'You can trust me, Sol. He's still a boy. And we take good care of him. Look at his grades.' She took some papers from her desk. 'He's the best student in the school. Even in conduct. I keep a close watch on him.'

"Next morning, we went out again. This time Ann joined us. She looked at him admiringly as he outpaced us down the street. 'He has blond hair and blue eyes, just like his father. There's very little of me in him. I would like for him to be just like his father.'

"'Even if he forgets his Jewish mother?' I added sardonically.

"'I don't care. All I want is his happiness. I don't want him to have any complexes.'

"'Catholic, not knowing anything of his Jewish heritage? Hating Jews!'

"'You must understand, Sol, there are no nondenominational schools in Poland.'

"'But that school, they teach him Catholicism. Only Catholicism,' I protested.

"'So what? One religion is as good as another.'

Her streak of stubbornness was showing. I knew that nothing I could say would change her mind. So, I switched the subject. 'Ann, why don't you remarry?'

"'I can't. I always think of his father. He was the most beautiful man I ever met. All those girls running after him, and he chose me, a Jewish girl. He was so noble, so nice, so gentle, so cultured. Everybody loved and respected him, even the tenants. How they cried when he passed away. I want to raise Adam in his image. I want him to have part of his father's culture, his nobility.'

"'Even at the expense of turning him against his own people?'

"'I don't care. I think that if I give him a good education, he'll be broad-minded enough to choose the right way when he is twenty-one.'

"'I hope you know what you're doing. He needs a father. There are too many women in his life.' I could see in her eyes that she resented this comment. 'Don't you know that boys always resent the people who raise them? What if he were to become a misogynist?'

"'What do you mean? Sol, he'll never hate me. He loves me.'

"'But still, if one day he becomes a woman-hater?'

"'Don't say that. He does everything I say. He tells me everything. For instance, one day he asked me quite innocently, "Mother, what does 'screwing' a girl mean? They say it's nice to open a girl's legs and put your thing in. I don't understand."

"'I must admit that I was shocked at first but tried not to let it show. There was a small contradiction in my strategy. I wanted him to get a head start in his education, so I sent him to school early, before other children his age. But at the same time that he developed a type of intellectual maturity, he's fallen behind his classmates in physical maturity. It was nothing that could be helped. The boys in his grade are already becoming aware of the opposite sex. I cautioned him not to listen to them, that they were vulgar. If he needed to defend himself, he could simply say that he is the son of a Count and Countess. Those boys aren't in the same social class as he. I told him not to associate with them.'

"'But Ann, what they said was quite normal. We both know that. Adam is going to be a very lonely little boy.'

"My sister became very stern. She was always insulted when I insinuated that Adam would grow up with some kind of psychological scar. That too was normal, but she couldn't accept it. It was an affront to her and her husband's integrity. 'Adam won't be lonely. I'm always here. So is his governess. Anyway, I don't want him associating with those dirty, nasty boys. He listens to me and faithfully follows my instructions.'

"'Yes, he does listen to you. But that's because you play upon false fears. You threaten to send him to a kibbutz. Why is he afraid of that if not for the reason that he has already been influenced by the boys and their parents who've instilled them with prejudice?'

"My sister couldn't answer me. Indeed, she fell silent. I think she realized that her mistake was already irreparable. It was the last time I saw her.

"War broke out in Europe. We heard what happened to the Jews and asked our allies for help but in vain, as you gentlemen well know. During the war I received no news about my family. Everyone who had relatives in Europe worried, but that was about the only thing we could do. All the real news we received was bad.

"In 1947, I met a man who had been in Paris. He knew Adam and told me that he had become somewhat of a delinquent. He had even been to jail. I was a liberal and tried to understand that war does strange things to people. On my next trip to Geneva, I took an excursion to Paris to find him. I didn't have an address, so I went to the St. Paul area where many of the Polish Jews lived. At the first café I asked for him, but nobody recognized the name. I launched into a description according to the facts I had heard and then they began to respond. Everyone was aware of his reputation. I was almost ashamed. 'Oh, that's Ted. He's an American MP. Yeah, we know him. What a tough customer he is.'

"I revealed that I was his long-lost uncle and asked how I could find him. Most of the men thought it was a mitzvah that I had come to pull him out of such bad habits. Someone who was probably involved in the same activities as Adam finally spoke up. 'He's in Germany, but I think he'll be back tomorrow night.'

"I announced that I would return and asked them to make sure that 'Ted' would wait for his Uncle Sol. I took a room in a nearby hotel and went sightseeing. What I saw did not please me at all. The French were rebuilding their country thanks to the Americans. They were a greedy people, and it struck me that since their country was being rebuilt for them, they considered themselves very important. I looked around and shuddered. They did not bother to correct the errors of the past. I felt sorry for any Jews who by some stretch of the imagination planned to raise families there. The filthy beast, la bête immonde, as they called it, was buried but not dead.

"The next night I returned to the café. The owner was waiting for me. 'He's here. Just got back an hour ago. I told him you were here, and he said to have you wait. He should be here any minute now.'

"I sat down and ordered a drink. I fixed my eyes on the door. Every time it opened, I leaned forward, thinking that it was Adam. I didn't know if I would recognize him because I hadn't seen him for so long.

"Then a man strode over to my table. 'Uncle Sol, how are you?' I couldn't believe that this tall, blond man was my sister's child. He was slim and had the appearance of a lady's man. His eyes were the most striking feature. There was a sort of wild look about them. We hugged each other.

"'Adam, after all these years!' I began to weep. Then we sat down together.

"'How have you been, Uncle,' inquired the boy cheerfully.

"'It's for me to ask you that, Adam. From what I understand, you've had a rough time over here.'

"He smiled. 'Yes, we've had a hard time here in Europe.'

"I knew that my sister had perished in the camps and hesitated to probe his feelings about her in our first reunion. I didn't want to risk pushing him away. Or perhaps it was a premonition that he'd say something I didn't want to hear. I decided to engage him on another level. 'Well, what have you been doing since the war?'

"'A little of this and a little of that.' He was very obtuse.

"'I don't want to be too direct, Adam, but I've heard some things about you that I couldn't really believe. They told me that you were a gangster, that you had been in jail.'

"'So?' came his answer.

"'I can't believe that your mother or father would want you to be like that. You come from such a good, noble family.'

"'Uncle, I respect you, but I'll level with you. I don't give a damn about what they would think.'

"'How can you say something like that?' I was profoundly hurt. 'They always tried to do the best for you.'

"'Perhaps. Perhaps, but they failed to prepare me for life. I was left alone and to survive I had to fight by my own rules. My teacher taught me about communism in the ghetto. When my mother's way no longer worked, I tried to follow his until I met him after the war and discovered that he too had lied to me. Everything I learned as a child turned out to be an enormous lie. When I came to France, I was determined to start things all over again. I created my own life with my own rules.'

"'But you could get a legitimate job here in France,' I offered hopefully.

"'Don't kid me, Uncle. You see for yourself what the French do. They sit by as the Americans supervise the reconstruction of their own country. When they need workers, they send DPs[23] like me into the mines or factories. Can you see me working in any of those places? It's almost like working hard labor for the Germans. I didn't live through years of war to slave in anybody's factory or coal mine.'

"'But Adam,' I pleaded, 'you need a job and money. You could even have ...'

"'I lost years of my youth and I had to catch up quickly. I needed a shortcut. I've got to make money effortlessly and rapidly. Tell me, Uncle, did we win or lose the war?' There was bitterness and irony in his voice.

"'We won,' I said optimistically.

"'All right. Then if we won, why should I have to live like a loser?'

"'I don't follow you.'

"'Listen, Uncle, when I was in the ghetto, a man told me that no Jew could survive the war, but if one, just one, managed to survive, then he would be covered with gold. During the war I was alone. When the war ended, I was still alone. I got used to it. But no one covered me with gold. I was pushed around by everybody and anybody. I got sick of it.'

"His bitterness made me feel distant, although I tried to comprehend his fallen aspirations. He seemed resigned to follow through with what he started. I accepted that and tried to be a good uncle and show some kind of interest in his work. 'How did you get started, Adam?'

"'How do you mean? As a gangster?'

"'Yes, I'm interested.'

"'Well, I came to France from Odessa with the Americans. I had studied English in school and during the time I spent with the Americans, I learned to speak it fluently. When I arrived in Paris, I decided to smuggle contraband. My English came in handy. I did nothing worse than I had done during the war. I only wanted to make some money because I had figured out that no one would cover me with gold. I had to do it myself. Eventually I went to jail. Perhaps they might refer to me as a hoodlum, but I'm Adam.'

"He looked at me. His eyes were odd, as if they were trying to convey something that defied verbalization.

"'I don't know, Adam. I still ...'

"'You condemn me, uncle, don't you? How can you? Did you help me during the war? You who were safe in Palestine? The only person who got me out of it alive was myself.'

"He was right. I hadn't the right to condemn. Still, I wanted him to change somehow. Perhaps I could help him now.

"'Adam, it's true what you say. I didn't help you during the war, but I can now. Come to Palestine with me. I'll get you a good job. You'll do okay.'

"'I have no intention of going into a kibbutz.'

"There was a glint of fear in his eyes. Then I remembered Ann's threats. It was that and maybe something else.

"'Uncle,' his eyes frowned now, 'I just got out of one ghetto. Do you really want to put me in another?'

"'You still want to be a gangster?'

"'Gangster? Maybe,' he paused. 'No. I'm living by my own rules. But you don't and can't understand that. Anyway, don't worry, uncle. Gangsterhood is only a shortcut to respectability.'

"'But how long will it last?' I wanted to know. He had Ann's stubborn streak in him. I was glad that she wasn't alive to see him now. 'Have you made any money?'

"'Yes. In the last couple years, I've made about a hundred thousand dollars.'

"'Don't you think that's enough? Don't you think you've had your revenge on society? Why don't you lead a normal life?'

"He smiled. 'I'll never have my revenge on society. Never,' he mused emphatically.

"'But you're a part of society. Society is the foundation of your existence, Adam.'

"'If I'm alive today, uncle, it's no thanks to society. I helped myself during and after the war. Instinct was my only foundation and I always took the initiative to act in my own hands. It has nothing to do with society except that society was always throwing obstacles onto my path.'

"'Your thinking is all wrong, Adam.' I was getting disgusted with his outlook on life. He had gone bad and there was nothing I could do. It was too late.

"'Don't start with that morality crap,' he raised his voice belligerently. 'Don't ever tell me how to think, please. I'll think the way I want to.'

"'How do you make all this money?'

"'I go to Belgium and Germany and bring back expensive things that can't be bought here. I might buy a load for one thousand dollars and sell it for five thousand.'

"I asked him about the people he met in his line of business, about the things he did. He explained them in detail, then he looked at his watch and said, 'We've been talking for hours. I'd like to get out of these clothes. Want to come to my room?'

"I agreed and followed him to a rather shoddy hotel. He had a small room with all the usual furnishings. He washed and shaved, while I remained silent and surveyed his belongings. 'Why so many pictures of Humphrey Bogart?'

"'I like him,' came the cursory answer.

"'Is he your idol?'

"'I don't have any idols, but when I have certain problems, I try to think of what one of his movie characters would do in my place. It helps.'

"'Would you go to work for the Zionists?'

"'Doing what?' He was surprised by the directness of my proposition.

"'Transporting people.'

"'I'll work for anybody who pays me.'

"'Listen, we have the means to take people from Marseille to Palestine. But we don't have a plan for getting them from the camps in Germany to Marseille. I'm convinced that you can do it. We have twenty-two people waiting to go to Marseille right now. Can you get them across the border safely?'

"'I'll do it for you, uncle. Just to prove I'm a good guy.'

"Two days later we went to Germany. There were nineteen men and three women at the Salzheim camp who were prepared to leave for Palestine. Adam left me there with them and returned in a few days with Polish Labor Guard uniforms. He gave them ID cards that we fixed up with pictures. He produced what appeared to be an official document authorizing him to take twenty-two Polish Labor Guards to France.

"'What about the women?' I asked.

"'They'll be nurses.'

"'And the rabbi? He refuses to shave off his beard. It will look ridiculous.'

"'Where is he?' asked Adam, visibly annoyed.

"I called the rabbi over. He really did look idiotic in his uniform. We tried to talk sense to him, but he stubbornly refused to cut his beard.

"'Okay, uncle. Don't worry. We'll have to take him anyway.'

"'But the papers? And his uniform ... This is sheer madness!'

"'Calm down. He'll be the group rabbi. What else?'

"Adam laughed. Me too. I thought he was crazy and told him so.

"'Will you stop worrying, it'll be okay. Why don't you come along? You can see how I operate. It might be useful for your organization.'

"'All right, but I won't be in your group.'

"'Coward!'

"'No. But I'm no fool either. I'm in too important a position at home to take this kind of risk. Yet I'd like to see what happens.' I suddenly became very enthusiastic about the whole thing. It was like a game.

"We boarded the train separately. The German border control was no obstacle, but the French came to demand papers. Naturally, the refugees signaled that they didn't have any. My nephew arrived and waved a paper with the twenty-two names on it. One of the officials checked the list and then stamped it. Ten hours later, we arrived in Marseille and took the refugees to the Palestinian transit center.

"This was about the same time that the war for independence erupted. While we stayed at the transit center, I introduced Adam to the commanding officer. 'He brought these people from Germany. Give him a hundred dollars per head.'

"The officer was a little surprised. 'Is he Jewish?' he inquired while inspecting Adam.

"I didn't know what to say because a Jew would never request money for such a mission. 'No. He's not,' I pronounced.

"After Adam was paid, I turned to him. 'You've performed a mitzvah for the Jews. Why don't you stay with us and see how the center is run?'

"Adam agreed, and we moved into a small Quonset hut at the edge of the transit center. We discussed the political and military situation. I thought I could work on him and perhaps persuade him to stay with us.

"Soon I believed that my influence was starting to take effect. One day, two of the men we had transported from Germany disappeared. They didn't want to go to a desert in the Middle East. Instead, they wanted to stay in France. The following day, the French police brought them back. The Zionists who ran the place administered a public humiliation to set an example for the others. As we stood there, I noticed a painful grimace on Adam's face at every insult hurled at them. It was the first time he exhibited any kind of real emotion. A little while later, we encountered the commandant at the mess hall.

He approached Adam directly and asked, 'Want to work for us? We need you to go on another rescue mission.'

"'No. I've decided not to work for you. I'm not a slave-trader.' He stared directly into the commandant's eyes.

"The commandant was astonished. 'What do you mean?'

"'Why did you abuse those guys?' asked Adam indignantly.

"'Because they were insincere. We paid to bring them here in order to give them passage to Palestine. They ran out on us.'

"'I don't see it that way,' stated Adam bluntly. 'They're just like me. They had a hard time and now all they want is to enjoy themselves. I can't contribute to anyone's unhappiness. I wouldn't help you bastards if you paid me a million dollars!'

"The commandant stalked away with a sour expression on his face.

"Later, when we were alone, Adam apologized to me. He admitted that he was sorry for letting me down but vowed not to help the Zionists, whom he compared to the Fascists.

"'Well, what are you going to do now?' I asked.

"'Don't worry, uncle. Right now, life is just a play. I call it the second underground. There are no risks involved.' He turned closer to my face and confided, 'What do I risk when I smuggle a couple of cameras? Three months in jail is nothing. Don't fret about me because I'll always manage. I've made it this far without you, and I'll make it the rest of the way. Thanks anyway, but you understand I hate fanatics.'

"'What do you mean by that?'

"'Nazis were fanatics. I fought them as long as they were a threat to my existence. Zionist fanaticism has replaced their brand of terror. I'll fight them too if I have to.'

"I couldn't take this harangue. His logic was twisted and although not directed at me personally, highly provocative. 'What exactly are you working for in life?' I asked, refusing to take the bait.

"'I don't know yet. I'll have to find out. I'm still young and have a long way to go. But what you offer me is not the least bit appealing. I have to find something pure. I'm looking for my gold.'

"'What gold?'

"'I'm covering myself with gold, like the man in the ghetto once told me. Since nobody else is interested, I'm taking the initiative myself.'

"'Can't you find another ideal for yourself somewhere?'

"'I don't know where it is. It must exist somewhere because life can't be this lousy. There'd be no reason to survive if not. I'm looking for something good, wherever it is.'

"'You know, Adam, when you talk about fanatics, you've become one yourself.'

"'Perhaps. Yeah, I could be a fanatic, about what I don't know. One thing I do know, I'm against your type of fanaticism. Goodbye, Uncle. I hope to see you again.'

"I gave him my address in Haifa before we parted."

"Did you ever see him again?" I asked.

"Yes. He came to Israel last year. I hadn't seen him in so long that when he came here, I was shocked.

"He was fifty-six but I recognized him at once. I was glad to see him here although I didn't know his reasons. He was quiet and somber as he ate dinner with my wife and family. He brought gifts for everyone. That pleased his cousins and aunt, who had heard only good things from me about their relative in Paris.

"After dinner we went for a walk around the city. It reminded me of the walks I used to take with him in Poland.

"'Uncle, I know you'll be glad to hear that I'm leading a very quiet life now. I have a legal business. I hope that pleases you.'

"'Yes, that does satisfy me. But the important person is you. Are you happy, Adam?'

"'Being legitimate and being happy aren't the same thing,' he replied.

"'I'm happy, Adam. I have a wife and children. I work for my country. For me that is happiness. What do you have?'

"'Nothing. I'm alone. The only future I have is death and before that, old age. Perhaps cancer. I won't let that happen to me.'

"'You're getting morbid, Adam. But I'm glad you've settled down. I was afraid that you'd end up in jail for a long time ... or even under the guillotine,' I joked.

"'Were you really worried about me, Uncle? Did you have a guilty conscience?'

"'Do I have a guilty conscience? What is a conscience?'

"'Don't you know?'

"'Yes, but I think we mean two completely different things by that word. Did you feel guilty about robbing people?'

"'No. As a matter of fact, I felt satisfied. As far as feeling guilty is concerned ... if I feel guilty, it's about things I haven't done. This world is so mean, the people so despicable, so hateful that I don't think I could ever repay the misery they have wrought upon myself and my brothers.'

"'Wait. When you say brothers, what do you mean? Jews?'

"'No. Just people in general. What have you done to help me or others? I can't pretend that I'm happy when I'm not. I only hope that I've relieved you by going legitimate.'

"After a few hours of walking and talking, he proposed we have a drink. I took him to the Dan Hotel where there was an American bar. He had a few drinks and relaxed. He even danced with a couple of the girls. As they returned to our table, he wanted to know if I was tired. I said no and pushed him to continue. He seemed happy, and I did not want to interrupt it.

"Then something happened. There was an old man sitting alone at a corner table. He was even older than I. Adam stopped in front of him and pushed away the girl he was dancing with. His eyes were wild, and he stood in front of the table staring at the old man. 'You goddamn bastard,' he shouted. The old man was afraid. He didn't know who the hell my nephew was, but Adam certainly recognized him from somewhere. 'Where's the gold?' he shrieked. 'Where's all that fucking gold?' repeated Adam as he knocked the table out of the way and tried to strangle the man. Everybody in the place rushed to the corner and finally pulled Adam away. He was in a frenzy and still struggling.

"I was nervous and worried. I thought maybe Adam was hallucinating or having a psychotic attack. That man had been in Israel since 1947 and as far as I knew, Adam had never been here before. He had simply assaulted a stranger.

"Adam finally calmed down sufficiently to apologize to me. He said that he wanted to talk to the old man and apologize to him personally.

"I went over to the old man who was recuperating from Adam's attack. I made the apology on his behalf and asked him if he would see Adam privately. He agreed.

"The next day Adam went to see him. He never told me what they talked about but claimed that everything had been cleared up.

"'Israel's in trouble, Uncle,' he stated without introducing the subject.

"'Since when did the welfare of Israel concern you?'

"'I'm not concerned about this goddamn country. But look at your people. Do you think that anybody's going to protect you when you're fighting against hundreds of millions of Arabs, against all humanity? Everybody hates you. Do you think the Americans will help you? You think they'll choose to defend little David's lion against the oil wells or the Russians? You have no luck. Like the old Jews, you'll fight. You'll fight but you will not survive. You'll disappear like heroes. The best you can expect is that all humanity will cry for you.'

"His diatribe against Israel left me speechless.

"'Don't worry, Uncle. I'll do something to help you.'

"'How much will it cost the government,' I inquired.

"'Nothing,' he shot back. 'It's on the house this time.'

"'You mean you're ... no fee?'

"'No fee.' He stared me in the face like a mensch.

"I didn't understand what he had in mind, but all the same I was a little bit frightened. Now that you come here with an investigation into the Berisov thing, I don't know what to think."

The room fell silent. Mr. David got up and walked to the window. He stared down at the city below.

"Did you see him again after that last conversation?" I asked.

"No, I did not."

Harris started to say something, but I interrupted him. "Mr. David, would you be willing to come to New York if it meant helping your nephew?"

"That depends, Mr. Miller. That depends if it will help Israel too."

I said nothing more but allowed Harris to ask him if we could meet with the old man whom Adam assaulted.

"The old man? Certainly. He only lives a few blocks from here. I'll bring him back."

Chapter 18. Greenberg's Prize

Adam's uncle left to find the old man. Harris sat on the rattan chair like a statue. He had nothing to say really. I think he was totally incapable of following the better part of the conversation we had just had. Words like conscience, morality and guilt weren't in his vocabulary. What about mine?

"Miller," he said, finally breaking the contemplative silence, "do you think the uncle here has any connection with Mossad?"

"Could be," I responded. "If he does, you can bet that they found out what happened when our boy Ted was here last year. Did you hear what he said when I asked him about flying to New York? If they know anything about Ted, it's probably already in Donaldson's dossier."

The trouble was that Donaldson might not tell us everything he knew.

That strategy session died as suddenly as it started. I poured another drink and lit a cigarette while Harris sat back in the chair and daydreamed.

The uncle returned about an hour later with an old man who looked to be in his late eighties. He wore a long white beard and had to be helped as he took every step with the utmost caution. The uncle explained why we were in Israel and what we wanted from him. His English was less than perfect but good enough to communicate. Mr. David left, saying that he would return shortly.

I approached the old man directly and asked how the fight with Adam had started.

"Why do you want to know?" He shook his head. "It's not very important. I said nothing to the police."

"Of course. Of course. We know that. But surely Mr. David emphasized how important it is for you to cooperate with our investigation," explained Harris respectfully. "Everything that concerns Adam is vital to us. He was very quiet for the last ten years. We want to know what provoked this sudden outburst. Why did he assault you?"

The old man stared into space. His skin was weathered and leathery. He spoke slowly and it was often difficult to understand him. "It was in the Warsaw Ghetto about forty years ago. I don't remember how long ago, really. I think I was about forty-five then. I met Adam there when the Germans sealed off the area. They made a curfew for the district. We couldn't go out after nine, so we would gather in our building and talk about the future. The situation was bad, very bad. We had no food and children were dying of hunger.

"In the particular building where I lived a lot of wealthy Jews had their apartments. The President of the Jewish Council, Dr. Cherniakoff lived there. Artists like Szlengel and Dann ... Dann ..." he stuttered on the name and then gave up trying to recall it. "They would come to sing for us. We gave them gifts so that they could eat and live. We were the aristocrats of the ghetto.

"A lady named Polanska lived on the second floor with her son. They came to listen and join the meetings. The boy was unlike others his age. I had the feeling that he didn't belong to us, to the ghetto. When I kibbitzed with him, he answered me in goyishe Polish. He didn't have a Jewish accent. This was very rare, as rare as his blond hair and blue eyes. If I ever saw a Jew who didn't look Jewish, it was him. 'What are you doing in the ghetto, child?' I questioned him one evening when his mother was absent.

"'I'm with my mother. She's Jewish. We came here from Lodz.'

"'You look like an Aryan. If I looked like you, I'd go over the wall.' That's the advice I gave him, but when I said that, I didn't know what was coming. It was when no one believed the rumors about the camps.

"I used to see him all the time. He would look at me and announce that he was on his way to school, as if I should care. One day he told me that he was getting bad grades. He said that he didn't like the ghetto.

"'Nobody likes being here. You're not so special,' I told him.

"'I understand that.' He was precocious at such an age. 'But I don't belong here. I don't like the people.'

"'Because they're Jewish,' I assumed.

"'I don't know. I never knew I was Jewish until I came here. I came here only because my mother is Jewish. I had to follow her because I always follow her. Everything she says is right. That's why I'm here.'

"'You're a good boy to listen to your mother. Still, if something happens, remember that you are one of the few who have a chance to go over the wall.'

"Sometime after that, the action started. It must have been in July 1942. The Germans brought in Ukrainian and Lithuanian ...'"

Harris interrupted him. "Mr. Greenberg, please spare us the details of the Holocaust. Try to concentrate on Adam. It's Adam whom we want to know about."

The old man turned his head toward Harris and grimaced as if he did not understand. But he did. His reaction was typical of people who were insulted if you didn't want to spend hours listening to their problems. His eyes were deeply buried in their fallen sockets. They teared intermittently, which led me to suspect that he had a cataract. He probably couldn't even see us very well.

His throat opened as if to drink all the air he could. I was afraid we were tiring him, so I put a glass of water in his hand. He pushed my arm away and reposed the glass on the night table without even looking. The glass rocked on the edge and fell over onto the carpet before I had a chance to catch it. The old man paid no attention to his clumsy error. He had made his way through the Holocaust and back to Adam.

"After the liberation I tried to find some of my friends but couldn't. This was a time of whirlwind courtships and marriages, a marriage craze. Everybody was afraid they wouldn't have a partner. Nobody wanted to be alone. They wanted to have families and rebuild the Jewish nation. I met a girl who had been in the camps. We married and immigrated to Israel in '47. We've lived here ever since, my wife, my children and I."

"Tell me, sir, why do you think Adam attacked you that night?" I wanted to keep him on the right track yet avoid being brutal with such a fragile old man.

"Don't worry about that. He apologized the next day."

Was the old man avoiding the fight out of shame or did he have something to hide? I tried to guide his thoughts one more time. "What did Adam say? What were his exact words when he apologized to you, Mr. Greenberg?"

"He said he was very sorry he tried to hurt me." The old man's voice faltered, and he swallowed hard. He grimaced in pain as if a hand had wiped across his face.

"I see him now like that night, like I see you gentlemen before me now. He said, 'Mr. Greenberg, I hope you recognize me.'

"At first I didn't remember. My memory is not good anymore. He helped me though.

"'It was a long time ago in the Warsaw Ghetto,' he said. 'I'm Adam, the little boy with a good face. I'm sorry for yesterday. I don't know what came over me. It was a very childish act, but when I saw you, I suddenly blamed you for everything. Do you remember the talks with Winarski and the rest? I was there all those times. You were the one who advised me to jump the wall, to integrate into the Polish community. Well, I did it. You also told me to survive by any means. Survival was the most important thing. I committed many crimes, things that under any other circumstances I would not have done. I kept what you told me in the back of my mind. You told me that if there was a survivor, he would be covered with gold. Well, I survived but nobody covered me with gold. I looked for the promised land but only found hell.

"'On the first day of liberation, the day we waited for so long ... after all that hardship, I thought I was the only Jew left because I hadn't met any others since I jumped the wall,' he said. 'I went to the RTRP[24] headquarters. The man at the door asked me what I wanted. I said I'm one of the last Jews. He smiled ironically and sent me to the office. I told the same story to the girl behind the desk. She replied that the RTRP had nothing to do with that problem. She gave me an address and said that the people there could help me. I left thinking that that was the place where I had to go to get covered with gold.

"'When I arrived at the address, there was a crowd of several hundred persons trying to get in the building. All of them wanted to be covered with gold. I was disappointed that I wasn't the only survivor. I was angry that I wasn't the exception. You may think I'm a monster, but I was jealous.

"'I decided to wait my turn in line anyway. When I finally reached the desk, I told the man, "I'm a Jew who survived. Cover me with gold." He smiled sympathetically and handed me one thousand zlotys. I left the building screaming angrily. Since then, I've never asked anybody for help.

"'Last night when I saw you, something inside me snapped. Suddenly I remembered everything I did to survive so in the end I could be covered with gold, as you'd once promised me. For me you were responsible. I saw you as the person who pushed me into all those senseless and unjustified things. But never mind. I'm here to say I'm sorry for attacking you. I really don't blame you, and maybe if I hadn't dreamed about the gold, I wouldn't have survived.'

"'You didn't hurt me last night, Adam.' I told him. 'Gold is the happiness that you have to build around you. I'm covered with gold. I have a wife and children. You could have done the same thing. You're younger than I am. You had more opportunities. You could have had many children and a happy family life.'

"'Is this the gold you were talking about?'

"'Yes.'"

The old man looked up at me and his eyes squinted. "This is a promised land, here in Israel." It was both an answer and a question at the same time.

"He asked me more. He said, 'Mr. Greenberg, maybe that's your kind of gold, but it's not the gold I was looking for.'

"'What kind of gold are you looking for, Adam?'

"'I don't know, but I've been looking and looking, and now I think my search is almost ended.'

"That was the end of our conversation," sighed the old man. "The boy was in a trance. I asked him how his search would end. All he replied was that when his search ended, everyone would know. His face was horrible, like a lunatic or fanatic."

"What kind of fanatic?" I asked.

"I don't know. He just apologized again and left."

"You know, Mr. Greenberg, I was a soldier," I said. "Most of the people I met who survived did so underhandedly. Please don't take it personally, but what did you do?"

"Nothing!" The old man said angrily. "I told you already that I didn't do nothing!"

"Are you trying to tell me that you just survived when all around you, younger men were being killed. How?"

"I don't know. I was in the ghetto in Warsaw. I went through the selections. They told me to live, so I lived. I went to Majdanek. There were more selections. They told me to live. Then they transferred me to Auschwitz. They sent people to death but let me live. I don't know, maybe the hand of God kept me alive."

"Are you sure? This interview is not on the record ..."

"Mr. Miller, I've done nothing wrong, nothing to be ashamed of."

I looked at him. "Mr. Greenberg, I'll tell you something you'll never believe. You might be responsible for the deaths of four and a half billion people."

He laughed. "Me responsible for the deaths of four and a half billion people? How? Why?"

"You don't know why?"

"No, I don't."

I was really sorry, and it wasn't necessary for him to know about something he couldn't stop. He had simply encouraged the boy to fight for survival in terms he could understand. No one could have predicted the weight a couple words might bring to bear years later. "Nothing, Mr. Greenberg, I was only joking. You're not responsible. Good night, Mr. Greenberg."

"Good night, Mr. Miller, Mr. Harris."

"Did you find out anything?" asked Mr. David, who had entered unnoticed. He seemed like a teenager compared to Greenberg.

"Yes," we replied in unison.

"Are you going to stay in Israel?" Our conversation simply ignored the old man who was content to reflect by himself.

"No. I'm afraid we have to go back to the States. The press conference is Monday and we have to finish our inquiry as quickly as possible."

"Well, if there's anything I can do for you, please contact me."

"Thank you, sir, but we've already kept you from your family for too long. We'll manage by ourselves."

The two Israelis left together. Harris and I escorted them, helping Greenberg to the lobby and into a taxi. We returned to the room and stretched out on the beds. Harris had been reasonably quiet lately and was beginning to loosen up.

"Hey, Johnny, let's go find some girls."

"No. I think I'll have some food sent up. You go out and enjoy yourself. And don't forget we have a plane to catch at 4 AM."

Harris frowned at me, then turned and walked slowly toward the door. "You feel okay, Johnny?"

"Yeah, but I'm just a bit tired. That's all. Happy hunting."

He opened the door and walked out. Then he stuck his head into the room. "You aren't sick or anything, are you?"

I swore at him and he closed the door for good this time.

About 2 AM he returned, looking rather upset.

"What's wrong with you?"

"This place is just as bad as the South."

"Really?"

"Yeah. You know after I left you, I found a discotheque-restaurant-type place. I started talking to this North African Jewess. We got along well. She taught me the latest dance in town. We got down to what we were both after and she agreed to come back to the room with me. We took a taxi back here and as I was paying the fare the driver urged me not to take her inside because she wasn't European. I thought he was kidding. Obviously, the management didn't say anything to me directly, but I got the message. We went to a more liberal hotel. Johnny, I can't get over it ... the Jews are racists among themselves in the promised land."

Harris lay down for a catnap. I couldn't sleep anymore so I opened up the book from the airport. Lauren Bacall's autobiography. I still didn't know why, but the subject intrigued me. I pored over the words in search of an answer.

Part IV - The Package

"Hell is other people." – Jean-Paul Sartre

Chapter 19. Lucini's Ted

Thursday, October 13, 1983 – "**Federal authorities have just released the picture of the man who has been held in custody for the assassination of Soviet Premier Berisov. The suspect is known as Tadeusz Szczepanski, a Polish refugee, who entered the United States on the stolen diplomatic passport of Rudolf Schleyer, a UN delegate from the Federal Republic of Germany. Although the suspect has claimed that he carried out the crime on the orders of U.S. intelligence, Rockwell Donaldson, the Director of the CIA, has denied that his agency had any connection with the murder. Unofficial sources in Washington report that an intensive investigation of the crime began almost immediately. The results are expected within the next few days.**" – *The New York Times*

I was nearing the conclusion of the book when I realized suddenly that Ted had been trying to construct a personality from the random moral axioms of movie scripts. He was recombining these fragments into a patchwork of beliefs that made him feel comfortable and unique. How many times had I heard the word "unique" in connection with Ted, from the people I had interviewed, from the depths of my own imagination and memory? I flipped back to the pages in Bacall's book where she cited John Huston's eulogy delivered at Bogart's funeral. "We have no reason to feel any sorrow for him, only for ourselves for having lost him. He is quite irreplaceable. There will never again be anybody like him."

Suddenly I saw the pattern in all its clarity. Bogart, Spade ... the undying legend. Ted was unique and unpredictable. No one would ever replace him either. I was stupid not to have understood this. I began to recall what had happened when I visited Ted in his apartment in 1957. It had all started with a telephone call. He invited me to his apartment, which was unusual. I used to meet him in the Parisian cafés, bars and restaurants. I had never been to his apartment. His voice sounded strange. "Johnny, please come to my place. I don't feel too well. I need a friend."

I took a cab, which drove me to a small building around Gare de l'Est. I mounted the staircases, as he had told me to do on the telephone and rang the doorbell. He opened the door slowly and said, "Thanks for coming, Johnny." He was solemn and acted ceremoniously as he ushered me into the living room.

A few things struck me simultaneously. Ted was sad, almost in tears. As far as I knew, this man had never cried in his life. Also, the apartment was upholstered in Humphrey Bogart movie posters. There were dozens of them, covering every available inch of the walls. Bogart smiling, Bogart grinning, Bogart brandishing a revolver, Bogart doing anything. Bogart scared like Ted at this particular moment. I briefly wondered what kind of act he was playing now. But he was not playing. It was the only time I saw him genuinely sad. I felt as if I were meeting a stranger for the first time.

"What's happened?" I asked.

"I bet you're surprised to see me crying, Johnny."

"Yes, I am," I admitted.

"It's the first time and the last time you'll see me like this," he stated.

"It's okay. It's human," I tried to console him.

"Yes, but I'm inhuman." There was a lump in his throat.

"Forget it." I tried to cheer him up. "What we need to do is celebrate."

"You're quite right, Johnny. Let's have a drink."

He limped over to the bar and poured a glass of vodka for himself and a whiskey for me. Handing me the glass, he lifted his own and proposed a toast. "To Bogie," he said.

We consumed several drinks in total silence and then he started to talk. Tears rolled down his unshaven cheeks as he spoke. He was indeed in an extraordinary state.

"I think I owe you an explanation, Johnny," he sobbed.

"You don't owe me anything," I replied. I poised myself to listen to him. I can't remember whether I felt like a cop, a priest or just a plain human being, but I knew that he needed to confide something.

"Want to stretch out on the couch?"

"Stop pulling that shrink stuff." He was annoyed by my suggestion. "I know how to stop the tears," he said, as if reading my mind. "John Huston said that we shouldn't cry for him because he got everything he wanted. But we should cry for ourselves because we lost him, and no one will ever replace him."

Suddenly his expression changed. I thought he was beginning to feel better. "I want to reveal something to you about my personal life, Johnny, but I want to keep it confidential between you and me," he said.

"You've got the word of a scout," I promised.

"Your word is shit. But I'll tell you anyway because I need to tell it to somebody, somehow, and now is the time. Of course, you see him all over my place."

"You mean ... Bogart?"

"Exactly. He died yesterday, January 14th, 1957. He was only fifty-seven years old."

"But Ted," I interjected, "you're only thirty. Myself thirty-four. We've got a long way to go."

"I know," he said somberly, "but from now on, I'll be all alone."

"No, Ted. You have friends, me, beautiful girls."

"That's not the same. He was like a father to me," he moped.

"But you never met him," I argued.

"Of course not, but my own father died when I was four. I never really met him either." He paused, lit a cigarette and cleared his throat.

"I'll explain. You see, Johnny, during the war, all the values espoused by my teachers and by my own mother were crushed by the Nazi invaders. I was searching for new values. At first, I admired the Nazis. Perhaps it was because they destroyed the world of hypocrisy that I was raised to respect. Perhaps it was simply because they symbolized the new reality. But as soon as they revealed themselves to be my enemy, I had to look for something else. I thought that Communism was an answer, but they rejected me as a bourgeois. I was not good enough for them. I decided to go west with you in '45. Remember?

"In France they looked upon me as a dirty foreigner. To the Americans, I was just another displaced person, a number. I couldn't embrace the values of people who treated me as their inferior. And then suddenly, I discovered Bogart's pictures. *The Maltese Falcon, Casablanca, To Have and To Have Not, The Big Sleep* – those were the ones that pleased me the most. I saw each of them several times. Spade, Rick, Marlowe were fused together in the person of Bogart. He created an honest, noble hero who fought his own way through a corrupt, hostile world. Suddenly I realized that I was a little like those Bogart characters myself. I also had to fight my own way through a dirty, stinking world. I adopted him as my father. I adopted those values. I tried to live my own life according to the way they would show me.

"Now I understand why you cried," I said. "You searched and searched until you found your idol and then he died. So now you're alone."

He was silent.

"But Ted, you make him sound like a Christ."

"Better than a Christ," he announced proudly. "Whenever I have a hard problem to solve, Johnny, I think about what Spade, Rick, Marlowe or Morgan would do in the same situation, and I do it. Now, with him gone, those values remain ingrained on my conscience. He gave me an example of how to live with the dignity of an individual. For the rest of my life, I'll stare at his pictures and they'll show me what to do. Up to now I haven't lived up to those characters, but from now on, I'll try to be just like them."

We cleared customs at Paris Orly at about 9 AM. I immediately went to the phone and called Mustapha. "Hey, this is Miller speaking. Did you find the professor for me?"

"When do you want to see him ... today?"

"As soon as possible. I have to be in New York tomorrow."

"Right. Meet me at La Coupole around noon. I'll be there with him," he guaranteed. "How about my boy, Tadek? A very neat job he did on Berisov. You could have knocked me over with a feather when I saw his face in the paper. A real slick job, heh? Too bad he won't get away with it."

"Yeah, yeah. Thanks for the commentary, Mustapha. At noon then. So long."

I found Harris and sent him to hail a cab. I stayed at the phone and dialed Lucini's number.

"Lucini, this is Johnny."

"How did things go?"

"So-so. I don't have time to talk about it now. Have you got the take-out order ready for me?" Somehow the Poles were on to me, but I still trusted Lucini and decided to take my chance. Nothing ventured, nothing gained.

"Everything's ready," came the quick response.

"Listen, I've an appointment at noon. I'll stop at your place before I go. I'm still at Orly so it'll be a few minutes before I get there."

"Okay, come anytime. I'll be waiting for you."

I hung up and hurried to the curb where Harris was waiting with the taxi door opened. We checked in at Lutetia Hotel. I washed, shaved and changed clothes. Then I went into Harris' room. "Johnny, do we really need to talk to this guy?" was the way he greeted me.

"Sometimes I wonder," I confessed. "But according to Mustapha, he's the only person to whom Ted ever confided his ideas. And let's face it, Ted didn't say much of anything to anyone, did he? This character might be able to help."

"He might," mused Harris.

"Listen, I have another appointment before we see the professor."

"Without me?" protested Harris.

"It's a girl," I smirked.

"Yeah, but this early in the day?"

"I'm going to make it a quickie. Besides she's busy the rest of the day. I'll meet you back here a little before noon and we'll go up to Montparnasse to see this guy."

I left Harris in the hotel wondering about my athletic abilities and got in a cab that I directed across the Seine to Passy, where Lucini lived.

"Man, what happened to you?" Lucini exclaimed as he opened the door. "Come on in. You look as if you haven't slept in five years."

I didn't want to relate the Polish episode to him, so I sloughed off his comment, saying that wine and women were responsible for my fatigue. "Where's the stuff?" I finally asked, noticing that it was getting late.

"Here." He reached underneath his sofa and handed me a package. "Seven kilos."

"And I deliver it to the same place?"

"No. You have to call this phone number when you arrive in New York. We're having trouble with the Chinese there. Call this number and you'll get instructions."

"And payment?"

"They pay me, I transfer your cut to the Swiss account, as usual. When are you coming back?"

"I don't know," I replied honestly, "with the international situation the way it looks."

"They'll find a way out," Lucini declared optimistically.

"That sounds strange coming from a Frenchman."

"A Corsican!" Lucini corrected me.

I fit the package in my briefcase and proposed a short drink. I explained to him that if everything went smoothly and my investigation ended successfully, I might have a choice of jobs. I could even become an executive at the Narcotics Bureau. Then we would be able to make some real money. I could make as many runs as we deemed necessary.

"Speaking of your investigation," said Lucini, "are you on this case?" He showed me a copy of France-Soir with Ted's picture emblazoned on the front page.

I was a bit shaken. "What makes you think I'm on that case?"

"Just a hunch. All I can tell you is that I knew this guy."

I wasn't really interested in revealing the extent of my involvement to him, but I was nevertheless curious to have what he knew. "A fellow-traveler in the cause for Corsican independence?" I asked jokingly.

"He was in the rackets here after the war. We crossed each other's paths from time to time. We almost came to blows when he recruited one of our Africans to pose as a black GI. He was selling contraband, moving in and out of the clubs we operated. But it finally worked out for our common interest because he ended up taking care of the bars that were giving me stiff competition."

"He continued to do that?"

"No. In '58 he went legitimate. He bought himself a few nightclubs. A few years later, he ran into some kind of trouble. He called me one day. 'Lucini,' he said, 'I need some help. Can you come to my place?'

"I took a taxi to his club. It was in the middle of the afternoon and he was alone. 'Nice place,' I complimented him.

"'I've got two more just like it.' He was kind of proud but worried. 'I can't be everywhere at the same time.'

"'How can I help?'

"'I need a machine gun. An Uzi will do fine.'

"I was really startled by that request. 'Are you crazy? If you spill blood, the cops will close you down.'

"'What else can I do when a bunch of fucking racketeers try to extort me?'

"I pointed out that he was in the same line himself not that long ago.

"'I know,' he replied, 'but it was I who screwed the others. I don't like being on the other end.'

"I thought about it and then proposed to rid him of his troubles on certain conditions.

"'Like hell!' He was furious. 'I won't pay you any lousy money for protection.'

"'Who said anything about paying?' I told him. 'It's a business proposition. It could work wonders for both of us. And you won't have to pay a cent.'

"'That sounds better.' He calmed down. 'I hate the idea of being screwed by a friend.'

"'Listen,' I explained, 'you've got three clubs right now. I can give you three good managers, protection, and spread the word that the places are in Lucini's territory. Nobody'll touch you.'

"'What'll I have to do in exchange?'

"'Simple. I'll put my whores in your clubs and use them to circulate drugs. The clubs will be filled. You'll make three times as much as you do now without investing anything. In fact, we'll start some more clubs with the profits I make. You can keep your profits if you like. Even so, we'll be partners, fifty-fifty.'

"'You mean you'd invest money in my bars? I don't get it. What's the catch? Suppose the cops close one of them. What then? I'd be out a lot of money.'

"'You're coming closer to the point. Tell me. How much money do you make per club?'

"'About eight thousand dollars a month.'

"'If they close your clubs, any one of them or all of them, I'll guarantee the money you lose for each month they're out of commission. How does that sound? Okay?'

"'Yes, but ...'

"'Listen, the real benefit is that the more clubs we have, the more circuits we'll have in the business. They'll never close all of them at the same time. The more clubs we have, the better the business.'

"'But what about the cops?'

"'It's nothing to worry about. I have contacts at the Préfecture de Police. I'm sure that most of the clubs will stay open. Perhaps they'll shut one or two occasionally to give the right appearance, but most of these places will run. Do you think I'd offer to invest my own money if this wasn't a sure bet?'

"'It sounds good as long as you get those thugs off my back. Nothing more I hate than being squeezed by ignorant hoodlums.' He paused to fill up our glasses and raised at toast. 'To the Union Corse. *Na Zdrowie!*'

"'To a crazy Polak!' I reciprocated the gesture.

"'I'd still be more comfortable with an Uzi,' commented Tadek.

"I laughed. We made the deal official, and it lasted for almost twenty years. Then he disappeared, until today when I saw his picture in the papers."

"He left his places and the girls to you?" I asked.

"He had staffed his clubs with competent, trustworthy people. Rarely, if ever, did we have any problems. He trained them well. As for finances, his presence wasn't even necessary. We settled our accounts once a month."

"Can I ask you a question? I'm not sure if you'll like it," I said.

"Go ahead. I'll decide."

"What's the relation between this Corsican independence movement and your Unione Corse?"

"Those bums have nothing to do with us," Lucini was annoyed.

"What's the difference?"

"I have explained it to you many times, you dumb Yankee. They want to keep the French out of Corsica, when we believe that we already have the French in our hands, ever since Napoleon. That's why we created the Corsican Union. Look here, Johnny, I have a medal for fighting against the Germans. Just like you have your Congressional Medal of Honor. It's the same thing."

"Still sounds like the Mafia to me."

"The American Mafia doesn't have members in the U.S. government!" He shouted as if I were stupid. "And worse still, your government isn't efficient without them."

"Well, we could include them in Washington, but it still wouldn't get us any oil."

"Because you Americans are stupid. You have the force to seize it, so seize it, for Chrissakes!"

"It might be a good idea, but it'll have to wait until the Mafia controls the government completely."

"That's not such a bad idea. You'll avoid a lot of stuff like your disgraceful retreat in Vietnam. But why are you so interested in the liberation movement in Corsica?"

"I was just wondering whether Ted could have any connection with them." I had by now dispensed with all pretext. Lucini was certain that I was on the investigation.

"Of course not. He was with us all the way. He even warned us to watch out."

"Watch out for what?"

"For Qaddafi. He's got Malta already and he's planting agents in Sicily. He's got more power in Sicily than the Italian government. As you know, the Mafia always goes with power, so maybe they are collaborating with him. His next step might be Sardinia or even Corsica. He finances these national autonomy movements with his oil money. The more the Europeans move toward consolidating their common market, the greater are the opportunities for his activities right here, like with the Basques in Spain, the Albanians in Yugoslavia. He already finances the Irish Republican Army and could move into Flanders or Brittany."

"So why doesn't your Unione Corse do something about it if he's so powerful?"

"Because we're waiting for you folks to move first, Uncle Sam," he replied sarcastically.

"Don't hold your breath. With Uncle Sam, you never know these days," I admonished him.

"Well, we can have one more drink anyway. To the times when American power stood for peace with profit. *Vive l'Amerique!*"

"Vive le SCUM," I countered.

"What's SCUM?"

"Society of Corrupted Universal Motherfuckers. You're a charter member. So long, Corsican SCUM."

"Bye, Yankee SCUM."

Chapter 20. The Professor's Entourage

I hurried back to the hotel. I wanted to leave the package in the safe deposit box before collecting Harris and going up to Montparnasse.

I found him in the Lutetia café talking to a blonde. How convenient, I thought. Had he followed me to Lucini's? I had no choice but to play along.

"Hi, old buddy. Don't waste your time," I said, surprising him. "She's five thousand francs a throw. A thousand dollars. You dig?"

"You mean she ..."

"What do you think? Maybe she goes for your looks or your charming personality? Let's go. I'm hungry and we have a previous engagement."

We left the whore wondering what she had done wrong and hailed a cab for La Coupole. The driver fought his way through traffic up Boulevard Raspail, past the shoppers, commuters and movie-goers, turned left onto Boulevard Montparnasse, and glided to a halt in front of Paris' grande dame of brasseries. Fishmongers wearing long aprons, rubber boots and gloves presided over the sidewalk raw bar. They shucked oysters, clams, crabs, sea urchins, and crayfish and rested them on shaved-ice serving trays draped in clean, fresh seaweed.

I entered through the bar, a tiny space compared with the rest of the massive dining room and saw Mustapha approaching us.

"You're right on time," he said, extending his hand warmly.

"Army training, Mustapha," I greeted him.

"Come on, I'll introduce you to 'the professor.' You're to call him just that. He doesn't want his name connected with this thing."

We moved toward a corner booth that was hidden by a cluster of university students. Seated at the table and surrounded by four pretty girls dressed decadently chic was a small man in British tweed. I guessed that he was about sixty-five or seventy years old. I immediately sized up the situation: a mandarin holding court among his students and acolytes. They acted like bodyguards to prevent any unauthorized vassals from having contact with him. He was obviously popular with this generation of students. He had silvery hair, a narrow, haggard face and mischievous eyes. This is no Frank Sinatra, I thought to myself, wondering what talents he possessed to merit the blanket of stylish young women in tight sweaters and jeans who stomped around on high-heeled boots that sometimes rose past their knees.

As we approached, Mustapha cut through the crowd and we followed. Perhaps they knew him. Perhaps they'd been notified of his visit. The girls squirmed out of the booth, leaving the professor hunched alone over the table. He looked like a tiny warlord who was contemplating the possibilities for victory of his warriors just departed for battle.

"Professor, Johnny Miller and Dave Harris," announced Mustapha. He shook hands with both of us and invited us to sit down with a graceful sweeping gesture.

"What are you drinking, Professor?" I asked.

"Vittel-menthe," he replied.

"Mustapha?" I turned to look up at the refined Arab hoodlum who had not sat down with us.

"Nothing, thanks," he replied.

When the waiter came, I ordered the three drinks. Mustapha bowed as if to excuse himself. "I'd better be going now," he said.

"Thanks for everything, Mustapha. But before you leave, please do me a favor if you're not too busy."

"Sure," said Mustapha. "A friend of Tadek's is a friend of mine too."

"Wait for me at the bar and I'll join you as soon as I've finished interviewing the professor. We'll have a few things to discuss."

"Okay with me," grinned Mustapha. "Especially since I see a nice Swedish blonde coming in. See you later, Mr. Harris, Professor." Mustapha disappeared into the crowd of students and lunchtime tourists.

"Mustapha said you want us to call you 'Professor,' but what is your real name?" I started out the discussion just like a cop.

"Pierre-Michel Boulet," he stated clearly.

"No kidding?" Harris' mouth was agape. "Not the real Pierre-Michel Boulet? We've heard a lot about you in the States." Sarcasm dripped from his comment although it was probably lost on the Frenchman.

"I'm afraid philosophy has never been one of my strong points," I confessed and then pulled out the two pictures of Ted that I handed to the professor. He studied them intensely. "Under what name did you know this man?" I asked curtly.

"Ted. I never knew his last name." The professor's English was excellent, not a trace of accent.

The waiter arrived with our drinks. "Professor, you know what we're up against. Our job is to find out as much as possible about Ted."

"I hate to disappoint, but I don't know much about his life."

"But you do know something, obviously."

"Yes, you see, we talked a lot. But they were chance meetings. Nothing more than that."

"What on earth did you two have to talk about? From what we've heard about him, well, ...?" Harris shrugged his shoulders.

"Philosophy, of course. His view of the world and mine. You know, I'm often accused of spending my life in cafés. It's true, though. I can't work anywhere else. A café has the advantage of being indifferent. The people who come here are independent of each other. Just imagine, if I were at home, I couldn't talk to you as I do now. There's my wife and children. When I'm working, they're a burden to me. Here, I feel free.

"About Ted, it's very strange because about a year before I met him, I'd decided to branch out. Philosophy in essay form is rather boring. I began to write plays and attempted a novel too. But I found that my dialogue was too abstract. I made notes of man-in-the street dialogues to liven up my work. At the end of each evening, I would go home and read what I had recorded each day. I'd choose the most interesting ones and throw away all the others. One that I saved was Ted's."

"Like a collection of the most interesting characters you'd ever met," I suggested.

"Yes, something like that. But before we enter into a bibliography of Ted's work, I'd better tell you a little bit about la Boîte. It was a café in St. Germain des Près. They've torn it down now. I met Ted there for the first time in 1949. La Boîte was frequented by all types – intellectuals, working girls, homosexuals, even a few students. Sometimes people fought. Sometimes they held discussions and then fought.

"One night, a blond fellow wearing an American army uniform and speaking German caught my ear. His German dialect opened a lot of old wounds. He was shouting like an SS man, but people were crowded around him, enjoying it. Most of them were laughing. I was curious. I asked the waiter about him. I was told that Ted was an American who spoke German fluently and came every night looking for girls. I told the waiter to invite him over to my table for a drink.

"He finally ambled over to me and asked if I thought he was German or American. I admitted that I believed he was an American. He began to laugh and ribbed me because I had listened to the waiter who repeated the same story to anyone who asked. I simply couldn't believe it when he told me he was Polish. I was quite surprised."

"Did you learn why he acted so strangely?"

"'Well,' he began to tell me, 'I was fighting in the war, but we were defeated by the Russians. For me there was no medal, no glory. When I wear this American uniform, I become the liberator of France. It's easy to get the chicks when you've got heroic glory pasted all over you.'

"'What about the language?' I inquired.

"'Oh,' he sniggered, 'it's completely crazy. I don't quite understand why I do it except that since the beginning of the war when I saw the SS men exercising all forms of authority, I wanted to become one. But they rejected me as a failure, as a human being. They murdered my family to prove it. I'm no expert, but I think that by acting German I refute their rejection of me as a human being. It seems plausible anyway.'

"I had no way to respond to him," confessed the professor. "All I did was to suggest that he read a few books so he might better articulate his identity. I suggested Dostoyevsky since he was a Slav, I mentioned Nietzsche, Sartre, and ..."

"Yourself," I grinned.

"You're quite right. You see, I thought that if he read a little, it would help complete his identity. It would round out the character of an individual I understood to be a man of action."

"Are you a man of action, Professor?" I demanded.

"I'm afraid not, therefore I am still incomplete. I can only go so far as to inspire other people to action." He admitted this squarely.

"From what I know, Professor, I remember seeing your picture associated with the movement to try Americans for war crimes in Vietnam. I also remember that you once interviewed Andreas Baader in prison. I'd refer to that as action. What about you, Professor?"

"Armchair action, only armchair action," he mumbled modestly. "Please don't confuse the issue, Mr. Miller. I have nothing against Americans, only those who directed the war in Vietnam and continue to support imperialism, Kissinger, McNamara, Weinberger and their corporate running dogs. Many of your own compatriots share my opinion ..."

"Okay, no hard feelings." The Vietnam War and Boulet's politics were distractions I was anxious to drop. "Let's return to Ted," I said. "When did you see him again?"

"Well, I met him a couple of years later. He was very upset, something about a girl. At first, he attacked me. 'You and your fuckin' idea of freedom. It stinks,' was the way he greeted me.

"I asked him to explain what prompted such a condemnation of my theories. 'I don't see the connection between your love affair and my logic of freedom.'

"'Well, I had a date with a chick here tonight ...'

"'... and she stood you up?' I guessed.

"'No,' he said belligerently. 'She's right here with another guy. I was so angry I wanted to beat him up, but she said that even if I did, she'd stay with him.'

"'So why attack me then?'

"'Because she referred to you and your philosophy.' He was shouting now, waving his finger in front of my face and blustering. 'She told me that she was free and could change her mind anytime she wanted!' He was really angry and stomped his foot whenever he emphasized a word.

"'Well, I agree with her,' I said.

"'You do? Well what about her word? The promises she made to me!'

"'It doesn't matter because, as you said, she is free to change her mind. She is free to do anything she wants to do, and so are you.'

"'Suppose I am free to slap your head!'

"'Why would you do that?' I didn't know whether he was serious but was taking no chances. He was a slim but powerful-looking man.

"'For poisoning the people's minds with your absurd idea of freedom! Your idea of freedom gives people all sorts of possibilities. They can betray, kill, denounce their best friends to the police. Your idea of freedom gives people a poor excuse to do anything. What about manhood, honor and dignity?'

"'I really don't see your point.'

"'With your philosophy of freedom,' he took a conciliatory yet dead serious tone, 'people can be bought and bribed with a clear conscience

... No, Professor, I believe in freedom but not your type of freedom.'

"'Then the books I recommended didn't help?'

"'They confused me, that's all. Those writers, your philosopher-kings, they all contradict each other. They made me feel dizzy, like I was drunk. From now on I don't listen to anybody. I'll create my own set of values,' he swore with conviction. 'The first act of my style of freedom is that I won't slap you. You're much too old and I respect your age. My only comment is that the generation of kids who are listening to you will no doubt be quite free,' there was a long pause, 'to kill each other!' He looked around the room and began to stare at a group of women who had just entered the place. 'Excuse me, but I see a pretty young face and I think it would be more enjoyable to be with her than you. No hard feelings?' And he left.

"I didn't see him for many years. I had heard that he fell in with the underworld. When I met him again it was 1958, and he was an established businessman. I ran into him in one of his own nightclubs. He was smiling. 'Hi Professor.'

"'Hi, Ted. What do you do here?'

"'I own this joint.'

"'Really?'

"'Yes. I have a couple of others just the same. Have a drink on the house,' he offered.

"'I'm with some friends,' I explained.

"'Drinks for everyone then!' He turned to the bartender and ordered him to serve everyone in the place a free drink.

"When we were finally alone, I confronted him with the rumors. 'I heard that you are associated with the underworld.'

"'That's none of your business, Professor,' he snapped.

"'But I'm genuinely worried. You haven't done anything illegal, have you?'

"'Of course, I have. All my life I've been breaking those kinds of laws. To live was illegal for my race in Poland. And then I was here alone in a foreign country. To go illegal is a new kind of warfare, Professor. My war didn't end in '45. By the way, what did you do during the war, Professor?'

"'Not much,' I confessed. 'I helped to organize passive resistance.'

"'And you did a lot of thinking,' he interrupted.

"'Of course.'

"'You spent the war sitting on your ass, thinking, while I was fighting in the Polish underground. Professor, you are a man of thought, I'm a man of action. When I joined the underground, it was not to become a hero. It was simply a question of survival. After the war I discovered I would have to use combat tactics in order to survive once again. But for now, for this short period in life, I have found some peace.'

"'Why no combat now?' I wanted to know.

"'Who knows. Maybe some circumstances will put my nerves to the test again. In that case, I'll have to go to war for a third time.'

"I attempted to order another round of drinks for my friends who were seated apart from us. He stopped me. 'No, no. You're my guests.'

"'Still with that honor and dignity,' I prodded him.

"'More than ever,' he responded without visible expression. 'You see, Professor, I never studied as much as you, but I have made three important journeys in life.'

"'I didn't realize you were such a traveler.'

"'It was not the kind of traveling you might think. My first voyage was through different political systems: fascist, communist, liberal and conservative democracies. You have to have seen them all in order to take a position. My second journey was among different classes of people: from the aristocracy into which I was born down to the gutter, passing through working people, bourgeois, gangsters, murderers, mercenaries, and retarded bums. I went through all of them.'

"'What about the third trip?' I asked anxiously.

"'Well, the third trip was my most important trip, but the most difficult to explain, especially to a guy like you.' He stared into my eyes accusingly.

"'I'm not a complete imbecile,' I tried to defend myself.

"'I know that, Professor, but the third trip was an odyssey between the extremes of human experience.'

"'I think I know what you're trying to describe, Ted. It's to kill and to be killed.'

"'That's right, Professor. Once you've made this trip, none of the other emotions count any longer. Once you've completed this sort of journey, you've covered all paths. The path leading from instinct to knowledge and back again.'

"'Well, I have often contemplated such experiences, but I never had the privilege of living through them.'

"'Professor,' his face was tense, and his lips quivered. 'I lived through them and I hesitate to call it a privilege. It was forced upon me in order to survive.'

"'Did you ever compromise your sense of honor and dignity to survive?'

"'Perhaps I did, but I was young and naive at the time. Since the end of your war in '45, I've understood that without honor and dignity, there is no sense to survival.'

"He excused himself and returned to his work. He wished me and my friends a pleasant evening. I didn't see him again for another ten years.

"It was in the spring of 1968 that we ran into each other. It was in the midst of the student uprisings.

"'You see, Professor, this is the generation you created. They're high on the concept of freedom that you offer. And now look at the mess they've started.'

"'Well, I can't blame them,' I said. 'They have their convictions. They are refusing a world of rules which they had no part in creating. I would gladly join but they would not have me. They don't trust the older generation. We are racists toward the young, they claim.'

"'You're really too much, Professor,' he said coldly. 'You ought to cross that line and join those bastards. I understand them also,' he added bitterly. 'When I came to France, there was no place for me either. I had to fight alone, and it was hard to get my place in the sun. And I risked my life and freedom. What do they risk? A day in jail? A policeman's truncheon? It's nothing compared to the Gestapo tortures and executions. They are basically cowards if they have to demonstrate in a big crowd. It makes them feel reassured. These demonstrations are bullshit!'

"'How can you say that!?'

"'Take a close look. They even have queers demonstrating. Transvestites, prostitutes and all kinds of freaks. And as far as racism is concerned, take my advice. I'm an expert. You're not a racist for the young, quite the contrary. This is the new racism against the old. The whole world is turned upside down. They're not fighting for democracy but hypocrisy. I hate hypocrisy. I once saw it. There's no longer anyone to set an example for them. Government leaders, people in the highest places – all they do is lie. They said prosperity was here to stay. It's not. They said the war in Indochina was over. It's still going on. They said that there would be no rising cost of living. It's going up every day. Read the press!'

"'What about you? Do you have a better example?' I argued.

"'Yes, I was lucky enough to have one.'

"'Where is he?'

"'Bogart died, but it doesn't matter. His values still live.'

"'What do you intend to do?'

"'I don't know. The world makes me sick and tired. Most of my friends are gone. I don't understand the new generation anymore. My business is running by itself. Sometimes I feel like locking myself in my apartment, not seeing anybody anymore. I don't belong anywhere.'

"'Watch what you're doing,' I cautioned him. 'If you withdraw, you'll find yourself in the desert.'

"'I'm tired of living in this jungle. I'll choose the desert instead.'

"'But you don't have to do it the hard way. Just adapt a little.'

"'Ha!' he sniggered. 'No, Professor, there will be no compromise,' he said harshly. 'Compromise signifies that all my past years were failures. Compromise would mean the end of Ted and his set of values. No, Professor.'

"'Hitler didn't want to compromise either. He committed suicide.'

"'Don't worry, Professor. Before I compromise or commit suicide, I'll take a whole bunch of others with me. I haven't yet figured it out, but I shall. In dying, I want to have a lot of company.'

"He left me standing there.

"The last time we met was about six months ago, here at La Coupole. My eyesight is very poor now. He called out my name to get my attention. 'Professor, it's me, Ted!'

"'Where have you been?'

"'Holed up some place.'

"'I don't understand.'

"'Don't you remember in '68 when I told you about choosing the desert or the war? Well, I'm going for the third war.'

"'What have you been doing?'

"He was quite incomprehensible.

"'Planning. Master-planning.'

"'What kind of planning?'

"'How to get even with this fucking world.'

"'What a morbid idea.'

"'On the contrary. You should be proud of me. It's the result of my reflections on your favorite subject, freedom. You see, Professor, your concept of freedom came from constantly sitting in your chair and thinking. I also thought a lot, and I decided that the world will find its freedom only in destruction. Violent destruction.'

"'Well, you're not the only one with that theory. All the terrorists think the same way. What surprises me is that you would reach this conclusion after fifty years of age. If I had only known the way you felt before, I could have introduced you to some organized fighters.'

"'You mean those terrorist bandits? The ones who blackmail the world?'

"'I would not refer to them as bandits. Today they are true freedom fighters. They counter the hypocritical, decadent Western policies. They remind me of you fighting in the Polish underground army. They are today's heroes.'

"'Do you actually fight with them, Professor?'

"'Of course not. I do some thinking for them. And I try to rehabilitate their image in the public's eyes by using certain media which are at my disposal. But I can still introduce you to them.'

"'No, Professor. There's no sense. My battle and theirs are not the same.'

"He was carrying a parcel, which he offered to me.

"'I'd like you to look at this Professor. It's a sample of my writing. I call it "The Five Days of Freedom." They were the days when I felt deeply and enjoyably about freedom – the freedom so dear to your heart, and mine. Of course, there were more than five days. There were thousands, but to write about each one of them would have presented too great a problem, so I cut it down to five days. The rest can be filled in by the reader's imagination. Maybe you'll find it comparable to your philosophy, or maybe it will strike you as a different type of freedom that you never dreamed of. I don't care if it will ever be published or not because I am not the kind of man to fight the world with a pen and paper, sitting on my ass like you. Lately, though, I have been sitting on my ass. Now I have to go. The time for action has arrived. I shall strike, and you'll remember me on that day, Professor.'

"'With honor and dignity?'

"'Always, Professor. Always.'

"I see the connection now," added the professor. "Berisov, this was his strike."

"Yes, Professor."

I wanted to say, "Eureka!" and puke all over this intellectual bastard. "That's exactly what we're investigating. Did you have any further contact with him?"

"No, but I have that copy of his writing, if you'd like to see it. It's at my home, which is only a ten-minute walk from here."

"Thanks, Professor, I'd appreciate it. Before we end this chat, what kind of person was he? What kind of impression did he make on you? Was he rational or irrational?"

"He was both, like everybody," explained the professor. "But what was most original about him was that he tried to keep values in a world where there are few. I think he was the only man I knew who truly belonged completely to himself. His convictions were unshakable. Nothing could make him change his mind or influence his character. That was his main problem: the conflict between his ideals and the reality of the world. It also made him attractive to other people. He was a romantic idealist, always reaching for unobtainable absolutes. Honor and dignity are very rare traits today. They were his treasured possessions that nothing and no one could purchase."

"May I ask you a question, Professor? Have you ever heard of Sam Spade or Rick Blaine?"

"No, I don't think so."

"Well, you must have seen some Bogart movies ..."

"Bogart! Of course. I saw them all. Years ago. But what does any of this have to do with Sam Spade or Rick Blaine?"

"It doesn't matter. Those were the names of his heroes, the ones Bogart portrayed. When I think of it, your descriptions of Ted remind me of a Bogart hero. You said he kept his values in a world where there were few. I just read that in a book, *Lauren Bacall, By Myself.*"

"I haven't read that book, but I did indeed say that about him. It's true, and your comparison may be exact. But weren't all of Bogart's heroes conventionally good? They never dreamed of destruction."

"Thank you, Professor."

He made a motion to one of his young women students. She came to the table and helped him up. Slowly, they walked to the door and left the restaurant in search of the book.

When they were gone, Harris turned to me. "How did you get this crazy idea about Ted and Bogart?"

"Well, things pop into my head when I read. Sometimes I get brainstorms. "We're policemen, aren't we?"

"Of course," said Harris with conviction.

"Now I've come up with a brainstorm for you, Dave. So far, you've had some nice tail on this trip. How'd you like another piece of ass tonight?"

"You mean it?" Harris asked skeptically.

"Yeah, that's why I had Mustapha wait by the bar – to keep you happy. I don't want you to turn into a misanthrope like this dude Ted."

I stared toward the bar until I caught Mustapha's eye. He had been sitting at the end of the bar talking to the Nordic-type girl. He now excused himself and walked to our table.

"Yes, Miller?"

"Can't you get a girl for my friend? You know he's a poor FBI agent who hates to spend Uncle Sam's money."

"You want me to get him a girl? I have plenty of girls working for me. It will be my gift to the U.S. and the FBI whom I admire so much."

"Make sure that she's clean," I whispered into his ear. "I don't want him bringing home any clap from Barbès because he'd get fired by the FBI." It'd serve him right, I thought to myself privately.

"Barbès?" asked Mustapha with surprise. "You think my girls are only from Barbès? I have some high-class stuff too."

"Take him and find a nice one. You can send one to my room at the Lutetia for later."

"Will do," smiled Mustapha.

They left and I was finally rid of Harris again. This time I wanted to do some legitimate thinking and didn't need that two-bit gumshoe in my face. I ordered another drink and practiced my French with a couple of the professor's young women while we waited for the mandarin to return. Soon the old man made his grand entry. The crowd split into two like the Red Sea parting for Moses. He deposited a package on the table as he squirmed into the booth. He was panting. A ten-minute walk for a guy his age was an athletic workout.

"I want to apologize to you, Professor. I have a bad habit of always being a cop. I have just one more question. You spoke to him about his ideas more than anyone else. What, specifically, could have motivated him to commit such an act?"

"He was perhaps trying to constrain the world to fit his imagination. By such an act, he would force the world to conform to his sense of morality." The professor paused, lit a cigarette and blew a puff into the air. "Maybe he was simply bored," he concluded.

"Bored!" I exclaimed. "I don't believe it. People don't risk the world's existence just because they are bored."

"You might be surprised. A colleague of mine in England, Dr. Colin Wilson, has elaborated a theory of murder claiming that mass murderers commit their crimes out of boredom. His book is called *The Psychology of Murder*. You can read it. It might help you as a policeman."

"Do you think his sense of honor and dignity would have led him to jeopardize his life, the lives of others?"

"I think, yes."

"Last question, Professor. Was he addicted to anything?"

"Not in the usual sense, if you are referring to drugs or alcohol. His only dope was danger."

My conclusion too.

I left the professor and his entourage and moved to the Select Bar Américain across Boulevard Montparnasse. I asked the waiter for a small table in the rear, a bottle of Perrier and total privacy. I slipped him a hundred-franc note just to make sure. Then I opened the parcel.

Chapter 21. "The Five Days of Freedom"

They might die at any minute. He looked at his mother, who was sitting on the other side of the room. She was completely oblivious to the danger that surrounded them. Still she was unable to protect him. He hated her. Because of her, he was still there. How many times could he have jumped the wall and mixed with the Aryans, as Max and Mr. Greenberg told him? Everybody told him that he could get away with it. Despite his religion, his accent and his looks were perfect. And now he was sitting trapped like a rat just because he couldn't leave her. When he was a little boy, she used to ask him, "Who do you love the most?" He would answer, "My mother." When she wanted to scare him, she would say, "You know what's going to happen to you?" He would shake his head. "I'm going to die and leave you all alone." He was scared of being left alone. Now he was going to die with her. He remembered how she had protected him at school when he was a child. Now she could no longer protect him.

They say that before you die, you see your past flash before your eyes. Now it was coming to him ... his mother, Karski ...

His mother was a really big lady. Countess Polanska. Sometimes he heard people laugh behind her back. "A Jewish countess! Who ever heard of a Jewish countess?" They were jealous. He didn't care.

During the summer he stayed on the estate in Lodz. Karski was there. In one way he was like Adam's mother, always talking to the boy about his father. His mother talked about how handsome he was, how she would like Adam to be like him. Although Adam had barely known his father, he pictured him in his dreams because of the way he had been portrayed. Karski would always begin his stories, "I remember the charge against the Bolsheviks in 1920. Your father insisted on participating even though he was a doctor. He was an officer, and it was his patriotic duty, he said, to charge the enemy with his fellow officers. The Colonel was riding with his sword in his hand and I was beside him. What a marvelous time it was! I promised him that if anything happened to him, I would always take care of his family."

Adam liked Karski. Technically, Karski was running his mother's estate. Adam went to school in Lodz, to a Polish school, Ksiedza Skorupki, because he was Polish. But sometimes people would tell him that he was Jewish. Half-Jewish. It sickened him. He couldn't understand why they said that.

When the war started, the Germans came to Lodz and to their estate. As soon as they arrived, they ordered all Jews to wear badges and herded them into the Lodz Ghetto. He and his mother were classified as Jews, and they were threatened. His mother didn't know what to do. But as usual, Karski came to the rescue. "Countess, you and Adam should go to Warsaw. Lodz is going to become part of the German Reich. In Warsaw there'll be more freedom. And don't worry, I'll take care of everything."

They followed his advice and, with but a few of their possessions, left the family estate behind. In Warsaw they rented an apartment near Karski's. Ever the loyal retainer, he too moved to the capital. It was 1939 and Adam was just 13.

During the first year nothing really important happened with the exception that the Jews were ordered to wear bands with the star of David. He didn't like to wear it. It burned his arm. His mother didn't care. A friend once asked him, "Why don't you like to wear the band? Are you ashamed of being a Jew?"

"Yes, I'm being treated differently, and I don't understand why I should be. I don't know why I deserve to be."

The situation changed rapidly. They heard rumors about kidnappings, about forced labor, about people being beaten up or killed. But they didn't believe them. Neither he nor his mother took them seriously. However, when they started to seal off the area for the ghetto in 1940, he grew concerned despite his mother's persistent blindness. He wanted to know why they were building a wall. He asked many people, but it was only Karski's answer he remembered. "It's no good. I hope you don't go inside. The Nazis don't build walls and put people inside just to release them afterwards. It will end badly, very badly."

On October 12, 1940, the order came for all Jews to move into the ghetto. The ghetto area was much too small to contain the half-million Jews already crowded into the city. There was only enough room for about twenty percent of them to live comfortably. Karski insisted that Adam and his mother should not move into the ghetto, but Adam's mother was reluctant to disobey. "Karski, there's a death penalty for any Jew who stays outside. In the ghetto, at least, there's nothing to fear." Karski didn't argue with her, and Adam, then only fourteen, had no choice but to follow his mother.

His mother had money and jewelry that she had brought from the estate at Lodz. Some of the jewelry was sold on the black market to pay for an apartment in a good area of the ghetto at 20 Chlodna Street. The President of the Jewish Council, Dr. Cherniakoff, lived there along with select families of the high intelligentsia. Karski delivered food because it was hard to buy in the ghetto. But on November 15, the ghetto was sealed to the world outside. No Aryans were allowed to enter, and no one could leave without a special pass.

In the beginning many Jews thought that the German measure was a good one. Although the life and the humiliation of the ghetto were painful, it gave them a sense of shared identity. Jews who were living outside under a borrowed identity were subject to a solitude that obliged them to deny themselves, to be always on edge. In the event of betrayal and discovery, they faced prison or death, whereas in the ghetto such dangers were for the moment nonexistent. Jews thought they were safer inside.

Certainly, people died from hunger, but due to his mother's wealth, Adam was well-nourished. On his way to school in the mornings, he had to step over dead bodies in the street. Sometimes they were covered with newspaper but not always. The first time he saw a corpse in the street, it shocked him. He ran home crying, "Mother, I just saw a dead man in the street!" The next day there were two or three corpses.

The day after, even more. The bodies became so commonplace that he learned to step over them and sublimated his emotions. Although a corpse can be an outrage, it does have a stupid serenity about it.

In Lodz, Adam had been a good student, but in the ghetto school he received bad grades. His teachers were angry and often scolded him. "Study harder, you're wasting yourself," they admonished.

"Is studying really necessary? You don't teach me how to survive," he protested.

"Is that what your mother told you?"

"Not at all. Anyway, I've started to have doubts about my mother."

One teacher, Abram Winarski, had known Adam from Lodz and reacted with surprise. "I remember when you believed everything she said. Why have you changed now?"

"Well, when I was young, everything that she did and said was consistent. But once in Lodz, a German soldier pushed me, and she said nothing. She, who was always protecting me, said nothing. From that moment on, I doubted everything she said, everything she did, and all the people in our circle whom she talked to. You know, I don't think she prepared me for reality."

"And what is reality?" asked the teacher.

"Germans are the reality now," Adam replied.

From November 15, 1940 to April 17, 1942, life in the ghetto went on as usual. Some people were making money, some lived frugally like Adam and his mother, while others starved to death. The ghetto had become an autonomous state. The Germans had even created a Jewish Police Service from the available young men. Adam wanted to join, but they didn't accept him because of his age. The policemen looked different because they sometimes wore high jackboots like the Germans. They also wore a hat with a Jewish star emblazoned on it. Except for that star, Adam envied them. Somehow, he would find a way to get a uniform.

The majority of the Jews Adam met in the ghetto were Orthodox. He had never lived in a Jewish community and was a stranger to their culture. He asked himself over and over, "Am I a Jew? Or am I a Pole?" He had nothing in common with the Jews and felt like a Pole, but the decision was not up to him. The Germans had decided that he was a Jew and put him into the ghetto. But even that didn't help him find himself.

Adam would walk the streets for hours, simply to be alone and to think. Sometimes he played on the dead bodies, jumping from one to another. When he tired of this game, he would stop in the Art Café where they gave shows. From time to time, he saw a few "bulls" sitting there. Everyone treated them with respect because they were smugglers. They would sit down and drink, eat and talk about their adventures on the other side. Adam admired their courage because they went to the other side. That's where I belong, he thought, not here.

The German authorities supplied only one-fifth of the food necessary for survival in the ghetto. Rumor had it that the rest of the food came from the smugglers. It was true. That's why everyone respected them. People had seen the smugglers at night unloading the trucks. They had seen them with their own eyes unlike the other rumors about kidnappings and exterminations. That was rubbish, but this was true.

In turn the smugglers lived better than most, but they risked their lives for this privilege. They helped everybody. There were some stupid people who said bad things about them, that they were making money off the people in the ghetto. So what? Adam didn't care. He looked up to the smugglers. They were his kind of people. On the other hand, he and his mother had money. They could buy food. There was always a way for them even without smugglers.

At the Art Café, he would sit at a table near the smugglers and listen attentively to stories of their exploits on the outside. Adam watched one particular man who always talked loudest. One night their eyes met.

"Hey, boy."

Adam didn't like very much being referred to as "boy" but respected the man. "Yes, sir," he replied.

"What are you doing here?"

"Having a drink."

"You're not Jewish, are you?"

"I don't know," said Adam truthfully. "What do you think?"

"Come on, cut the crap. My name is Max. What's yours?"

"Adam."

"Well, Adam, are you Jewish?"

"I told you, Max, I don't know. They told me I was, so I'm here."

"You're Christian?"

"On my father's side."

"Want some vodka?"

Adam had never tasted vodka. He was too young. But Max impressed him, and he was flattered to be asked to drink with such a great man.

"Of course." Adam drank a couple of rounds with them.

"You're lucky," Max said. "With your face, blond hair and blue eyes. You don't even have an accent when you talk. Look at me. I can't speak Polish or even Yiddish properly. I used to be a porter in a railroad station. You know, boy, everybody's bitching in the ghetto. People are dying. But people are dying every day, all over the world. Here, me and my friends keep people from dying. We bring them food. Now I have an important job and people respect me." Max smiled at Adam. "I could use a boy like you. With your face, you could go through easily. I bet you could even survive easily there. Come see me here tomorrow. We'll talk."

Adam returned the next day. He felt proud in his company and continued to meet him at the café. Max was respected and some of it seemed to rub off on him.

One day Max asked, "Would you like to go with me to the other side?"

"Outside is death. At least here we don't take any risks. On the other side, we are sure to die," ventured Adam.

Max laughed. "You don't trust your old friend, Max?"

Adam's first trip to the other side came in the spring of 1942. He went in a truck with Max and his gang of smugglers. They went through the gate without a hitch. Nobody asked for passes. They went to the big German food distribution depot for the Warsaw area. Max got out of the truck and spoke to a German officer like an old friend. Then he called Adam over and introduced him as his new "secretary."

The officer smiled at him. He wore a strange uniform, probably that of a German administrator. "What's your full name, young man?"

"*Ich heisse Adam Polanski.*"

"*Du kannst gut Deutsch sprechen.*"

"*Danke,*" replied Adam, adding impulsively, "*Meine Mutter ist deutsche.*"

"Too bad," the German, whose name was Kraussmeyer, sighed. "But what can we do? The Führer's orders are law, so you have to stay in the ghetto."

They began to load the truck, and during the operation Adam ran to find Max. "I'd like to visit a friend of mine. He doesn't live far from here."

"Okay but hurry up. We're leaving in an hour."

Adam went to Karski's Warsaw apartment. He was at home and overjoyed to see him. "Count Polanski," he exclaimed and embraced the boy as if he were his own son. "Is it really you?"

"Yes, Karski, but I can't stay long. I've just come for a visit."

"You should stay. You should bring your mother here. Something is in the wind. I've heard rumors from the country. Since the war started with the Soviets, the Germans are killing everybody in East Poland."

"How you exaggerate everything," Adam laughed.

"I heard it through the underground," Karski said.

Adam stopped laughing. "You're serious, aren't you?" He stared into Karski's face. It was immobile. "What's happening out there?"

"In all the towns, everywhere you meet Jews, they all tell the same tale. Einsatzkommando squads come into a town and kill all the Jews." Seeing that the boy still didn't believe him, Karski added, "Even the Poles say the same thing. Einsatzkommandos mean death to the Jews."

"But we are here under the General Government. We're not in the Soviet Union. Maybe they do that because they want to take revenge on the Jews in Russia because they started the Soviet revolution. But here in Europe, we're in a civilized country and nothing like that can happen."

"I hope you're right for your sake, Count Polanski. But still I don't trust the Germans. If you ever need any help, remember I'm always here. I'll never leave Warsaw while you and your mother are here. I promised your father I would take care of you."

With Karski's sad face and the frightening thought of the Einsatzkommandos still fresh in his mind, Adam found his way back to the depot and Max. They returned in the truck laden with food.

Once back in the ghetto, Adam pushed to the back of his mind the sad part of his conversation. At home, his mother asked him why he was so unhappy, but he didn't say anything because he knew she would never understand. As a matter of fact, she was playing bridge with the wives of Drs. Rosenbloom and Grajevski and another woman. She had inquired out of politeness. She really didn't care what he thought or why he was depressed. His mother was happy because she could play hostess, the Countess Polanska, wife of the late, venerated Count Polanski, M.D. She was happy because she could serve her guests sandwiches, and they were happy to be able to eat and pretend that their lives were normal. They played bridge completely oblivious to what was going on around them.

Rumors started to seep into the ghetto about the exterminations of Jews in the towns of Lublin and Belzec. Yet the Warsaw Jews chose to believe that everybody was being sent to the East to work. Adam knew better. When he finally told his mother of the danger, she simply laughed it off. "Danger, ha! What do you want to do, go to the other side? The only thing that awaits us on the other side is death. Don't you read the German orders? We are supposed to stay here. And here we live peacefully."

All she cared about were clothes and arranging the furniture she had brought so carefully from Lodz to Warsaw. And those damn crystal glasses! She was always worried when there were ashes on the carpet. Adam was tired of her ridiculous games.

More rumors were circulating. This time from the town of Chelmno where Jews, it was said, were being murdered en masse. Still, the ghetto did not believe. "It's probably the caprice of the local authorities," was the most popular comment. There were also countervailing rumors, deployed by German propaganda, to the effect that life in the labor camps was pleasant, and that workers were fed and paid reasonably well. In fact, the information about the exterminations was so cruel that nobody dared to believe it, until April 17 and 18, 1942. During a nighttime raid, the Germans shot 30 people whom they had roused from sleep and dragged into the street. Now mass murder had come to the Warsaw Ghetto. The next morning the Germans announced that those people were executed because they were helping to finance the underground. It was only the second time that Adam had heard the word, underground. On July 22, the Germans posted proclamations in the ghetto announcing the evacuation of all Jews to the East. Six thousand men were to proceed to the Umschlagplatz or Transfer Area where they would be given three kilos of bread and one kilo of jelly.

During the first days, a few people went voluntarily. Adam was walking along the street when he ran into Max, who was wearing a Jewish Police uniform. Get yourself a uniform," he counseled. "The Jewish Police are going to be the last evacuated."

"But where? Can you get me one?"

"I think so. C'mon."

Max brought him to the Art Café where they sat down with the band of smugglers. Max spoke to them demonstratively in Yiddish, most of which Adam couldn't understand. He was staring out the window feeling excluded when he saw his teacher, Winarski, go by. He looked tired. Adam rose to invite him inside. "Teacher! Come in here for a moment, please."

Winarski saw Adam and entered.

"Who's he?" Max inquired as Winarski approached their table.

"My teacher," replied Adam. He's a Communist. He's the one who always says that Jews have to fight."

"Oh! Nice to meet you." Max extended his hand to the teacher, who hesitated, looking at him uneasily. "You don't want to shake my hand," grunted Max. "You think you're better than me?" Max withdrew his hand and cocked it into a menacing fist.

"Max, don't," Adam pleaded. "He's not like you, but he's a good man."

"I don't like him."

"I don't like you either," retorted the teacher. "You make money off poor people who are dying of hunger."

"What do you mean? If my friends and I hadn't smuggled food, nobody would have lived. Nobody would have food. The only good thing that was done in the goddamn place, we did it. Didn't we, boys?" The other smugglers nodded their agreement.

"But you sell food only to those who can buy it. To the others you give nothing."

"That's not true. We give a part of our food to the poor. Anyway, how do you think we pay for the food? With air? We have to buy it too. Don't forget that."

Adam looked at his teacher and then at Max. He didn't know who was right. Perhaps they both were, but as he was one of the well-fed, he leaned toward Max's point of view. "Listen, teacher. Max is a courageous man. If you're thinking of organizing a resistance group, Max is your man."

"I don't think so, Adam. He's in the police uniform."

"Yeah, but I'm not a member of the force," Max confessed. "I just wear it to protect myself in the raids."

"He's really a good man, teacher. You can trust Max."

"Okay, Max. I'll try to keep in touch with you."

Adam accompanied his teacher to the door. "Do you really think it's bad?" he wanted to know.

"Yes. Evacuation means death," Winarski intoned solemnly. "The Germans have us. They sentence one group to death, while they give another one the hope of survival. They're playing one side against the other. Soon the point will come when a Jew will send his brother to death in order to save his own life." The teacher went his way, and Adam returned to the table.

"So, the revolutionary thinker left," declared Max to his friends' amusement.

"Yeah," smiled Adam, who did not want to condemn his teacher.

"Well, I've got your Jewish Police papers and uniform." He passed a large box to Adam. "Go in back and put it on."

Ten minutes later Adam reappeared.

"You look fine. I think you'd look good in any uniform, even a Nazi one," observed Max ironically.

"You can't imagine how long I wanted to be a Nazi. Why was I born half Jewish?" lamented Adam.

"You can't help what you were born. Don't think about it. We aren't safe. We don't know when or where we're going. We don't know how long this transfer will last. But the uniform will protect you for now."

In the uniform, Adam was able to roam all over the ghetto, even in areas that were being raided. Sometimes, a few of his police "colleagues" looked at him suspiciously but said nothing.

On July 25, Adam met his teacher again. "Come to my apartment," said Winarski. "I want to talk to you. Adam followed him obediently and once inside, the teacher stared directly into his eyes. "Would you like to fight?"

"Against whom?"

"The Germans, of course!"

"I will, but not by myself. Do you have others?"

"Not for the moment. We're beginning to organize, but I had you in mind. What would you do if I sent you to the other side as a liaison?"

I'd run away at the first opportunity, Adam thought to himself, but declared, "I'd go."

"You wouldn't run away, would you?" asked Winarski.

"No, teacher. I promise on my honor."

But things were moving faster, and he soon lost contact with his teacher and Max too. It was now September 11. The radio and newspaper told everybody to group themselves in the four blocks of the ghetto. There the final selection of the "action" was to take place. "Action" was German code for liquidating the ghetto and sending its residents to the death camps. It had been 51 days, and it was over: There were 50,000 left out of the original 500,000 Jews.

The final blow came in the form of a man from Treblinka. Adam had never heard of this place, but someone said that it wasn't far from Bialystok. The man said that he had come back to Warsaw by train, hidden under a pile of clothes. "Nobody goes East to work, only to die. You are either shot or sent to the gas chamber." Even then nobody wanted to believe that the Germans could kill people so coldly. "Me, because I was strong, I worked in the Sonderkommando. I helped empty the gas chambers of corpses. I also took people to places where they were to be shot. Every night when I slept, I had nightmares. I saw the living, dead bodies praying to me for life and mercy. When I woke up, I found that I hadn't been dreaming. It was real, horribly real. Babies, women, children, everybody. I'm warning you, don't go to the East. Deportation is death."

Some Jews in the ghetto still refused to believe these reports and defended the German Kultur and all their contributions to civilization. Others were scared and confused. Some were defiant. Beat the Jews. Take away our civil rights. But exterminate us in cold blood? Never!

Then the ZOB took over. They posted proclamations throughout the ghetto: NO JEW WILL GO VOLUNTARILY TO THE EAST. EVERYONE MUST STAY AND FIGHT.

From September 12, after the action ended, until January 18, there were evenings of endless discussions about what to do. It was during these discussions in early January that Adam saw Winarski again.

"Well, teacher. I see you're organizing fighting units. Count me in."

"I don't trust you," he replied. "If I sent you to the other side, you'd run away."

"I could've run when I went with Max, but I didn't."

"It's dangerous on the other side."

"That's what Max said too. Max told me that I should go over the wall, that I was one of the few who could survive." Adam thought about his conversations with Max, who had cautioned him about being alone on the other side, and the dilemma of abandoning his mother to survive.

"We need somebody to tell the truth, to tell how the rest of us died," Max had said.

"You have to leave her." It sounded inhuman to Adam to leave his mother. Yet sometimes he dreamed of doing just that. She wasn't able to protect him. On the other hand, he couldn't imagine living without her. "Adam," Max had continued, "I know that one day you'll do it, so remember, there'll be a million dangers. But you know the Christian religion. You don't look like a Jew. And most important, you don't have an accent. But watch out for blackmailers. You'll take a room and become a new man. But you'll have to play it cool."

"You do think I should go?"

"Yeah."

"Why don't you go?" he had asked.

Max had laughed. "Look at me. I have a bad face. For me, it's finished."

"What do you mean?"

"I know too much. Remember my buddies who sat in the Art Café with me all the time? They were shot by the Gestapo."

"Why?"

"Because they knew too much. Someone tipped me off in time. I did a lot of business with the Germans. If the SS finds me, they'll shoot me on the spot. In the ghetto, they can't reach me for the time being."

"What are you going to do?"

"Go to the camps. There, I'll be able to survive. But I can't go on the other side. You can, though."

"I'll try, Max. I'll do my best."

While Adam had been daydreaming, Winarski had stepped away and was now involved in the discussion on the other side of the room. Every night it was the same topic: What to do? There was Wolenski, a very assimilated Jew like Adam. He didn't identify with other Jews in the ghetto either and was always shouting and very excited. Adam felt like Wolenski, but he couldn't understand why he was so excited.

There was Moshe, who was an anti-Communist Jew. "You're a Communist, Winarski," he complained. "The Communists are running the ghetto now. I lost most of my goods because of the Germans. Now you take whatever the Germans left for the Party. They want to fight. For what? For whom? Look, we've already lost four-fifths of our people. Do you think we can fight the whole German army? France, Belgium and Holland capitulated. All Poland surrendered. How do you expect us to win?"

There was Shlomo, an Orthodox Jew who for Adam was one of the worst because he represented the religious attitude and traditions. "You see, the Aryan nations believe in heroism and military power. In the Jewish tradition, power is moral courage coming from religious sources over a thousand years old. Man's goal cannot be bought by material or military means."

They pray because they think that through prayer, they will have more power to kill the Germans, thought Adam.

Shlomo kept rambling on, saying nothing. "God won't permit the destruction of the Jewish nation. We have to wait for a miracle. Fighting the Germans is nonsense. They'll exterminate us within a few days. You believe in the Allies. So why do you despair? Now you believe that the Red Army will win. Trust and you shall be free."

Wolenski had been getting steadily angrier as Shlomo spoke and finally exploded. "Miracles!" he screamed. "All you people ever talk about is miracles. There are no miracles! There are only 450,000 corpses, who used to be alive here in this ghetto."

"Where was your God then, Shlomo?" added Winarski who could not resist provoking him too.

"You're a Communist. You don't believe in God. You wouldn't understand. You're almost like a goy," retorted Shlomo.

Wolenski was right to oppose Shlomo. The Jews had been living for many centuries like bums. They had never been their own masters. They were always being thrown out of some country or other and defended themselves by escaping or with money but never with guns. There had hardly been a case in modern history where a Jew had killed anyone in his own self-defense.

In the first action in the ghetto, 400,000 went to the slaughter without any resistance. One young German hoodlum could take 100 people, and nobody had the courage to attack him in order to save his own life. When a Jew was trying to form a resistance group in the ghetto, it was like Lot trying to find ten just men. Everybody had their own problems – wife, husband, children, duties. Nobody wanted to die for the others, and each thought he would be the only one to survive. There were no ten selfless men in a town condemned to destruction.

But there was a change in the situation. Winarski was trying to form armed resistance groups and always said, "There are only two ways to die, like sheep or fighting. And you know which one I choose."

"I'm with you," Wolenski raised his hand softly into the air.

Then Moshe said, "I'm an old man. I can't fight and I don't like Communists, but I'll give you money to buy guns."

"Thank you, Moshe. You've finally realized that it's not the Party now, only the people."

"No fighting. Just pray to God. Everything that God does is good, and His universe is good," Shlomo droned his chant.

Finally, Winarski could stand no more. "Even extermination!"

"Yes, even extermination. It must serve His mysterious purpose," replied Shlomo.

Adam was revolted by this. "Shlomo, although you're a Jew, you sound like a Catholic priest. They also told me about God's mysterious ways." Face-to-face with an Orthodox Jew, Adam felt emboldened. "Most of you are twenty years older than me, but I don't respect you. None of you, especially Shlomo. You disgust me. All of you preach death in some form or another. I want to live!"

"But we all want to," they seemed to say in unison.

"But you can't. I have a chance. I'm going to jump the wall."

"That's desertion!" Winarski shouted.

A man named Greenberg, who had only been listening silently, suddenly defended Adam. "Don't call it desertion. We know that we're all going to die. We need a witness. Somebody who will know. Somebody who will tell what happened. He should leave if he feels that way."

"You're wrong," Winarski shot back. "The boy is a very selfish young man. If I sent him on the other side, he wouldn't come back. He won't help us."

That's how the discussion ended that night, but these went on every night for three months. The general feeling was that what had happened to 400,000 of their people would happen to them too unless they defended themselves. Everybody had the same opinion. If a burden was divided into 1,000 pieces, it would be much easier to bear.

Adam found Greenberg a few days later. "You're the only person other than Max who told me that I could live on the other side. Do you really think I have a chance?"

"You might. But don't imagine that life there is going to be easy for you. First, you'll be lonely, in constant solitude. You'll have to be vigilant all the time. If you lose control over yourself, you know what will happen, don't you? Prison camp. Torture. Death."

"But I do have a chance . . ?"

"You have, but remember, you've lived in the ghetto a long time.

You come from a different social class, so you'll be easy to spot. No man goes through Hell without having a mark on him."

"But Max said I have a good face and no Jewish accent."

"That's not enough. You'll also have to be a great actor. You'll have to act naturally in the part of somebody else. You'll live in a universe apart, which follows different laws. You'll need papers, an ID card. Anybody can sell you phony ones, but they will not be replaced in the police files. On the first control, if you're not confirmed, all they have to do is pull down your pants. They'll see who you are. Also, there's the birth certificate, which is only given by the clergy. It makes you a Christian. You will need to obtain an authentic one somewhere, somehow."

"I think that with the right connections they'll be easy to get."

"Easy or not, I don't know. But suppose you have all these papers. There are the neighbors. You'll live alone. They'll wonder where you came from. Who is the new young man who just rented a room? Why doesn't he have much luggage? Why doesn't he have a family? Why doesn't he receive any mail? You see, you have many problems to solve. And over there every new man will attract suspicion."

"What should I do?"

"Stick with the Germans. I don't say that Germans are better than Poles, but it will be much harder for them to recognize you as a Jew. Stick very close to them. You'll be relatively safe."

"I should go then?"

"By all means you should. I'm just sorry I can't make it easier. You should go because here in the ghetto, we're all going to die. On the other side you might die too, but there is a small possibility of survival. If you are one of the very few Jews or half-Jews in your case who survive, you'll be covered with gold, my boy. You'll be covered with gold."

"Anything else?"

"Don't speak German. All Poles think that Jews speak German."

"But I never met any Jews who spoke pure German."

"Well, they speak Yiddish which is based on German. Therefore, if somebody speaks German who isn't German, the Poles automatically think he's a Jew."

"But I don't speak Yiddish. My German is pure."

"Do as you think best. But there'll be nobody out there to give you advice. Oh, yes. You know there are blackmailers who hunt Jews. They go into the street and stop the first person they meet. 'Are you a Jew?' they ask. If the person isn't, he tells them to get lost. If they take him to the police, he'll be released. But a Jew can't allow that. And now, when there are so many of us on the other side, their job is easy. No document is going to protect you from the blackmailers."

"What do they do if they catch a Jew?"

"First, they take his money. If he doesn't have any, it depends. Most of the time, they sell him to the Gestapo. You see, some of them are in the pay of the Gestapo. Others belong to an underground organization that wants to rid Poland of both Jews and Nazis."

"So, can you tell me what to do, where to go?"

"No, I can't. I can simply warn you about where the danger lays. Even the Poles, the good ones who help Jews, are sentenced to death. There is no way to obtain addresses for help. Everybody is afraid of everybody else. They're afraid of torture and death. But it's the chance you have to take. Right now, there is a real chance of making it. And I think you'll make it. Follow your instincts and think about the gold you're going to be covered with. And one more thing. Don't ever look or be sad. Christians never look sad. They don't have a death sentence hanging over them. Only Jews do, therefore they look sad. You must be and look carefree. Fight what you feel inside you. Keep smiling all the time. Do you think you can be an actor twenty-four hours a day?"

"I don't know, but I'll try, sir."

"You'll have to appear relaxed even when you're very tense. Slowly your heart will turn to stone. You'll be very lonely and there'll be nobody to share your secrets with. When you meet Jews, you'll have to swear at them, kick them, tell them they're no good. You won't be able to trust the priests. You'll have to be vigilant. You'll have to be another person, a goy, cruel, sadistic, happy. You'll have to make friends. That will be difficult. Perhaps even a professional actor wouldn't be able to play this part. Can you?"

"I'll try. I'll try."

"Yes, you try. Just follow your instincts and think about the gold you'll be covered with. Think about the gold!"

And yet Adam still didn't jump. He stayed with his mother and eventually they were transferred to Swietojerska Street to work in the Brush Shop there. It was a time of relative peace.

On January 18, 1943, a new action started. Adam saw Max again for the last time that day. "The Germans have surrounded the area. We're going to fight," declared Max.

"Can I fight, too?"

"You're too young. Go into hiding."

"I'll go over the wall."

"It's too late now. Go into hiding. I'll get in touch with you later."

"What are you going to do?"

"I'm staying here for now. I still have friends who can protect me."

"I hope to see you again, Max."

"If not after this action, then after the war."

It was the third day that Adam, his mother, and the others had been hiding in a small room. It was hot and they were running out of food and water. Suddenly, Adam heard German voices outside. They had discovered the concealed door and were battering it. This was the end. It was hard to describe the feeling of fear. Adam knew that he was going to die soon. Before, it had been a question of days. Now it was a question of minutes. His fear of death was not a Christian fear of death. He was not afraid of what was going to happen in the afterlife. All he thought of was pain, how they were going to kill him. Were they going to torture him? How much pain does a bullet or a knife in the belly cause? How long does the pain last? If he had had poison, he would have taken it then and there. He was afraid of pain. He began regretting life. He was only sixteen, and all the beautiful things that he should have done, the women he should have loved, the beautiful life he should have led, everything was going to be taken away from him in minutes.

Five minutes later, the door gave in and the room was filled with Germans. "Raus, Raus!" they shouted. Adam didn't expect that. He thought that they would enter shooting, but they simply threw them out of the room.

They were not the only ones. There were already many people standing in the courtyard who had been ousted from the surrounding buildings. He saw a few dead bodies lying face down with fresh blood still flowing from their wounds. The Germans were pushing people into ranks of five. They were supposed to stay like that until told to do otherwise.

"There is going to be a selection," someone to his left whispered.

"There may be a small chance some of us will survive," mumbled another voice.

"They're not going to exterminate us all."

"Maybe not."

They stood in groups. Beside Adam was his mother and behind him, Benjamin, the freight porter who had been working with Max, and Sarah, his little sister. He didn't look at the rest. The Germans were pushing them in front of a committee composed of three SS men with hardened faces, holding whips in their hands. "To the left! To the right!" the senior officer barked. As the groups approached them, they turned in the appointed direction. To the left meant survival until the next time. To the right meant death.

Adam's turn came. He walked forward with his mother, removing his glasses in order to look more like a worker than an intellectual. He believed that the Germans might spare him if they thought they could use him in the shops. They stood in front of the men. The SS man looked at him and then at his mother. "Left!" he shouted at Adam. "Right!" he shouted to his mother. Adam saw the whip strike her face and the ugly red mark it made. He ran to the left and she to the right. He was free ... if only for a minute. For her, it was death. But he was glad, he was glad to be one of those chosen to live. He was numb at the thought that his mother was going to die and that he was going to live. Maybe for only five minutes longer, but it was life.

Then something happened. Benjamin took out a knife, rushed forward, and stabbed the German officer in the heart. The SS man fell slowly to his knees. There was a surprised look on his face and on the faces of all the people in the yard. The other Germans, who were armed with machine guns, opened fire in all directions. There were screams and shouts. People were running, looking for a place to hide. In the melée, Adam ran towards the hallway staircase. He ran up the stairs, then he heard footsteps behind him. Germans, he thought. Then he heard a voice. "Wait for me!" It was Sarah.

He stopped. "Come on, then," he called. We'll hide on the fifth floor. I know a little place where we can go from here to number 34."

There had been passages made in the cellars and in the attics in the houses, so that people could move freely from house to house without being seen on the street. 34 Ogrodowa Street was a warehouse used by the ghetto smugglers and considered relatively safe.

Sarah and Adam peered out the window into the yard. The Germans were still firing. If he lived five minutes more, it would be a miracle. The Germans couldn't believe that a Jew was able to kill one of them. Adam stared into the yard. There were bodies everywhere. He could still hear screams. Then came a German with a flame-thrower to set fire to all the bodies. Many of the Jews were not dead, only wounded. As they were burning one could hear inhuman screams. The stench of burning human flesh was almost unbearable. He turned away from the window. His mother's face flashed across his mind, but it didn't remain long. His first concern was how to survive for another five minutes.

Now they had reached the fifth floor and gone through to number 34. The shooting and screaming ebbed and gradually stopped. Probably everybody was dead. He didn't know. He didn't care. Sarah was next to him. He said nothing to her. He was too wrapped up in his own thoughts.

It was January and darkness came early. It was after five. "What's going to happen now?" asked Sarah.

"I don't know," he responded. At first, he wanted five minutes more to live. Now he contemplated another half-hour.

"What are we going to do?"

"I don't know," he repeated, annoyed with her question. He wanted to go to the other side. He knew that Karski would help him. How stupid he had been not to have jumped earlier, but then he suppressed that thought because it made no difference anymore.

With darkness, the Germans had probably pulled out. Adam looked through the window. Jewish orderlies were taking away the dead bodies and putting them on carts to be buried. Some others were washing the blood stains away.

"Is everything okay?" Sarah asked stupidly.

"Nothing is okay." He looked at her. "They've stopped killing for today, but tomorrow they'll start again. How do you think we'll survive then? There's no chance of survival here. But maybe on the other side."

"You're going over the wall? Take me with you," Sarah pleaded.

"It'll be hard. The wall is guarded, but I have a chance. Here we have no chance at all."

"Kiss me."

"What? Now!"

"Kiss me."

"Now? Are you crazy?" He kissed her on the cheek.

"No. Not that way. I want to be kissed like a woman."

"There's no time."

"It's now or never. I'm still a virgin. I might die in a half-hour, maybe tomorrow, maybe next week. I want to make love with you now." She caressed him all over.

"Not now, Sarah. Not now. There's no time for it. Wait until we get on the other side. After we jump the wall." He pushed her away.

He hoped she wasn't offended. Many times, he had dreamed of making love to Sarah, but he'd been afraid of what his mother would say or what the neighbors would say. Anyway, there was no place to do it. For that matter, he was a virgin himself. Most of all, fear of dying and torture killed his sexual feelings.

"We'll make love, but we must get over the wall first," he repeated. "I'll go outside and see what's happening. Then I'll come back and get you. You see, there's a 9:00 curfew in Warsaw. It's a little after 7:30 now. I'll have very little time to scout the area and make a plan. Now that it's dark, we'll have a better chance. I'll be back."

"All right, Adam. I'll wait here for you."

He went downstairs and mixed with the people who were cleaning up the yard and moving the bodies. He didn't see his mother's body. He was glad. Now he would remember her as she had been when she was alive. He was finally clear of the courtyard when he saw one of the Jewish policemen he knew coming toward him.

"Have the Germans pulled out?" he inquired.

"Yeah. Hey, you know what happened?"

"No, what?" Adam responded.

"You know Benjamin, the porter? Well, he killed one of them there." The man pointed to the yard from where Adam had just come. "For the first time, we have a few resistance groups. The Germans pulled out."

"Do they still guard the walls?"

"Sure, but no more than usual. The action is over until the next time," he gestured.

"Of course. They were supposed to burn down the ghetto, but because of the resistance ... well, I think we have a couple months more."

But Adam didn't want to wait any longer. He had been in the ghetto too long. He didn't belong there. He found a couple of guys whom he had met through Max. They helped him find the ladder Max used to scale the wall. Now he was going to use it for the same purpose.

Having reached the top of the wall, Adam looked cautiously to the left, then right. Calmly, he observed the German guard pacing. He looked at his watch. The soldier took eight minutes, four to the left and four to the right. He disappeared and came back again. Adam ignored his promise to Sarah. It was a choice of life or making love. To hell with making love. Life is more important. It's now or never. He jumped and hit the ground as the guard turned the corner into the back street. Adam ran to the wall of the house across the street. He was breathing heavily.

January 18, 1943. His first day of freedom was beginning in darkness. He had to make ten yards very quietly. Suddenly, two men appeared from nowhere. He thought they might be friends of the smugglers, who had helped him with the ladder, but very quickly he changed his mind.

"Hey, Jew. We saw you jump!"

Adam was trapped.

"Come on, Jew. How much money have you got on you?"

"A little," answered Adam.

"Give us the money or we'll take you to the Germans. There's one right over there. He'll be happy to see you, I'm sure."

"I'll give you the money, but you have to take me somewhere. I have no place to sleep."

The two men looked at each other. "Okay, we'll take you with us."

They didn't live far from the ghetto, just a few blocks away on Sapiezynska Street. They went up to the gate and rang the bell. The concierge opened the gate. "Who's there?" she asked.

"It's us with one of our friends. He's okay," answered one of the blackmailers.

She closed the gates behind them and looked at Adam suspiciously. Then she returned inside.

The three of them made their way upstairs, and seeing his blackmailers in the hallway light, Adam guessed their ages at around 19 or 20, only a few years older than he.

"Well, Jew-boy," one said, once they were inside the apartment, "how much money do you have?"

He had 20 little swine[25] sewn in his jacket and about 600 zlotys in his pocket. "I've got 600 zlotys. But it would be nice if you'd leave me something, or else I won't be able to eat tomorrow."

"Look, boy. If you leave here tomorrow, you won't need the zlotys because the Germans will catch you. We'll just keep it all."

It was nearly 9:00, and after that no one could be on the street past curfew without a special permit. In a pitiful voice he asked, "Can I at least stay in your place tonight?"

"Okay, you can stay. You see, we're nice guys. We hate what the Germans do to you Jews. But, you know, we have to make a living. When we see a guy like you jump the wall, we try to get some money."

"Yes, I understand."

For some unknown reason, they became cheerful and offered Adam some vodka. They told him that their names were Stacho and Wojtek. The three young men talked for a long time. After one of their infrequent pauses, Wojtek said, "Hey Stacho, he doesn't look like a Jew, does he?"

"No, he doesn't," answered Wojtek with some hesitation.

"I think he could mix. Would you like to do that, Jew-boy?"

"Yes, I would, but I've no chance now. You've taken all my money," said Adam.

"Look, we'll make a deal. With your face, you can pass, and we'll cover you. You have no place to sleep so you can stay here. You just spot a few Jews and bring them to us. We'll take care of you."

"Fifty-fifty?" Adam proposed.

They laughed. "That would be too good. No, we take everything. We're offering you your life. As long as you cooperate, we'll feed you and protect you. What more do you want? Life is everything, can't you see that? We don't have to die, but you do. If that's not good enough for you, we'll hand you over to the first German we find, and you'll see."

"Okay, it's a deal," clipped Adam.

"Good boy. He's a good fucking Jew-boy."

"Don't call him a fucking Jew-boy," said Stacho. "He's one of us now. Respect him. Just call him a Jew."

"No. We won't even call him a Jew. What's your name?"

"Adam."

"Well, Adam, if we make some money together, you have nothing to worry about."

Then Wojtek opened another bottle of vodka and produced some sausages. They started to stuff themselves.

Adam was very tired. The long day's events were too much for him. He still didn't know what was going to happen to him, especially with these guys. "Is there a place where I can sleep?"

They motioned to a couch at the back of the room. Adam lay down and closed his eyes. He saw Sarah's face, then his mother's. Here he was in the blackmailers' apartment with a few gold coins in his jacket lining that they didn't know about. He fell asleep on his first night of freedom.

Stacho and Wojtek were shaking him now. "Come on, wake up and have some breakfast. Look, try to bring somebody here. We'll meet you at 6:00 tonight. Okay?"

"Give me some money," he demanded.

"What do you need with money?"

"To buy a paper or coffee, to take the streetcar."

"All right," Wojtek conceded. "Stacho, give him a hundred zlotys. But bring us a good fish. You hear," he warned Adam.

Adam left the apartment quickly. It was cold outside. This was the first time he had walked along the streets of Warsaw in more than two years. He remembered Greenberg's advice to keep smiling. "The worst thing against you will be your face. It will betray you. The Jews are sick with fear and it shows on their faces, especially in the eyes." Adam walked along with a big grin on his face. He smiled at everybody. Some people looked at him very strangely. Maybe he smiled too much. Maybe they thought he was a Jew. Then he figured out that it was because he had that silly grin on his face. Thereafter Adam decided to look happy and to relax. "Relax. Be calm. Don't be afraid. Go to see Karski." He repeated this to himself over and over.

To reach Karski's place, he had to cross Warsaw in the direction of the Vistula, for he now lived in a suburb called Powisle. It took about an hour to get there. When he finally arrived, he rang the doorbell. A little girl answered. "Who is it?" she asked.

"A friend of Karski's. Is your papa home?"

"Papa's gone away. He'll be home tomorrow night."

That was a stroke of bad luck. Adam didn't know what to do. He left the building, bought a paper, but all the time he was trying to think of what he could do. It was nearly 9 AM. Karski wasn't at home. He had a day and a half in front of him. He took streetcars for a couple of hours, jumping off one onto another. He went to the end of the line and took another one. He was trying to think of a place where he could spend the night. He couldn't return to the blackmailers without a victim. And this blackmailing business was something that he didn't want to have anything to do with.

Then he remembered a little villa in Otwock, another Warsaw suburb that had been bombed in 1939. He went there quite often to play before they were confined to the ghetto. There he could sleep in the ruins. He decided to take the last train and spend the night there. Meanwhile he had a lot of time to kill. He went to the movies. Of course, it was an old German film about their military victories on all fronts. All the evil characters were Jews. Naturally, they were murdered in the end, to the applause of the Germans in the audience. He sat through it three times. Then he was fed up with that nonsense and left. It was about 5:30 in the evening, but the last train didn't leave until 7:30.

He was going towards the main station when he heard people running. He looked around and saw them racing in all directions. "It's a raid," someone shouted. He saw German cars blocking all streets in the area. The Germans also raided Polish cities for slave labor to replace the Germans sent to the front. There he was in the middle of that mess with no papers, no certificates, with nothing at all to show. Your first day of freedom will be your last, he thought. His heart stopped for a second. There was a lump in his throat. He closed his eyes and could feel the torture and beating he knew would come. And there would be no help. How long would the torture last?

The Germans got out of the trucks and closed off the area. He didn't know how far back, but for all he knew, it was the whole area of the city where he was. How could he protect himself? What could he do? All he had with him was a small medallion. It was a little Nazi swastika he'd found in the street one day just at the beginning of the war. It had probably fallen from the pocket of one of the Gestapo officials. He remembered how angry everybody was when he showed it around, especially his mother and their neighbors. He didn't know why he carried it with him, but he enjoyed carrying something in his pocket that was forbidden. Maybe because everyone was always on at him about how bad it was.

The Germans started moving slowly through the streets, checking papers. Those Poles who worked with the Germans were released. All others were put into trucks and taken away. Nobody knew where. Maybe labor camps, maybe concentration camps. But Adam knew what would happen to him. They would find out that he hadn't any papers, make him take down his pants. They would shoot him when they saw his circumcised penis.

Then he spotted a young man about his age, blond and looking quite scared. He hit on an idea. He went over to the boy. "Are you worried?"

"Yeah. What about you?"

"I'm okay. What's wrong?"

"I have papers, but I've heard that the Germans take everybody."

"You have working papers, don't you?"

"Yes."

"Maybe I can help you. Come with me."

The young man followed him without hesitation. Adam wondered why, but it really didn't matter. His instinct taught him to always make quick decisions and to be able to adapt himself to any changes or obstacles.

He pinned the Nazi badge to the underside of his lapel and then searched the faces of the German guards. He chose one who was not too young or too old and who looked the least intelligent of the lot. He went up to him, pulling the young man by the arm. Adam looked the guard straight in the eyes and showed him the swastika. He addressed the guard authoritatively, explaining in near-perfect German that he had taken custody of the young man. *"Herr Unteroffizier, dieser Mann geht mit mir. Ist alles in Ordnung? Du kannst lassen uns gehen."*

The German snapped to attention and let them go through.

"Man! Where did you learn to speak German like that?"

Suddenly he realized that he might have made a mistake. Greenberg had told him not to speak German. But now it was too late. The damage was done. But on the other hand, he didn't speak Yiddish, so his accent was pure. That is what he repeated to himself in order to quell the rising fear of being discovered. "I speak German well because I am German."

The young man's eyes opened wide in astonishment. "You're not a very good German. You helped me. Why?" asked the young man once they were outside the zone.

"I'll explain over a drink," Adam replied.

They found a café and sat down.

"My name is Tadek," the young man introduced himself finally.

"Mine is Adam." They ordered vodka. Adam took his time. He

needed a place to sleep. Maybe Tadek would offer his room.

"You're German, really?"

"Yes, but I didn't choose to be born that."

"I don't blame you for being German."

"My father was Polish, and my mother was German. I'm a Volksdeutsche[26]. But my heart is with Poland and the Poles. When I saw you in trouble, I was thinking about my younger brother. I tried to help you. Maybe you can help me too."

"If I can, I will."

"My situation with the Germans is very bad. You see, I think that Germany is going to lose the war. I would like to get in touch with the underground. I could give them a lot of information. If you could put me in contact with them, I'd be grateful." He was taking a chance here and he knew it.

"That's easy, Adam," said Tadek. "I'm in the underground."

"Do you trust me?"

"Well, you saved my life. That's good enough reason in my opinion for me to trust you."

Adam looked at his watch. "It's almost 8:00. I've missed my train."

"Don't worry, you can sleep at my place."

Adam accepted with joy. That's what he'd been waiting for. Last night there was no future for him, only death, and now he was free. Tomorrow, what about tomorrow? That was the mystery, which nobody could foresee, but in his life, the future was every minute, every second. He had to use every second to the utmost, because it might be his last. Only one thing troubled him, though ... no papers. What would he do if there were a landlord or concierge where Tadek lived?

They walked to Tadek's house. It was almost 9:00 when they arrived. Tadek rang the bell and the concierge opened the door. She looked suspiciously at Adam.

"I brought a German friend with me tonight. A good German. His mother was German."

Adam showed her his badge.

"Oh," she said. "*Kommen Sie ein, bitte.*"

They went into the concierge's apartment.

"Do you live here, Tadek?" asked Adam.

"Yes, this is my rooming house. She's my landlady. But she's okay. She's a nice woman. She knows I'm in the underground and hides my gun here. Magda," he called the concierge, "show him my gun."

"Are you out of your mind?"

"Come on. Show it to him. He's a good friend. He saved my life today."

"I guess you know what you're doing," she said and, from a cabinet behind the table, opened a drawer and removed a "vis."

"When I'm called out on a job, I take it with me," explained Tadek.

Turning to Magda, he asked her for some vodka.

"You've had enough, Tadek."

"But this is a special occasion. Adam here saved my life."

Reluctant to share her vodka, Magda stared at him for a minute. Tadek got the message. "Oh, okay. If you feel that way about it ... Come on," he motioned to Adam, "Let's go."

Adam followed him up the landing and into his room. There were two beds. "You can have that one," Tadek pointed to a small cot.

"Thanks." Adam stretched out on the bed, exhausted. "I would like to join the underground. What kind of underground are you in?"

"I belong to a very special group, NSZ. You've heard about us?"

"I have." You bet he'd heard about them. They were Polish Nazis and hated Jews even more than the Germans. Adam now found himself in a ticklish situation. He knew that even one tiny slip, one unthinking action or word meant instant death.

"Yes, I'm in NSZ. We fight everybody – Germans, Russians, Jews, Ukrainians. Poland for the pure Poles. That's our aim. If you stick with us, you'll be with the winner."

"In that case, I'll stick with you." What else could he say?

"Good. If everything goes okay, I'll introduce you to our chief."

"I'd like that. It bothers me to work for the Germans and not do anything for Poland," added Adam.

"Hey, with the action, a lot of Jews are in town."

"Yeah, I know. Plenty of those bastards." Adam was thinking how to extricate himself from this situation as soon as possible. "You know what I do?"

"No. Tell me."

"I look for them. When I find them, I take all the money they have. They have no choice but to give it to me. If they don't, I take them to the Gestapo, and they shoot them."

"You don't like Jews either?"

"I hate those no-good bastards."

"You're the kind of man NSZ needs. Come to think of it, I'm a little short right now. If we could get hold of a couple of Jews and get money, we could buy more vodka."

"Well, I know where one is hiding."

"Where?"

"He's hiding in Otwock." Adam thought about the bombed-out villa where he'd been planning to sleep that night.

"Let's go there tomorrow, then."

"Okay." Adam drifted into oblivion on his second night of freedom.

In the morning, Tadek woke him up. "Come on. Magda's fixed us some coffee, real coffee. Afterwards, we have some work to do."

"What work?" Adam was still sleepy.

"Remember? The Jew in Otwock?"

"Oh, yeah."

"How much money do you think he has?"

"Don't know. I met him by accident. My friend got 600 zlotys off him but doesn't understand that Jews are animals and gave him 100 back. He's hiding in the villa."

"Good. Very good. I think he has plenty of swine on him. We'll take everything he's got. And you know what we'll do afterwards?"

"Turn him over to the Gestapo?"

"No, we'll shoot him ourselves. He won't talk then. Nobody will suspect us. Anyway, we'll be doing him a favor because he's going to die sooner or later."

"You're right. Let's go."

They went down to Magda's and had their coffee. Tadek took his gun. Adam saw Jania, Magda's daughter, for the first time. She was watching him intently. Her eyes bothered him but just for the moment. He was thinking about the job he had to do on his second day of freedom.

Tadek and Adam left the house and headed for the station. They took the train to Otwock. Adam remembered the way although he hadn't been there in over two years. The old villa was situated off the main road outside the town. There was a pile of debris adjacent to the house, revealing a hole that appeared to lead into the basement. Adam had played there before. "He's hiding in there, Tadek. You want to go first, or shall I?"

"You'd better go. He knows you."

Adam disappeared into the dark, wondering exactly what he was supposed to do. He knew what he wanted from Tadek. He wanted his identity, his papers, his gun, and his freedom. Adam waited in the hole for ten minutes, then emerged saying, "He's offering us 10,000 zlotys."

"That's a lot of money." Tadek smiled. "Come on, let's get it."

"Tadek. Do me a favor?"

"What?"

"Have you ever killed a Jew?"

"Of course," answered Tadek.

"I'm half-German and would you believe it, I've never killed a Jew," Adam began. "Give me your gun. I'd like to kill the sonofabitch. Go inside, grab him and bring him out. I'll shoot him here. I want to see how a Jew dies."

"With pleasure." Tadek handed Adam the gun and crawled into the hole.

"Hey, Jew. Where are you?" he shouted. "It's dark in here. I don't see him," he called to Adam.

Adam crawled into the hole behind Tadek. "He must be hiding." Then he threw a pebble to his left. A noise came from the left, and he said, "Light a match. You'll see him then."

Tadek struck a match. Adam could see the outline of his head as he held the match directly in front of his face. He raised the gun and fired. Tadek lunged forward when the bullet entered his brain. Adam quickly reached out to the body and hurriedly took the matches from his still-warm hand. He struck one. He could see the blood and brain oozing from the hole in his skull.

It was the first time Adam had killed a man.

He was happy.

He was still alive.

He started to smile. Then he stopped smiling. Adam grabbed all of Tadek's papers and left the hole, dragging Tadek's body behind him. Once outside, he stopped for a few seconds to catch his breath and regain his strength. Then he found a rock and smashed Tadek's face to a pulp. If they think it is a Jew, there'll be no investigation, he thought. Then he pulled down the pants and smashed the corpse's penis. He did the same to its hands in case of fingerprint identification. Very satisfied with his work, he took a stick and wrote in the dirt, LIVED LIKE A DIRTY JEW, DIED LIKE A DIRTY JEW. Then he left the ruins. He wasn't worried anymore. No one could identify Tadek now.

It was 11:00. Adam had Tadek's papers and a gun. He had lived one-and-a-half days more. It was a small victory.

He took the train back to Warsaw and felt much better with Tadek's ID card, even though the picture wasn't his. But then, he and Tadek were almost the same age. No matter what happened, he had something to show. That was the important thing. As he walked the streets of Warsaw, he caressed the gun in his pocket. That lovely cold toy, that little warm toy that gave life and death at the same time. He felt a new sensation, freedom. For two years, he had been the prey. Now he was both the hunted and the hunter, all because of that little toy. If someone tried to blackmail him, he would say nothing. The gun would speak for him. He had a new feeling of self-confidence. Now when he smiled, it would not be the same as before, there would be sincerity behind it, because the gun gave him a feeling of security. Now he was walking not as a victim who could suffer at the hands of anybody who asked him, "Are you a Jew?" Now he was walking like a tiger in the street, and he knew that anyone who crossed him would die before he did. He liked those words. "Tiger in the street." He repeated them over and over.

But he had no lair. Where would he sleep? He could go back to Tadek's, but what would he tell Magda, "Just one more night"? There were always hotels, but with the ID picture not exactly resembling him, he would never pass the intense scrutiny, especially now that so many Jews were hiding on the Aryan side. Never before had he heard so much talk about Jews. It was the topic of all the conversations, even on the train.

"Did you hear? My neighbor was hiding two Jews. The police found the men and shot them. They shot her, too."

"Well, everyone knows there's the death penalty for hiding Jews."

"Those goddamn Jews! Why don't they stay in the ghetto where they belong?"

"Anybody who hides them is stupid. They can die for that. It's not worth the blood of a Pole."

"Good. If they hide those dirty bastards, they deserve to die."

"They're not good Poles, if they do things like that."

"I hate the Germans, but that's one point on which I agree with them. Even if they lose the war, we won't have a Jewish problem. If there's one thing I'll be grateful for, it's for doing our dirty work."

Once he heard someone say, "Well, you can like them, you can dislike them. But you shouldn't kill them like animals."

"How would you like to see them destroyed, like royalty?"

"They're solving the Jewish problem for us, so what are you carping about?"

"Poor people. They're human just like we are. They shouldn't be treated that way."

Adam had been listening without saying a word. He was bitter. He hadn't intended to say anything, but something inside told him that he'd better. "Why are you sorry for them? Those bastards never worked hard. They lived on us Poles. They exploited us. Let them die. I think the Germans are doing a good job. Anyway, like you said, it saves us the fucking trouble."

Some people looked at him with admiration. Others with contempt. He felt great.

After wandering around the city during the afternoon, Adam decided to go to Tadek's. It was nearly six. Magda opened the door as usual. "Oh, the German," she said.

"*Bitten Sie. Ich heise Adam*," he greeted her politely in perfect German.

"Herr Adam, where is Tadek?"

"He's not coming tonight. He's on a mission. I'm staying here. Please put my gun in the same place you put his."

Magda took it but didn't seem to recognize it as Tadek's. He had taken a chance and won another gamble. She looked at him with admiration and asked, "You belong to us, too?"

"Yes. You see, I'm half-German. My father was Polish and my mother, German. But my heart is always with Poland."

"Would you like some vodka?"

"Yes, thank you."

They went into her apartment. That night Jania was at home. She was a beautiful girl and very sexy. Adam had the feeling that Magda was trying to fix up something between the two of them.

"Jania, you've met Herr Adam. He's half-German, but his soul is all Polish. He's staying here because Tadek is on a mission."

"Oh?" Jania looked at him and her blue eyes twinkled. Magda left the room.

Adam felt uncomfortable. "Where did your mother go?"

"What do you want with her?"

"I'm a guest in her house. This is the first night I've been here without Tadek and ..."

"That is why she wants you to make yourself at home and feel at ease." Jania moved slowly over to him and started to kiss him. He pushed her away.

She was surprised. "Don't you like me? A lot of guys around here want to sleep with me. I can sleep with anybody I choose. You're Tadek's friend. You're half-German. You're special."

"Listen, Jania. No matter what my feelings are toward you, I can't make love when I think Tadek is in danger."

"What about tomorrow?"

"Okay. Tomorrow."

"Kiss me."

He kissed her. Jania's body was warm and yielding to the touch. She was very sensuous and aroused in him a feeling that he'd never had before. No, that's not exactly true. It aroused in him a feeling that had never been so strong.

Adam had never had a woman, yet within the space of 48 hours, he'd had more propositions than he knew what to do with. He had never made love to a woman, but he wanted to. He wanted to make love to Jania and to Sarah, and to the girls he saw in cafés. But if I make love to Jania, she'll find out, he thought. This fucking Jewish habit of cutting the dick. I'm lucky they don't cut the ear. He smiled to himself. Jania, thinking he was smiling at her, smiled back. No, I can't take the chance. "We'll have time tomorrow," he told her.

"I'll be waiting."

There was a knock on the door. "Can I come in?" asked Magda.

"Of course," said Jania. Magda came in with a surprised look on her face.

"Your daughter is very charming, but my mind is on Tadek at the moment. I'll stay here tonight, but tomorrow I ..."

"Please, come back," pleaded Jania.

"I respect your mother, Jania," he said, trying to get himself out of the mess without raising any suspicion. "What do you say, Magda?"

"Of course, Herr Adam. Come back, please. You're always welcome here."

"Since you put it that way, I'll come back. I promise. Now I'd better get some sleep."

"I'll fix you breakfast in the morning."

"Thank you." Adam went to Tadek's room and slept heavily. His third day of freedom was over.

The next morning it was not Magda, but Jania who brought his breakfast. She looked tempting. Her blue eyes lingered over his body, which was covered by the sheet.

"Is Tadek back?" he inquired.

"No, and that's strange."

"Just between me and you, he went on a special, very dangerous assignment. It's top secret and he might not return for a few days. I'll be here tonight, though."

Jania smiled.

"If Tadek doesn't return, I'll be here," he stated again.

"Okay." She looked at his jacket and saw the Nazi badge. "Why do you wear that?"

"Because I'm partly one of them." He hoped she would dislike him and leave him alone. On the contrary, she seemed fascinated.

"Are you really a Nazi?" she asked.

"No. It's not my fault that my mother was German. I feel like a Pole, so I work with you people because I want to help."

"That's great! You don't have to do it. You don't have to help us. I admire Tadek because he's an underground fighter, but I think what you're doing is even more noble because you are one of the masters. But you identify with us."

Jania looked at him and smiled. Her eyes were filled with admiration, like a child who meets her idol for the first time. At that moment, Adam wanted to grab her and make love to her. His yearning was almost unbearable. But he couldn't take the chance of letting her discover his secret. It was only then that he came to the sad realization that he could not make love no matter how much he wanted to, no matter how much he needed to until the end of the war. He was almost seventeen. How long would the war last?

Adam attacked his breakfast. It was as if he hadn't eaten in a long time. She sat there watching him, not saying a word. How he wished that she would go away. "Tonight, Jania," he said when he had finished. She took the tray and left. He dressed quickly and left the house.

January 21, 1943, this was his fourth day of freedom. He thought that Karski should be home by now. Adam caught the tram for Powisle. He went to Karski's and rang the bell. Karski himself opened the door. When he saw the boy, his face went pale as if he had seen a ghost. "Count Polanski!"

"Shhh. Call me Tadek, please."

"Tadek, I'm so glad, so glad to see you." Karski embraced the boy. "Please, come in."

"Are you alone?"

"No. My wife and children are here."

"When did you get married?"

"Last year. The children are hers by a former marriage."

"Congratulations, but you must keep certain parts of my life secret. I don't want your wife to know."

"But she's a good woman."

"I can't trust anyone unless he's dead. Nowadays you can't trust anybody. Keep it a secret. Don't tell her I'm a Jew."

"Who's there?" called a voice.

"It's a friend. Remember I told you about the Polish Colonel I used to work for during the war in 1920? It's his son."

"Oh!" Karski's wife exclaimed as she entered the room. She was not very sexy, but then what could he expect? Karski was 45. She was probably just a few years younger. "I'm very happy to meet you. Want something to eat?"

"Of course he does," said Karski.

"Thank you, Karski," Adam smiled. "Your wife is very charming."

Karski smiled as if he was glad to have the approval of the young boy. "Make yourself comfortable."

Karski and Adam sat down and made small talk. Twenty minutes later, the food was ready. It was eaten in relative silence, except for the children asking Adam awkward questions about himself.

"Take the children in the other room," said Karski to his wife when they had completed the meal. When she returned, he told her, "The son of my Colonel works for the underground as I do."

"I understand." She was a good Polish woman. She hurried to clear the table and brought them some coffee and vodka. Then she disappeared.

"You see, my boy. We know how to handle women."

"Of course, we do. I escaped the ghetto three nights ago. I came to see you immediately, but you were away."

"Then you were the one who came to the door. You should have warned me. I would have waited for you."

"It happened quite unexpectedly. The Germans don't announce their plans in advance."

"Yes, of course not," he said. "What can I do for you, sire?"

"Stop calling me 'sire' for a start. Tadek is my name now."

"Yes, I'll try to remember."

"I've got papers, but the picture isn't mine. Look." He pulled out Tadek's papers and gave them to Karski. "I've got a gun too." He showed it to him. "But I have no place to sleep. What I want to do is join the underground. Can you help me?"

"Yes, I told you I'm in the underground myself. Almost everybody is nowadays."

"I want to be in the active part."

"Active?"

"I have nothing more to lose. I'm taking a risk just being here. There's already a price on my head because I'm a Jew. By joining the underground, I can do something good at least."

"As you wish. I'll talk to my chief."

"I have a lot of things I want you to do for me. The papers first, the ID card. Can you fix it?"

Karski studied the papers, and Adam saw from his facial expression that he did not recognize the boy's picture, which was good. Then he handed him the card. "It'll be hard. What kind of papers do you want?"

"The best."

Karski looked embarrassed. "You know, Tadek, to get good papers is a difficult thing to do, but to have the best you have to be real. You have to substitute yourself for somebody else and that will take time."

"Those papers are the best. Only the picture and fingerprints need changing."

"What do you mean?"

"The guy who owned them really existed, but he's dead now. All you have to do is, through your group, make me him." Adam pointed to the name on the card. "Tadeusz Szczepanski . That's going to be my name. He used to live at number 12 Nowogrodzka Street. Give that information to the underground. That way, it'll be easy for me to have the same documents and replace him."

"But they may find out," Karski suggested.

"He belonged to NSZ."

"You killed him." Karski looked at Adam with a certain fascination and then said, "I see."

"Nothing can be traced to me."

They finished the coffee and vodka. "Well, to do all this, I have to meet my contact. What are you going to do?"

"What I've been doing for the last two days. I'll wander around the town."

"Okay, be careful. Let's meet here this evening. 5:00. All right?"

They left the apartment separately. Adam strolled through Powisle. He walked slowly, not noticing the time or where he was going. He walked until he found himself in front of the ghetto walls. They seemed to attract him. People were still living inside those walls, if you can call it living, waiting for death.

He could hear sporadic shooting from inside. Had somebody died fighting? Then he heard a child's voice near him. "Who was killed, mommy? Was it a man or a Jew?"

"Don't worry, darling. It was only a Jew," a woman spoke reassuringly.

Some people were sympathetic to Jews. "I wouldn't treat my dog the way the Germans treat the Jews," asserted one voice.

"At least they're fighting. I guess they don't want to be slaughtered like sheep anymore," suggested another.

"They can't do much. Look, the troops have machine guns," someone commented.

"I heard they killed a lot of SS men," replied another.

Adam heard one woman wailing. "Why couldn't King Hitler have done it peacefully? They've burned all those houses. The Jews lived in such luxury. Now all that gold and luxury is going up in smoke."

Then he heard a man's voice. "What's going on? I smell smoke."

"They're burning the ghetto."

"Oh," the man said, "then it isn't so serious."

Adam suddenly saw two German guards on duty. It's not very healthy for me to stay here, he thought, and he hopped a streetcar.

Once again, he heard the discussions. Two men were arguing. "You goddamn Jew," one said. Adam froze. He looked at the person being spoken to and the man wasn't scared at all. He wasn't a Jew, or at least, he didn't look like one. Then he understood that to call a person a Jew was like calling him a bastard, just another insult. A Jew would feel that epithet deeply. A Gentile would just laugh. Adam was learning fast how to act like an Aryan. He was glad that no one had insulted him in that way. He preferred to be called a no-good sonofabitch or a motherfucker.

There was tension on the tram. He saw a man staring at him and he stared back. The man's eyes penetrated Adam. He began to wonder, does he know? Is he suspicious? They always told him in the ghetto that the Aryans could recognize a Jew by the expression in his eyes. Adam looked at the man and smiled proudly. Then he flapped his jacket lapel to display the Nazi badge. The people's faces changed. Fear crept into their eyes. Now they were afraid. Fear. Always fear.

Adam decided to look everyone in the face with pride in order to scare off the blackmailers and to make their hunt as difficult as possible. He didn't have the doctored ID papers, but even if he did have them, they were no protection against blackmailers. He thought about the gun he was carrying and composed a new look, a look that no Pole could imagine the Jews having. Then he went into the German compartment and he felt safe. The Germans welcomed him with an air of complicity and friendship. He returned that look. It was so restful to be among Germans. They couldn't detect him as Poles could.

When the tram reached its destination, he took another one back to the center of Warsaw. Each time he boarded a tram, he heard the same thing. The Germans were fighting major battles against the Red Army in Stalingrad and the British in Egypt where Rommel's advance had stalled, but these stupid people had only one topic of conversation – Jews, Jews, Jews.

Suddenly he realized that he was the only one silent when everybody was talking. He had to participate. "Those fucking Jews are no good. I thank the Germans for exterminating them. Poland in the future will be rid of them," he stated to no one in particular.

People looked at him with an air of satisfaction and approval. At that moment Adam felt no fear. Too much fear, every minute, every second can exhaust you mentally. It can exhaust you to the point where you feel nothing, not even fear. Now Adam was mentally exhausted. He got off at the next stop and walked along the street, thinking. What danger surrounds you when you become another person? When you take someone else's identity? You can begin to forget that your existence is make-believe. You are so preoccupied with making everyone else believe that you are that person that you forget about the danger. But the moment when the realization of danger returns and penetrates your awareness, you are vulnerable. One slip and it's all over.

Adam had been walking along, oblivious to what was happening around him. He was brought rudely back to reality when he looked up and saw two men arguing. They were about 200 meters in front of him. As he moved closer, he realized that one was a Jew and the other, a blackmailer. Something forced him to intercede for his brother. "What's going on here!" he interrupted, flashing his Nazi badge.

"Sir," said the Pole, "this man is a Jew. I think we should take him to the Gestapo."

"Okay, Jew, do you have any money? Or shall we take you in?"

"I promise you, I don't have any money," the man said fearfully.

"You see, he's been saying that for the last five minutes, but I know he's a Jew. All Jews have money."

Just a few meters on, there was a vacant lot surrounded by a high fence. "We'll settle this over there without witnesses." Adam invited the blackmailer to follow him. The conversation started again once the three men were behind the fence. "Okay, Jew-boy, empty your pockets." The man had about 1,000 zlotys.

"You see. You see!" the Pole said excitedly. "What about the lining of his coat and pants?" The Pole picked up the money that was on the ground.

"Frisk him to make sure." The Pole found 5,000 zlotys and 50 swine, which he gathered up eagerly.

"You dirty lying bastard," the Pole shouted venomously while striking the man across the face.

"What are you going to do with me? You have my money. Let me go now," pleaded the Jew.

"We should take you to the Gestapo," shouted the Pole.

Adam looked at the money in the Pole's hand. "Let me have that." He grabbed it.

"But, sir ..." The blackmailer never finished his sentence because Adam pulled his gun and shot him through the heart.

The Jew stood trembling, figuring that he was next. Instead, Adam handed him half the money.

"Get out of here and be quick about it." The Jew looked at him gratefully and walked away quickly.

Adam looked at his watch. It was nearly 3:00. A few hours to kill before his appointment with Karski. He felt uneasy with all those Poles around him. "Stick with the Germans," Greenberg had advised.

Adam roamed around till he found a German police station. He looked at it and smiled. Two Germans came out and stared at him. "Hello, Polish boy. What are you doing here?"

"Nothing. I was just admiring the building and your uniforms."

"Would you like to be one of us?" asked one of the guards.

"Yes, but I'm Polish."

"That doesn't matter. You should see the Chief. Now there's a way for all good Poles to wear this uniform."

"Really?" Adam went into the station.

"Are you hungry?" the other one asked.

"Well, if you have anything to eat ..."

"Okay, come in here." The guard took him into an alcove where another German was sitting. "This is a very nice Polish boy. He's hungry. Give him something to eat. He'll sweep the floor for us." They prepared him some hot soup and sausage.

It turned out that he was in a German military police station because there were a few German prisoners waiting in a big cell. Adam smiled and thanked them for the meal. He requested a broom and swept the stationhouse floor. Time passed quickly, and it was nearly 4:30 when he asked permission to return home.

"Come here again and talk to us," said one German. "You need to practice your German although I must say that for a Pole you speak very well."

Adam left the post and headed for Karski's. When he arrived, Karski, code-named Krol in the underground, was waiting for him. "Everything's okay. I talked to my Chief. They accept your story. You know that there are a lot of people in different sections of the Home Army. Everyone is suspicious so you must be aware and careful always. I will get you two sets of IDs. The command will know you as Hans Bauer, the son of a Polish woman and German father. For civilian purposes, you can keep the name Tadeusz Szczepanski . All I need now are your fingerprints and a photo. In the morning you'll have your papers." He removed two ID cards from a folder and opened an ink pad on his desk. Adam put his fingerprints on them.

"Where do I have my picture taken?" asked Adam.

Karski pointed to a trunk and removed a camera from it. Adam followed him into another room where Karski took his photo. It was done. Karski would get the film developed and deliver the complete set of papers in the morning.

"Now you're perfectly legal. Where are you staying?"

"In Tadek's house." He told him about Jania and Magda.

"Well, that's not good, only a temporary solution. You see, in the Home Army, you're never supposed to sleep where you're listed officially. Stay there tonight if you can trust her. I'll get you another room as quickly as possible.

"Renting another room could be dangerous," Adam ventured. "You know how people are today. A new guy comes. They think he's from the ghetto."

"It won't be a problem," Karski said. "I know a lot of people in Warsaw. I'll tell them that you're my nephew. That's what I told the Chief." Suddenly Karski fell silent.

"What's wrong?"

"I had to swear."

"Swear? Swear what?"

"That you are my nephew. I had to swear on the Bible that everything I said was true. It was the first time I swore to a lie," he admitted sadly. "But I couldn't forget what I promised your father. When the war's over, I'll go to confession. If I survive, that is."

"We'll try, won't we?"

"Yes, we'll try."

Adam returned to Magda's later that night. He found her and Jania looking very worried because Tadek was still absent. He told them that Tadek had been captured by the Germans and sent to work in a German factory. He told them that he was trying to help him out and that with his influence, Tadek would be treated well.

Magda accepted Adam's story and seemed impressed that he had enough influence to help Tadek back in Germany. She wanted to believe him because it confirmed her admiration for the Nazis. If all Poles became Nazis, she thought, the Germans would leave Poland alone. The Poles had to be Nazis to be free, to become masters of their own destiny. She envied Germans and but hated them for occupying Poland. Adam, with his German-Polish identity, fulfilled her ideals more than Tadek had. Although Tadek was in the NSZ, he was not of the master race as Adam was.

"Can you really do something for him?"

"I'll try," lied Adam.

"It'll be very lonely here without him," said Magda.

"Well, I'll come once in a while."

"You will?"

"Of course. I like you. You've been very kind to me too."

"Why not?" Magda smiled.

"I'll replace Tadek. You can have my gun for safekeeping overnight." Adam removed the pistol from his pocket and offered it to her.

She took it and smiled. "Now, you're really one of us."

"Yes," he yawned. "And I'm very tired. I need some sleep." He went upstairs to Tadek's room and lay on his bed. Ten minutes later, there was a knock on the door. Jania entered. "Do you need anything?" she asked.

"No, thank you," replied Adam, courteously.

She sat on the bed, leaned over and kissed him. "Why don't you want to make love to me?"

Adam pushed her away gently. "Look at me, Jania. There is nothing I want more than to make love to you but unfortunately I can't."

"Why? Are you sick or something?"

"No, but when I joined the underground, I swore that I wouldn't make love until the war was over. I took the solemn oath on the Cross."

Jania looked sad. "But the war could last for years."

"No, dear. It will finish in a year or two. And what is that in our lives? We're still young. Afterwards we can be together for the rest of our lives. Please don't tempt me here. I made a vow."

She said she understood and left the room but returned to wake him the next morning, January 22, 1943, his fifth day of freedom. His fifth day of freedom and he was still alive. She brought him some breakfast and returned his gun. "Are you going to inquire about Tadek?"

"Yes. I have to be at the rendezvous at noon." He finished his breakfast. "Would you like to take a walk?" They walked through Saski Gardens holding hands. Adam was the first to speak. "Can I trust you?"

"Of course, you can. Tadek used to trust me all the time. I'm one of you. I'm in the underground too."

"This is a very delicate matter. My role is more important than you can imagine. If the Germans find out I work for the underground, they'll shoot me and that'll ruin my chances for helping Tadek. You understand?"

"Yes."

"Don't ask questions, but I'm going to stay in your house under Tadek's name. This must be kept secret. Anyway, I won't come to sleep in your place very often."

"Come anytime you want."

He smiled. "But sometimes I'll be on very important assignments, so I'll have to know what is going on. Here's my plan. Don't even tell your mother. The fewer people know, the better. You meet me here at this spot every day at 12:15 to let me know if the Germans have been looking for me, do you understand?"

Her eyes widened.

"Repeat it," demanded Adam.

She did. "Good girl. Let's have a beer."

They found a café and ordered beer and cakes. Then Adam bent over to kiss her. "I have to go to work now."

"Take care of yourself," whispered Jania.

"Don't worry. I will."

Take care of himself. That's exactly what he had been doing for four days. Four days, which seemed like forty years.

Karski was waiting for Adam as they'd agreed. "It's fantastic how you're always on time," Adam observed.

"In this business, if you're late, you might be dead or in jail," warned

Karski. "Here are your two ID cards, one for Tadeusz Szczepanski, the other for Hans Bauer, along with his German working papers."

"Working papers? What do I do?"

"You sell newspapers. The Home Army might use you as a liaison. You have to remain in town. You'll be protected from deportation. Here's your little green paper from Magda's."

He shoved all the documents into his waistcoat pocket. "What other papers do you have?" Karski asked. "Pictures?"

"None."

"Very suspicious. Every man carries pictures of his girlfriend, his parents. I'll give you some from my album. Here. Put them in your wallet. Here are some letters. Let's go."

"Where?"

"To your new apartment. I told the landlady you were my nephew."

"But won't it look suspicious without any luggage? No mail?"

"I thought of that too. I'll write you every so often and if you like you can write to yourself. As far as luggage is concerned, I've got an old suitcase you can use, and we'll buy another one."

They went to the center of Warsaw and bought a suitcase, a few shirts, ties, socks, underwear and other things that would make it look as if Adam were really moving from another city.

The apartment was on Solec Street, not far from Powisle. The landlady was a fiftyish woman.

"This is my nephew, Tadek," announced Karski.

"Ah, yes. Come in. The room is ready." She took them to Adam's new home.

"If he misbehaves or causes any trouble, just let me know."

"He looks like a very nice young man. I think we'll get along just fine."

Adam put his luggage on the bed and looked around the room. It was sparsely furnished but adequate for his needs. There was a wardrobe, two chairs, a table, two lamps, and a little hotplate for cooking.

They went downstairs where the landlady had poured vodka and they cordially toasted to the memory of her husband and son, both of whom died fighting the Germans. They talked politely for an hour until Karski announced he was taking his nephew on a walk to familiarize him with the layout of Warsaw.

"We have to go now," Karski said after an hour of talking and drinking. "We have a lot to do."

"What kind of job does your nephew have?"

"He sells newspapers. Starts work tomorrow."

"I hope I'll get one free."

"You will," promised Adam.

Once outside, Karski explained, "Now you meet your contact. His name is Grat. We have an appointment with him at 3:00 sharp. Not one minute earlier nor one minute later. It's at the tram stop. He knows me. I'll walk in front. You follow me and he'll follow you. We ride three stops and then get off at the Saski Gardens."

Everything happened the way Karski said. Adam saw a young man, maybe a year or two older than he was, follow them onto the streetcar. All of them got off at Saski Gardens. Karski and Grat greeted each other. Then Karski introduced Adam to Grat as "Hans." Grat gave him instructions on where to report for work, how to act and dress, and what to look out for. He then waved to Karski and left.

Adam returned with Karski to his house. They said little more to each other until Karski gave him a paternal slap on the back. "Well, you're all set now. You've got your papers, working cards and you're in the Home Army," stated Karski, satisfied at having fulfilled his obligation to the Count.

"That was quick," observed Adam.

"If it wasn't like that, you'd die."

"True. Very true," Adam agreed.

"Any more problems?"

"Yeah. Something still bothers me. There are two blackmailers in

Warsaw who caught me the night I jumped the wall. I'll never be safe as long as they live." He explained exactly what had happened.

"What do you intend to do?"

"Kill them tonight."

"Why not wait until tomorrow?"

"What if I meet them while I'm working? No, I can't take that chance."

"Do you know where they live?"

"Yes, but you don't have to go with me."

"It'll be better if I accompany you. But don't tell anybody about this because we're not supposed to execute anyone without orders from the Chief."

Arriving at Sapiezynska Street, they stopped two gates from the blackmailers' house. They must have had a hard-working day, he thought, because they didn't show up till a quarter to nine. Adam pointed them out, and they watched them go into the house. "Give them five minutes and then we go in," he said calmly.

Five minutes passed. They approached the gate and rang the bell. The concierge opened the door.

"What do you want?"

"We're friends of Stacho and Wojtek. We have business with them."

"All right. Come in."

They went up the stairs to the first floor. The concierge was watching. Adam could feel her eyes on his back but didn't turn around. Did she recognize him from his earlier visit? They stopped in front of the door. Adam knocked, and then told Karski to wait outside. The door opened.

"Well, well, well. What have we here?" Wojtek pulled him roughly into the room. "Stacho, look, it's our Jew-boy. We haven't seen him for three days, but I told you he'd come back."

Stacho, who was lying on the bed, looked up from his newspaper. "Hello, Jew-boy. Looking for a place to sleep? For some money? You have a deal maybe?"

"Yeah. I found three Jews. Rich Jews," stated Adam.

"That's what we like to hear, rich Jews. Poor Jews are bad business. We don't even blackmail them. It wastes our time."

"You see," said Wojtek, "I told you we could trust him. It's a good thing we didn't give him to the Gestapo. This boy is very cooperative. He's going to give us a lot of money, he's going to make us rich."

"That's right. I know three addresses, and I'll take you to the places," Adam reassured them.

"How much money do they have?" asked Wojtek excitedly. "Do they have only zlotys?"

"No. They have gold and jewelry, too."

"Do you hear, Stacho? They have jewelry, too. And you wanted to turn him over. You stupid ..." He raised his arm as if to strike Stacho. Then he thought better of it. "He's a good Jew-boy. If they were all like you, everything would be fine. We could live together forever and cooperate."

"Listen, you guys. Don't you have any vodka? This is a night to celebrate. You're going to be rich," suggested Adam.

"Yeah, let's celebrate." Wojtek went to get the vodka.

"Want to hear something funny?" announced Adam.

"What?" they said in unison.

"I blackmailed a Jew."

They started to laugh. They laughed until tears rolled down their cheeks and they spilled their vodka. "You did what?" smiled Wojtek when he finally calmed down.

"He blackmailed a Jew," said Stacho from his position on the bed. "How much did he give you?"

"1,000 zlotys."

"Give them to me," demanded Wojtek, moving toward Adam, his hand outstretched. At the same time, Stacho rose on the bed.

"Sure." As he spoke, Adam pulled out the gun and fired point-blank into Wojtek. Neither one realized what had happened because just as Stacho put one foot on the floor, Adam took one great step and fired a bullet into his heart. His body was thrown back onto the bed by the bullet's impact. It made a bizarre sight. Wojtek lying in a pool of blood, face down with one hand outstretched, and Stacho with his body doubled backed on one leg and the other dangling over the side of the bed.

Adam heard voices on the landings. "What happened? Who's shooting?"

"It's a raid."

"Were they Germans?"

"What happened? Gestapo?"

"Polish Home Army. We've just executed two traitors," announced Karski as Adam stepped into the hall. "It's all over. You can go back to your rooms. We're representing the Home Army. Two traitors have just been executed. That's all. Please go back to your rooms and forget everything you've heard tonight."

Adam and Karski were strangers to the people who lived in the house, but they seemed to respect and listen to anybody who had a gun. Adam had learned that a gun was the first key to freedom. He felt like a master. Some people came to kiss his hand.

"There are still young boys who are willing to fight and die for the freedom of Poland," someone said.

Others seemed frightened, but everybody treated them with respect and, above all, caution. Then it appeared as if one man was preparing to leave.

"Where do you think you're going? You can't leave this house," warned Karski.

"Why?" asked the man.

"Curfew."

"But I have authorization," he objected. "Here, see?" He pulled some documents from his coat pocket. Karksi glanced through them and handed them to Adam, who read them and gave them back to the man.

"Maybe you work for the Gestapo and want to report this," Karski stated bluntly, turning first to Adam and then the man.

"No, no," the man insisted, fearful of what had just happened. "I work on the night shift. Please, they'll ..."

"You ... will ... stay ... here," said Adam quietly and firmly while staring the man straight in the eye.

"Yes, sir!" The man ran back upstairs.

"Everybody stays here until 6:00 tomorrow morning. Nobody leaves," Adam announced.

Karski and Adam took up positions in the lobby. A few men joined them in their vigil. The young men asked questions about the Home Army. Some wanted to join. But they gave very obscure information. The old men reminisced about the old days when they fought against the Bolsheviks. A few stories were very interesting, but most were very boring. They were both tired. When pressed for more specific answers about the Home Army, Karski said, "We're only soldiers. We carry out orders. We don't give out information. We simply don't know."

One old man took their side and chided the youngsters for not understanding their situation and wasting time with foolish questions.

"What shall we do with the bodies?" someone asked.

"Report them to the police an hour after we leave. They'll take care of it. Anyway, it's not much of a loss."

At 6:00, when everybody was free to go, Karski and Adam left with a final warning. "Wait here for 20 minutes. If anyone opens the door or tries to follow us, we'll shoot. Is that clear?"

They exited the house, caught a tram and returned to Karski's. On the way back, Adam felt great. He was no longer afraid. After being vulnerable to death all the time, his fear began to dissipate. Living constantly in fear, he'd died a thousand times, but now he was beginning to realize that death can only come once. He was in the underground now, and it was much better inside it than being a Jew on the outside. Anybody could betray a Jew without any risks. In the underground, it was different. Even his death would likely be avenged by comrades.

It was a hard life. After those four days of freedom in which he died a thousand times, his heart turned to stone. He had denied his own identity. But he had learned the art of dissimulation. Nothing could matter. Nothing held him to life anymore. Unconsciously, he had been preparing himself for death. He didn't think that he would survive. He knew for sure that he would die. Yet he'd survived at least for four days in a situation where millions would have died. He was nearly seventeen. To make death easier, he tried to convince himself that life was not important. Nothing was important. Eating, not important. Making love, not important. Going to the movies, not important. Walking, not important. And once he had assured himself that nothing was important, he felt that death would come easy. But he felt a kind of emptiness.

Then, he touched the gun. Only the gun gave him a feeling of freedom. He could kill without pity. He knew that now. He knew how dangerous he was. He was a tiger in the street. He knew that any German, any Pole, anybody who came up to him with the idea of blackmail or any other proposition that didn't suit him would be dead. Everyone was in danger of dying just as he was. Perhaps even more so because he had nothing to lose, and they had everything to lose. This was freedom. This was his sense of freedom.

January 22, 1943, the fifth day was ending ... his fifth day of freedom.

Chapter 22. Johnny's Ted Again

When I finished reading the manuscript, I relaxed in the bar for a few more minutes. I ordered a glass of Muscadet. It was cold and bitter, almost as bitter as Ted's interpretation of freedom. Freedom to him, and to all those who had survived the horrors of the camps, was a curse. He wished he had died with the others, and his living was worse than an eternal hell because his impulse to survive monopolized every waking minute. It constantly dominated his perception of others and twisted the most commonplace situations into potentially deadly events. As an involuntary action, he could not help but live out his nightmare. Those who surrounded him knew only a zombie in an awakened state. What they knew of him was no more than what one could know of a corpse. Statistics, the number of days he had spent in jail, the amount of money he had earned on the black market or in the legitimate world of business – to him these were all just a rush of events, places and numbers which flashed by as he tried to relive those glorious days of freedom.

I decided to go back to my hotel and rest, but as I opened the door, I remembered Mustapha's little surprise. She was waiting on the bed. An exotic beast, she reminded me of Ted's women.

When it was over, I leaned back on the bed and reflected. It was too heavy to continue thinking about Ted at the moment. I got dressed again and went to the lobby. I found a vacant phone booth and called Donaldson.

"Nick speaking. Is that you, Bobby? Put the scrambler on."

There was a thirty-second pause. I surveyed the empty hotel lobby. No one but the night crew and a team of janitors dressed in green jump-suits. They didn't know how lucky they were to have escaped the hell of a ghetto teeming with dying flesh.

"Thanks for not waking me this time. What's new?" asked Donaldson.

"Plenty. Harris and I will be in the city tomorrow. We take the 9 AM plane out of here."

"I'll be there at the airport to meet you."

"Don't forget to bring a half-million dollars with you."

"What for?" He sounded surprised.

"My little trip to Poland wasn't as easy as you said it would be. I ran into a lot of trouble."

Donaldson became angry and defensive. "I never agreed to anything! This was part of the mission. You were supposed to obey ..."

"Yes. And it was also supposed to be easy. But it wasn't." I spoke curtly.

"But do you have the paper?" Donaldson would try to find out as much as he could before he agreed to any further deals.

"I have everything. Just be sure you have everything with you."

"You must be joking."

"This is no joke! I'm explaining this to you now because it will be hard to do tomorrow. Have the money with you!" I insisted.

"And if not ...?"

"Then no paper! As far as I know this wasn't part of the mission at all."

"We'll talk."

"I've had enough talk. Just bring the money. No money, no deal." I hung up and returned upstairs to my room.

As much as I wanted to forget about the manuscript and get in a good night's sleep, I couldn't help thinking about those "Five Days of Freedom." They filled in the parts of Ted's existence that no one had witnessed. They presented as clear a picture of Ted as anyone could ever have. I was still unsure whether all this personal information would be enough to do the trick. He's thinking about being covered with gold. Well, the United States government has enough gold to cover him. Why should I worry?

But I did. I believed that it would be much more complicated than handing him a bundle of money. The manuscript had mentioned that every Jew who survived the Holocaust would be covered with gold and that was an obvious impossibility. Then I also had doubts about what Ted meant by the expression, gold. Was it possible that in his crazy melodramatic dream world, gold signified something more than material wealth? Freedom from the agony of existence? Power to annihilate the world?

My mind went back to the last time I had seen Ted. It was 1966 in Paris. He had several night clubs. He was moody though. I saw by the expression in his eyes nevertheless that he was happy to see me. "Hello, Johnny."

"I came to say goodbye, Ted," I started off.

"Leaving Paris?" he asked with a puzzled look on his face.

"You read the papers, don't you?"

"Well, I read the newspapers, yes, but what does it have to do with you?" he inquired, not quite sure of my point.

"De Gaulle is kicking us out," I stated flatly.

"You'll have to go to Belgium or Germany. It's not that far." It showed on his face that he really didn't want to lose contact with me.

"I don't know," I pondered. "I've applied for a new job but there haven't been any definite answers yet." I had absolutely no intention of telling him about my new arrangement with Lucini nor about my job with the narcotics squad. He no longer seemed like the old Ted. I didn't know how reliable he would be.

"Stop in and see me if you ever return to Paris. The girls and drinks will be on the house."

"Speaking about the girls," I interjected, "how's your love life?"

"It doesn't exist anymore," he replied curtly.

"I don't understand ..."

"I'll explain as simply as I know how. I've stopped fucking

completely. I've abandoned women."

"But why?" I was surprised. "For Christ's sake ..."

"I think it's a matter of age ... and competition," he admitted after a brief second of reflection. "I felt my youth evaporating. My pride was hurt. I had powerful competition from a younger generation, so I decided to solve that problem by retiring from sex. I not only rejected the competitors, but I put myself outside of them."

"Don't you miss all that fun? You, who used to have a different girl every night?"

"In a way, you're right," he conceded. "I do miss it."

"Well ..." I extended my arm in an uncomprehending gesture.

"There was too big a price to pay for it. That price was a matter of my honor and dignity. For me they have the highest value. I wouldn't trade them for sexual pleasures with a woman." He spat out the word "woman" as if it was synonymous with "whore."

"But it must be horrible to live like this."

He waved his hand in a disgusted manner. "Shit! It's all shit! I think that dignity today is the most important thing. I accomplished that. I don't want to lose it."

"I still don't understand why it should stop you from enjoying a woman."

"You see," he revealed, "you still don't understand, and you are a man. The idea of dignity is incompatible with a woman's mind. They prefer that you love them and throw your dignity away. For me, dignity is more important than love. I've got a different goal now because a man must always have a goal."

"What's your goal now, Ted?" I asked, trying to figure out his logic.

He smiled. "Remember that button we talked about."

"A button," I hesitated, "a button ..."

"I've been thinking about this button constantly. If I could only find it."

My mind was kind of hazy. We'd spoken about so many things

together. "Please tell me again, Ted. What kind of button are you searching for?"

He paced around the room. "You see? You forgot," he exclaimed. "The button, the right button is the one I could push and destroy the whole fucking world!" He was getting hysterical. I tried to calm him down.

"Don't be so bitter. Life can be beautiful even without women. Don't you enjoy flowers in the spring, the sun and a nice summer day?"

It didn't calm him. He became worse, and he started shouting, "I don't! Don't talk to me about nature. I remember people being executed on a nice summer day with the sun shining upon a field of beautiful flowers! Nature is indifferent to human problems. It's inhuman," he snarled.

I didn't know what to say. I felt like having a drink. "I need a drink," I proposed. "You need one too. Let's have it."

"Now you're speaking my language. We won't have one drink. We'll have a bottle or two if necessary."

That night I got drunk like I'd never gotten drunk before. All I remember is that he insisted that I return to visit him whenever I came to Paris. I assured him that I would, knowing that I'd never visit him again because he was so depressing. Even the alcohol couldn't lighten his spirits.

"I am sure that we shall meet again in the future," he said, trying to read my thoughts.

It sounded like a premonition, and I knew that it would come true. I remember that we shook hands and I left.

If there was only one person whom Ted talked to with all his heart, it was me. I knew more about him than even the professor who had seen him six months ago. And I was hoping that in the near future he would trust me again, and I'd be able to conduct my mission to a successful ending and make him change his mind about that statement.

I was the only one who had the keys to his mind. I thought about that and fell asleep.

Part V - The Incorruptibles

"The police are gangsters who failed." – Lucky Luciano

Chapter 23. Harris's Threat

Friday, October 14, 1983 – "After three days of scrupulous deliberation in our council chambers and in accordance with a unanimous decision made by the highest representatives of the free and united Arab republics, all petroleum exportation will be stopped at noon tomorrow. We shall not comply with the frivolous whims of infidel superpowers, nor shall we contribute to the destruction of Almighty Allah's beautiful earth at the hands of Zionist scoundrels. The utmost precautions have been taken to assure our security lest anyone attempt to take what is not theirs by force." – *Communiqué, Council of Ministers, Arab League Conference, Baghdad, Iraq*

I don't know how long I'd been sleeping, but I could hear Harris' voice in the distance. "Johnny, wake up. Johnny."

"What? Are we in New York already?"

"No. I want to talk to you."

"Christ. Right now? What about?"

"Something very important," he said mysteriously and then looked around. "Everybody's asleep. I don't think we'll be overheard."

"Okay, shoot. What's it all about, the girls?"

"Be serious, Johnny. His tone was muted, and I had no idea what was to follow. "I know you have fourteen pounds of heroin in your luggage."

How did he know that? I was stunned but tried to keep my composure. "Excuse me?"

"You heard me. Fourteen pounds of horse, seven kilos to be exact, which you are so graciously delivering for Monsieur Lucini Spaggiari. He gave it to you in Paris."

"Anything else you want to tell me?" He knew about Spaggiari. But how? Nobody knew about us except the Polish State Security.

"You have an account in a bank in Geneva. Credit Suisse. There's three million dollars in account number 1256-8YZ-917."

I knew then that he wasn't bluffing. I also realized that there wasn't anything I could do about it. Maybe he'd left a note somewhere about the whole thing. I played it cool. "I'm listening."

"You see, Johnny, it's all your fault. I was a good cop, a real Elliot Ness, as you liked to say. But during this trip you pressured me into changing myself. I never went with loose women. I didn't drink much either. You forced me into a different lifestyle, Johnny, and I'll tell you something, I enjoyed it. I'm really grateful to you. You know I'm not stupid, just not as experienced as you. But you were an excellent teacher. Now I don't want to give it up. I want your money. I want to live the way you taught me, and I can't do that on my salary. If you don't hand it over to me, then all I have to do is to tip off customs when we leave the plane. You can refuse, but at your age, old man, twenty years on the inside will be hard to take. Get my message?"

I could always deny what he said. But where had he gotten his information? During his investigation for my Treasury Department application? During his investigation for my special job? If he had known, he would have turned me in right away. "How did you get your information?"

"From my French connection, the DST[27]," he smirked condescendingly.

I was shocked. Was Spaggiari's Union Corse really infiltrated by the police? How could he not know? It couldn't have been a setup because I already knew enough about Lucini's network to shut him down if push came to shove.

"How did you find out from them?" I demanded.

"The DST is a sophisticated outfit. They were trained by MI5 in

London during the war. After the liberation they were instrumental in hunting Nazi war criminals and French collaborators. But De Gaulle didn't trust the Brits when it came to Communists. He knew the Soviets obtained our A-bomb research from British double agents and sought our help to prevent them from infiltrating his government. Since then, the FBI and DST have shared a lot of intelligence. All our work against the Camorra and Mafia was indispensable for their surveillance of the Coriscans," he concluded.

For my own selfish reasons, I'd let Harris wander off too often. Hell, I had encouraged it. I was flying without a parachute now. "I don't believe it," I challenged him.

But the son-of-a-bitch was right. He smiled a hypnotic little grin as if to inform me that he was taking hold of my consciousness and erasing a small detail or two. I couldn't do a goddamn thing. It was worse than a brainwashing.

"I can't give you the money now. I have to write to Switzerland and then call them with my code name. I can't very well do all that on the plane."

"Don't play me for a fool. I'll never let you get through customs if I don't get that money."

"Be reasonable, Harris. What can I do? If I had it on me, I'd give it to you right now. Believe me. Besides we have something more important to do. If we don't finish this job, the money won't be any good to either of us. There won't be a world left to spend it in."

"Don't give me that bullshit. You sound like a broken record. I'm not a part of the investigation, you know."

An idea flashed through my mind. The heavy din of the jet engines whirred in the darkened plane. I had to come up with a solution that would catch him faster than he was thinking and leave him no alternative but to accept it on the spur of the moment.

"If you want to make some money, I mean real money, I can make you a better proposition."

"What kind of proposition?" he snapped nervously.

"I'll give you fifty percent of my business. You'll get half of what I have on hand as soon as we finish with Shipansky and half of whatever comes in afterwards. And believe me, there's a lot more money to be made with my connections and our cover."

"Let me think about that a while," he said.

I waited anxiously for him to take the bait. He stared out the window as if there were a long parade going by. He turned and looked at me with a combination of greed and distrust. "If you're on the level," he offered timidly, "it's a deal."

"Yeah, I'm on the level. How can I be otherwise?"

"When will I get the first payment?"

"As soon as we're through with Shipansky, we'll head for Geneva, and I'll give you a million-and-a-half to open a numbered account. But even before that, I'll give you half of what I'll get from what I'm carrying now."

"How long will that be?"

"A day or two. Remember we'll both be busy with debriefings on this case."

We both smiled and shook hands, then ordered Johnny Walker from the hostess. "To our deal," I offered a toast.

"To the deal," he responded.

While I drank, I was already figuring how I could get rid of him for good. I had no intention of giving him even a penny.

When we landed at JFK, I wasn't sure of myself or Harris. He could change his mind at any moment. We walked down the ramp and proceeded through customs without a hitch. A chauffeur held up a sign printed MR. HARRIS. We followed him outdoors to a limousine where Donaldson and Haverson were waiting, the motor running. The airport was enveloped by a cold October fog that felt like a wet slap in the face.

"Just don't play with me," whispered Harris as the chauffeur held open the door.

Chapter 24. Donaldson's Plan

We shook hands with our bosses. The chauffeur navigated around the terminals and headed onto the highway toward Manhattan. No one spoke but, just as we approached the Midtown Tunnel to Manhattan, the chauffeur slowed down and pulled to the side of the tollbooths.

"Come with me, Harris," announced Haverson. We'll rendezvous in a few hours with the entire chess set."

Harris didn't protest. They exited our limo and got into another car waiting in the breakdown lane. They were just as anxious to be alone as I was to be with Donaldson. Harris could tell his version of what had happened plus correlate his notes with my absences. I was certain that I was tailed at some point during my escapades in Europe. Harris and Haverson would try to figure things out.

As we were now alone, Donaldson should have been more anxious to talk. Instead, he kept his mouth shut, and I had to offer the first sacrificial words. "Did you bring the money?"

"Are you blackmailing me?" Donaldson wanted to know.

"I'm just asking to be compensated for my mistreatment in Poland."

"Tell me about it," he asked.

I explained what had happened in detail.

"Well," he responded, "you were OSS and you were a soldier. That type of thing shouldn't surprise you."

"Look, Donaldson, don't forget that I'm no longer a soldier, and I'm tired of playing cloak-and-dagger games for nothing."

"How shall I justify the payments from our outfit?" he asked indignantly.

"You're unbelievable," I began to lecture him. "You're playing me for a sucker. Since when does the CIA have to justify their distribution of funds?"

"Well, you know the FOIA. We can't do what we were doing before."

"I'm not asking for new money," I said sarcastically. "I'll take what you've accumulated already. From the Mafia, the Chinese Triad, and the Israelis along with a few private investments here and there. Shall I recite them all to you?"

"No. You've said enough. Let's get down to the business at hand." He shut up briefly as if his pause would make me forget what I was arguing about. My eyes persistently stared him away from backing down. Then he declared, "You're pulling a fast one on me, Johnny."

"Yes. I'm pulling it now. I won't give you the code from the Polish general." I was calm yet firm in my blackmail. One of Ted's several personalities would have been proud of me.

"Can't I appeal to your patriotism? This is a national emergency."

"Fuck it! While you're talking, I've raised it to six hundred grand. I'll up the ante some more if I don't get it in the next few minutes."

"Don't get nervous. I get the message."

The car was weaving through city traffic. No words were said. Chunks of the skyscrapers whizzed by. The sky was an inky grey smudge. People moved about on the sidewalks, briefcases and shopping bags swinging rhythmically by their sides. Women strutted along with a determination I hadn't noticed in Europe where they were still relatively passive creatures. Shit, they didn't seem to care if the world was about to go down the tubes. Two things were on their minds, money and sex. No different than men. The interior of that smudge was papered in green and pink, and that's what drove everyone.

We headed downtown and the car halted at a dilapidated office building on the corner of Nassau and Beekman Streets. I waited while Donaldson went inside. Twenty minutes later, he brought me a briefcase filled with money.

"We have to hurry, we're late."

"Your fault," I replied while verifying the cash. It was all there.

The car went up over a curbstone onto the esplanade of Pace University and through the City Hall parking lot. We headed down Broadway two blocks, then across Church Street to the World Trade Center garage. Underground, there was a lighted portico where a doorman waited.

We took an elevator up the North Tower to the 53rd floor. Entering the room, I felt like I had never left ten days ago. Same plush carpeting, same mahogany conference table and the same configuration of imbeciles staring at each other as if the answers were written in their wrinkled foreheads. Haverson; Goldman of Secret Service; O'Brien from the Joint Chiefs; Berlinger from the Energy Department; Kramer, DIA; Secretary of State McClellan; and Tarnovsky, the National Security Advisor. They were all waiting to hear me reveal the big secret. A secret guarded perhaps for centuries and more profound than the Talmud, aiming right in on the meaning of life itself. I suppressed a hysterical laugh when I thought of the hooded Rosicrucians, those little gremlins who frolicked on the back pages of popular magazines demanding five dollars from the reader to tell him the Big Secret. Indeed, it was excruciatingly funny because the big secret in this case was that there was no secret. That's what I discovered on this God-forsaken mission, and I was anxious to see how Donaldson would explain that to these pinstriped pinheads.

"Where's Donaldson?" asked Tarnovsky.

"He'll be here in a minute," I said as I noticed Haverson duck out of the room.

Time was now compressed into this conference room. Everything seemed to hinge on the outcome of this assembly. Would there be another war? Another Holocaust that would create a new generation of Shipanskys? They played familiar bureaucratic games – paper clip un-doers, pencil fidgets and necktie-pullers.

Tarnovsky sat still. If he had one ounce of Polak left in him, it meant he was pickled in vodka. I kept expecting him to turn my way and offer to exchange my dollars for zlotys at a rate better than anywhere else. Could be he's thinking of another Final Solution, I thought. I wondered how many members of his family were left in the old country to spit on the ruins of the Warsaw Ghetto and curse the Jews for bringing the Russians to their country.

Reflecting on my contempt for these alphabet agencies and their self-serving chieftains, I wondered how different were they really from Lucini's Union Corse or Schlaube's allegiances to German thugs? Nazis, Red Army Faction – it only mattered to him that they were Germans. Even the Israelis, after what they experienced in the Holocaust, reverted to old tribal ways. Clan loyalties, ancestral territories were the alpha and omega of international diplomacy.

O'Brien, for example, the gutsy Irish general, where would he be without the Kennedys? Probably a lonely staff sergeant in the barracks checking the boys into bed and then sneaking off for a round of watery beer at the NCO commissary. I would have started to speculate on his IRA connection, but everyone motioned over my head as the double doors swung open. It was a real saloon entrance for the two DC gunslingers, "Dead Eye" Haverson and "Sorrowful" Donaldson.

For all the ceremony involved, they took their places as clumsily as a couple of Senate pages. I'll have to go to the movies if I want to see this done professionally, I made a note to myself.

"Dead Eye" glanced fleetingly at "Sorrowful." The cue was given, and the FBI director began. "Gentlemen, my agency and that of my distinguished colleague, Mr. Donaldson, have been receiving daily reports from our agents in the field. I must admit that I have often disagreed with Mr. Donaldson's conclusions. But in the last week, I have learned from our collaboration that his agency is a well-disciplined outfit. They have relentlessly pursued every lead and extended their investigation to all domains in this current situation. In connection with the Berisov assassination and the antagonistic attitude of the oil cartel, I hope you will accept his report, which will be submitted to the President as soon as this meeting is over. Naturally, any one of you may make further recommendations, which will be recorded and presented to the POTUS at the same time as this report."

"Well," said Tarnovsky, "as you probably know, POTUS is leaving for Uppsala, Sweden, tonight. He has scheduled an emergency summit with Kuslov, the new Soviet premier. I shall personally hand the report to him. You can make any observations you want. They shall be noted and delivered along with the materials that Mr. Donaldson has prepared for us."

At the mention of his name, Donaldson stood. He opened a large briefcase and piled eight dossiers on the table. Their shiny plastic covers gleamed in the light as he leaned over and passed them around to the other officials.

Everyone rifled through the pages, but they didn't have time for a detailed look. Donaldson's copy remained closed in front of him on the desk. He spoke extemporaneously.

"I'd like to begin by going straight to the heart of the matter, gentlemen. My original suspicions that the murder of Berisov was part of a plot to undermine our strategy for global security has indeed been confirmed by my agent. Shipansky was perhaps insane when he killed Berisov, but what really matters is that he became a part of world terrorist organizations in their plot to ignite a war between the superpowers."

Donaldson paused. He glanced down at the report. The others continued to feverishly browse from page to page.

How could that fucker have possibly prepared his report so quickly? I'd only been back for several hours.

"I won't reiterate the details of this memorandum, gentlemen," Donaldson said, interrupting their study-hall concentrations. "I just want you to reflect on this situation for several moments. Let's ask ourselves a simple question. Who would benefit from this monstrous destruction? The answer must be somebody as crazy as Hitler or a group of fanatics ideologically motivated by a totalitarian cause." He stopped and glared at his baffled audience.

"You'll reply that it was Shipansky, a lonely, demented creature with illusions of grandeur. A bitter victim of the war whose twisted mind led him to identify with the person who was responsible for his and his people's suffering. I reject that theory. Period.

"I had my answer ten days ago, but I needed more evidence to sustain my theory. I sent this man to Europe to confirm my conviction that Ted Shipansky acted on the direct orders of the German Red Army Faction." He pointed at me and grinned.

"I don't have to remind you of the legacy of the Red Army Faction. Their operatives kidnapped Rudolf Schleyer in order to secure his identity papers so that the assassin could penetrate the UN. When Shipansky got inside, he did as he was told. He pulled the trigger. When the mission had been completed, the terrorists killed Schleyer. They had no further use for him."

I was stunned. That wasn't the truth. The RAF had indeed funded Ted and provided him with Schleyer's ID but had intended him to blow up the UN building, not to assassinate Berisov. Without the details of my meeting in Germany, the memorandum was not only incomplete, it was a fraud. But I was only there to listen and was paid handsomely to shut up. I sat back and waited to hear the rest of his fantastic revelations.

"Organized terrorism has been on the march since the war ended. Its original and final goal was to destabilize Western governments and destroy political democracy. I shall not refer to it as exclusively Communist because, as you realize, there are other beliefs which are used to brainwash masses of people in the overpopulated, underfed regions of the world. Latin America and the Caribbean have been assaulted by Communists, that is true. But think of the Middle East, where our entire Central Treaty Organization has been destroyed by Islam. This radical fundamentalist movement is equipped with weapons equal to or even more powerful than Communism. Think of the strategic advantages of a religion which can mobilize ninety-five percent of a nation when its leaders call for a jihad. It makes Vietnam look like a sandbox rebellion in comparison. This movement is now eroding the imbalanced southern flank of NATO. It is more useful for penetrating the backwards regions of Africa than Communism. It also takes advantage of internecine squabbles among Communists.

While Vietnam warred with China, militant Islam recruited deeply in the Philippines, Malaysia and Indonesia. Islam and its agents even penetrated into the Soviet Union. Terrorism is on the rise there although it is not publicized. That's against the Party's policy. They never even report street crimes. But we know they exist.

"Our intelligence originally detected trouble in the Soviet Dagestan bordering Iran in the oil-producing area of Baku. It was led by a man who claimed to be a servant of Allah. He proposed a plan to liberate his fellow Muslims from godless Communism. He was protected by the peasants, rich and poor alike. Several incidents touched off a wave of nationalist movements among the Kazakhs, Kirghiz, Tajiks, Turkmens, Uzbeks, Chechnyans, Karakalpaks, Badakhshans, Nagorno-Karabakhs, all the peoples around the Aral, Black, and Caspian Seas. This represents seventy million out of the total Soviet population claiming an allegiance to Islam. Khomeini's revolution stirred them up and the invasion of Afghanistan gave them an excuse to mobilize, but it wasn't long before they gained a momentum all their own."

"But who the hell is behind this?" demanded Tarnovsky.

"Wait," shouted Donaldson, upset at the interruption. "I'll tell you everything in time. But I want you gentlemen to have a chronological sense of exactly what has been happening.

"This self-styled prophet was insane. He hated the progress that the American way of life offered to his people. He decried Communism in the USSR and China. Zionism was his preferred enemy. His party, the only party, was the Party of God, Hezbollah.

"Khomeini?" Berlinger was ready to play a schoolboy's game of twenty questions.

"No," reprimanded schoolmaster Donaldson. "Khomeini was too apprehensive about the Soviet Union to start that kind of trouble. He paid no attention to Afghanistan and ignored this movement for the same reason. This new fundamentalist movement threatened the strategic position of Iran and therefore his own revolution.

"Arafat?" ventured McClellan.

"No!" scolded Donaldson. "This man used Arafat. He used the Fatah killers and all those terrorist groups."

"Castro?" tried McClellan again.

"No!" exclaimed the CIA mogul. "On the contrary, he used a different strategy from Castro. Castro put his troops at the disposition of the Soviet Union. This man wanted to play superpower himself. He wanted to exploit the Palestinian operatives in his network in exactly the same way the KGB was using Castro."

"You mean he stole the whole organizational plan from the KGB?" suggested Kramer, who couldn't believe that an entire strategy could be copied.

"Yes, you see this man took up the vision of an immense Islamic power and a strategic return to the Middle Ages when Europe retreated in defeat after the Crusades. He had everything including tools, ideology, willpower, and money. Tools furnished by the KGB; the ideology of militant Islam; petrodollars; and the willpower of an insane mind. What is most extraordinary, gentlemen, this man had an atomic bomb!"

"The atomic bomb?" sputtered Goldman.

"Yes! The Pakistani and Libyan leaders told him that there was a Hindu bomb, a Jewish bomb, a Christian bomb and an atheist bomb. 'We must acquire an Islamic bomb,' they concluded. Through a combination of intrigue, intelligence and stubbornness, they achieved this goal. Not only did they construct a nuclear arsenal, but they did it under our noses. And we didn't detect it until it was too late."

Donaldson paused to wipe the sweat off his forehead. All this drama had taken a toll on his usually calm appearance. His shirt collar was soaked, his sleeves clung to the perspiration on his arms.

"Who is this man?" persisted Tarnovsky.

"I'd like to take a brief rest, gentlemen," announced Donaldson without looking at Tarnovsky. "But here's what we'll do," he proposed as he suddenly swung his torso toward the president's National Security Advisor. His mouth hung open and he peered at Tarnovsky like a crazed reptile.

"What!" exclaimed Tarnovsky with a metallic sarcasm that resounded across the room.

"We'll play a game," offered Donaldson with a comic smile.

"Are you out of your mind!" bellowed the frustrated Tarnovsky.

"Well, it'll be part game and part exercise in intelligence activity. From what I've told you, you should have a very good idea of who the man is. Now please, everybody writes the name of his candidate on a scrap of paper. Fold it and put it at my little section of the table here. We'll see how many intelligent people we have here. And don't cheat. Don't look at the memorandum and don't ask Haverson because he already knows the answer." Donaldson smiled murderously. "Between acts, I'll excuse myself. I want to take a leak and wash my hands and face. You'll play?" he surveyed the bewildered faces who offered no opposition. "Good. Johnny," he raised his chin toward my seat, "come with me."

I went with him into the toilet. "How do you like my game?" His words were enveloped in the odor of urinal soap.

"Okay," I responded hesitantly. "But it's not true," I added.

"No. Basically, it is true. Only your contribution is half-true. But it'll be true enough for Uncle Sam, so it's good enough for me. And good for you too," he grimaced as he glanced at his trousers in the mirror. I couldn't tell whether it was a compromising smile or his prostate kicking up. "Don't forget the money I paid you."

"I just wonder about one thing," I mused. "Your expression, the one you used to explain Shipansky's action as pulling the trigger. Where did you get that?"

"Get what?"

"The word 'trigger,' dammit!"

"What's with you, Miller? Are you hiding something?"

"No. Just this word, 'trigger.'"

"Why? It's a good expression and I'd use it again. Why?" He didn't really seem to care but was intrigued by my new linguistic infatuation.

"For your money, I'll let you know that Trigger was Shipansky's code name in the Polish Home Army."

"Fits fine, doesn't it, Johnny? Trigger is for guns like Ted. Miller is for money like a blackmailer." His lips quivered with the second phrase. "And I am for Uncle Sam."

"You're full of shit. You're for the CIA."

"And the CIA is always for what's best for the USA."

"You would try and feed me that kind of bullshit. It may be good enough for those suckers in there ..."

"We're in a hurry to find out the results of my quiz game, remember. Let's get back in there," he guided me toward the door. I think that he suddenly became paranoid about his own agency. Perhaps they had bugged the toilets.

"That was a long piss," General O'Brien greeted us as we entered the room.

"How long was it?" challenged Donaldson.

"You took fifteen minutes ..."

"Let's go back to our quiz show." He shrugged off O'Brien's comments and began to open the crumpled papers. He did so with relish as if he were opening little clams to toss down his throat. "Yes, all six of them," he asserted, "they all seemed to name the same man. You're all losers," he declared with a frown.

"How dare you!" shrieked the outraged Secretary of State.

"It was a game, McClellan," stated a poker-faced Donaldson.

"We never bet any money," stammered Goldman.

"That's because your bookie isn't here," quipped Donaldson.

"That's enough," shouted Haverson. "Please read the name."

"Colonel Qaddafi of Libya. All six papers. You've missed the point," laughed Donaldson triumphantly. "You should have understood from what I explained about Arafat that Qaddafi too was just a front man."

Donaldson suddenly shifted gears into a more business-like discourse. That game was over. His amusing little game based on such a big fat lie.

"You don't know his name. Excuse me for my stroke of sadism. His name is Imam Hamidullah, although he calls himself Mahdi. To Muslims everywhere, the Mahdi is the promised Messiah who will liberate them from the yoke of oppression. The Mahdi alone is capable of uniting the Muslim world into the largest, most highly charged army the world has ever known. He represents a power superior to that of Arafat, Khomeini and Qaddafi combined."

"But you're talking about a religious prophet!"

"Wait a minute!" Goldman chimed in amidst the disorder that Donaldson's stunning announcement had evoked. "You should be aware of the deep internal divisions in the Muslim world. The Shi'a hate the Sunnis. They've never been able to conceal this animosity, much less mend their quarrels."

"Very astute, Goldman. Very smart. But that is his genius. Imam Hamidullah has solved that problem. His existence as Mahdi is the end of that problem ... and perhaps our end also."

The crescendo of murmurs died down and the seven men looked at Donaldson sheepishly. He had achieved his desired effect and no longer needed to hide anything from them.

"Imam Hamidullah first appeared in Lebanon several years before the outbreak of civil war in 1975. He associated with the Shi'a minority and studied at a Shi'a seminary. Although an undistinguished scholar, Hamidullah captivated his fellow students and later on his devotees. He was straight as an arrow, yet his style and language reflected the 1960s youth culture. His reputation spread to every mosque in the Middle East. He was revered. He even journeyed to Qom, Iran's holy city, the Vatican of Shi'ism.

"Hamidullah returned to Lebanon in 1982 during the Israeli invasion. He trained and fought with the Shi'ite Amal militia. The contacts he established there were invaluable.

"Then, if you will recall, although I admit it is an obscure detail of history, he began stalking the U.S. contingent in Lebanon. He was spotted just a day before the bombing of the U.S. Embassy, and then he disappeared into thin air.

"Khomeini accused Qaddafi of kidnapping him. We thought this kidnapping signified a permanent rift between revolutionary Shi'ism and the Sunni radicals. But Qaddafi knew better, and Khomeini soon figured things out. According to Shi'a belief, the twelfth or hidden imam has been walking the earth since the time of Mohammed. He was imbued with the power to make himself invisible. Only when he came out into open and announced his presence would Muslims know that their Redeemer, the Mahdi, had arrived.

"Hamidullah wasn't kidnapped by Qaddafi, although he traveled to Libya on his own free will to coordinate and command the jihad. He supervised the construction of the bomb, blessed the efforts of radical mullahs everywhere, and above all convinced many Sunnis that he indeed was the Madhi promised in the Hadith, the compiled sayings of Muhammad. His genius resided in his ability to convince others that he was the infallible reincarnation of the hidden imam.

Donaldson collapsed into silence to survey the impact of his revelations.

"He's our man!" shouted a wild-eyed McClellan.

Tarnovsky was the next to react. "I'll report this to the president immediately. There's still a piece of information missing, though. You mention that Miller learned of the German Red Army's involvement in this plot. But that doesn't jive, Mr. Director." Tarnovsky smiled. He thought he had caught Donaldson in a logical trap. "Why would the Commies and anarchists participate in a project that meant their eventual destruction! To them, as to us, Islam must surely mean an even greater repression than fascism."

Donaldson bent his arms and crouched over the table. His eyes shifted around the room to make certain he had everyone's attention. Then he answered Tarnovsky with another bombshell. "Gentleman, Hamidullah is an American citizen. You know him as Kabala Murat, the Black Panther who fled to Cuba in 1967. In the minds of international terrorists of all stripes, he's from 'the belly of the beast' – Compton, California, to be precise. That universally connects him to all those marginals opposed to our security interests. Kabala

Murat, my friends, is the apotheosis of J. Edgar Hoover's nightmarish prediction of a Black Messiah. We believed we resolved this problem when we targeted Malcolm X and King, but this fish slipped through our net. Castro provided him a convenient cover. We followed him to Angola and Ethiopia with the Cuban forces and classified him as a Communist operative. Even the Russians believed this when he toured the Soviet Union, where he was lauded as a hero of the workers' revolution and his picture displayed in classrooms from Leningrad to Vladivostok."

Kabala Murat! Things were beginning to make sense. Montague Jefferson's slick operation and his luxurious Harlem digs, the seductive girlfriend offering booze and hard-bop were nothing more than deceptions. Could there be a more effective ploy than to conceal religious fanaticism behind a veil of hedonism? The bon-vivant terrorist cover. I'd missed it, but evidently so had the FBI and CIA. Focused as they were on hunting Communists, Cold War-style, they had ignored the varied religious cults that flourished in Cuba even under Castro. Santeria, candomblé, and Islam too were used by captive Africans and their children to resist slavery. Perhaps Hoover worried about a Black Messiah, but his understanding of subversion was limited by his own racist instincts. Mine too.

"Yet we ignored his biography totally," Donaldson continued. "Murat's parents came from Newark, New Jersey, where they followed the teachings of Noble Drew Ali, the original Black Muslim and founder of an organization called the Moorish Science Temple of America. Just before World War I, a Shi'a immigrant came to town from Beirut and condemned Ali's creed as un-Islamic. He publicly embarrassed Ali who couldn't read Arabic and didn't even own a copy of the Qur'an. He'd substituted a forgery called "The Circle 7 Koran" that the stranger exposed as a bunch of mystical gibberish and nonsense.

"Ali was so embarrassed that he ran away to Chicago and absconded with all the temple's funds. The stranger, Sheikh Dusé Mohamed, took over and began teaching Arabic and authentic Islamic worship. Murat's parents were youngsters. The sheikh took them under his wing, encouraged them to marry, and eventually sent them to proselytize in Los Angeles. When they had a child in 1932, the sheikh took all responsibility for the boy's education. He saw to it that Kabala learned Arabic and became a hafiz, or Qur'an reciter. As young man, the boy fought the draft and was imprisoned during the Korean War. In the federal penitentiary, he met Eldridge Cleaver, who brought him into the Black Panther Party when he was released in the early 1960s. The FBI only noticed Murat when he first went to prison, and they had no idea about Sheikh Dusé Mohamed and his disciples. Shoddy work that we're all doomed to pay for now," concluded Donaldson with an icy glance toward Haverson.

"Where does Miller come in as so important?" questioned Tarnovsky.

"Mr. Miller's role has been very useful. Haverson and I investigated a microdot he returned to us from Poland."

"Why did you send him to Poland if you already knew about the extent and degree of German terrorist involvement?"

"Please don't interrupt me," barked Donaldson, angry that anyone would second-guess his operations. "The microdot was handed to Mr. Miller in a very unconventional way by one of our agents who had infiltrated into a high position on the Polish Central Committee. The microdot contained information about the wave of terrorist outbreaks in the Soviet Union. This was the evidence we needed to confirm that Hamidullah and his terrorist gang had also targeted the Soviet Union and their satellites. Maybe they hate us Christians and Jews, but atheistic Communists are the lowest order of infidels to them. The microdot was a long-awaited piece of information, gentlemen. It also gave us the newest deployment plans for the Warsaw Pact units. I'm sure that you'll be interested to see them, O'Brien. All the details are in the memorandum."

"You did a good job, Miller," volunteered Berlinger.

"The CIA made a good choice," Donaldson spoke to take credit where he thought it was due. "Now you understand my insistence on sending him to Europe."

"One more critical question," asked Haverson, breaking a personal silence that betrayed his embarrassment over the FBI's glaring failure. "How did you learn of this Imam Hamidullah?"

"Without going into details, our mole in Warsaw belongs to the Catholic underground that has penetrated the official church hierarchy, the government bureaucracy, and the Communist Party too," explained Donaldson. "These Polish operatives even encouraged it to the degree that it was undermining Russian hegemony in Central Asia. The local rebellions demoralized the Red Army and heartened those in Warsaw who contemplated resistance themselves. Before backing Hamidullah with money and arms, however, they conducted a thorough investigation. Ironically, they tried to warn us about the bombing of our embassy in Lebanon."

The officials mused. Some protested and demanded to know the mole's identity but Donaldson wouldn't budge. Others wanted to know more about Murat and where he is now. "I cannot reveal anything further in an ongoing investigation. As we speak, Mr. Haverson," he leaned toward the FBI director, "our analysts are forwarding a top-secret report on the Hamidullah network to your Joint Terrorism Task Force. Hopefully, we'll never ignore another threat like this one."

"I'll be damned," swore Tarnovsky. "I better leave now so I can report to the President before he takes off for Sweden. Naturally, I'll need a copy for the President and another one for Kuslov."

Donaldson pushed a buzzer and asked one of his aides to come to the conference room. The doors swung open almost instantly and a young Marine lieutenant entered. He was carrying a bulky briefcase. Without a word, he marched over to Donaldson's place and deposited the leather box in front of his chief. He reached into his pocket and took out a key. Donaldson did the same and they placed their two keys in the lock. It opened like a Swiss safety-deposit box.

"I hope there's nothing embarrassing in there for the Russians," counseled Tarnovsky.

"Look, Tarnovsky, if I were an idiot I wouldn't be working for the company. Here's a Russian copy for Kuslov. It contains neither the references to their internal problems nor our Warsaw mole. I've prepared an alternative copy of the doctored version in English if they want to see 'the original.' You never know with them." He spoke like an experienced spook who was as familiar with the Russian quirks as with his wife's bedmates whenever he was away on assignment. "And here's the complete one for the President himself. You advise him how to handle it."

"Don't worry. I do my job as well as you do yours."

"I hope so, and I do worry," Donaldson added to annoy him more than anything else.

The second bureaucrat to rise was General O'Brien. "I must go too, gentlemen. I'm due back in Washington later this afternoon. The red alert is still in effect, and I'll confide a nasty little secret to you. As of this morning, our strategic command lost track of ten moveable silos. We're not sure where they are, no one is. The computer was programmed to institute a camouflage pattern during red alert, but since the red alert tests never lasted more than twenty-four hours, we had no idea that the machine could outwit us. If we don't locate the missiles in time, the consequences could be disastrous."

"You better hurry," offered Donaldson without the least sign of concern. "There's not much time left." Berlinger and Kramer excused themselves at the same time.

"I shall be in constant communication with our NATO friends," stated McClellan.

"Make sure you tell them only what they need to know," commanded Donaldson, dejected now by his colleagues' incompetence in a crisis of such dimension. "Christ," he remarked, "I'm depressed. I have to do all the thinking for you monkeys."

When they had all filed out, I was the only one left with him besides the Marine. He excused the soldier and turned to me. "I am really worried."

"You worry too much ..."

"That's not the point, Miller. If these guys are so incompetent, think about that jackass in the Oval Office. Suppose he doesn't know how to handle Kuslov."

"We'll never know about it in that case," I offered.

"You mean you're not worried?" asked Donaldson, expecting a serious answer.

I disappointed him when I said, "Why should I? I've got more than a half-million dollars."

"If the bomb comes, you'll have nothing. Just concentrate on how to handle Shipansky, our 'Trigger.'" We acknowledged each other without smiling.

"I will, but remember you promised I'd have a free hand in dealing with him."

"Don't worry. For him there'll be plenty cash. Anything he wants. We're not footing the bill for that. NSA pays that ticket." He paused and stared at the desk. I knew he was thinking about the payoff he had made to me. The fucker knew all along I'd have trouble in Poland. He just thought he could get away without paying a cent.

The searing pain of my torture and the cold, damp feeling of the cell clamped down on my brain. "Admit it, Donaldson," I interjected, "that half million was the best investment you ever made in your life."

"I don't get you ..."

"Don't pretend. Thanks to me, you've acquired an unlimited budget for yourself and the company. If I had realized, I might have demanded more."

"You bastard! If you had, you'd be dead now."

"That I know, you cheap bastard, and I don't intend to ask for more. I just want Wilson's job. Head of the DEA."

"It's yours. You almost deserve it, and besides that Wilson is a lousy guy."

"One more thing before I see Shipansky. Is anything you told those dummies true?"

"What difference does it make to you, Miller?"

"Well. for example, if we're dealing with a national emergency, red alert and all that, I don't suppose the president should be advised to act if it's all a part of a paranoid boogieman fantasy."

"What makes you think it's a fantasy?" Donaldson was clearly annoyed.

"You said you and Haverson studied the microdot and inserted that information into the memorandum. You didn't have time. It was a phony statement and the memorandum must have been written beforehand."

"Look, whether it's fantasy, half-fantasy or pure truth, it doesn't matter as long as it serves the president and our country's interests. So what if the memorandum was prepared in advance!"

"And whatever serves the country's interests serves the company ..."

"You're catching on, Miller. I'm even starting to like you. How'd you like to be on my staff?" he proposed.

"I wouldn't. I'm long past the age for spying. Wilson's job will be sufficient."

"But working with the agency is more exciting." He was baiting me now. All he wanted to do was confirm his suspicions about me. I had nothing to hide, but still wouldn't tell him anything. With Wilson out of the way and with Spaggiari easily replaceable on the other end, I'd make all the loot I needed. The DEA, I thought, how crooked can you get? This scumbag was playing with the lives of billions. We're all scum, but Donaldson was the biggest of all.

"On the other hand, Donaldson, I'll offer you a job. A place in HELL!"

"Never heard of it."

"I know. It's a very exclusive outfit, sort of like Bohemian Grove. You could probably be its chairman."

"Thanks, but what would I have to do?"

"Nothing. Act yourself. I've got no time for further details. Trigger, remember? See you later."

Donaldson called the Marine back into the room. He carried

the same briefcase but this time he pulled out a bunch of papers authorizing me to take complete control of the prisoner. My meeting with Trigger had been set for 9 AM the next morning. That left me with the rest of the evening to draw up a plan that might account for his strange way of thinking. I also had the chance to finally get a decent night's sleep. First, though, there was a small business deal to take care of.

I left the building with my luggage and my own attaché case in one hand, and the one with Donaldson's cash in the other. I hailed a taxi and told the driver to cruise until he found a vacant phone booth. He weaved through traffic and finally slowed down as we approached the East Fifties. He stopped in front of a booth at the corner of Fifth Avenue and East 56th Street. I got out with my things but asked him to wait.

In the booth, I punched the seven digits given to me by Spaggiari. A voice answered at the other end. No greetings, no formalities. I was the only caller they had been waiting for all day. All the voice said was to be at the drop point in the parking lot of the Good News Church in Teaneck, New Jersey. I was to wait for a Mark IV.

I had the cabbie take me across town to the Port Authority, where I changed to a bus headed for Jersey. I wasn't taking any chances with the agency or the real cops, or even with Harris for that matter.

The exchange went smoothly. I returned to Manhattan and checked into the Intercontinental Hotel. I could afford luxury at this point. As I looked around the plush lobby staring into the well-manicured house plants, I felt a stab of fear rip through my body. What if Donaldson's apprehensions were justified? I would have spent years just hoarding my money for no reason at all. I'd die a death as banal as a motherless pauper in Bangladesh. There would be nothing separating us in the common grave we would share, not even a distinctive fat smile written across my radiation-scarred face.

Part VI - The Puritans

"To remain noble, man must be the master of four virtues: courage, insight, understanding and solitude. For solitude is a virtue with us, a need for a clean life, to divorce all contacts with other men and society that is impure. All contacts with society will make the man, sooner or later, ordinary. The noble type of man regards himself as arbiter of values; he does not need to be approved of, he passes judgment.... Many men die too late and sometimes too soon. Few manage to depart at the right time." – Frederick Nietzsche

Chapter 25. Cop or Friend?

Saturday, October 15, 1983 – None of the familiar demons haunted my sleep, yet I did not feel refreshed when I awoke. I glided around the white-carpeted suite as if its luxury was a derisive suggestion that I did not belong there. I could have a dozen places like this with the money I was making. Perhaps I could rent a penthouse with a commanding view of the East River, but I would have to get used to the smell of affluence. My suitcase world was incontestably filled with nice rooms, maid service and first-class travel arrangements. I was used to tipping bellboys, waiters and flunkies. That was a sign of identification with them and not at all commensurate with the style of a wealthy hoodlum. No big tips. Discretion would have to be adopted as a rule and, furthermore, the women would have to be narrowed down to nameless whores with whom I could agree upon a set price, be it for a night's worth of fucking or a month's vacation on a Greek island. If pressed to articulate this apparent regulation so necessary to my changed position, I assume it could be called a lowering of one's values. It's an attitude that answers the silly riddle of why the rich get richer: They have nowhere to go but down amongst everyone they cheated on the way up, and as any elementary schoolkid knows, the downhill slide is the easiest. Constantly haunted by my dead platoon mates, I was already halfway to hell anyway. There was no problem for me. I'd get used to it and wind up enjoying it as much as that Polish sonofabitch relished torturing his prisoners.

I moved around the suite delicately to avoid offending its dignity. I took a quick shower instead of dawdling in the tub like a peasant in his monthly bath. I shaved and dressed, putting on the grey suit that was financed by my last meeting with Wilson. Was he still sore about that sucker punch I gave him before helping myself to a few big bills from his wallet, I wondered? Nice suit though, a Brooks Brothers Golden Fleece made-to-measure. It was a uniform in a sense. I had worn it throughout my mission in Europe. The agents who followed my itinerary watched me as if I were an enemy soldier moving around behind the lines. They scrutinized the cut and material of the suit. To them it was an indication of my rank. Their perceptions were sharp. They were capable of distinguishing a well-tailored Italian suit from the ready-to-wear copy manufactured for famous department stores. The more I regarded the suit as my uniform, the easier it made my rehearsing in the mirror. From what I knew about Ted, he was bound to respect a uniform even if I had long since lost his trust.

The next step was to simply present my case to him. I wasted no further gestures on the mirror and left the hotel, passing by the reception to request that the room be reserved for another night. I didn't know how long I'd have to wait here in New York. If all went well, I'd be out of town by the weekend.

The one flaw in Donaldson's scheme to save the world had nothing to do with Ted. It was Harris. He was to accompany me to the clandestine cell where Ted was being held, but he would have no authority to listen to our conversation. Haverson probably just wanted to guarantee his share of whatever Donaldson had promised him for his support in front of the brass. Haverson was Donaldson's problem like Harris was mine. To come out of this as the administration's top dog, Donaldson had to conceal our extracurricular activities from Haverson. Knowledge of my payment, for instance, could become the subject of the Inspector General's report or a Congressional inquiry. Those things take on a life of their own, and who knows what more dirt might emerge?

Like having an old friend who's chronically broke, I had no trouble locating my "problem." He was waiting in front of the hotel in a chauffeured limo. I carefully placed my attaché case in the back seat between us. The driver sped away before the door was completely shut. Soon we were heading downtown. We exchanged pro forma jokes about our debriefings. Harris related what he had heard about the report given inside and tried to get me to confirm it. I nodded occasionally in order not to cut him off. Talking to him like an equal was something I'd had enough of. The bastard was trying to rip me off and we both knew it. At the moment there was no plan to diminish his threat so talking to him was pointless. He seemed compliant with my attitude and obligingly fell silent.

We drove to Lower Manhattan and pulled up in front of an ordinary-looking apartment building. "We're here," said the driver. "Just go inside. It's a secure fortress."

Harris and I got out and walked up the steps. SECURITY ACCOUNTING SERVICES read a bronze plaque to the side of the door. I pushed it open and we went in. We entered an austere waiting room. There was an empty reception window with a NO SMOKING sign in English and Chinese.

The door closed behind us. "May we see identification?"

We turned to see two armed men. I presented my attaché case to one of them so that he could open it without any suspicion. He gingerly took the small leather suitcase and held it level with his eyes. He flicked the locks in a peculiar fashion by tapping them with a pencil and then signaled his partner to pass a magnetic wand over it. They weren't taking any chances.

When the case was finally opened and my identification verified, the guard spoke again. "What is your purpose here, Mr. Miller?"

"If you allow me, I will take my orders from the case."

He nodded. I rifled through my files.

Moments later, I was standing in the middle of a stark room. A streak of light penetrated through a dirty window placed three or four feet above eye level. It was small enough so that even a kid would have trouble climbing through. It was barred.

At first, I saw no one. Then I looked behind me. Ted was sitting in the corner, his arms folded, hands resting on his knees, his unshaven head leaning against the wall. His eyes were closed. I thought he was asleep.

"Ted," I half-whispered. He moved his head sharply, but he made no further effort to answer. "Ted," I repeated a little louder this time, "It's me, Johnny Miller."

He opened his eyes and stared in disbelief. Then he got up slowly and walked toward me. There was hardly any expression on his face. "Miller? Well, it really is you. I thought at first it was a new inquisitor, but when I heard your name ... It really is you."

He stopped in front of me and stared at my face. I couldn't read anything in his eyes.

"You haven't changed much," he said. "Just a little older. And you've put on some weight, that's all." He put his hands on my shoulders and then took them away. "Just a little older," he mused and turned his hunched-gorilla back to my face.

I surveyed the room. There was a tray of uneaten breakfast. Four or five unopened packs of cigarettes lay on a small table. On one side of the dingy room there were two beds pushed together to make a large double bed. It was messy and unmade. The sheets looked disgustingly filthy. It was a typical Ted hangout, right down to the bars on the windows, which were a familiar fixture in his Parisian apartments. For the brief time he had been residing there, it was certainly cluttered. Books were scattered about. Solzhenitsyn's *In the First Circle*, Chandler's *Simple Art of Murder*, Ian Kershaw's two-volume biography of Hitler, and Koestler's *Darkness at Noon*. Still fighting the war, still trying to understand if people choose sides for reasons other than pure survival. I looked around and inspected the walls and corners, underneath the bed and mattress, but I couldn't find any microphones. Donaldson had apparently kept his word.

I placed my attaché case on the small night table and opened it. I removed Lauren Bacall's *By Myself* and handed it to Ted in a silent offering. He received it with all the grace of a primitive god, starved for the enlightenment he knows his worshippers will never achieve.

"They sent you?" he interjected after thumbing through the book like it was an old friend. He wore a horrible expression on his face. I couldn't believe that a human being could project such an ugly appearance without the help of cosmetics. In the middle of his forehead was a two-and-a-half-inch gash. Barely healed, it looked like he had been scratched by a wild animal. His hair was still blond but eaten away and patchy. It stood up on its ends in an unfashionable crewcut which had neither been trained nor combed for the past few days. Cigarette burns stained his fine lips. His ears looked as if they had been glued on as an afterthought by a careless barber who had accidentally shaved them off.

He stood straight up and did his best not to reveal the middle-aged girth which surrounded his waist rather harmlessly. His clothes were dirty, a navy-blue military shirt, pants with the waist belted so tight that it must have left a permanent crease in his belly. Nothing but his shoes were in order. They were a brown pair of wing tips, heavily polished and gleaming. They reflected the abrupt movements we made around one another and mirrored all the heat and tension that hung over the room. I studied them closely and finally perceived his eyes staring down at the floor in search of whatever he thought had caught my attention. His eyes bulged out like those of the cadavers of skeletons I had seen somewhere. They were the remains of Jews who had been executed during the Spanish Inquisition and hidden away in the sub-cellar of a Madrid church. The eyes were raving mad and the sockets turned upwards and to the side in the most hideously distorted manner.

"Yeah, they sent me," I began.

"They want you to make me talk, don't they?" he shouted maniacally. "But they're mistaken." Then he sneered. "Nobody will make me withdraw my statement." He looked at me, twisted his head slightly and softened his voice. "Did you come as a cop or ... a friend?"

"Both," I admitted. From my attaché case, I took out a pile of folders. "I've investigated you. I've read your manuscript. Here's the report. It might amuse you. You know me well. We met often enough, although nobody knew about it except us. But I've found out a lot about you these last few days."

He laughed. "What did you find out, Johnny? Nobody who knew me could have told you anything, or they couldn't have told you the truth."

"I don't pretend to know the truth." I put the papers on the floor next to the bed. "You'd better eat something. How'd you like it if I round up some kielbasa and a quart of vodka? That okay? I'll be back. We'll talk then. I don't pretend to know the truth. I know it!"

I left without hearing or expecting a response to my suggestion. On the way out of the room I turned and stared into his eyes, which had been fixed not on the papers but on the book. I left the way I had been brought in, remembering to tell the guards that I would return at noon. Harris was reading a magazine in the room where I'd left him. "You finished already?"

"Are you kidding? I haven't even started. Come on, I've got some shopping to do."

"What!"

Harris followed me out the door and into the street. I looked for a taxi and instantly realized that we would have to settle for the chauffeured limo which had delivered us. The precautions were made for a purpose and, no matter how ridiculous I thought they were, there was only one way of leaving if you planned to return.

As I climbed into the back seat, Harris whispered orders into the driver's ear. No doubt he warned him against acceding to any unusual request but simultaneously advised him not to disobey anything I asked. It must have been that way because the driver didn't even turn his head to get Harris' nod when I asked that we be driven to a delicatessen located on Second Avenue in the East Village. Not knowing what the hell this driver had on me, or whether he was working for the Bureau, Harris or the KGB, I kept my mouth shut until Harris and I were alone in a booth at the rear of the restaurant.

"What happened?" Harris quizzed impatiently.

"Shit. Those security precautions border on the ridiculous. Must be the Bureau ..." I didn't wait for a response to such a pejorative remark. Instead I turned to the jukebox and began flipping through the selections. "Doesn't this joint remind you of Stein's place?"

"Not really." Harris was by now sickened by my comments. His real character was beginning to show through. I didn't like it. On the other hand, there was no way to get out of conversing with him. My silence would only prompt him to suspect I might not go along with our little deal. And he was a man who thought he had me by the balls.

For the moment he did.

"He's a strange guy," I volunteered.

"Could have fooled me," replied Harris sarcastically.

"No, I mean it, Harris. I don't know if I'll be able to crack this nut. Even with all we've got on him, with Donaldson's report, and with any kind of rational appeal that could be made, I'm just not sure he'll bite. That's why I took this break immediately. Boy, he's depressing. I can't imagine spending the entire day in there with him, but if I have to, I'd rather fortify myself first. I suppose I fooled myself this morning by thinking that it was going to be a quick shot in the arm and then I'd ..."

"You'd what? You, sonofabitch," interjected Harris. "Remember that it's my party now. Don't think that I'll lose you in all this confusion. Donaldson may have a lot of authority at the moment, but as soon as this is resolved one way or another, it'll be back to the regular ways of conducting business. Maybe we've got just as many things on Donaldson as we have on you, Miller. I wouldn't take chances hiding behind him. He's liable to drop you like a hot potato. You'll be ruined. Perhaps you'll get a stinking medal for saving us, but you'll be back to where you were after the war, hero."

"There'll be nothing in it for you either," I retorted.

"Deal is a deal," menaced the brave man who had succumbed to the most primary of all torture methods in Poland.

"Okay," I agreed. "No need to go overboard." I knew he had been bluffing all along but didn't expect him to come out with something as stupid as a threat to Donaldson. Better not to say anything more, I noted to myself. I cracked a supercilious smile as if to let Harris know his threat was as childish as the gangster routine he was trying to pull on me.

I ordered bagels and lox while Harris settled for a nice plate of bacon and eggs. I also asked the waiter to wrap up a bottle of Polish vodka and a pound of cooked kielbasa and put it on the bill. Harris shoveled the breakfast down like the greedy little miser he was. I would have done likewise but caught myself and remembered the lesson taught to me by the Intercontinental Hotel's furnishings and appointments this morning. Small, slow bites. Yes, the affluent were in a hurry most of the time, but they never ever finished everything on their plates. Not like Max. No, I wouldn't follow his example. He was a hood but nothing more.

To Harris' surprise, I ordered a screwdriver. "I told you I had to fortify myself!" was my justification to his reproach for drinking so early in the day.

We lingered in the booth for some time, perusing the newspapers and eyeing the women who sauntered in after a Friday night crowded with sweaty disco partners, cocaine, and neurotic fucking on the carpet. At about 11:30 AM we paid the bill, picked up the package at the front counter and found the chauffeur waiting where we'd left him.

"He's a loyal hound." I nudged Harris as we approached the car.

"Shut up and do what you have to. I'll take care of the rest until we've made our split."

His statement was as ordinary as any one of the post-European Harris comments, but at that moment I resolved to get him. Even if all my efforts failed where Ted was concerned, I'd take care of Harris so he wouldn't even have the privilege of getting his genes mutated in a nuclear rainstorm.

Chapter 26. Ted's Adam, Adam's Ted

"I've read it. I looked through it. You don't know shit about me. This is all in pieces, and I'm not so sure they're even accurate." Ted was speaking. I was back in the room again. This time there could be no further excuses. I'd leave here a winner or a loser, but I was in here until the moment when Ted and I could reach an understanding. It looked like a long afternoon ahead of me.

"I know," I replied as calmly as a psychiatrist. "Why don't you help me put it together?" I unwrapped the bottle and pulled out two plastic cups I'd brought along with a piece of kielbasa. "Want some vodka?"

"Vodka? Yes, I would." I poured his straight and made myself a weak screwdriver with the orange juice that was abandoned on his breakfast tray. Ted began to leaf through the papers. He looked up and grinned, showing me his tobacco-stained teeth. "Stein, I should have killed that bastard a long time ago!"

"I know what you mean. I've got a similar problem. There's not any time for that now though. Let's get you and me out of here and then we'll worry about settling accounts."

"Max," he continued, reminiscing, apparently not heeding my advice. "A big likeable slob. You should have seen his face when he saw me in that Nazi uniform, when he talked about the German interpreter in Trawniki. Johnny, the look on his face ..." Ted laughed.

"Was he fat then?"

"Around two-fifty."

"Well, he's gained another fifty pounds," I informed him.

"Monty, he was a good guy. I really liked him. Too bad he didn't stick with me. He wouldn't have such strange ideas now."

His ideas would probably be much worse, I thought. "I like his ideas better than yours," I challenged Ted with an insulting statement.

"What do you know about my ideas?" he shot back with a laugh.

"Nothing really," I admitted dryly. I wanted him to talk so I shut up.

"Franek Juraski – Grat -- a romantic idealist like me in my youth. He still fights for his utopia. Mercenaries. Most people don't like them, but I know he's not doing it for the money. It's the ideal. I understand him, but I could never have joined him."

"Why not?"

"For one, I don't believe in a good world anymore. Secondly, when he and I were so close during a time of great danger, I was afraid to admit to him that I was a Jew."

"You think he suspected back then?"

Ted shook his head no, then said, "Ah, Mustapha. A hood but trustworthy. We just had a misunderstanding about women."

"But you never had any misunderstanding with Spaggiari when it came to women, did you?"

"Well, women were his line, his business. I had nothing to do with it except to keep my boys in order and collect the profits. Women were his business, nightclubs mine. We made the deal that way, and it stayed just like that right up until the end when I left the business."

Ted thumbed through the profiles I had scribbled in the dossier. He seemed interested only in what these characters had to do directly with him. His ego was as dominant as ever. One could surmise that this Shipansky, the weird Pole that had as many lives as the situation required, was the most selfish man in the world. It was one prescription for survival.

Comments muttered in Polish broke my thoughts. Ted had found an interesting passage. "The Professor?" I guessed.

"Yeah. I can't make up my mind about him. He didn't help me much. But he did make me conscious of many things I didn't notice before. He encouraged me to read more. Most of it was deep stuff that made my head spin. Nausea, that's the title of one of the books he gave me to read. That's what it gave me too! At the time I was all for changing the word "philosophy" to nausea. That's what it did to me, and I could swear that's the most accurate diagnosis of whatever's bothering the people who scribble that crap.

"Look," he changed his tone, "you're prying. You know all these little details about my life, and everything I know of you has been reduced to a few basic categories. I'll ask you one more time. Did you come here as a cop or a friend?"

"Like I said before, both. I was sent here as a cop, but I'm still your friend. You saved my life, remember? The government doesn't want much from you. Only a retraction of your statement. We know, and you know, that the agency didn't order you to kill Berisov."

"Why are they so eager to get me to withdraw my statement?"

"Don't fuck around with me," I snapped. "Your act might start World War Three. I'm aware of what you planned. Regardless of your reasons, I at least found out what your objective was. I know the truth."

"Do you?" he challenged me but without emotion. He wasn't surprised that the plot was so obvious. Instead, he was simply curious to see who could figure it out. His way of evaluating the intelligence of others turned out to be a very dangerous game. Even Donaldson, with all his Machiavellian power tactics, would never dare to propose such a deadly game.

"The Russians have mobilized," I said.

"A conventional war won't resolve anything," he stated with overwhelming confidence.

"We've mobilized too. Monday there's to be a press conference from Sweden. If nothing is resolved by then, the world may be destroyed. You could help."

"And you could be smart about it. What the fuck are you doing in this dump on the last weekend of the world? You should be out screwing, drinking, lying and spending money."

"The government will do anything you want. They'll let you out of here, give you financial resources or a new identity. You can live any place you want with all the protection necessary."

"I can live any place I want with all the necessary protection?"

"Yes. Sure. Think of it!"

"But that's just like being here in prison," he reasoned.

I was stuck. "You could have plastic surgery. No one would recognize you then," I emphasized.

He smiled again.

"All you have to do is say that you killed Berisov for personal reasons, because the Russians killed your family. Any goddamn thing."

"That's all?"

"That's it in a nutshell."

"Do you mind if I tell you a few things about me, as a friend?"

"Go ahead," I said. He seemed so closed off from everybody that I suddenly wanted to learn as much as possible.

"I don't think you have an exact understanding of me. I fought in the war, but it got me nothing. Greenberg's words were always with me. 'If you survive, you'll be covered with gold.' I survived all right, but nobody covered me with gold. I'll tell you something. The first day after the liberation, all I had was twenty dollars' worth of zlotys and a loaf of bread. That was my gold. Those were the seeds that Greenberg expected to blossom into a garden of Eden," he spoke with cynicism and irony. "That was when I felt the emptiness. The massacres, the tortures, the dead bodies – were they worth only twenty dollars in zlotys and a loaf of bread? The things I did to survive. I killed friends and enemies alike. It didn't matter to me. The only thing that mattered was survival. And if I survived, according to that old phony, Greenberg, the world would belong to me. But was it all only worth twenty dollars and a loaf of bread? I keep coming back to that. It's no mistake. I may be senile, or my brain may be burnt by the speed I've taken to wake up and the barbiturates I've taken to sleep, yet it's no mistake that I keep coming back to that question. For me it's as important as a fancy debate about dialectical materialism." He stopped abruptly and folded his arms. He stared down at the floor.

Ten minutes of silence passed until I decided to console him, not really knowing if it would help but feeling sorry for this poor bastard. "Listen, Ted, I know life wasn't easy for you. But it wasn't easy for me either. Now you're leaving the world hanging between peace and war. You can make a contribution to peace. It might help you feel better about all this history. We all want to live, don't we?"

He looked up. "I like what you said just then. 'We all want to live, don't we?' Johnny, can you imagine that there are people who are sick and tired of this absurd life?"

"That's possible," I confessed. "But I'm not convinced that all this misanthropy of yours isn't based on an exaggeration of the truth. Maybe you prefer to look at things this way. Perhaps you're a lazy creature, and it's much easier to fabricate a justification for doing nothing rather than admit that you're insignificant like everyone else. All that stuff in your memoirs, was it really true?"

"Most of the things really happened," he replied forthrightly and added, "you may have a point about my being lazy. I'll concede that to you, but it was the feeling of solitude that was the biggest determining factor. I was alone. I couldn't communicate with people. My life was upside down. I tried to set up my own values. I knew that death was the only true value because we all have to die. I based my way of thinking on inevitable death. In the war years, the feeling of anguish, loneliness and solitude hung over me. I knew how to escape it through danger. I needed it then and I still do. Being without danger was like being dead; the danger of death gave me the urge to live. That's why all through my life I had to create danger. In order to live. On the other hand, I wanted to be sincere. Now I know that it was impossible. At the time I used to beat my head against the wall trying. I did it in order to situate myself as the judge of hypocrites. I hate hypocrites more than anything. But in order to have the right to judge and to hate – and believe me, I hate everybody – I had to prove that I was better than them. After the war started me off on this track, I continued to destroy all the things that connected me with life. I began to prepare myself totally and completely for death. I holed up in my apartment to think about the problem. You must think I'm crazy," he smiled wistfully.

He was right, but I couldn't let him know it. "No, I don't."

He continued as if he had not heard. "I had the impression that the war was hell and that afterward we would have heaven. I was disappointed. I survived. Nothing happened to me except one disappointment after another. The famous gold that Greenberg used to rave about never came. And nobody gave a damn about me! On the contrary!"

He was raving now.

"I was sick of being treated as a Jew by the Nazis, as a bourgeois by the Communists, and as a dirty foreigner by all the others. Old people rejected me as too young. Then I aged myself and the young people rejected me. Worse still, women rejected me. The world went on rejecting me just as it had rejected me during the war. Nothing and no one helped me. No help, no gold," he repeated. "The only thing I could do was strike back and reject all the others." He frowned. "What a goddamn fool I was! They went right on living despite me. As I said, when I rejected everything, nothing came back."

He paused.

"You've been a soldier, Johnny."

"Of course," I assured him.

"In a real battle?"

"Certainly, but you know that."

"That's not the point."

He seemed annoyed that I would dare to contradict his train of thought. "You always had the opportunity to relax after an operation. Even in the battle zone, there was occasional downtime, right?"

"Naturally."

"Well, in the underground it was impossible. I was on the front line for three years, and I knew that I would not survive. It was hard to survive, especially since I I felt like a condemned man no matter where I turned."

"How do you mean?" I asked.

"Once as an ordinary underground soldier and again as a Jew. In order to make my death easy, since I couldn't avoid it, I started to prepare for it. Remember my story?"

"Yes, 'The Five Days of Freedom.'"

"Well, I was dying a thousand times a day. It was an illusion because I wasn't really dying. Yet I was always in front of a German execution squad. I knew that I was going to die for I had been sentenced to death. To make it easier, I tried to break all the ties I had to life. Without the fear of dying, there is no longer the fear of God or the fear of the fear of the unknown as some people say. No! There was only regret for everything I would miss out on. To make it easier for myself, I kept repeating, nothing is important. Nothing is important. Fucking, drinking, eating, reading a good book or watching a good movie. All counted for nothing. I was emptying myself, trying to convince myself that nothing really mattered, rejecting everything in life, making myself completely empty. So that when I faced the execution squad or was walking into the gas chamber, there would be nothing more to lose. I succeeded well. Maybe too well, because now when the danger of death no longer exists, I still feel empty. All those values of life I rejected didn't come back. Nothing came back. I felt like a dead man, like a walking corpse, just like in that movie where Boris Karloff played a corpse who returned from the grave to haunt the people who executed him. But I wasn't an ordinary creature. I simply performed normal physiological functions without any human feelings at all. If you die a thousand times a day and you remove everything from yourself, there is no possibility of resurrection.

"It would be too difficult, no, impossible to make you understand all those things. When the war was finished, I had a choice, the void or compromise. Compromise seemed like the world I lost when we moved into the ghetto. It was filled with self-satisfied people or perhaps strivers trying to attain the good life. It began with a career, marriage, and children. With no idea how to get started or where it would lead, I concluded that it was not only beyond my reach but also the path to endless frustration and failure. 'Better the void,' I told myself. By then I was used to it. Like a man who knows that a toothache can never be cured until the dentist extracts the rotten tooth, I knew that the void would disappear only when my life was extracted from my body. I laughed when I remembered how much I struggled to survive during the war, when something inside me kept repeating, 'Nothing is important but to survive. Nothing is important but to survive.' It was like a broken record, my Greenberg record. I think about everything I did to survive, and now I don't even care if I die tomorrow, in an hour or in a few minutes.

"You know, Johnny, somehow the Professor was right. When I closed myself off in my apartment, I created a desert. I was never very good at physics, but I know one axiom, that emptiness must be filled up. Gradually over all these years, my void filled up with hate, Johnny! A tremendous hate against the whole world.

"I tried Israel, but that was no solution. Even there nobody understood, and it was no Promised Land for me. And back in Paris, shut away in my apartment, I felt that the whole world was sneering at me. Suddenly I saw what I had to do. What I needed was one violent action to smash the whole world along with myself, as Samson did."

"But Samson only smashed the Philistines," I interrupted. "You want to smash friends and enemies alike."

"Yes!" he shouted. "The whole damned world. Then there'll be no one left to sit in judgment on me. It took years to put my plan together, and it's worked perfectly up to now."

I was thinking while he talked. He was crazy like a mad dog and my job was to bring him around to reason.

"Johnny, remember the man in the tower? His name was Charles Whitman."

"No, I can't say that I do."

"The man who went berserk and barricaded himself in a tower on some university campus in Texas and killed sixteen people and then was shot by the police. I knew just how he felt. But even if I killed two hundred people, it wouldn't solve my problem. I wanted to settle my account with humanity once and for all by taking everybody with me. Then I remembered Gavrilo Princip who killed twenty million people with a single shot."

"Who?" I asked.

"The man who assassinated the Archduke of Austria-Hungary and with that one shot started World War One. It took twenty million lives. Now with all the new weapons, all those nuclear warheads, Johnny… I killed Berisov and said that the CIA told me to do it because I hoped that my one shot would destroy the whole fucking world. I may outdo Princip yet."

I wanted to laugh. The whole thing was so ridiculous. But the situation at the moment was no laughing matter, and he was dead serious. Before I could say anything, he continued in a softer tone.

"I've had one hero for the last thirty years. I told you. Remember? Humphrey Bogart playing Sam Spade in *The Maltese Falcon*. I saw the picture for the first time soon after the war, and I've seen it at least thirty times since. It inspired me. There was a man who created his own moral code. Once he decided what was right or wrong, nothing could budge him, neither love nor money. He acted on his own principles. After the war I adopted Sam Spade's morality to preserve my honor and dignity, but there was one problem. Because I was a human being, I was no better than the rest. Then I suddenly recalled what Hitler had said, 'If we lose this war, we will drag half of the world down with us.'"

Ted's voice rose to a shrill pitch, and his gestures resembled those of Hitler. "I decided to do him one better and take the entire world with me! This is my final solution!!"

He calmed himself almost immediately and commented in a level tone, "It took me years to work out a decent plan."

"The Red Army Faction told me all the details," I said. I wanted to bring him back to reason if it were possible. "You mentioned Samson a minute ago. But what about Sodom and Gomorrah? The Lord told Lot that he would not destroy them if ten just men could be found."

"Lot didn't find them," laughed Ted. "And I didn't find them either. Except maybe Karski. Leave out Stein, that punk! Max and Lucini were good guys and Franek. That makes four. Schlaube, five. Mustapha, six. Forget Greenberg and my uncle and the Professor. And you, Johnny, seven. The teacher Winarski was a no-good bastard too. I don't think there was anybody else. You seven guys are the best I've known. Sorry, Johnny, but going by the Bible, there aren't ten to be found. The Bible means nothing to me now anyway. It's Sam Spade or Rick Blaine, or Marlowe or Steve Morgan."

"But you're wrong," I argued. "Those characters were apostles of love. They worked on love. You're operating on hate. You admitted it yourself just a few minutes ago."

"Yes, but those scripts were written more than thirty-five years ago when there was still hope, still a chance that things might turn out for the best. Now it's lost and on top of that, Bogart's gone. I have to make my own decisions and draw my own conclusions. Perhaps Bogie would do the same thing if he were alive. It's a chance I'll have to take."

"You've gone completely overboard," I reacted in frustration.

"I call myself an individualist," he continued, paying no attention at all to my comment, "because I didn't belong anywhere. Most individuals are powerless, and I had to prove that it's still possible for one individual to influence the course of history. This is the end of history. Marx thought he could do it, but his plans failed. This is the end of the line for me and for everybody else too."

"Look," I proposed, "the government wants to do everything it can for you if you'll listen to reason. Money. Situation. Anything. You talk about being covered with gold. If that's what you want, they'll do it."

"You really think so?"

For a moment he seemed to be lured by the bait, but then he quickly drifted off as if I had never made any such offer. I was finding myself increasingly pressed into the role of a cop and I think that he wanted it that way.

I stared around the room. Nothing had changed. All that had

moved were the shadows and the level in the bottle of vodka. Time was closing in. I believed that he was close to a catatonic trance and if I didn't make some kind of spectacular appeal to his conscience, it too would dissolve into nothing, leaving me with a pre-cortical animal. He sipped on his vodka, then gulped it down. Several times he made an effort to speak and then swallowed his first syllable.

"I couldn't help being born in Poland or being half-Jewish," he finally said. "But one thing is certain, one of these days I'm going to die and so is everybody else. Okay, I decided how I would live my life. I chose to be Ted. When I was young, I couldn't choose anything. Everything was decided for me. I believed everything my mother, teachers and elders told me. In a way, I took them for gods. Their word was law, the Ten Commandments. When the Nazis came, I was thirteen. I'll tell you something. When I saw Germans parade along the street in their beautiful black boots, I wanted to be a Nazi too. But they rejected me. They didn't want me. To them I was a Jew. Sure, I'd heard the word Jew in my mother's house, but she never told me that I was Jewish. My mother used to be everything to me. Then the Nazis began to push us around. I lost my idol because she failed to protect herself. How would she ever succeed in protecting me?

"After that, it was one rejection after another and out of them I created Ted. Even the name is false, but that doesn't matter. All that came out of the glorious life I'd been dreaming of was Ted. I decided to lead a clean life. I'd done a little 'cleaning' before so that was no obstacle. Then I created an exclusive little club in which I was President, Vice President, Treasurer and the only member. It was called Ted Szczepanski ."

As he paused, I suddenly saw my chance to get his mind off himself. "Listen, Ted," I spoke like a friend now, "I've read your manuscript and I've listened to you. You speak of dignity and honor constantly, but it seems to me that you're full of self-pity."

He started to protest, but I wouldn't allow him to interrupt. "Wait a minute! Let me finish. You're not the only one who's had troubles. You're not really alone in this world at all." I was clutching at straws as he looked at me for the first time with a semblance of interest,

ROBERT DANNIN & TONY GAWRON

albeit primitive.

I explained my problem with Harris. "You see, Ted, my life is also a waste. I discovered yesterday that I'm going to lose everything I worked for. I feel like blowing my brains out. I have nothing left. You're not the only one who's had a raw deal, but at least I try to solve my problems without destroying the world."

To weaken him even more, I pulled out my last shot. "I'd have a void too if it weren't leased out already."

"What are you talking about?" he asked curiously.

I had stumbled onto the right dialect and tapped directly into his twisted imagination.

"I'm talking about Harris, the FBI agent assigned to shadow me on this case. He's my secret sharer, unwelcome of course. He's learned everything about my old capers with you and even a deal I just pulled off with Spaggiari in France. It was inevitable, but now he can ruin my life. I don't know how to handle it. If I had you outside of this place, I'm sure you would come up with a solution. Maybe you could do a little cleaning for me. Only one person."

"Well, I'd be pleased to help." The idea of a 'cleaning' excited him.

"Don't worry about it, Ted. I have a few contacts. Like I said, there's nothing you can do for me in jail. Even if you wanted to."

"Johnny, you don't look very happy about your so-called solution," he sympathized. "Look, I can help you even though I'm here in jail."

"How?"

"I can help you if you're willing."

"I don't see the point."

"Do you have a paper and an envelope?"

I took out some stationery from the attaché case. Ted reached out and grabbed the sheet of paper with his dirty fingers. He hastily scribbled a few words, then grabbed the envelope. He sealed it and handed it back to me.

"Give it to Max," he glowered. "It'll take care of Harris."

I took the envelope and clutched it for a moment, then shoved it into my inside jacket pocket. "Thanks, Ted," I said. Then, to emphasize the conspiracy into which we had just entered, I stretched my arms out to the side. "But if a war comes, what good will it do me? I want to survive."

"We all have to die sooner or later."

"I'd rather it be later in my case, if you don't mind."

"Johnny, why do you cling to life so tenaciously?"

"With Harris out of the way, I won't be clinging to anyone or anything," I announced. "And then I can begin to enjoy life."

He shook his head and smiled wisely. "Listen, Johnny, there's no real place in the world for people like us. We're the last of the individualists and we don't belong. We'll never belong to a world that has committed itself to closing the gap that separates men from ants. Our every act is a protest by the last of the free individualists."

He began pacing back and forth in the room. "That's why I hatched the plan to knock off Berisov."

"But Ted, you've spent too much time and energy on an enterprise that's doomed to fail."

"I don't think so, Johnny."

He stopped pacing and turned to face me. "It won't fail. It's out of the question." His eyes pitched upward in their sockets and looked at the ceiling. "How many minutes for the missiles to hit New York?"

Back to his solution. I wasn't sure whether I'd talked him into anything but a final gesture to preserve the honor of a friendship he'd rather do without. "I don't know exactly," I answered carefully. "I haven't read up on it lately, but I believe that the SALT II treaty limited the trajectory time to somewhere around seven minutes for land-based missiles and three minutes for air-and-sea-launched warheads."

"Three to seven minutes," he repeated. "Then I'll get all the gold I was promised." His face jerked as in a seizure. I hadn't noticed it until now but his whole body was jittery. Half an hour earlier, a cigarette had flown out of his hand. There were several personalities inside Ted, each one vying for dominance. It was no ordinary case of dissociative identity, however, because even the collective force of the other personalities could not conquer the consuming death wish that Ted harbored. That lethal impulsion sank its roots into each of the repressed individuals because they had each been in a situation where they died a thousand times a day and were at present prisoners of the void. Ted was the original hollow man. He was an individualist and consequently had many dimensions, each of which suffered from a similar despondency. The others were only one-dimensional figures. Although hollow, they accepted it and lived with it. But poor Ted's despair was fathomless.

"Look, you killed Berisov ten days ago and nothing has happened yet. For ten days, every government in the world has been knocking itself out to prevent the missiles from being launched. They'll likely succeed in thwarting your plan. If they do, they'll gang up on you, and you will be their only victim, apart from Berisov."

He stared at me as if he had never considered that the world might see through his game and save its own wretched existence. He had operated on the assumption that deep down everyone wanted to die. My presence had driven home the point that his plan had been conceived in a desert and that there was no guarantee it would work. "On the other hand, you can have freedom and all the real gold you want. I'll get it for you. Isn't that worth anything to you?"

"What do you mean?"

"I mean the real money. Let's go back to that," I suggested. "I can promise you that the government will give you anything you ask if you'll simply retract your claim of CIA involvement."

He looked at me in astonishment. "Johnny," he asked after a moment's deliberation, "are you trying to bribe me?"

"Not at all," I protested, despite growing confidence that my proposed bribe might work. "The government realized from my investigation what a raw deal you got after the war. The world failed you. The government is willing to make that clear and make it up to you. You can think of it as their special Marshall Plan for Ted."

"Where and when?" he asked.

"Any time and place you choose, but on one condition; you must tell the truth at a television press conference on Monday and state specifically that the CIA was not involved. You can always say that you shot Berisov because the Russians did away with your family."

"I don't have a family," he offered rather naively.

"It doesn't matter. Say that Qaddafi engineered the project or that the Red Army Faction concocted it. Any statement that will clear the CIA will do."

"Now I see why they chose you for this mission," he deduced. "They know that I saved your life in Poland."

"That's right." I couldn't help feeling that I was reasoning with a little kid, Adam perhaps. "Now give me the chance to save yours. How much money do you want?"

He was silent for a minute. Then he whispered, "Ten million bucks. Not a cent less." Just like in the old days, he leaned closer and said, "I'll cut you in for ten percent."

"That's up to you. Shall we shake on it?"

"Can I trust you, Johnny?" His eyes stared directly into mine.

"Of course," I said. "Didn't I trust you with my drug-running and my trouble with Harris?"

"That's true. But I want the money before the press conference," he insisted.

"You'll get it tomorrow," I promised.

"And before I speak, they've got to tell the whole world what a rotten shake I got."

"They will. Now let's shake hands on it."

He mumbled to himself in Polish and then suddenly burst into an uncharacteristic smile. "Of course, Johnny!" We shook hands like a couple of long-lost pals.

"I've to go now," I announced hurriedly. "Can I have them bring you something else? You'd better eat. It takes a lot of energy to spend ten million. Anyway, I'll see you at the press conference."

"What do you mean?" he became very angry. "You'll see me here first! And bring the money."

"Naturally," I reassured him.

"Don't forget," he reminded me. "And don't forget Max, for your own sake."

"I won't. Look at it this way," I smiled at him. "You'll be able to hang out with that fat slob, eat and drink yourself silly." We both laughed and I left.

It was now 5 PM and Harris was sitting in the waiting room where I had left him. He was reading Fortune magazine, practicing for his cool millions, no doubt.

"What about the call to Geneva?" he demanded upon seeing me.

"Whoa! Just a second, man. I haven't finished yet, and besides it's 11:00 at night in Switzerland. No bank is open before Monday morning. I've got to get my report ready for tomorrow's meeting."

Harris frowned but said nothing.

"See you at 9 AM."

I left him there, still leafing through *Fortune*.

I didn't forget Max. I phoned him immediately and scheduled to meet him across from Stein's place in Brooklyn that evening.

"Let's walk, Max," I suggested.

"I saw Ted this afternoon. We had a long talk and he gave me this envelope for you." I fished it out of my pocket and gave it to him. Max extracted Ted's note and held it close to his face. His expression remained implacable. "I'll need some dope about this guy," he stated. The chill October wind rippled our suits. As we walked further down Flatbush Avenue, I told him everything he needed to know.

"It's got to be done fast and clean," I insisted. "As for expenses, I figured on about fifty thousand. That sound okay?"

Max chuckled. "Not a thing. For friends like you and Ted, it's a favor. What else was the war for? And it seems from this that you've worked things out with him too." He glanced up at the tombstone-dark sky and jerked his thumb upward. "No bombs yet, huh?"

"We'll know after tomorrow," I cautioned.

"If the bombs don't fall," he joked, "you'll owe me a favor in the future sometime."

"Isn't there anything I can do now?" I asked.

"Sure," Max turned to me with a serious look on his face. "Buy me another kishke."

Chapter 27. Whose Millions?

Sunday, October 16, 1983 – I slept well that night. I had manipulated everyone I could and even some with whom I had had no contact. If I could get ten million for Ted, why not get another two million for myself? That way, I'd be set for the rest of my life.

At 9 AM, I showed up at the World Trade Center and found everyone there with the exception of Harris. Nobody seemed to notice his absence. Good old Max.

All the faces were tensed with the suspense of my forthcoming report. When I smiled, they figured I must have some good news.

"Well, Miller, did you manage to bring him around a little?" asked Donaldson.

"Better than that, sir," I tried to hide my pleasure. "He'll withdraw his earlier statement entirely and swear that his only reason for killing Berisov was purely personal."

Everyone relaxed.

"But," I continued, "it will cost you some money. He wants me to deliver twelve million dollars in cash to him today. Otherwise, no deal. Naturally, he wants a guarantee of safe conduct out of the country. But the thing he's most insistent about is that before he retracts his statement, a high government official must declare that his act was understandable, although regrettable. I told him what you'd said. Can you deliver on this?"

"Of course," said Donaldson, indignantly.

"Twelve million is a lot of money, a hell of a lot of money," argued McClellan. He tugged at his lapel. I saw that he was full of shit and only looking to see if anyone would agree with him.

"It's cheaper than World War Three," said Donaldson in defense of his unilateral decision. "Besides, we can always get it back afterwards," he added rather nervously.

Goldman cleared his throat. "Everything about this guy is so irrational. Suppose that at the last minute he changes his mind and refuses to retract the statement. What then?"

"Kill the bastard!" growled O'Brien.

Haverson smiled at me in a superior way. "Johnny seems to think he's won this guy over." He stretched out his hand toward me. "But that's just one man's opinion. We'd better work out an alternative. As General O'Brien suggests, we can get rid of Shipansky, but it'll have to be done in a way suitable to the Soviets."

We sat there thinking. As far as I was concerned, it didn't make any difference whether Ted came through or not as long as we could avoid a war.

Donaldson had left the room to telephone the presidential delegation in Sweden and now returned. Looking at his face, I could tell that the matter of twelve million had been settled.

"Miller," he said, "there's an executive order on the way up. Treasury will pay out twelve million in cash to you. Washington is calling the New York office. You know where it is, right across Broadway on Maiden Lane. Get over there quickly."

"Sir," interrupted Tarnovsky, "we have to consider alternatives in case Miller's plan fails."

"We're dealing with a madman," added O'Brien. "There's no guarantee this'll work."

"He can always be eliminated during an attempted escape," Donaldson emphasized. "We can make it public immediately. The Soviets will understand, plus we'll be able to recover the money."

All these bloodthirsty vampires, after all the work I'd done, now they were considering terminating the subject. It kept worrying me. I'd have to give ten million to Ted and then somehow get away with my two-million share. Better for them to just concentrate on my idea. The conference room smelled of expensive cigars. The aroma was distinctively Montecristo, a Canary Island blend, good but miles behind the taste of a pure Havana. I'd have given anything for a Cohiba at that moment, but I shrugged off the temptation with the thought that I'd soon be able to buy a case of them.

"Miller," Donaldson interrupted my daydream, "you'd better get going. Treasury people are waiting for you."

I excused myself and headed for the door. The upturned faces nodded at me with respect. I'd pulled them out of a tight situation so far and except for the money, they were grateful. Somewhere in their idiot minds, they were grateful.

Haverson leaned over to me and shook my hand, then he held it for a second too long. I knew something was up.

"How come Harris didn't show today?"

"Don't ask me," I replied. "He's usually dependable." So was Hoffa, I thought.

I left them at the table working out their alternatives and hurried to the elevators.

There was no trouble at the Treasury Department. But it turned out to be quite a bundle and I had nothing to carry it in. "Lend me a couple of duffel bags and I'll return them on Monday."

"Sure," said the cashier cheerfully. "If they can trust you with twelve million, I guess I can trust you with two bags." He packed them for me and then asked whether I needed an escort.

I refused.

"Twelve million and no escort. It sounds pretty risky to me."

"Look," I confided to him, "nobody knows but you, me and the President. And I'll tell you, if something happens to me, everyone's going to know about it."

I took an ordinary cab back to the Intercontinental and divvied up the cash, one duffel bag containing Ted's ten million and the other with my two, which I parked downstairs in the hotel's safe. I've earned that by saving the world, I congratulated myself.

I took "Greenberg's gold" to my meeting with Ted. When I reached SECURITY ACCOUNTING SERVICES, the guard inside pointed a gun at me.

"Again?" I acted surprised. "Don't you recognize me? I was here all yesterday afternoon."

"I recognize you all right, but what've you got in that bag there?"

"Ten million dollars," I responded with a straight face.

The guard started to laugh. "Ten million dollars," he repeated. "Just like that, I suppose. Okay, let's see it."

When he opened the bag, he almost collapsed.

"Is it for him?"

"Exactly. Executive order from the White House."

Ted was sitting where I had left him the night before.

"Here's your present," I greeted him. "That's our part of the bargain," I asserted a little coldly, then bent down and opened the bag in front of him.

"I didn't think you'd be back so soon," he remarked in a gruff, froggy voice. He hadn't slept as far as I guessed. I had the feeling he was happy not to be alone.

"In an emergency, we're damned quick with these small business loans," I kidded him.

He began to count the packets of bills without saying a word. I assured him that it was all there, but he carried on his miserly counting. Then suddenly he handed a bunch of packets to me. "Your commission, as promised. Just like the old days." He was playing the honor and dignity role and put on a trustworthy guise.

"Thanks, Ted." I took the money – yet another million for me – and we exchanged a firm double-hander, a handshake to acknowledge our mutual sovereignty.

"Here's to the future," I saluted him with a fistful of hundred-dollar bills.

"Our future," he corrected me, and then flashed that Trigger-happy smile. And the US government is going to broadcast that statement about me?"

"Of course."

He wanted reassurance, which I gave him without hesitating. "Everything has been arranged – the money, the safe conduct, the statement, everything."

"I kind of trust you, Miller. If not for you, I'd never go through with this kind of a deal."

"I know how you feel. I've really got to split, but I want to thank you for the favor you requested from Max."

"There's just one more thing."

"What's that?" I hoped it was nothing to sink the entire operation.

"I want you to keep this money for me. I don't trust the people here, and you're a friend. You can get it into a Geneva account for me."

"Thanks for the trust," I said.

"You deserve it," he replied. "And it'll all be yours if something happens to me."

"Nothing will."

"Everybody's mortal," he stated. Now he looked even more lonely than when I had entered the room. He was defenseless. He'd been beaten and now he was beaten again. I was almost sorry for the poor bastard.

"You'll outlive us all," I joked. I picked up the duffel and flashed him one last smile as he sat down again with his back to me.

"Bring me another bottle of vodka for the press conference," he half-mumbled, half-demanded.

"Whatever you want." It came out as a barely audible whisper.

Later, I called Max from my suite. He was out so I had to leave my number with his wife, requesting that she make every attempt to locate him. After what seemed like an endless hour, the phone rang. "What's new?" Max gurgled. He had something in his mouth. "You need another favor?" He swallowed on the word favor.

"Yes, I do, Max. I need to see you right away."

"It's for Ted, but I can't explain over the phone. Can you get over here?"

There was a pause. "Better if we meet in the usual place," he decided. "How about something to munch on? A light supper? I'll buy you the kishke this time."

"Okay," I agreed. "I'll be there in about seventy-five minutes."

I got dressed and had the doorman get me a cab for Brooklyn. Max was already waiting at the place and greeted me with a big smile. "You got complaints about the service?"

"No, I smiled thinly. "The service was fine, but Ted's given me one more thing to do. Can you handle a few million? Get it into a Swiss account?"

"That's easy and I like doing that. You know that I took over Lansky's business when he died."

On the way to Max's little Jewish restaurant, I explained further. "It's the money the government paid Ted to retract that damned statement on TV tomorrow. He asked me to get it out of the country before the press conference."

"You have it already?"

"It's locked up at the Intercontinental. It's actually a lot, twelve million dollars."

"Ritzy, Johnny. Very ritzy!" Max liked to needle me for the sake of teasing a cop. He'd done it many times, but he had a way and a tone that reassured me that he was a genuine prankster. "Good," he said thoughtfully. "We'll handle it the Lansky way. Something he learned in Israel called hawala. It's an Arab method actually," Max explained. "You give me the cash and a password, I give it to a hawa here who calls his hawa in Switzerland, or wherever. You designate an agent over there who contacts the hawa and gives him your password in exchange for the money minus the commission. Swiss bankers do it all the time. The hawas keep their own accounts. Nothing's ever recorded on paper. Works like a charm.

"You have a Swiss bank in mind, Johnny?"

"It's 1256-8YZ-917 at Credit Suisse in Geneva. I keep the code myself. Twelve million bucks, Max."

"That's all right," he counseled. "You come to my house in the morning. It'll cost you the usual one percent."

The waiter set the plate of kishkes in front of Max and returned to the kitchen. "Listen, Max, there's one more thing. I need a new passport, driver's license – the works."

Max stared at me suspiciously as he shoved an entire kishke into his face. "What you got in mind?" he chomped.

"I want to quit the scene," I confessed. "I'm going to meet up with Ted somewhere over there."

"I'll need some photos and twenty-five grand."

"I have everything with me." I handed him an envelope with the pictures and the money in it. He peeked into the envelope and saw that the amount was not correct. All he had to do was feel it, actually. "There's more than twenty-five here," he asserted expertly.

"That's right, smart bastard. It's double."

"Why fifty?" he screwed up his nose.

"I'd like two passports, two complete sets of ID's. All the information is there on how to construct the new identities."

He took the envelope and put it into his plastic shopping bag, the only briefcase I'd ever seen him use. "I got Harris' papers. I could make you a special price," he grinned.

"You trying to make me sore? You know as well as I do that the cops are already out looking for Harris."

His grin widened. "I know that. I also know that you don't dig my Jewish sense of humor."

"I guess you're right," I said, "but let's eat. The rest of these kishkes are getting cold." Max polished off his helping enthusiastically. "What about the twelve million?" He looked up as if to say he was finished and had business to take care of.

"Send your driver to my hotel as soon as Geneva confirms the account."

"One more question," Max requested as if reading my thoughts. "What names are you asking for?"

"Jake Calhoun for one, Robert Munroe for the other. I've made myself a couple of years younger. I never look my age."

"No problem." He pushed his empty plate away. "Well, I've got to take off right away. You gave me a pretty tall order."

Out on the street, we exchanged hugs. "See you in the morning." He hurried away, wobbling down the street as I turned my back and looked for a cab.

Back at the hotel, I inspected all my papers and destroyed any that would give the cops a lead on my whereabouts. Then I packed one suitcase with enough clothes to last a couple of days. Finally, I poured myself a Jack Daniels and settled down to watch a movie on the tube.

Epilogue - The Cleaning

"'Operation Cleaning' shall be the code name for all undertakings by the Broom Squad. The aim of this operation is to dispose of traitors and negative elements in society." – Polish Home Army Directive (1942)

"All acts are acts of power on the outside world. There is no act without enough power to modify reality." – Gerard Mendel, Paris

Chapter 28. Ted's Final Solution

Monday, October 17, 1983 – At 5:30 AM, I was awakened by a call from the hotel concierge. One of Max's drivers was waiting for me downstairs. I dressed, brushed my hair, then slugged the last shot of Tennessee whiskey that remained from the evening. At the front desk I paid the cashier and had him lead me to the vault where I retrieved the duffels. Max's driver, Benny, escorted me to his car and we headed to Brooklyn following the early morning traffic southbound on the FDR toward the Williamsburg Bridge.

It was still dark when we pulled up in front of Max's building. It looked crummier than ever in the dark.

As soon as we reached the stoop, the door swung open. One of the same hoods who had been there the first day was on duty. "Mr. Calhoun?" he asked.

"That's right."

He led me into the big messy room. "Max is on the phone in the office. He'll be right with you." A few minutes later, Max entered and greeted me. "I just need the cash and your password. Then call your guy in Switzerland."

I picked up the bags and followed him into the office, which was a lot neater than his living room. From the smaller bag, my two million, I counted out a hundred twenty thousand to Max and recited the passcode. He squeezed into a Windsor chair behind the desk and punched a number into the phone. After a minute he recited the code and quickly hung up. "Your turn now," he pushed the phone toward me on the other side of the desk. "Give him the password and instruct him to contact al-Safir Import/Export. He'll understand."

I called Geneva. When I got Credit Suisse, I asked for Herr

Ubrechler. A few seconds later, he spoke into the phone. "Ubrechler here ..."

"Herr Ubrechler, this is Robert Munroe in New York, account holder 1256-8YZ-917. I am expecting a transfer from al-Safir Import/Export, my authorization code is M-A-G-N-U-M-4-7-5-7-6-0-0."

He repeated the account number and password. "Mr. Munroe, this transaction will take approximately an hour," he explained. "I shall await your further instructions." He hung up without waiting for my reply.

Max had disappeared, and I found him back in the living room. He was sitting on the sofa drinking a dark pink liquid from what appeared to be a glass flowerpot with a rounded bowl and long fluted rim.

"It'll be an hour, but I want to give the banker further instructions," I reported.

Max leaned over to his coffee table, shoved away a stack of unread newspapers, and deposited the half-empty vessel. He tilted his head up toward me and let out a long, voluble belch. It lasted for a few seconds, enough time to envelop the room with a sweetish, pungent odor.

I was nearly overcome by the fumes. "What kind of concoction is that?"

"Cold beet borscht with sour cream, Johnny. Breakfast of champions. Would you like to try some?"

I declined politely but picked up a newspaper and eased into a recliner. More dead Marines in Beirut. Protests against U.S. nuclear missiles in West Germany but support for them from the French president, of all people. A Polish Communist Party meeting in Warsaw amidst infighting and criticism from Moscow. No wonder they'd been so touchy. A former CIA agent on trial for hiring the Aryan Brotherhood to murder his ex-wife. Nazis and Communists, terrorists and spooks. When would it ever end?

"Ubrechler here," the other end answered.

I identified myself and account number. "Did you receive about twelve million US dollars for my account?" I waited impatiently as he checked.

"Yes, that account has received exactly eleven million seven-hundred ten-thousand dollars. How would you like that handled?" That checked out. One percent plus 50 thousand for the IDs to Max. Another one percent to the hawala.

"Put it on six-month term CD's, banking acceptance, please."

"Very well, sir," said Ubrechler respectfully.

"I'll be in Geneva in a couple of days," I added, "and I hope that you will do me the honor of dining with me."

"With pleasure," he affirmed. "And how is the weather in New York?"

"Clear and cool," I answered. "And in Geneva?" I returned the cordiality.

"About the same."

"By the way, Herr Ubrechler," I asked, "what is the interest rate today?"

"About twelve percent, but with this terrorist crisis on, it fluctuates hourly."

"That's the way it goes," I commented and following another exchange, I hung up.

"Everything set?" asked Max.

"Set, all set, Kishke Max." I had to smile.

"Good." Max picked up a manila envelope from the desk and handed it to me. "Here's the rest of the favor, passports and everything else."

It took me about ten minutes to read through both sets of documents. They were legitimate.

"Max, there's nothing at all discount about your services. I mean that as a compliment."

"Don't mention it, Mr. Calhoun," he replied, smiling happily. "Let's have Benny drive us."

The young hood came out of the shadows and followed us down a tiny corridor to the back door, which opened into a small courtyard. He scooted in front and opened the car door. As soon as Max and I had squeezed into the back, Benny put himself behind the wheel and started out.

We cruised into the city just ahead of the morning traffic jams and wound up at the Lexington Avenue entrance to the hotel.

"So long, Max. I'll never forget you. But one thing worries me. When are you going to swear off kishkes?"

"Why do you ask?"

"You're a typical Jew," I teased him. "Answering a question with another question. What for?"

"You just did it too," laughed Max.

"It must be contagious. That's what I get for hanging around disreputable characters like you. But you're a great guy anyway. I don't know anybody better to do business with."

"Make sure you don't."

I couldn't tell whether it was meant as a joke or a threat, but there was no time to find out. At the end of his sentence, Max rolled up the window and shouted at Benny to move. When I looked up from the sidewalk, they were already lost in the traffic.

I mounted the stairs to the lobby and bought a couple of newspapers and magazines and returned to my room. I dropped onto the couch and devoured the journalistic hogwash to see what kind of predictions they were making about our press conference. The whole world seemed to be clutching at this last straw.

At noon I started out for the TWA office on Fifth Avenue. There was a seductive brunette behind the counter, but I didn't flirt with her. Too much was on my mind.

"This evening's flight to Geneva, please. Business class, round trip." I figured it was better just to play it safe.

The bitch was trying like hell to stir up my libido. She was probably schooled in gentlemen seeking same-day passages to Switzerland. I ignored her silent advances. "There's a 7:58 flight this evening," she sighed, having apparently abandoned her hopes of finding a sucker in me. "Your name and passport, please."

"Calhoun. Jake Calhoun." I repeated my new identity as I readied my wallet and slid the passport toward her on the counter.

"Your local phone, Mr. Calhoun." She peeked at me with a beckoning smile.

"I just arrived from upstate, so I don't have any place you can call me. I'll call TWA to reconfirm the departure time."

"Call at 4:00," she recommended. "But there shouldn't be any problems today."

If there was to be a problem today it wouldn't be the exclusive concern of transatlantic airline passengers, I thought to myself. I counted out the cash, pocketed the ticket and began to look for a cab. I had an appointment with Haverson.

The next few hours were going to be crowded for everyone, for Ted, for me and for the entire world. My one thought was that Ted had better come through with his part of the agreement. I wanted to be able to spend all that money.

At 2:00, Haverson was waiting for me in his office. "We still haven't heard from your partner, Harris." His voice was full of consternation, although I didn't know whether it was real or not. "He's just disappeared. I hope you can handle Shipansky alone."

"I'll handle him," I proclaimed modestly. "You boys get the details ironed out after I left yesterday?"

"Green plan, red plan – we're in business. POTUS is in Sweden with Kuslov right now." He leaned closer to me. "Now, because the conference is at 5:00, I want you to pick up Shipansky as soon as we're finished here. I don't want to attract any attention. There'll be an unmarked car, just like before but a different driver. We removed the other guy as a precaution. He might have something to do with our missing Harris. The press conference will take place in one of the studios at 30 Rock. The driver is instructed. We won't release the time until after you're inside, so you shouldn't have any problem with photographers. We've also dropped some false rumors in the press and we've even scheduled a couple of dummy operations at some of the different studios across town."

I arrived at SECURITY ACCOUNTING SERVICES just at 3:30. I sat in the waiting room as before. Then two guards brought Ted in and left us alone. He was as grubby as ever. "Hello, Johnny," he said eagerly.

"Hi Ted," I answered. "You ready?"

"Yup." His smile reassured me. "Did you manage to transfer the money?"

"That's the first thing I did. I'll give you the account number as soon as you're free."

"That's okay," he smiled again, then as if he suddenly recalled a forgotten detail, "How's Max? I bet he charged you an arm and a leg."

"One percent, thanks to you. The only other thing he asked for was kishkes."

Ted laughed. "Max will never change." He seemed happier than I had ever seen him before, and I was anxious to get the whole thing over, fearing his mood might change.

"It's time to go," I announced.

"Okay. Did you bring more vodka?"

"Yes, here it is." I opened a brown paper bag and handed him a quart of Polish vodka. He examined it and slipped the bottle back into the bag, grasping it tightly. We passed my friend, the guard, who watched us glumly as he fidgeted with his holster.

The car was waiting in front. Behind was another car full of agents. We didn't talk much during the trip. I guess Ted had talked himself dry. He seemed interested in the skyscrapers we passed as he strained to look up through the sealed bullet-proof window. I was thinking about my millions in Switzerland and the possibilities of making more through my promotion and the Spaggiari connection. When we reached the RCA building, there were several pedestrians milling around but Haverson's decoys had succeeded in keeping most of the press away. Several people stared at our little group, but Ted was hidden in the midst of a black cloud of FBI agents. We rushed him in a side entrance and directly to an elevator. He was installed in a small make-up room before any of the NBC technicians or other employees realized who the new guest was.

I watched Ted as we waited. He still had that happy appearance, but he remained silent and withdrawn. At 4:30 we were ready to go. TV cameras were in place. The agents brought him out and led him to the podium, which was filled with mikes. A studio technician approached but was abruptly shoved away.

Ted was standing before the world very calmly. No symptoms of stage fright at all. I stared at him from the wings. I found a few reasons to like him.

Within fifteen minutes, the journalists began to file into the studio. Each was carefully screened and searched. A hundred in all were to sit facing the man who held the destiny of the world in his hands. Despite the apparent orderliness, the press corps began to murmur. Their muffled comments grew to a din and there were several outbursts. "The statement! Mr. Shipansky! Mr. Shipansky, how long have you been with the CIA?"

Ted smiled down at the men but did not answer. He nodded occasionally as if to salute his name.

I moved over to the mikes. "Okay, ladies and gentlemen. Hold your tempers. You'll get a statement." Ted and I smiled at each other. "But this afternoon's program doesn't begin with him."

The NBC men quieted them down. Ted and I were waved back into the wings and an announcer took his place in front of the mikes. He began to talk smoothly. "Ladies and gentlemen of the press, at this critical moment in world history, we are to hear some reassuring words from Ronald McClellan, the Secretary of State. Secretary McClellan."

McClellan, heavy and grey-haired, strode quickly to the mikes from the opposite wing. I didn't even realize that he was in the building, so tight were the security precautions. In spite of his set smile, he looked worn and tired. He cleared his throat and began.

"Fellow Americans, citizens of the world, I speak to you today in the name of the President, the Congress and the entire administration. For the past ten days, we have done everything in our power to preserve world peace in the face of the regrettable assassination of Soviet Premier Berisov. Now we have persuaded Ted Shipansky, the assassin, to speak honestly, to retract his statement implicating the United States and the Central Intelligence Agency in his act. But before bringing him forward to reveal the truth, we wish to make it perfectly clear that not only we, but the whole world failed this man when he most needed some recognition. As a mere boy in Poland, he was forced into a clandestine life when his family was deported to a concentration camp. When the Soviet Union entered Warsaw, his friends were deported to Siberia, but he survived. At the end of the war, he had nothing left to him, neither family nor nation, neither friends nor a sympathetic face – and he was barely an adult. Like many other victims of the war, he became an outcast. Along with other nations of the world, we admit our neglect. At one point we even refused to allow him to enter our country for a visit. It is such neglect and mistreatment that pushed him to commit his crime. It is such inhumanity that has put this planet on the brink of total destruction. Even greater suffering would follow a nuclear war, and we are determined to prevent that. We hope we have succeeded. In a moment, Ted Shipansky will retract his statement and reveal to you that his act was fueled by personal and individual concerns, in no way guided by the Central Intelligence Agency nor any other organization connected to the government of the United States. Thank you – and may we all pray for peace!"

When McClellan stopped, the room grew tense. He stepped back and wiped his forehead with his handkerchief. I nudged Ted, who smiled contentedly. He stood up, shook off a passing cramp in his left leg and walked up to the microphones. He stared out at the press corps and the cameras that were broadcasting his image over the entire world. After a moment of silence, the crowd became restive once again, although there were no catcalls.

Suddenly Ted raised his right hand in a "Heil Hitler!" salute. Everyone in the room shuddered, but I caught on. He was playing Hitler now. He smiled that mad-dog grin of his. He was enjoying all the public attention, all matters under his control. No wonder he tried to prolong this moment. He had his money and his kicks too!

"First, I'd like to clear up some misunderstanding. My real name is not Ted Shipansky. It's Adam Polanski," he stated as his arm fell to his side.

So far, so good, I whispered under my breath.

He continued. "All I ask you, ladies and gentlemen, is to be patient. In about one half hour, you shall all be covered with gold."

This signaled to me now that something was wrong. Gold meant nuclear fallout in Ted's lexicon. I looked at McClellan who had joined me on the side. "Let me speak to him immediately," I suggested nervously.

"Wait. He's going to talk," was McClellan's overconfident reply. But it was too late.

"I have only one thing to say," he began to shout, "and it is perfectly clear. Despite all the bribes and pressure brought to bear on me, I repeat once again and for the last time, the CIA paid me to kill Berisov."

I stared at Ted in shock and disbelief. "He double-crossed me," I said aloud. The stricken faces of Donaldson and McClellan loomed to my left.

"You failed, Miller!" Donaldson cursed me.

"Not yet! You've got to let me speak to him alone."

I rushed to the podium and grabbed Ted. I pulled him away from the mikes and pushed him into the wing. "Leave him alone!" I shouted at the agents who had swarmed onto the stage. I was clutching Ted's arm tightly, but he made no protest at the discomfort. He wasn't angry. All I could say into his face was "Why? Why? Why, Ted? You've signed your own death warrant!"

He grinned at me. "I signed it for me and for everybody. You should've known me better than that. You should have realized that it was useless to bribe me."

"What are you trying to say?"

"Johnny, neither Sam Spade nor Rick Blaine. Not Marlowe, not Morgan, none of them would have allowed themselves to be compromised. And there are no longer any good guys to stand by. The whole world is rotten," he explained calmly. "Let's celebrate!" He took the bottle out of his pocket and downed a mouthful of vodka. He looked like a Pole juicing himself up before battle. "Come on, Johnny, have a drink!"

I thought perhaps it was not too late. I clutched at one last hope. "Ted," I shouted, trying to get through to him, "you don't know about the alternative. They're going to shoot you right away if you don't change the statement. They'll shoot you now!"

He smiled. "I'll die a few minutes before everybody else. They'll join me later. Have a drink," he insisted.

I grabbed the bottle and took a swallow too. I needed it badly. He took the bottle back from me and had another drink. Then he said, "Sorry Rick, this isn't bourbon on the rocks. It's only vodka but this is my drink and my great day. Here's to you, Spade." He put down the bottle and spoke with irony. "See you soon, Adolph. I hope I've fulfilled your prophecy. Operation Cleaning is on!"

He looked at his watch. Everything he did was cold and deliberate. He seemed reasonable if not sane, but I knew I couldn't get through to him anymore. My mind was racing. Where did I fail? I thought I had all the keys to Ted's mind. Where did I slip? Nowhere, I said to myself. His unpredictable behavior was the only constant in the established pattern. Nobody could bribe Spade, Rick, Marlowe or Morgan. He fooled me. Or did I ask to be fooled? I forgot the pattern and believed his promise. I slipped. I ignored the pattern because I was blinded by all that money I was taking from the government.

I got scared. Ted was a dead man, and I would have to act fast before they recovered from the shock and began searching for the money and me. That is, if we didn't all die in a nuclear explosion.

"I failed, Donaldson. He's all yours now," I turned to the man who masterminded this whole goddamn investigation.

"Well, at least we have the other alternative. Let's apply it immediately and with discretion."

The FBI agents took Ted from my grasp. "See you later, kid." He looked up at me as they hustled him out of the studio.

I took off in the other direction. With all the confusion, nobody noticed my exit. I needed to get to my plane. I grabbed a cab for Max's house.

"Anything I can do, Johnny?" He greeted me as usual.

"My plane leaves Kennedy at eight. Can you get me to the airport?"

"Sure, sure, intoned Max. "One of my sons will drive you. Moshe, he's thirty-five, my oldest."

I looked up to see an intelligent-looking man. Healthy and much slimmer than Max, he had a typical American face. A varsity man all the way.

"I'm glad I took that extra passport, Max. I may need it at Kennedy."

"Good thinking, Johnny. You could work with me if you stuck around. Moshe here will be taking over soon. I'm considering retirement in Florida if this fucking heart doesn't get me first." Max was thinking about his personal health, a condo and an electric golf cart in Palm Beach. I was dreaming about my money in Switzerland. At a time like this, it was unbelievable!

"Come, Johnny. You look a little haggard. Sit down and take a load off your feet," suggested Max. He then bent over and turned on the television. The news was being broadcast from Washington. I heard exactly what I had expected.

"We repeat," announced the newscaster, "that Ted Shipansky, alias Adam Polanski, was shot in an attempt to escape federal custody. An FBI agent was wounded. The assassin was killed immediately by a bullet in the head."

"Too bad for Ted," Max turned to me, seemingly oblivious to the other news surrounding the head-spinning tumble of events. "I liked him. You liked him too, didn't you?"

I nodded my head yes. I wasn't sure whether I really liked him or not. Anyway, he'd made me rich. He'd also helped to get rid of Harris. In a way, I suppose I also helped him to solve his problems, although it was purely unintentional. The only thing we could hope for was that the President would manage to save the world so I could enjoy the cash Ted bequeathed me.

"Let have a drink to Ted's memory," suggested Max solemnly.

"Sorry, I didn't bring the kishke," I apologized.

"You were in a hurry. A Polish pickle will do," Max excused me.

Another newscaster came on the screen and announced, "The White House has officially announced that the President and Soviet Premier Kuslov met today in Uppsala, Sweden. Their discussions concerned the present world situation. Further details will be released as they are learned, and this network will bring you a report direct from Sweden. Stay tuned for other bulletins."

I thought about Ted. To hell with his purity, his Bogart, his honor and dignity, although I had to admit that he had followed his principles as far as he could. But he could never realize that the world was even bigger and tougher than he was. I was convinced that they'd make some sort of deal in Sweden. The world had become a world of deals and compromises – a rotten world, but I was used to it.

"My plane!"

Max got up to see me off and Moshe automatically stood up. I said goodbye again to Max. Moshe drove me to the airport. I was tense but tried not to show it.

The next obstacle was to pass through the gate with ticket and passport made out to Calhoun. Despite the precautions Max had taken, they'd eventually uncover my tracks. I tried to keep moving in the terminal so nobody would see my face long enough to remember it. I slipped through the metal detectors and passport control smoothly and proceeded in haste to my boarding gate. Passengers were already boarding. I glided through onto the plane but didn't relax until we were out over the ocean.

I sat back in my seat and ordered a single malt scotch. The hostess was pretty. I offered her a drink.

"Never on duty, sir." She seemed interested, however.

"Well, when are you off duty?" I inquired.

"In about seven hours, in Geneva."

"How long will you stay?"

"About twenty-four hours," she cooed.

"What about there? I'll buy you a drink there," I offered.

"I don't know," she teased.

"Well, why not?" I played her game. "You could show me the town. I'll buy you a watch."

"I've got a whole collection of watches." She was sassy. "I'm selling them myself now. I prefer cash."

My charm was wearing thin. I was getting old, I admitted. But I had all the cash I needed. "Is it a deal?"

"A deal." She licked her lips.

I'd have the afternoon to track down my money and then in the evening, I'd teach that fresh bitch a little discipline.

Neither Donaldson nor Haverson would order an official investigation. They'd look foolish. But they would certainly unleash their private hounds on my trail. They might be looking for a guy named Jake Calhoun, but I'd already be Robert Munroe. I'd switch the number on my accounts. If the Polish government knew about them, I reasoned, then it would be possible for others to find out.

Donaldson would be furious. His political position was weakened and, although it was his harebrained scheme that was in the process of failing, he'd no doubt take it all out on me – especially when he learned of the missing money. I wouldn't be safe anywhere. With his connections, I might be killed by a terrorist, a refugee, a ski instructor, or even the stewardess. I'd need plastic surgery. I could get the pictures of my new face to Max and he'd arrange for another new passport. I'd kill the surgeon afterwards.

Suddenly all my speculations were interrupted by the in-flight television. It was the same announcer from this afternoon at Max's. Behind him stood Sweden's landmark Uppsala Castle.

"Ladies and gentlemen, the President of the United States of America."

A cringe of suspense wriggled through the pressurized cabin. I looked back to see the stewardesses grouped together in a small knot near the galley. The pilot emerged from the cockpit and strode calmly past the first-class passengers and joined the multitude in the tourist cabin.

The President's familiar face flashed onto the screen. He looked weary. He stood at a podium but did not speak. Another voice spoke off-screen.

"Three days of secret meetings in Uppsala, Sweden between the American and Soviet leaders have produced the following joint communiqué, which we now broadcast via satellite to audiences around the world. First, the President of the United States will speak. Afterwards, the Soviet Premier will read his statement."

"Citizens of the United States, citizens of the world." The sound switched to the President's tense yet confident voice. He smiled. "For the past ten days, following the death of Premier Berisov of the Soviet Union, the threat to peace has grown daily. It has taken three days of discussions between Premier Kuslov, myself, and other world leaders to bring this crisis to a constructive conclusion, the details of which I shall now outline. It is our firm hope that these plans will permit us and our progeny to live in peace and prosperity."

The first part of the speech was almost a verbatim repetition of what I'd heard at Donaldson's big show. Yet certain things were missing. The President didn't accuse the Soviet Union or the KGB of harboring and financing terrorists. Instead, he said, "We have agreed on the common principle of putting an end to all terrorist activities that promote death and destruction all over the world."

The other part of the speech was new to me and much more interesting. "To prevent the danger of the Mahdi plot, Premier Kuslov, myself, Prime Minister Mukherjee of India, President Dao of China,

French President Jean-Monod and British Prime Minister Burgess worked out a number of security measures that will be beneficial to everyone. Indeed, there may be resistance to these decisions in certain quarters. To those who may contest our plans, I must say that there is no chance of reversing the decisions that have been made with the full support of myself and my esteemed colleagues here in Sweden. We have realized that substantive preventive measures were absolutely necessary to diminish the threat of thermonuclear war, which hung over the world as the result of the actions of a madman. The United Nations was no forum for our discussions. We were in complete agreement that the UN has become a meaningless organization and furthermore a forum for all but constructive solutions.

"This meeting, my fellow citizens, is the most important since Yalta at the close of World War Two." He paused to allow the effect of the words to be felt. "Even more important," he added as an afterthought designed to fortify the impact of what followed. "Our decisions were implemented at the moment of our agreement yesterday at midnight Washington time. They will continue to be applied even now as I am speaking to you. In 1979 we were not ready. Now we are ready.

"Several military operations have unfolded simultaneously. By the invitation of moderate Arab nations, we have deployed our armed forces to protect the oil fields on the Arabian Peninsula. The same invitation for protection was requested by the Lebanese government, which asked for our help in restoring order to a country torn apart by senseless fratricidal conflict. At the same time, our 101st Airborne division landed troops in Mosul and Kirkuk and proclaimed the independence of Kurdistan. Our 82nd Airborne division has flown into Tehran and spread out to meet the advancing spearhead of the Soviet Special Forces. Descending from the Caspian Sea, the Soviets declared the liberation of Armenia and Baluchistan.

"Some operations concern our Marines, who have landed at Abadan while armored divisions are progressing toward Tehran and Mosul. In the Mediterranean, our air cavalry took over the Libyan nuclear installations and our logistics forces helped our Egyptian allies to proceed in their operations against Libya and Yemen. We have expressed our disinterest in Afghanistan to the Soviets as well as our desire to see them use the port of Abadan for commercial and peaceful purposes. After signing a non-aggression pact with China, the Indian army occupied all Pakistani nuclear installations.

"But these military events, the details of which you shall soon learn, are secondary. The main negotiations were the fruits of diplomacy. We have arranged to convince the Soviet Union and China to sign a mutual non-aggression pact and friendship treaty. The Chinese henceforth have surrendered their claims to Siberian regions while the Soviets will permit the Beijing government to restore order in Southeast Asia. Joining this agreement are Japan and the two Koreas. Japan has offered formal apologies and reparations to China and Korea for wartime atrocities committed by the Imperial Army. Furthermore, Japan and the Soviet Union have agreed to jointly administer the Kuril Islands under the aegis of the newly formed Northeast Asia Federation. A formal treaty guaranteed by the United States, China, Japan and the Soviet Union will finally end the Korean war and foster the economic development of North Korea with the goal of political reunification with the South.

"I want to assure you that no colonial regimes will be created as a result of our operations. We shall not repeat the same errors that brought us to the brink of war with the only other nation in the world capable of helping us solve the technical problems of humanity. All we have done was to liberate certain nations from the clutches of regressive history. Our desire is to move forward together into a common, sustainable future. Accordingly, our priorities have been devoted to guaranteeing the peaceful use of the world's resources and commercial routes.

"To cover the expenses of our protection, the Arabian countries have announced that the price of oil will be cut in half. For the time being, the province of Khuzistan will be administered by the Saudi Arabian government. We know that they will develop and distribute this resource wisely. Finally, part of the oil profits will go directly to the world's underdeveloped countries so that they may feed their starving millions.

"To commemorate this modern feat of diplomacy, myself and Premier Kuslov have agreed to meet one year from today in Tehran to open the next and hopefully most successful SALT meetings. We shall do this in the spirit of the first Tehran conference between Roosevelt and Stalin.

"Naturally, all my decisions will be subjected to the scrutiny of Congress, according to the democratic principles of our Constitution.

"Ladies and gentlemen, goodnight. Sleep well, people of the world.

"And now, my friends in America, I should like to introduce my friend, Premier Kuslov."

The American and Soviet leaders hugged and kissed each other for the television screen. That image was transmitted all over the world via satellite, and it made me sick. I couldn't look at the picture anymore, especially with two politicians acting like a couple of lovers.

Something made me think about Ted. He was a man like Bogart who tried to keep some values in a world where there were few. But Ted, like all good Bogart characters, was a loser. The world was Bogart's more than it was Ted's. I wondered whether there would be anyone else in the modern world to replace them. But I didn't feel any sorrow and I didn't cry. With this unexpected solution, I would now be richer than before. The dollar would rise in value. I succeeded. I was a winner.

There's nothing like a good clean conscience for a restful sleep. And as far as a conscience was concerned, I didn't have one.

Glossary

[1] Drug Enforcement Agency

[2] Demobilized members of Polish Home Army plus liberated Polish prisoners employed by the American Army to guard German prisoners of war and ammunition depots.

[3] An ancient Jewish coinage first minted some 450 years after the Babylonian conquest, around 135 BCE, by John Hyrcanus I, King and High Priest of Judea.

[4] The SS Main Economic and Administrative Office (*SS Wirtschafts und Verwaltungshauptamt*), abbreviated SS-WVHA, was a Nazi organization responsible for managing the finances, supply systems and business projects for the Allgemeine-SS. It also ran the concentration camps and was instrumental in the implementation of the Final Solution through such subsidiary offices as the Concentration Camps Inspectorate and SS camp guards.

[5] ZOB (*Żydowska Organizacja Bojowa*) The Jewish Combat Organization was a World War II resistance movement in occupied Poland, which was instrumental in engineering the Warsaw Ghetto Uprising.

[6] "Shops" were factories in ghetto areas that utilized Jewish slave labor.

[7] CID, the United States Army Criminal Investigation Command, investigates felony crimes and serious violations of military law and the United States Code within the US Army.

[8] Broom Squad. Section of the Polish Home Army underground charged with carrying out political assassinations.

[9] KEDYW or *Kierownictwo Dywersji* ("Directorate of Diversion") was a Polish World War II Home Army unit that conducted active and passive sabotage, propaganda, and armed operations against German forces and collaborators.

[10] (Committee of Civilian Warfare) used to direct the operations of the Polish Home Army, Underground and other armed organizations. Dependent on the London-based Polish government-in-exile.

[11] Vis, a Polish handgun, equivalent to an American Colt-45.

[12] In October 1939, Hitler annexed western Polish areas and the Free City of Danzig. The area was incorporated into the Reich as Reichsgau Danzig-West Prussia. Ethnic German and their children were recognized as citizens.

[13] NSZ or *Narodowe Siły Zbrojne* (National Armed Forces) was a Polish anti-Nazi and later anti-Soviet military organization which was part of Poland's World War II resistance movement. The NSZ fought occupying German and Soviet forces as well as Soviet-allied Polish Communist partisan forces such as Gwardia Ludowa and Armia Ludowa. The NSZ was the third-largest Polish resistance movement of World War II, after the Home Army and Bataliony Chłopskie. The number of its soldiers ranged from 70,000 to 75,000.

[14] Grey Scouts. Teenagers employed by the Polish Home Army to paste anti-German posters and underground communiqués on the walls of the city.

[15] Silent Killings

[16] Translator

[17] FLN, National Liberation Front, is a nationalist political party in Algeria. It was the principal nationalist movement during the Algerian War and the sole legal and ruling political party of the Algerian state until other parties were legalized in 1989.

[18] Sturmbannführer was a Nazi Party paramilitary rank equivalent to major that was used in several Nazi organizations, such as the SA, SS, and the NSFK. Translated as "assault unit leader," the rank originated from German shock troop units of the First World War.

[19] Operation Erntefest[19], Operation Harvest Festival, was the liquidation of those remaining in Jewish concentration camps in the General Government, initiated November 3, 1943.

[20] Part of Poland under German administration.

[21] Bundesnachrichtendienst (Federal Intelligence Service) is the foreign intelligence agency of Germany.

[22] Bureau of Narcotics

[23] Displaced Person

[24] The Provisional Government of the Republic of Poland (Polish: *Rząd Tymczasowy Rzeczypospolitej Polskiej* or RTRP. The establishment of the RTRP was an important step in strengthening the control of the Polish Workers' Party and Union of Soviet Socialist Republics in Poland.

[25] Swine is Polish slang for ten gold Russian rubles, the most common gold piece in Poland, legally circulated until 1917.

[26] Literally, German-folk, a term invented by Hitler to designate German-speakers living outside Germany and Austria, mainly in central and eastern Europe. *Volksdeutsche* were considered to embody Aryan racial stock and accorded quasi-citizenship under German rule. The Nazi Party (NSDAP) recruited and them as a fifth-column to undermine independent governments in Czechoslovakia, Poland, the Balkan states, and elsewhere.

[27] DST, *Direction de la Surveillance du Territoire*, was the equivalent of the FBI in France until reorganized in 2008.